# The Fate of Saul's Progeny in the Reign of David

# The Fate of Saul's Progeny in the Reign of David

Cephas T. A. Tushima

◆PICKWICK *Publications* • Eugene, Oregon

THE FATE OF SAUL'S PROGENY IN THE REIGN OF DAVID

Copyright © 2011 Cephas T. A. Tushima. All rights reserved. Except for brief quotations in critical publications or reviews, no part of this book may be reproduced in any manner without prior written permission from the publisher. Write: Permissions, Wipf and Stock Publishers, 199 W. 8th Ave., Suite 3, Eugene, OR 97401.

Pickwick Publications
An Imprint of Wipf and Stock Publishers
199 W. 8th Ave., Suite 3
Eugene, OR 97401

www.wipfandstock.com

ISBN 13: 978-1-60899-994-1

*Cataloguing-in-Publication data:*

Tushima, Cephas T. A.

    The fate of Saul's progeny in the reign of David / Cephas T. A. Tushima, with a foreword by Tremper Longman III.

    xxiv + 348 pp. ; 23 cm. Includes bibliographical references and index.

    ISBN 13: 978-1-60899-994-1

    1. Bible as literature. 2. Bible. O.T. Samuel—Criticism, interpretation, etc. 3. David, King of Israel. 4. Saul, King of Israel. 5. Ethics. I. Longman, Tremper. II. Title.

BS1325.52 T255 2011

Manufactured in the U.S.A.

*To*

*My grandmothers, Akohol Atum and Ade-ember Anju;*

*and*

*My mother, Rachel Kposoga Tushima,*

*The women who impacted my life immensely*

*in my most impressionable years.*

# Contents

*List of Tables / viii*
*Foreword by Tremper Longman III / ix*
*Preface / xi*
*Acknowledgments / xvii*
*List of Abbreviations / xx*

1  Introduction / 1
2  A Survey of the Interpretive History of 1–2 Samuel / 26
3  Narrative Criticism / 63
4  The Contest for the Succession to the Throne of Saul (2 Samuel 2–4) / 111
5  David and Michal / 159
6  David and Mephibosheth / 224
7  An Integrative Reading of Research Findings / 271
8  Conclusion: Truths from David's Dealings with the Saulides / 314

*Bibliography / 325*
*Index / 341*

# Tables

| | |
|---|---|
| Table 1 | Examples of Prophecies/Promises in the Torah and their Fulfillment in Samuel / 8 |
| Table 2 | A Sample Survey of Common Motifs/Themes in the Song of Hannah and the Song of David in 2 Samuel / 12 |
| Table 3 | The Evaluation of Israel's Leaders vis-à-vis Israel's Fortunes in its Conflict with the Philistines / 14 |
| Table 4 | The Comparison of the Ark Motif Occurrences in both 1 and 2 Samuel / 191 |
| Table 5 | Compositional Motific Similarities between 1 and 2 Samuel / 192 |

# Foreword

THE STORY OF SAUL and David is vivid and compelling drawing the reader into a narrative of gripping action and complex characters. Typical of the best Hebrew narrative, the narrator of the Saul and David story rarely reveals the motivations of characters and even more sparingly provides moral evaluation of its characters' actions, preferring a strategy of showing rather than telling the story. Readers are expected to enter into the story with their imagination and to do their own evaluations.

The masterfully written account of Saul and David leaves plenty to the readerly imagination. Some readers have a tendency to simplify and turn Saul into a bad character and David into a hero, both military and spiritual. More recently, scholars have reversed this traditional reading to turn Saul into a tragic rather than evil figure and David into a villain (see the work of Gunn, Halpern, and McKenzie, cited and evaluated by Tushima). In response, other scholars, both literary (Borgman) and biblical (Long), have presented sophisticated literary readings of Saul and David that have defended the traditional reading.

It is into this deeply contested interpretive territory that Cephas Tushima enters with his own sensitive and provocative reading of the biblical text. He does so with a full knowledge of these previous efforts, their successes and failures, and gives a very persuasive reading. As his title indicates (The Fate of Saul's Progeny in the Reign of David), his study focuses on a particular important indicator of the narrative's assessment of David's character, namely how he treats the surviving children of his predecessor.

I am pleased to recommend Tushima's work not just for his skill as an interpreter of ancient Hebrew literature, but also because of his skill as a biblical theologian. While many scholars are content to analyze the text, Tushima is interested in navigating the theological issues that his reading of David, which punctures a typical traditional-positive reading of David, raises. In particular, how does a David, shown by Tushima to be no great moral hero when judged by the Deuteronomic code, become so important to royal theology and in particular the development of a messianic expectation?

It is a particular joy to introduce this work because Tushima was my student for a number of years. Even after I left Westminster Theological Seminary for Westmont College, we maintained a professional and personal relationship. Through his diligent research and sharp insight, he taught me much about both narrative analysis as well as the proper interpretation of the Saul and David story. Now that the book is published I expect that it will have the same impact on future readers.

Tremper Longman<br>
Robert H. Gundry Professor of Biblical Studies<br>
Westmont College

# Preface

THE LITERARY RICHES OF biblical Hebrew narrative have consistently intrigued its readers through all ages. The story of David, in particular, has been a fascination of both the academy and popular culture in all of Western civilization and the spheres of its influence. In spite of the myriads of readings of this story, due to the depth of the narrative's riches, many of its facets remain unexplored. I set out, in this book, to explore only a small tributary of this literary Amazon: The relationship between David and Saul's heirs. A few things underpin my particular approach to this enterprise, namely, the desire to 1) be comprehensive and systematic in my study of all the heirs of King Saul in the Davidic era; 2) be consistent in my evaluation of these narratives on the basis of the Deuteronomic Code, and not on grounds extraneous to the biblical text itself, since the study assumes the Deuteronomistic redaction of Samuel; 3) be consistent in my application of a narrative critical approach to all the passages studied; 4) carry out my study within the context of contemporary secondary literature on the topic through an in-depth discussion, analysis, and critique of such literature; and 5) carefully sketch out the outworking of the biblical theological and redemptive historical import of the themes and motifs that arise from this work.

In its comprehensive analysis of the fate of Saul's heirs, this study shows that David, like other ancient Near Eastern usurpers, perpetrated heinous injustices against the vanquished house of Saul. The study evaluates the relationships between David and Saul's heirs, with the underlying theme of justice, drawing upon the provisions for justice in the covenant community in the book of Deuteronomy. Because no separate narrative of Saul's descendants exists in the Bible, this study focuses on the story of David and its interconnection with the fate of the Saulides to determine the factors that lay behind the tragedies that befell them, specifically whether these tragedies were due to continuing divine retribution, pure happenstance, or Davidic orchestration. The passages studied for this purpose are 1 Sam 18:17—19:17; 25:39–44; 2 Sam 2–4, 6, 9, 16:1–4; 19:25–31 [ET 19:24–30]; 21:1–14. A close reading of these texts brings us to the conclusion that David was, for the most part, unjust and calculating in his dealings with the Saulides. Thematic and motific threads arising from this study (such as the impact of human conduct on the environment, the tension between election and the character of God's servants, the dynamics of sacred space and sacred typonyms, the Judahite [Davidic] kingship, the monarchy, marriage, and Zion theology) are subsequently discussed within their contexts in Israel's (and Jewish) traditions for their biblical theological and redemptive historical import.

Chapter 1 lays out the primary concern of this work, the investigation of the fates of Saul's heirs in David's reign. It also situates Samuel in its DtrH context, highlighting the thematic and motific connections between Samuel and the Torah, not the least of which is the theme of justice—the undergirding criterion for evaluating David's dealings with the Saulides in the book. The chapter also necessarily demonstrates the literary unity of the books of Samuel, because my reading of the narrative as it relates to the Saulides disregards the consensus position regarding the boundaries of the Succession Narrative (SN). By this, I included in my study 2 Sam 21, which, along with the last three chapters of the book, is usually severed from the rest of the book's narrative and branded as an appendix.

Chapter 2 is an overview of the history of the critical study of the books of Samuel, beginning from the early nineteenth century. It also highlights pivotal points in Samuel scholarship in the twentieth century, leading up to where we are early in the twenty-first century. The general overview is followed with a narrower focus on a review of selected literature that is centered either on David (2 Samuel) or on Saul (1 Samuel). Additionally, the review also considers the methodological approaches that have been employed, and their underlying presuppositions.

The third chapter considers the exegetical methodology approach of the book. In it, I survey the use of contemporary literary criticism in biblical studies (with particular emphasis on biblical narrative). The literature is studied with a view to underscoring the generative factors, development, and growth of contemporary literary criticism, with especial attention paid to narrative criticism. I, therefore, survey the different forms of this approach and the direction in which the studies that adopt them take. Finally, I discuss the various elements essential in narrative criticism. It would be foolhardy to attempt to discuss every literary device that is used in narrative criticism, so I simply review some of the more salient elements or devices. These devices (along with those not specifically reviewed here but discussed in the course of data analysis) serve as heuristic tools in reading our texts.

Chapter 4 is where I begin to delve into the core of the study. The death of Saul and his three sons is recorded in 1 Sam 31–2 Sam 1. In 2 Sam 2 civil war breaks out as David is crowned king over the house of Judah at Hebron. We begin to encounter David's confrontation with the Saulides in 2 Sam 3 during the civil war years. Here we begin the literary analysis of the report of the initial civil war, Abner's negotiations with David, Abner's death, and the death of Ishbosheth.

The focus in chapter 5 is on the relationship between David and Michal. Because of the enduring nature of a marriage relationship, my investigation here goes back to the story of their marriage in the History of David's Rise (HDR). I read the return of Michal to David by Abner as still part of the HDR. I give close attention to the implications of the return of Michal to David after she had been Paltiel's wife. I explore this issue in its legal, ethical, and theological dimensions.

This is followed with an analysis of the estranged relationship between David and Michal (encapsulated in their conversation at the end of the ark procession). Some of the issues I tackle at this point, besides the literary analysis, include the cultic nature and significance of this episode and the literary genre of the woman at the window and its implications for Michal's story. I also carefully examine the enigmatic conclusion of the episode with the narrator's notice that Michal had no children at the time of her death. My proposition is that Michal was not barren, as the passage has been traditionally read, but was bereft of her sons in the Gibeonite sacrifice.

I concluded the chapter with the consideration of the murder of Michal's five sons and her two half-brothers. I necessarily had to deal with the textual difficulties of 2 Sam 21:1–14, and why I have elected to follow the Masoretic Text (MT) rather than the ancient translations, as most scholars and modern translations do. I discuss the genealogical mix-up with a comparative analysis of similar situations both in the books of Samuel and in the Chronicler's history. Ultimately, my primary concern is with the murder itself. I explore the nature of the reported oracle, and the nature of the "sacrifice" of the Saulides. All these are studied in light of the Deuteronomic Code and the import it ought to have borne on that incident.

In chapter 6, I engage the complex dealings of David with Mephibosheth, the lame son of Jonathan—David's supposed best friend, who had even abdicated his right to his father's throne for David. I begin the discussion with a look at the triumphant David and the presumed restoration of Mephibosheth. I glean through the narrative in order to discern possible motivations for David's unusual kindness to a Sualide, the family line of which David had unremitting suspicion.

We follow the checkered fortunes of Mephibosheth as they mutate with the whims of David in the vagaries of the latter's trouble-plagued political history. From the zenith of David's triumph we journey with a Mephibosheth who is invested with his grandfather's estate, even if he has no control over it, to the nadir of David's disgrace, where the humbled Mephibosheth is dispossessed of what he never asked for in the first instance. When the dust of rebellion settles, we are found alongside Mephibosheth in the train of those who had come to grace the return of the king. We watch with the hapless Mephibosheth as a David, who, with a compromised integrity and a conscience sullied by the bribes of Ziba, is unable to look the two contenders for the estate of Saul in the eye and give a just judgment, but rather resorts to a face-saving compromise verdict, which Mephibosheth rejects off-handedly. What pulled David to such abysmal moral depths? These matters squarely engage our attention.

Chapter 7 consists of an integrative reading of the research findings. It has two main parts. The first part is concerned with an evaluation of the dealings of David and/or his retainers with the Saulides, studied in the light of Torah instruction, especially as spelled out in the Deuteronomic Code. We assume an exilic final redaction of the Deuteronomistic History, hence the need to evaluate the accounts with the ideological/theological presuppositions that underpin the entire history in the context of the exile.

The second part of the chapter focuses on the biblical theological implications of the study. This draws out the significance the book may have held for the Golah community as they sought a new direction for their future. Seeing astride the biblical terrain the colossus that David is, I attempt to make sense of Yahweh's choice of him: I seek to find reasons for the fascination of the biblical writers with David. I also correlate the way I have read these biblical narratives to other biblical data with similar concerns.

The concluding chapter, chapter 8, lays out a summary of the project, highlighting the significant findings of the research. It also includes the inferences and conclusions drawn from the study. Finally, it evaluates the success of the project, thereby indicating the contribution this project has made to the body of knowledge in the study of biblical narrative.

The highlights of the significant contributions of this book include its introduction of new concepts and terminology in literary critical theory, especially but not exclusively, with respect to the Bible. Such new concepts/terms include intra-textual consciousness, stitch-word(s), historarity (and its adjectival form, historary), dishabilledly, and plotlet. Important likewise is my understanding of the dual authorship of biblical narratives. Accenting to the divine authorship of the Bible, I concluded that the divine author identifies with, but is not subsumed by, the narrator's voice. On this note, I proffered intra-textual consciousness (undergird by the fact of the divine author's position of super-agency and super-perception) as the basis for understanding all elements of biblical narratives including the narrator's point of view.

# Acknowledgments

THE PRESENT BOOK IS a revision of my PhD dissertation. It, therefore, has been a long journey that I could not have made all alone. Constrained by both time and space, I am unable to acknowledge every source of support and encouragement. I will, however, enumerate just a few out of the myriad of God's people who have supported my family and me through the valleys and hills of this journey.

My foremost appreciation goes to my mentor, Dr. Tremper Longman III, whose penetrating inquiries into the whats, whys, and hows of what I was doing in my research set me on the path of critical reappraisal of my work at crucial junctures. This often led me to change course—whether in substantial or peripheral matters. The present work is a direct result of such vital guidance. Likewise, his suggestions of additional resources for me to consult were very helpful. Dr. Longman even graciously went beyond the call of duty by correcting technical errors that escaped both my proofreaders and me. I am equally thankful to him for accepting to write the forward of the present volume.

Also to be thanked are my professors at Westminster Theological Seminary. First of all, I am highly indebted to my late faculty advisor, Prof. J. Alan Groves, who helped shaped my interest in the Deuteronomistic History. Through the opportunity he accorded me to work for him as a research/teaching assistant, Prof. Groves afforded me such privileged exposure and experience in our discipline that will continue to inform my work for years to come. I am equally indebted to my former professor, Steve Taylor, who recognized my potential and would not watch me fall by the wayside on account of financial constraints. The initiative he took on my behalf resulted in a scholarship that allowed me to complete my studies at Westminster. I also extend gratitude to the other professors in my department (Drs. Peter Enns, Kirk Lowery, Dan McCartney, Vern Poythress, J. Douglas Green, and Prof. Michael Kelly), from whom I have learned immensely as I studied under them.

I am thankful to Rev. Dwight Singer (my mentor during my studies at ECWA Theological Seminary, Jos, Nigeria), who introduced me to the Hebrew Scriptures and the Hebrew Language. On a personal level, Rev. Singer also worked hard to make possible my "Coming to America." I am equally thankful to Dr. V. Philips Long (Regent College, Vancouver, B.C., Canada), the external reader of my dissertation, whose kind affirmations have been a huge encouragement, while his constructive criticisms helped me tighten my arguments in places and correct outright mistakes in others.

I wish to also mention a few, from many of God's people, who supported us at different points during our sojourn in America. These include Westminster Theological Seminary (for my scholarship awards) as well as several church congregations both in U.S. and Nigeria. On an individual level, my appreciation goes to Mr. Allen Kwaghkor, Dondo and Eva Ahire, Emmanuel and Olubusola Eshiet, Daniel and Mbanan Sugh, Saaondo and Eunice Anom, Solomon and Doo Asen, Daniel and Comfort Agogo, Paul Martin, Lorrain Martin and her family, Stephen and Karen Dunn, Luke and Linda Brown, Daniel and Joan Lloyd (and the Lloyd family), Bob and Vicki Winter, Joseph and Mae Jane Sun, Bill and Dottie Roberts, Teddy and Judy White, Dorothy Carson, and Leanne Bickel. To you, and all the others I am unable to name, I say, thank you for your labors of love. The Lord is not unjust as to forget your sacrifices for the sake of his people (Heb 6:10).

My gratitude likewise goes to my immediate and extended family. I want thank the members of both the Dugeri Aber (my wife's) and the Tushima Anju (my own) families for their support and encouragement right from when we first answered the call to the ministry to the present. I am particularly thankful to my wife (Nguhemen) and daughter (Iyuana Salome), who had endured many years of my being around but not available. Without your sacrifices, this book would not have been possible.

I similarly appreciate the invaluable instructions on writing style I received from Leslie Altena (of Westminster Seminary Writing Center). I wish to also thank Henry Whitney, Janice Kuhlmann, Denise Hoover, and Dr. Kenneth Davis, who painstakingly proofread the initial dissertation manuscripts. A big thank you to Dr. Robin Parry, my editor at Wipf and Stock, for his professional help and the wonderful working relationship I have had with him on this project. While I appreciate their assistance, I am solely responsible for any errors that may still subsist in the present volume.

Above all, I am most grateful to the Almighty God and my Lord and Savior Jesus Christ, who loved me before the foundation of the world and called me from my mother's womb to be his servant. To him be glory and honor forevermore.

Cephas T. A. Tushima<br>2011

# Abbreviations

| | |
|---|---|
| AB | Anchor Bible |
| AnBib | Analecta Biblica |
| ANE | Ancient Near East |
| AOTC | Abingdon Old Testament Commentaries |
| Apollos OTC | Apollos Old Testament Commentaries |
| *Basor* | *Bulletin of American Schools of Oriental Research* |
| BCE | Before the Common Era |
| *Bib* | *Biblica* |
| *BibSac* | *Bibliotheca Sacra* |
| BO | Biblica et Orientalia |
| BST | The Bible Speaks Today |
| *BZAW* | *Beihefte zur Zeitschrift für die alttestamentliche Wissenshaft* |
| CBQ | Catholic Biblical Quarterly |
| CTC | Christian Theology in Context |
| *DOTHB* | *Dictionary of Old Testament Historical Books* |
| DSB | The Daily Study Bible |
| Dtr | The Deuteronomist |
| DtrH | Deuteronomistic History |
| EA | El-Amarna tablets. According to the edition of J. A. Knudtzon. *Die el-Amarna-Tafeln*. Leipzig, 1908–1915. Reprint, Aalen, 1964. Continued in A. F. Rainey, *El-Amarna Tablets, 359–79*. 2d revised ed. Kevelaer, 1978. |

| | |
|---|---|
| FCB | The Feminist Companion to the Bible |
| FCI | Foundations of Contemporary Interpretation |
| FOTL | The Forms of Old Testament Literature |
| FTMT | Fortress Texts in Modern Theology |
| GBS | Guides to Biblical Scholarship |
| HDR | History of David's Rise |
| HSM | Harvard Semitic Monographs |
| HSR | History of Saul's Rise |
| HDR | History of David's Rise |
| HTIBS | Historic Texts and Interpreters in Biblical Scholarship |
| *HUCA* | *Hebrew University College Annual* |
| ICC | International Critical Commentary |
| *IEJ* | *Israel Exploration Journal* |
| *ISBE* | *International Standard Bible Encyclopedia* |
| ITC | International Theological Commentary series |
| *JBL* | *Journal of Biblical Literature* |
| *JETS* | *Journal of the Evangelical Theological Society* |
| *JFSR* | *Journal of Feminist Studies in Religion* |
| *JSNT* | *Journal for the Study of the New Testament* |
| *JSOT* | *Journal for the Study of the Old Testament* |
| JSOTSup | Journal for the Study of the Old Testament: Supplement Series |
| *JSS* | *Journal of Semitic Studies* |
| *JTS* | *Journal of Theological Studies* |
| K & D | Keil, C. F., and F. Delitzsch, *Biblical Commentary on the Old Testament*. 10 vols. Peabody, MA: Hendrickson, 2001. A Reprint from the English edition originally published by T. & T. Clark, Edinburgh, 1866–1891. |

| | | |
|---|---|---|
| LBI | Library of Biblical Interpretation | |
| LNTS | Library of New Testament Studies | |
| MBA | Middle Bronze Age | |
| *MQR* | *Mennonite Quarterly Review* | |
| MT | Masoretic Text | |
| NAC | New American Commentary | |
| NCB | New Century Bible | |
| NIBCOT | New International Biblical Commentary on the Old Testament | |
| NICOT | New International Commentary on the Old Testament | |
| *NIDOTTE* | *New International Dictionary of Old Testament Theology and Exegesis* | |
| NIVAC | NIV Application Commentary | |
| NT | New Testament | |
| *NTS* | *New Testament Studies* | |
| OT | Old Testament | |
| OTL | Old Testament Library | |
| SBL | Society of Biblical Literature | |
| SBLEJL | Society of Biblical Literature Early Judaism and Its Literature | |
| SBT | Studies in Biblical Theology | |
| SHANE | Studies in the History of the Ancient Near East | |
| SHBC | Smyth and Helwys Bible Commentary | |
| SN | The Succession Narrative | |
| STDJ | Studies on the Texts of the Desert of Judah | |
| TAC | The American Commentary | |
| TOTC | Tyndale Old Testament Commentaries | |
| *TSK* | *Theologische Studien und Kritiken* | |
| *TynBul* | *Tyndale Bulletin* | |

| | |
|---|---|
| *UF* | *Ugarit-Forschungen* |
| *VT* | *Vetus Testamentum* |
| *ZAW* | *Zeitschrift für die alttestamentliche Wissenschaft* |

# 1

# Introduction

THE THREEFOLD DIVINE PROMISE to Abraham (of blessing, progeny, and land) remained of vital importance to Israelite life (both at the national and individual levels) through the centuries.[1] Progeny is the evidence of Yahweh's blessings (cf. Gen 15:1–2). One way this blessedness manifests is in the care children provided for their aged parents. Besides, children also saw to the proper burial of their parents. A fitting burial meant ultimately "being gathered" to the ancestral tomb so that the family continued to be together even after death.[2] More importantly, children served as security for the family and ensured the continuing life of the family within the covenant community. John H. Walton and Victor H. Matthews, commenting on Gen 11:30, observe, "Failure to produce an heir was a major calamity for a family in the ancient world because it

---

1. Keil writes of four promises to Abraham, namely, numerous offspring, blessings (material and spiritual), a great name, and the status of a possessor and dispenser of divine blessing (K & D 1, 122). He understands the promise of land to be a part of the command to Abraham to leave the land of his birth. We note, however, that this divine promise is repeated several times to Abraham, Isaac, and Jacob. A number of these repetitions mention the three aspects of the promise as blessing, progeny, and the land of Canaan, though not everyone of the repetition has all of the elements (cf. Gen 12:1–3; 13:14–16; 17:1–8; 18:18–19; 22:15–18; 26:3–4; 28:13–14).

2. Explaining the OT concept of family, Drinkard, Jr., expatiates, "Even in death the Hebrew ideal placed one with their family. One common Old Testament expression for death is 'to lie down with one's ancestors' (1 Kgs 1:21, 22, and frequently in Kings and Chronicles). Another common phrase is 'to be gathered to one's people' (Gen 25:8, 17; 35:29; 49:29, 33; etc). Both these phrases and archaeological and biblical records indicate that family tombs were common. At Sarah's death, Abraham purchased a cave and field at Machpelah to use for a burial cave or family tomb. Later Abraham, Isaac and Rebekah, Jacob and Leah were also buried in the same family tomb" (Drinkard, "Family in the Old Testament," 485–501).

meant a disruption in the generational inheritance pattern and left no one to care for the couple in their old age."[3]

The land itself was reckoned as a fief that Yahweh had bequeathed to Israel (Lev 25:23; 2 Chr 7:20; Ps 85:1). Thus, each individual family land was viewed as Yahweh's inheritance (Hos 9:3; Joel 2:18; 3:2; Isa 8:8), for which Israel was just a steward. Therefore, land as Israel's inheritance, was not subject to a perpetual transfer outside of the family, clan, or tribal allotment (cf. Num 27:7–11; 36:1–12; 1 Kgs 21:1–3; Ezek 46:18). This accounted for the desire of everyone in Israel to have children, especially sons, who would ensure the perpetuity of Yahweh's inheritance (i.e., land holdings) within the family.[4] Of course, the children themselves were seen as Yahweh's inheritance, on loan, as it were, to their parents (Ps 127:3; Ruth 4:3–5; cf. Gen 4:1, 25; 30:1–2; 1 Sam 1:19–20; 2:20–21).

In this light, the extermination of any family line (or tribe) in Israel was not taken lightly (cf. Judg 21:2–3). The annihilation of a person's family in Israel was an extreme manifestation of divine retribution— the severest kind of punishment reserved for the most heinous forms of blasphemy or apostasy (Josh 7:1, 24–25; Num 16:27–33; 1 Kgs 14:7–11; 16:1–4; 21:18–24). It is surprising, then, that a systematic study of the fortunes of the progeny of Israel's first king (which was all but wiped out) has not generated interest in the scholarly community. Our interest in this study is heightened by the fact that aside from the central matter of succession to the throne of Israel, the motifs of burial (for Saul and his deceased sons in the ancestral tomb, a function one's progeny performed) and the inheritance of the land (left behind by Saul) are interlaced in David's complicated dealings with Saul's house. Additionally,

---

3. Walton and Matthews, *Genesis–Deuteronomy*, 35.

4. Wright captures the intricacies of the relationship between the people, the land, and Yahweh well, as he writes on the Hebrew term נחל (both as a noun and as verb), "The most common literal meaning of both refers to the division of the land within the kinship structure of Israel and thus signifies the permanent family property allotted to the tribes, clans, and households of Israel. The sense of kinship and of specially significant property inherent in the words leads to a wide metaphorical use, of which the most theologically important is the use of both nom. and vb. to express the relationship between Israel and Yahweh. There is a flexible 'triangular' usage of both *nhl* and *nahalâ* to signify the land as Israel's inheritance, the land as Yahweh's inheritance, Israel as Yahweh's inheritance, and even Yahweh as Israel's (or at least the Levites' inheritance)" ("נחל," *NIDOTTE*, III, 77–81). For more on the discussion of נחל see Lewis, "The Ancestral Estate (נחלת אלהים)," 597–612.

the many tragedies that befell this family make one wonder whether it was the curse rather than the blessing that was operative within it.

In this book, I have investigated the fortunes of the surviving Saulides during the reign of David, the goal of this investigation being to establish whether the fate of individual Saulides recorded in Samuel was due to divine retribution, on account of their father, or pure happenstance. Attempts have also been made, on the basis of textual evidence, to determine the role of King David in their fates: whether the tragedies that befell the Saulides were orchestrated by a Davidic containment policy directed at the house of Saul or they were precipitated by other factors.

Consequently, I have examined the accounts in 2 Samuel (relevant passages from chapters 3 to 21) to see *if* and *how* the actions of King David were directly or indirectly determinative of the plight of Saul's heirs. Careful attention has been paid to providing explanations of and for the actions (and inactions) of David and other prominent characters in the Samuel narrative that impacted the Saulides negatively. Subsequently, I evaluated the tragedies of each of the Saulides in the light of Deuteronomic provisions for maintaining justice within the covenant community.

Finally, I embarked up a biblical theological integrative reading of the research findings. The aim of this integrative reading is to determine any relationship between this particular way of construing these data and the rest of the biblical text. In view of David's stature in the Bible, it is imperative to reconcile his prominent place in redemptive history with his flawed portrayal in Samuel.

The significance of this project lies in the conscious effort to carry out a systematic study of the story of the Saulides after the downfall of their progenitor. In other words, its goal is to add to the existing body of literature a systematic account of the fate of King Saul's progeny during the reign of David.

Moreover, that the book of Deuteronomy serves as a prologue to the entire Deuteronomistic History (DtrH) is one of the few issues that a great many practitioners in the biblical scholarly guild seem to be agreed upon. Yet little effort has been expended in consciously evaluating the DtrH texts on the basis of the teachings of Deuteronomy. In this book, I have evaluated the narratives of the Saulides in 2 Sam 3–21 solely on the basis of the Torah instructions in Deuteronomy. Closely related to the preceding, I have endeavored to show how the theme of justice (arising from Deuteronomy) is highlighted in 2 Samuel for the *Golah* community as a means of pointing the way forward for them in the messiness of life in the exile.

Furthermore, there has been a growing scholarly recognition of the unity of the books of Samuel. This is often illustrated with the thanksgiving hymns of Hannah and David (at the beginning of 1 Samuel and the end of 2 Samuel respectively). This study will illustrate this unity with other salient motific concerns that interweave the two books.

Unlike many of the works that are reviewed in the second chapter of his book, my concern in this book is not to do an all-encompassing evaluation of the entire Succession Narrative (SN). Neither is it an adventure in historical reconstructionism. Rather, it is a venture in a literary understanding of the story of the Saulides who survived their progenitor, King Saul, after his demise during the Philistine conflict at Mt. Gilboa. Thus, my focus has been to read the relevant portions of the MT text of 2 Samuel as it narrates the story of Saul's progeny. My study therefore is focused primarily on those chapters of 2 Samuel that make specific reference to Saulides (especially chapters 2–4, 6, 9, 16:1–4, 19:25–31 [ET 24–30]; and 21:1–14). However, because David's dealings with Michal date to the History of David's Rise (HDR) era, I also considered 1 Sam 18:17–19:17; 25:39–44.

## READING SAMUEL IN ITS LITERARY CONTEXTS

### Samuel and the Torah

This study presupposes the organic nature of the development of the biblical canon. Therefore, in considering the justice theme as a yardstick for evaluating David's reign in Samuel, it is important to take a look at that theme's moorings in the Torah. Walter Brueggemann paradigmatically lays out the pattern of the development of tradition in Israel.[5] Explaining the pattern of the growth of Israel's tradition, he observes that Israel as a community of faith had precious memories (traditions) of God's dealings with her; which memories she considered normative. As a people, they were also constantly being buffeted by the pressures and tensions of historical existence. Therefore, Israel's sacred texts were the product of ongoing engagement of remembered traditions with historical pressures

---

5. Brueggemann "Introduction," 11–12.

that were shaping her life. "Sometimes Israel's situation invited strong affirmations, of enormous insight and power. At other times the cultural context sorely tried the tradition, evoking reactions merely defensive and parochial. But in each case, and therefore behind every text, there was a moment of meeting; and out of that came a new affirmation and a fresh statement of faith."[6] Accordingly, Israel's tradition was alive and growing in the ongoing experiences of the nation. Therefore, according to this paradigm, the principal question to ask of any text of the Hebrew Bible is: "What in this text can we discern of the meeting between memory and the historical pressure?"[7] Thus one question we seek to answer as we study the text of Samuel is to find the linkage between it and the past tradition as deposited in the Torah.

Writing on the portrayal of the prophet Samuel in the book that bears his name, Robert D. Bergen rightly observes, "The writer's portrayal of this prophet/judge functions as a bridge between the text of 1, 2 Samuel and the Torah"; it has the goal of communicating "hope to a people who doubted the status of Israel's covenant promises, especially that of return to the Promised Land (cf. Deut 30:3–5)."[8] In conjoining Israel's contemporary existential situation with the memory of its tradition, in a deliberative mode in order to persuade Israel to choose the path of hope, the writer of Samuel employed different media to re-enact and enliven the Torah traditions. These include the use of narrative analogies, theological themes, and literary motifs. Bergen has so well documented these linkages of the books of Samuel to the Torah that one forbears reproducing them here.[9] Nevertheless, key points in these similarities are highlighted here for emphasis.

The lives of the two most important figures in the books of Samuel have been cast in the shape that captures the images of the most important figures of the Torah, using narrative analogy. The image of the prophet Samuel in the book that bears his name is cast in a mold that corresponds to that of the long-foreseen prophet who is like Moses (Deut 18:15–18). Bergen draws out this similarity as follows:

---

6. Brueggemann "Introduction," 11.
7. Malchow, *Social Justice in the Hebrew Bible*, xv.
8. Bergen, *1, 2 Samuel*, 35–36.
9. Bergen, *1, 2 Samuel*, 35–53.

> Both Samuel and Moses were raised in environments outside their own homes. Both received their initial revelations from God in solitude, in the presence of a burning object, with their name being mentioned twice by God at the beginning of the encounter. During the first encounter with the Lord both were told of divine judgments that would come against the authority structures in which they were reared. Both were called prophets, and unlike any others in the Torah and Former Prophets, both were called "faithful." Both spoke words of judgment against leaders who had abused the Israelites. Both personally killed one oppressor of Israelites and then went into a season of self-imposed exile. Both wrote down regulations that were deposited before the Lord. Both performed some priestly duties, yet neither was ever termed a priest. Both acted as judges and were responsible for major transitions in Israelite history. Both had two named sons, none of whom played significant roles in later history. At the Lord's direction both anointed individuals who led Israel to fight against—and defeat—the inhabitants of Jerusalem, act in behalf of the Gibeonites, and conquer the Promised Land.[10]

In like manner, Bergen makes a case that the author of Samuel discreetly selected and arranged the events in the life of David so that it is a literary hologram of the history and destiny of Israel, beginning with the patriarchs, through the exodus, to the exile and the return therefrom:

> Like Abraham and Isaac, Israel's founding patriarchs, David was a shepherd (1 Sam 16:11); like Joseph he received a divine promise during his youth that he would be leader of his people (1 Sam 16:12); like Joseph also he faithfully served in a king's court (1 Sam 19–22); like Moses and Israel in Egypt, youthful David defeated a seemingly invincible opponent (1 Sam 17:32ff.); like Israel, David had an extended experience in the wilderness that involved moving from place to place (1 Sam 22:1ff.); like Israel he fought and defeated the Amalekites during his time in the wilderness (1 Sam 30:1ff.); like Israel, David received prophetic blessings from an opponent during his wilderness experience (1 Sam 26:25); like Israel, David re-entered the land but took control of it only gradually over a period of time (2 Sam 2:1ff.); like Israel, David conquered Jerusalem and established it as the nation's capital (2 Sam 5:6ff.); like Israel, David possessed the Promised Land and defeated enemies on every side (2 Sam 8:1ff.); like Israel, David committed grievous violations of the Torah that resulted in di-

---

10. Bergen, *1, 2 Samuel*, 35.

## Introduction

vine judgment and escalating internal problems (2 Sam 11:1ff.); like Israel, David was forced to go into exile east of the Jordan river (2 Sam 15:13ff.) and resided, like a later Davidic king, in a capital city previously considered hostile (2 Sam 17:24); like Israel, David ultimately returned from exile to Jerusalem (2 Sam 19:11ff.); like Israel, David experienced opposition from people in the land following his return from exile (2 Sam 20:1ff.)[11]

The theological themes of the Torah that are picked up in the Samuel books include those of Covenant (2 Sam 7:8–17; cf. Gen 15:18–21; 17:4–14, 19, 21; Exod 2:24; 24:8; Num 25:12–13); Land (1 Sam 7:14; 27:8–10; 2 Sam 8:3–9; cf. also 1 Sam 4:10; 31:7; 2 Sam 15:14; 17:22); and the presence of God among or with his people (cf. Gen 39:2, 21; Exod 33:3, 15–17; Deut 4:7; 1 Sam 3:19; 16:13, 18; 18:12, 14, 28; 2 Sam 5:10; 7:3). The leitmotifs of the Torah that the author of Samuel incorporates in his works include those of the barren woman (cf. Gen 11:30; 25:2; 29:31; 1 Sam 1); the shepherd (cf. Gen 4:2; 12:6; 26:14; 30:29–31; 38:13; Exod 3:1)—in which case Saul is shown to be an incompetent shepherd (1 Sam 9:1–5, as a proleptic portrayal of his kingship) while David is portrayed as a faithful shepherd (1 Sam 17:34–37, and to a degree a reflection of his anticipated reign); the use of the shepherd's instrument for deliverance (Moses in Exod 4:17; 7:12, 20; 8:17; 9:23; 10:13; and David in 1 Sam 17:40, 50); taking refuge with and yet outwitting Philistine kings (cf. Gen 20:1–18; 26:1–11; 1 Sam 27:1ff.); the dramatic echoes of fratricide (cf. Gen 4:8; 2 Sam 13:20–29; 14:4–7); the younger sibling surpassing the elders (Gen 4:2–5; 17:18–21; 25:23; 37:3–8; 38:29; 48:14–20; Exod 6:20; 1 Sam 1:4–5, 20; 16:11–12; 2 Sam 12:24–25).[12]

Thus, the books of Samuel served as a witness to the Torah, and in this capacity they function to reiterate and clarify the message of the Torah. Consequently, as shown in the table 1 below, in a number of places, these books demonstrate that the prophecy/promise pronounced in the Torah has now been fulfilled.

---

11. Bergen, *1, 2 Samuel*, 36–37.

12. For a detail discussion of these themes and motifs see Bergen, *1, 2 Samuel*, 43–53.

**TABLE 1:** Examples of Prophecies/Promises in the Torah and their Fulfillment in Samuel

| Prophecy/Promise | Place first made | Place where fulfillment is recorded |
|---|---|---|
| The rise of kingship | Gen 36:31; 17:6, 16 | 1 Sam 8:5 |
| The rise of a Judahite dynasty | Gen 49:10 | 2 Sam 7:8–16 |
| The rise of a destroyer of Moab & Edom | Num 24:17–19; Exod 14:14; cf. Num 24:20 | 1 Sam 14:47–48; 15:7–8 and 1 Sam 30:17; 2 Sam 8:2, 12–13 |
| Lasting priesthood to Eleazarite family | Num 25:13 | Eleazarites not Elides (1 Kgs 2:27); fulfillment (1 Kgs 2:35) |

### *Samuel and Deuteronomy*

In addition to the ways in which the books of Samuel are linked to the Torah, there are also a number of ways in which they are connected particularly to Deuteronomy. It has already been pointed out above that by narrative analogy, the author of these books showed that, in some respects, the prophet Samuel was the coming prophet like Moses (Deut 18:15–19).[13] Similarly, the prediction concerning Israel asking for a king "like all the nations" and the condition on which they were to appoint the person—the one whom "the Lord chooses" (Deut 17:14–15)—finds fulfillment in Samuel (1 Sam 8:5; 9:17; 10:1; 16:1–13).

In the same way, Deuteronomy's provision that Israel shall worship at a central sanctuary at the place of Yahweh's choosing (Deut 12:5–7, 14, 21, 26; 16:1–16) finds its fulfillment in Samuel (2 Sam 6). Indeed, the condition for arriving at the place of Yahweh's choosing was that Yahweh will give Israel rest from all their enemies round about them so that they dwell in safety (Deut 12:9–11). This condition was perfectly met in the reign of David, as recorded in Samuel. The Philistines were the unwavering troublers of Israel throughout the judges' era even up to the end of the reign of Saul. It was David that finally put to rest this trouble (2 Sam 5:18–25). This silencing of the Philistine made possible, as we shall see later, the recovery of Ark of the Covenant from Kiriath-jearim,

---

13. See my above reference (footnote 10 above) to Bergen's erudite discussion of this issue.

near which the Philistine had a garrison that restricted Israel's access to the Ark, thereby limiting Israel's worship of Yahweh as was anticipated in the wilderness (1 Sam 10:5; 13:3-4; cf. 14:18[14]). However, the resounding defeat of the Philistine in 2 Sam 5:18-25 made possible the removal the Ark from Gibeonite territory to a central place that was readily accessible to all Israel in 2 Sam 6. In fact, the *pax Davidide*[15] was what made the contemplation of the construction of a befitting temple at the central sanctuary conceivable (2 Sam 7:1-2). All this is a direct fulfillment of the expectation as annunciated in the wilderness (Deut 12:9-10).

Another way in which the connection between Deuteronomy and Samuel can be seen is in the ambiguous stance both books have toward the monarchy (whether they are critical or supportive of it).[16] Deuteronomy's prediction of Israel asking for a king is couched in language that may be reckoned as being negative: They asked that a king be appointed over them "like all the nations round about us" (כְּכָל־הַגּוֹיִם אֲשֶׁר סְבִיבֹתָי) (Deut 17:14). This demand in some ways undercut Israel's call, as Deuteronomy shows, to be distinct from other nations (a theme to which we shall also return later in the book). Yet, the positive element is that Yahweh will choose for them who would be their king at that moment. This ambiguity toward kingship resurfaces in Samuel (1 Sam 8—12). The negative element relates to Israelite demand for a king over them like the nations, using the exact Deuteronomic language (1 Sam 8:5, 19-20), and Samuel's unrelenting reprimand of them (1 Sam 8:6, 10-18; 12:7-25), while the positive element again comes from Yahweh not only acquiescing to their demand (1 Sam 8:7), but also being the one choosing for them their first two kings (1 Sam 9:15-17; 10:1, 20-25; 16:1-13).

---

14. For a fuller discussion of this particular passage see chapter 5 of this book.

15. My own term for the peace brought about by David's pacification and subjugation of all the nations that surrounded and often plundered Israel (2 Sam 5:18-25; 8:1-14).

16. This ambiguity in Deuteronomy and Samuel toward kingship has often been understand to mean the deuteronomists' attitude toward the monarchy, on which scholarly opinions range from those who take it be pro-monarchic, anti-monarchic, and/or a combination of both voices. For further discussion of this see Rost, *The Succession to the Throne of David*; Noth, *The Deuteronomistic History*; McKenzie and Graham, *The History of Israel's Traditions*; Klein, *1 Samuel*, xxviii; Keys, *The Wages of Sin*, 22; Gordon. *I & II Samuel*, 27; Frolov, "Succession Narrative," 97-98; Brueggemann, "Appendix," 395-97; Laato, "Psalm 132," 56-60; Clements, "The Deuteronomic Interpretation," 398-410; McCarter, *1 Samuel*, 161-62.

Other ways in which the special bond between Deuteronomy and Samuel can be seen include, first, the destruction of Amalek. The injunction to Israel to destroy the Amalekites given in Deuteronomy (25:17–19) was never fulfilled in any other book of the Former Prophets but in Samuel (cf. 1 Sam 14:48; 15:1–11, 28; 27:8; 28:18; 30:1–18; 2 Sam 1:1-15; 8:9–12). Indeed, most of the references to the Amalekites in the only other book of the Former Prophets that mentions them deals more with their oppression of Israel than their destruction by Israel (Jdg 3:13; 6:3, 33; 7:12; 10:12; 12:15). Second, the unique position of Israel as Yahweh's treasured people is spoken about more often in Deuteronomy than any other book in the Torah (cf. Deut 7:6; 14:2; 26:18; 27:9; 28:9). It is no accident that it is also in Samuel that this motif comes up in one of the most important passages of the Former Prophets, if not the entire Hebrew Scriptures (2 Sam 7:23–24). Third, in its prescription of the right cult, Deuteronomy also required the right manner of slaughtering and eating of meat: It must not be eaten with its blood (Deut 12:15–12, 23); and in all the annals of Israel, it is only in Samuel that the concern for the observance of this ordinance comes to expression (1 Sam 14:32–35).

Furthermore, it is to be noted that it is no coincidence that both institutions of monarchy and the prophetic office predicted in Deuteronomy (Deut 17:14–20; 18:15–19) should arise and become established in Samuel. It is similarly significant that the prophetic tradition of standing up to kings when they overreached themselves and threatened the religion of Yahweh would begin in Samuel.[17] One can even say that Samuel is the linking bridge between the Torah and the latter part of the Former Prophets cum the Latter Prophets, where prophetic denunciation of the overreaching actions (violations of the Torah) of monarchs is very pronounced.

## Samuel as a Literary Unity

Though the present study is concerned primarily with selected texts from 2 Samuel, it is important to remember that the immediate context of 2 Samuel is the two books of Samuel. These books entered the Hebrew canon as one book. Several evidences can be adduced to substantiate this claim. The number of books in the Hebrew canon in Second Temple literature is a good case in point. The deutero-canonical book of *2 Esdras*

---

17. McConville, *Grace in the End*, 26.

(14:45) indicates that the Hebrew Bible published by Ezra consisted of twenty-four books. Josephus (*Against Apion* 1.37–40), on the other hand, indicates that there were twenty-two books. There are different ways in which the disparity between the two accounts is accounted for. While the translator of Josephus's works into the English language, William Whiston, proposes that Canticles and Ezra were not included,[18] Roger T. Beckwith in his analysis suggests that Ecclesiastes and Canticles are the books missing from Josephus's list.[19] By whichever of the reckonings, the implication is that our present books of Samuel, just like the books of Kings, were counted as one book.

The MT of Samuel also leaves us clues that point to the unity of the books of Samuel. The Masoretes had the practice of indicating the halfway point of each book of the Hebrew Bible and noting the total number of words in a book at the end of each book. In the case of Samuel, the halfway point is found in 1 Samuel 28:24 and the notes containing the total number of words is found at the end of 2 Samuel.[20]

Additionally, the author/redactor of Samuel employs numerous literary features in ways that show the unity of these books, not the least of which is the thanksgiving song of Hannah (1 Sam 2) and David's psalm (2 Sam 22). On the literary function of the two songs, Ronald F. Youngblood writes, "These two remarkably similar hymns of praise thus constitute a kind of *inclusio*, framing the main contents of the books and reminding us that the two books were originally one."[21] Several other factors serve to substantiate the above view. One has to do with the position of the songs: Hannah's coming toward the beginning of the narrative and David's toward its end. Besides, it is generally accepted that the Song of Hannah had a different setting than its present one. Hans Wilhelm Hertzberg lists a number of reasons for accepting that the hymn was inserted where it is now from a different setting. The natural flow of 1 Sam 1:28 with 2:11 (without a lacuna) is one such reason; also, the content of the song is only peripherally connected with Hannah.[22]

---

18. *The Complete Works of Josephus*, 776, fn. g.

19. Beckwith, "Formation of the Hebrew Bible," 49–51.

20. Cartledge says that such a practice would be incorrect except the Masoretes had considered Samuel to be one book (Cartledge, *1 & 2 Samuel*, 349).

21. Youngblood, "1, 2 Samuel," 579.

22. Hertzberg, *I & II Samuel*, 29. For a contrary opinion see John T. Willis, "The Song of Hannah and Psalm 113," 139–54; esp. 140–52.

The probable reason for the insertion of Hannah's song in its present contexts is the fact that it highlights a number of motifs that are constitutive of the ethos of the Samuel books. Similarly, the Song of David, at the end, re-echoes the same motifs to recap what has been presented in the books. A few of these motifs common to the two framing Songs are shown in Table 2.[23]

**TABLE 2:** A Sample Survey of Common Motifs/Themes in the Song of Hannah and The Song of David in Second Book of Samuel

| S/N | Common Term/Concept | Ref. In 1 Samuel | Ref. In 2 Samuel |
|---|---|---|---|
| 1 | "horn" (קרן) as a symbol of strength | 2:1, 10 | 22:3 |
| 2 | "enemies" (אויב) | 2:1 | 22:1, 4, 38, 41, 49 |
| 3 | Yahweh as the "rock" (צור) who brings salvation (ישעה) | 2:1, 2 | 22:3, 32, 47 |
| 4 | Reversal of fates in favor of the humble (or oppressed) | 2:3–5, 7–9 | 22:28 |
| 5 | Yahweh thunders (ירעם) against his enemies (the enemies of his oppressed ones) | 2:10 | 22:14 |
| 6 | Yahweh descends/acts from heaven (שמים) for the sake of the oppressed | 2:10 | 22:10 |
| 7 | Reference to "the anointed" (משיחו) of Yahweh (the king) receiving a gift from him (strength or steadfast love) | 2:10 | 22:51 |
| 8 | Yahweh brings one person down to Sheol (שאול) and another out of it | 2:6 | 22:5–8, 17 |

Both songs contain the image of a suffering righteous one receiving deliverance from Yahweh. Simultaneously, Yahweh's wrath is thunderously visited on the proud/oppressor. Yahweh's role as an impartial, just judge is anchored in his ability to weigh the deeds of men (1 Sam 2:3),

---

23. For a similar comparison of Hannah's Song with David's Psalm, see Dillard and Longman, *An Introduction to the Old Testament*, 141. Hertzberg has also made a similar comparison of Hannah's Song with other ancient songs (Hertzberg, *I & II Samuel*, 146–48).

a clear innuendo to his ability to look beyond outward appearances but penetrate to the realms of the heart and motives (cf. 1 Sam 16:7; cf. Prov 16:2; 21:2; 24:12). This alerts the reader to the fact that in spite of human schemes to perpetrate injustice with grand concealment devices (such as the schemes of Saul and David; cf. 1 Sam 18:17–25; 2 Sam 11:15, 27b), Yahweh, the great judge, sees and holds them accountable. Similarly, Klein observes that the reversals of social conditions as contained in the songs are portrayed in the books of Samuel as the regular behavior of Yahweh, and Yahweh takes positive actions for the weak, while the sated and self-reliant (often oppressors) experience his reversing judgment.[24] By this indirect means, the author of Samuel advocates for justice in the behalf of the oppressed.

The advocacy for social justice commonly associated with the classical prophets of the seventh and eighth centuries often involved the critique, by the prophets, of the nature of the interaction between the king, the priest (and the cult), and the people. All these three institutions (the monarchy, the priesthood [and the cult, esp. at the central sanctuary], and the prophetic office) find their common confluence in the man Samuel.[25] Of these three, the priesthood was the most ancient. Yet by Samuel's time it had become decadent. Samuel, therefore, appeared on the scene as a reformer. It is reasonable to surmise that cult centralization, which became more established with the erection of the Jerusalem temple, began to blossom during this reform era of Samuel. His was not a spatial centralization; altars were still maintained at several high places (examples include Mizpah, Bethlehem, Gilgal, and Ramah). The centralizing factor was the priest (Samuel himself). It can be safely inferred that at all these altars only Samuel could offer acceptable sacrifices to Yahweh on the people's behalf. It was on this point that King Saul first fumbled, resulting in Samuel's pronouncement of the doom of the king's nascent dynasty (1 Sam 13:8–14).

---

24. Klein, *1 Samuel*, 16–17.

25. Ackroyd observes, "Kingship, holy place, priesthood—three themes which were eventually to be of fundamental importance in Old Testament thought. They are shown here linked together in the figure of Samuel with whom the book opens; and with him is linked too that other great line of religious influence which so dominates the period of the monarchy and beyond—the prophetic movement" (Ackroyd, *The First Book of Samuel*, 1971, 7–8). In his sequel to the volume quoted above Ackroyd notes, "The other great line of religious influence which is linked with Samuel is the prophetic movement; this too is developed in 2 Samuel" (Ackroyd, *The Second Book of Samuel*, 8).

There are other motific and thematic features that unite the books. An example is how the personal fortunes of Israel's leaders in the "all-Israel" era are intricately connected with how Israel fared militarily on their watch in Israel's ongoing struggles against the Philistines. There are four major leaders in 1–2 Samuel, namely, Eli, Samuel, Saul, and David. During the reign of each of these leaders, Israel had a military confrontation with the Philistines. There is almost an alternating pattern: Israel suffered defeat at the hands of the Philistines at the end of Eli's judgeship, enjoyed victory at the beginning of Samuel's, endured defeat at the end of Saul's reign, and experienced victory at the beginning of David's. This pattern is illustrated in table 3 below:

**TABLE 3:** The Evaluation of Israel's Leaders vis-à-vis Israel's Fortunes in its Conflict with the Philistines

| Outcome of Israel–Philistine war in leader's reign | | Evaluation of leaders in Samuel | |
|---|---|---|---|
| Ending Defeat | Beginning Victory | | |
| Eli (1 Sam 4:1–18) | | Negative | |
| | Samuel (1 Sam 7:1–14) | | Positive |
| Saul (1 Sam 31:1–10; 2 Sam 1:1–4) | | Negative | |
| David (near ending defeat 2 Sam 21:15–22) | David (2 Sam 5:18–25; 8:1) | Ambiguity (Somewhat positive/negative) | |

Of these four leaders, those defeated by the Philistines at the end of their reigns are depicted in a bad light, while those with victory at the beginning of their reigns are portrayed more positively. Thus, Eli and Saul are roundly condemned. Samuel receives the greatest approval (cf. 1 Sam 12), even though his children had a problem similar to that of Eli's children (1 Sam 8:1–2; cf. 1 Sam 2:22). Yet the damnation of Eli as a person (1 Sam 2:27–30) contrasts sharply with the high integrity of Samuel (1 Sam 12:3–5).

There is some ambiguity in the presentation of David in the present shape of the books. There are two major accounts of conflict with the Philistines in which he is involved, both at the beginning and the end of his reign. In the conflicts at the beginning of his reign, he is victorious over the Philistines (2 Sam 5, 8), and this is the time in which David is still viewed very positively. On the other hand, in the conflicts toward the end of David's life, when he is not being portrayed in the best light, the Philistines had prevailed over David but for the help of his lieutenants (2 Sam 21:15–22). This latter episode in David's life is reminiscent of 1 Sam 17–18, where Saul is saved from the Philistines temporarily only by the help of his servant David.

Closely related to the above is the existence of three factors that had destabilizing potential for Israel's leadership, namely, Yahwistic religion, the perennial Philistine threat, and successor-in-waiting (David, the son of Jesse, in the case of Saul).[26] These destabilizing forces created uncertainty for Saul, his reign, and his dynasty. Indeed, in 1 Samuel, we see all these three forces play out against Saul, once set in motion, until they brought his life to ruin. Second Samuel unveils how David dealt with these factors that had these threatening potential. For David, these forces were the ever-present Philistine threat, Yahwistic religion (how David dealt with this is considered in our discussion of 2 Sam 6 in chapter 4 of this book), and the house of Saul (as the successors-in-waiting). How David would navigate this potential minefield would determine his survival and the perpetuity of his dynasty. His retainers compromised Saul's house effectively enough to ensure his ascendancy (2 Sam 1–4); and he had routed the Philistines at the beginning of his reign. What remained was how to secure Yahweh's favor and to pacify the house of Saul so that it would pose no further threat. Ultimately, the struggle for the succession to the throne of Israel, between the houses of David and Saul, is evident in David's confrontation with Michal bat Saul in ch. 6.

Another major uniting theme operative in the books of Samuel is this: the tone for understanding the narratives about David in 2 Samuel is set in 1 Samuel (cf. 12:3–4). Samuel—who, as we have seen, has been cast as the prophet like Moses—is shown in this passage to be the embodi-

---

26. These forces were present for all of the four leaders in the "all-Israel" era in Samuel. For Eli, his sons' misconduct at the Yahwistic shrine (1 Sam 1:2:12–17, 22–25), the Philistine threat (1 Sam 4), and the presence of a successor-in-waiting, Samuel (1 Sam 2:11, 26; 3:1–9) all made possible the swift unleashing of divine retribution.

ment of the ideal Deuteronomic leader. The question that hangs over the work is, with the transition to the new type of leadership, will there be a king who will fit this Deuteronomic ideal of leadership? In other words, will there be another Moses? As we shall see, both kings mentioned in Samuel failed the test. Indeed, most of the kings in the books of Kings did even more pitifully, with the singular exception of Josiah (who alone of all Israel's kings is, like Samuel, cast in the mold of Moses).[27] The characterization of Samuel in this passage, as one who embodies the essence of Torah obedience, coming at the twilight of charismatic leadership of the judges and the dawn of monarchical leadership, then, is to form the template against which the kings were to be viewed.

---

27. Friedman shows that Josiah was a king like no other in Israel by pointing out that the DtrH is composed with Moses and Josiah constitution an *inclusio* that frames the entire document. The Josiah pericope in 1 Kgs 22–23 echoes matters (both thematic and phraseological) that are associated with Moses in Deuteronomy in ways that are not found in any other figure throughout the DtrH (Friedman, "From Egypt to Egypt," 171–73). Examples of this include:

1. The phrase "none arose like him" or the like, used of Moses in Deut 34:10 is not used of anyone unreservedly except Josiah (2 Kgs 23:5). Similar phrases are used of David (1 Kgs 15:5) and Hezekiah (18:5), but there are qualifications with them both: for David it was the Bathsheba affair and for Hezekiah it was his nonchalant and non-repentant attitude toward God's reproof (2 Kgs 20:16–19).

2. No other king competes with Josiah in fulfilling the law's requirement of wholehearted commitment to Yahweh (Deut 6:5; cf. 2 Kgs 23:25).

3. Josiah, in obedience to the law, inquires of the Lord (2 Kgs 22:13, 18; cf. Deut 17:8–12).

4. No king, except Josiah, fulfills the law's requirement (of both Israel in general, and kings in particular) to obey the Lord without "turning to the right or left" (Deut 17:11, 20; 28:14; cf. 2 Kgs 22:13, 18).

5. Josiah alone, of all the kings, carries out Moses' command that the Law be read in the "ears" of the people (Deut 31:11; cf. 2 Kgs 23:2).

6. Moses' action of smashing, burning, and grinding the golden calf (Deut 9:21) finds its only other counterpart in Josiah's actions (2 Kgs 23:6, 14).

7. The Law's requirement that the person Israel appoint as king be the one Yahweh chooses finds unsurpassed fulfillment in Josiah as his reign was predicted hundreds of years before his time (Deut 17:15; 1 Kgs 13:2).

## The So-called Appendix and the Rest of Samuel

Modern critical scholarship has dubbed 2 Sam 21–24 as an appendix in the belief that it is disruptive of the flow of the SN found in 2 Sam 9–20 plus 1 Kgs 1–2. It is beyond the nature and scope of the present project to go into the prehistory of the text of Samuel. Whatever that pre-history may be, it is demonstrable that these four chapters, in their present location in the text of Samuel, play a vital role in the literary shape this text assumes. The framing function that the songs of Hannah and David have played in the book has already been discussed above. I will presently point out additional ways in which these chapters are more than the insertion of a clumsy redactor.

The last four chapters of 2 Samuel (21–24) in their canonical place shape the books of Samuel in various ways. On the larger scale of the two books, 2 Sam 22–24, as the closing chapters, corresponds to the opening chapters of 1 Samuel (1–2), in a number of subtle ways:

1. The song in 1 Sam 2 corresponds to the songs in 2 Sam 22. The former is anticipatory thanksgiving (with regards to the monarchy); the latter is thanksgiving *post eventum*.

2. The sanctuary (at Shiloh) in 1 Sam 1 is replaced by the altar now built (on the threshing floor of Araunah in Jerusalem), where the temple eventually will stand in 2 Sam 24 (cf. 1 Chr 21:18–19; 22:1).

3. The book begins with a journey to *a* central sanctuary and ends with a journey to a site that will become *the* central sanctuary.

4. There is a petition offered at the sanctuary for life at the beginning (a son for one who had not begotten a child) and another petition for life at the end (to be spared from a plague).

5. The answer of the opening petition provides a man of prayer (Samuel) for Israel; the last petition provides a place of prayer (the temple site) for Israel. The results of the two prayers respectively adumbrate the religious shift from dynamic personal relations with the deity to the static rituals/formalism of the temple *cultus*.

6. The first petitioner (Hannah) cries to God for a grief that is no fault of hers; the last petitioner (David) seeks God's face for grief he caused others.

The use of the term "appendix" in referring to chapters 21–24 is in itself indicative of the conscious shaping of the text of Samuel. As many other commentators have done, Gordon sets these chapters in chiastic formation as follows:[28]

    *a* famine story (21:1–14)
        *b* warrior exploits (21:15–22)
            *c* psalm (22:2–51)
            $c_1$ oracle (23:1–7)
        $b_1$ warrior exploits and warrior list (23:8–39)
    $a_1$ plague story (24:1–25).

The superb chiasm displayed in the arrangements of these chapters evinces skillful editorial work.[29] The negative perception of these chapters by a majority of scholars is captured in the words of Tony W. Cartledge, who writes that scholars generally regard 1 Kgs 1–2 "as a direct continuation of 2 Samuel 20, with 2 Samuel 21–24 being a later insertion into the narrative flow. These chapters contain an artistically arranged series of appendices that collect and present miscellaneous memories of David that are displaced from their historical context. As such, they add little to the historical understanding of David's rule; their function is to add color and flesh to our understanding of David, his times, and his supporters."[30] Indeed, concerning the extermination of the Saulide Seven,[31] Cartledge goes on to posit the possibility that this story occurred chronologically between chapters 8 and 9. He writes, "[I]t most likely took place during the early years of his kingship, shortly after the establishment of Jerusalem as David's city and the center of Israel's government."[32]

While I disagree with Cartledge's low perception of these chapters, I could not agree more with his view that the chronological location of

---

28. Gordon, *1 & 2 Samuel*, 45.

29. In a similar vein Keys says, "2 Samuel 21–24 is a compilation that has been deliberately planned, not something that is the result of chance. Its mechanical structure leads to the conclusion that its present order was the work of an editor who arranged the material in this way for a specific reason" (Keys, *The Wages of Sin*, 83).

30. Cartledge, *1 & 2 Samuel*, 634.

31. The "Saulide Seven" is my own short-hand term for referring to Saul's two sons (from Rizpah) and five grandsons (from Michal) who were murdered in 2 Sam 21.

32. Cartledge, *1 & 2 Samuel*, 635–36.

the events recorded here belongs earlier in the narrative.³³ I also disagree with Cartledge in accounting for why these chapters (the so-called appendix) have been placed where they are found in the present text of Samuel. For example, Cartledge says that the story of the murder of the Saulide Seven was excised from its original setting in the earlier story of David because it "casts David in something of a bad light and interrupts the smooth flow of David's rise to power."³⁴ This does not make logical sense. A nasty story is nasty anywhere and anytime; it does not matter where it is placed in a narrative. In fact, it is worse, in my judgment, to place it at the end of someone's life story, when he ought to be "putting his house in order" (to borrow the biblical phrase) before death approaches. On the contrary, the murder of the Saulide Seven was placed where it is to bring closure to the fate of Saul's dynasty and a logical conclusion to David's era, thereby paving way for the History of Solomon's Rise that comes up in 1 Kings. Within the setting of David's reign, it forms an *inclusio* with the first mention of a Saulide (Michal) in confrontation with David at the beginning. Thus, as I see, it has everything to do with the succession to the throne of Israel: showing how David vanquished and supplanted the house of Saul.

## THE THEME OF JUSTICE IN DEUTERONOMISTIC HISTORY

In evaluating David's relationships to the Saulides from a Deuteronomic theological perspective, one pivotal ingredient is the theme of justice, as already hinted at above. The concept of justice in the Hebrew Scriptures is conveyed in the word מִשְׁפָּט, translated in English versions as "justice or judgment."³⁵ Usually, it is found in conjunction with its complemen-

---

33. For similar perspectives see Keys, *The Wages of Sin*, 83.

34. Cartledge, *1 & 2 Samuel*, 635–36. Gordon explains that the purpose of the shuffling of the material in these chapters to their present location was "to make up a kind of epilogue on David's reign. Since David cuts such a sorry figure in 1 Kgs 1–2 their inclusion at this point is more appropriate" (*1 & 2 Samuel*, 45). Again, in my estimation, the mixture of murder, poor judgment (in the case of the census) with psalms and heroic achievements of subordinates does not necessarily make David look prettier. Nevertheless, Gordon makes a valid point in highlighting the deliberate effort on the part of the final editors of this narrative to sever it from the following History of Solomon's Rise.

35. All the different entries in BDB under מִשְׁפָּט have something to do with justice—the administration of justice, those who administer it, rules governing its administration, etc. A sample of these include the understanding of מִשְׁפָּט, as "process, procedure, litigation before judges;" "place, court seat of judgment;" "sentence, decision of judg-

tary word pair counterpart צְדָקָה, which is often rendered in English translations as "righteousness," but not infrequently also as "justice." This word pair even more richly embodies the thematic of justice, when used as a hendiadys or combined in a parallelism (Gen 18:19; Deut 32:4; 33:21; 2 Sam 8:15; 1 Kgs 10:9; Job 37:23; Pss 72:2; 103:6; Prov 21:3; Isa 56:1; 58:2–7). Justice (and righteousness) is imbued with the qualities of integrity in purpose, rectitude in conduct, and equity in social dealings; it is a negation of oppression, decadence, and inequity. It closely approximates our modern concept of social justice.[36]

It is beyond doubt that justice is a major theme in the Old Testament. Christopher J. H. Wright writes, "No idea is more all-pervasive in the Old Testament than that God is a God of righteousness and justice."[37] Wright says, moreover, that behind Israel's detailed laws "stands a fundamental theological and ethical truth concerning the character of God himself—his justice."[38] This theme is aptly encapsulated, for instance, in Deut 10:16–18 thus: "Circumcise your hearts, therefore, and do not be stiff-necked any longer. For the LORD your God is God of gods and Lord of lords, the great God, mighty and awesome, who shows no partiality and accepts no bribes. He defends the cause of the fatherless and the widow, and loves the alien, giving him food and clothing" (NIV). This passage is a reminder that in Israel's Scriptures, justice derives from Yahweh, his character, his saving acts on oppressed Israel's behalf, and his covenant.

---

ment;" "justice, right, rectitude;" "one's (legal) right, privilege, due;" and something or conduct that is "proper, fitting, measure," i.e., being in the right or proper measure or fitting in accordance with the norm, nature, or custom (BDB, 1048–49).

36. Reimer notes that the first occurrence of this word pair as a hendiadys is in 2 Sam 8:15 and goes on to say, "Since the pair forms a hendiadys, precise and distinct meanings for each of the partners should not be sought. Rather, together they represent the ideal of social justice, an ideal lauded by the Queen of Sheba concerning Solomon's kingship in 1 Kgs 10:9, forming part of the excellence of his impressive administration" (Reimer, צדק, *NIDOTTE* 3:744–69). While Reimer's characterization of the word pair of משפט and צדק is on target, his understanding of Queen of Sheba's statement as acclaiming the justice practiced by Solomon seems apropos. The Queen of Sheba, no doubt, rightly understood the purpose of leadership (in this instance kingship) in Israel under Yahweh to be the administration of justice and righteousness. However, as to whether Solomon actually practiced it is another matter entirely; she certainly did not say that much.

37. Wright, *Living as the People of God*, 133.

38. Ibid., 133.

In modern scholarship, Bruce C. Birch points out that Gerhard von Rad drew widespread attention to the fact that such themes as righteousness (צדקה) in the OT can be understood only in terms of relationship.[39] Rad himself, for instance, writes, "Ancient Israel did not in fact measure a line of conduct or an act by an ideal norm, but by the specific relationship in which the partner had at the time to prove himself true. Every relationship brings with it certain claims upon conduct, and the satisfaction of these claims, which issue from the relationship and in which alone the relationship can persist, is described by our term צדק."[40] This emphasis on interpersonal relationships within the Israelite covenant community cannot be gainsaid by anyone acquainted with the Scriptures. However, the emphasis never existed in a vacuum. It derived directly from Yahweh's covenant relationship with Abraham that was reinforced in Israel's encounter with Yahweh in his redemptive act for their liberation in the Exodus-event, which eventuated in his self-disclosure to them in the Sinaitic Covenant.

In his discussion of צדקה, Birch likewise says, "Yahweh's righteousness was not an abstract norm but was seen in God's concrete acts to establish and preserve relationship. For Israel this divine righteousness is known in God's action to establish Israel in deliverance and preserve community in covenant."[41] Indeed, the Exodus-event, including the Sinaitic covenant, had such a profound effect on Israel that throughout its history, this redemptive act of Yahweh became the prism through which her people viewed all their existence and destiny. Consequently, it is on this covenant that the ethical appeals in the Torah for brotherly love are predicated. The book of Deuteronomy is replete with examples of such ethical appeals (e.g., Deut 1:16; 4:13–14, 31; 5:1–4; 9:9–11; 15:1–11).

Indeed, the Torah is not so much a legislative code as it is a fundamental directive principle (law) of the Covenant that obligates the covenant people, in fidelity and submission, to the great King, Yahweh. In discussing Old Testament ethics, Hendrik van Oyen equally demonstrates how central that the Torah is to the concept.[42] Thus the theme of

---

39. Birch, *Let Justice Roll Down*, 154.

40. Rad, *Old Testament Theology*, 371. Rad himself drew upon Cremer's *Biblisch-theologisches Wörterbuch*, 273–75 For similar views see also Reimer, צדק, in *NIDOTTE* 3:744–69.

41. Birch, *Let Justice Roll Down*, 154.

42. In his discussion of OT ethics, Oyen, highlighting the rootedness of OT ethical injunctions in the Covenant and its code, writes, "Il ne faut cependant pas oublier que,

justice in the books of Samuel (particularly in the relationships between David and the Saulides), as I demonstrate in this study, takes its cue from the justice of Yahweh and finds expression in interpersonal relationships and is guided by the demands of the Mosaic Covenant stipulations (the Torah—particularly the book of Deuteronomy for this study).

Because Israel's prophets have articulated this theme so clearly and strongly, many students of the Bible often fail to recognize that justice is also articulated—with equal force—if not with the same clarity—in other parts of the OT. Léon Epzstein, for example, focuses on the eighth and seventh centuries in his study of social justice in ancient Israel because he believes "that it was at this stage, at the time of the first great writing prophets, that the problem of social justice was raised with unparalleled strength and keenness and that it prefigured what was going to come next in the history of the Jewish people."[43]

The corpus of the Former Prophets is particularly susceptible to this misunderstanding. By dissecting this corpus and assigning its various parts to different sources or successive layers of redactors, many scholars too easily dismiss the presence of concern for justice in it. Commenting on 1 Sam 8:11–17, Klein writes, "[T]he highly polemic tone of vv. 11–17 has led many to see here a document based on bitter experience with later Israelite kingship itself. Since deuteronomistic language is absent from these verses and *since social inequities are not among Dtr's major concerns elsewhere*, it is probable that the historian is incorporating a previously existing document" (emphasis added).[44] The important question, as I see it, is not whether the redactor is incorporating an earlier text or making his own composition. Rather, the issue to wrestle with is, why did he incorporate this material in his compilation? There are others, however, who still insist "justice is the persistent theme of the stories from Genesis to the books of Samuel."[45] It is my hope that this study has

---

comme c'est le cas chez les prêtres et prohètes, dans ces exhortation simples et quotidiennes, la *tora* intervient constamment comme loi fondamentale de l'allaince d'où ces exhortations tirent leur origine.... Toute une série d'obligations qui doivent exprimer la fidélité et a soumission du vassal au suzerain. On doit se représenter la nature de la *tora* comme un fait analogue, obligeant le people de l'alliance à l'égard du grand roi, le Seigneur Yahvé" (Oyen, *Éthique De L'Ancien Testament*, 85).

43. Epzstein, *Social Justice*, xii.

44. Klein, *1 Samuel*, 74.

45. Schulte, *Die Entstehung der*, 94; as quoted in Adamiak, *Justice and History in the Old Testament*, 9.

demonstrated that justice is a vital theme constitutive of the ideology of the books of Samuel.

One basic assumption of this work is that the books of the Former Prophets were preceded by the writing of most of Deuteronomy and were greatly undergirded by Deuteronomic theology. One central tenet of Deuteronomic ideology is retributive theology. The retributive theology of Deuteronomy, with its ardent call to choose wise living in obedience to the Torah, classically expressed in (but not limited to) chapters 27, 28, and 30 in the themes of blessing and cursing, and life and death, constitute the basic background of the stories around the major characters in Samuel.[46]

Granting that the final redaction of the Former Prophets was accomplished in the exilic period, as I assume in this work, a major concern in the compilation of 1–2 Samuel had to do with the communication and reinforcement of religious beliefs of unparalleled import to the writer and his contemporaries. The purpose of this was, in a deliberative manner (speaking in a rhetorical critical fashion),[47] to help the *Golah* community choose the way of the Torah—the way of life. On this note, from a DtrH perspective, A. A. Anderson notes that the books from Deuteronomy to Kings were the work of the exilic community seeking answers for such troubling questions as these: What went wrong that the great hopes of the conquest and Davidic periods should come to nothing? How, if there is a time of restoration, can the people so organize their life that the future will be better? He concludes, "The whole work—Deuteronomy to 2 Kings—appears to be concerned with this, and answers the questions in terms of God's promise, his giving of the land of Canaan, his care of his people, and the disobedience of leaders and people to his demands, their turning away to other forms of worship, their failure to conform to certain standards of justice and right. It should not surprise us to find, in the Second Book of Samuel, some

---

46. Carlson anchors his dissertation on the story of David, as discussed in the next chapter, on this motif of "blessing and cursing." It is a pity that his work failed to generate the kind of attention it deserves. For more details on this see his *David, the Chosen King*.

47. In ancient rhetoric, there were three primary ways in which arguments were crafted (inventions), namely, judicial, deliberative, and epideictic inventions. For a detail discussion of these see Weima's "What Does Aristotle Have to do with Paul?" 459–61.

passages in which the emphasis rests on this final consideration of the meaning of judgment and the nature of hope."[48]

At the heart of these religious beliefs lay the issue of obedience to Yahweh (cf. 1 Sam 2:35; 12:14; 13:13–14; 15:22; 2 Sam 7:14; 11:27; 12:9–10). This call to obedience also takes its cue from Deuteronomy (cf. Deut. 4:30; 5:27; 6:3, 24; 9:23; 11:13, 27; 12:28; 13:4, 18; 15:5; 26:17; 27:10; 28:1–2, 15, 45, 62; 30:2, 10, 16–17). Indeed, the call to obedience in Deuteronomy assumes the proportion of a call for *imitatio Dei*. In the NT, Paul echoes this in his demand, Γίνεσθε οὖν μιμηταὶ τοῦ θεοῦ, "Be imitators of God" (Eph 5:1; cf. 1 Cor 11:1; Phil 2:5; 1 Thess 1:6). Deuteronomy 13:5 (EV 13:4) piles up verbs to express this idea thus, "You shall *follow* the LORD your God and *fear* Him; and you shall *keep* His commandments, *listen* to His voice, *serve* Him, and *cling* to Him" (NASB, emphasis added). Yahweh had displayed his wisdom in giving Israel the Torah: "Keep them and do them, for that will be your *wisdom and your understanding* in the sight of the peoples, who, when they hear all these *statutes*, will say, 'Surely this great nation is a *wise and understanding people*.' For what great nation is there that has a god so near to it as the LORD our God is to us, whenever we call upon him? And what great nation is there, that has *statutes and rules so righteous as all this law* that I set before you today?" (Deut 4:6–8 ESV; emphasis added). At the core of this righteous Law, within the context of the covenant community, is the theme of justice. In Deut 32, for instance, as Moses set out to proclaim the name (i.e., character) of Yahweh (v. 3) to his people, he proclaimed Yahweh's justice (verse 4).

Thus, Israel, as Yahweh's covenant community, was expected to show its wise obedience to Yahweh in three major areas: aversion to idolatry, that is, monotheistic Yahwism (Deut 4:15–20; 5:7–9a; 8:10–11; 11:16; 13:1–16; 17:2–7; 29:18; 32:10–26); passionate and correct observance of the cult, epitomized by worship at the central sanctuary at the place of Yahweh's choosing (Deut 12:1–14; 14:22–27; 18:6–14; 26:1–16); and justice in the covenant community, that is right relationship (Deut 1:16–17;

---

48. Anderson, *2 Samuel*, 4–5. Bergen, striking a similar note, observes, "Certainly a central purpose for writing 1, 2 Samuel was to communicate and reinforce religious beliefs of profound importance to the writer and his community. This 'overarching theological perspective' served as the framework into which historical and literary data were woven. The primary theological purpose was to support the teaching of the Torah and thus ... to provide guidance and hope for Israel's exilic community" (Bergen, *1, 2 Samuel*, 43).

10:17–18; 16:18–19; 17:8–13; 24:17–18; 25:1–2; 27:19; 32:4). These are the areas in which Israel (led by its kings) had failed woefully, the consequence of which was captivity and exile. Therefore, the effort to point the *Golah* community to the origins of its plight and to subsequently show it the way forward constituted the *raison d'être* for the traditions set forth in the books of Samuel and, indeed, the Former Prophets.

## CONCLUSION

This chapter, a general introduction, began by spotlighting the significance of the tripartite Abrahamic covenant promises of blessing, progeny, and land in the interlaced story of David and Saul's heirs. This set the requisite context for articulating the study problem, the significance of the study, and, lastly, the contribution this project makes to the study of Samuel. The chapter also highlighted the relationship between the Torah, especially Deuteronomy, and Samuel. It likewise demonstrates the literary unity of the books of Samuel. It is necessary to articulate the unity of the book because our reading of the narrative as it relates to the Saulides disregards the consensus position regarding the boundaries of the SN. By this, we include in our study 2 Sam 21, which, along with the last three chapters of the book, is usually severed from the rest of the book's narrative and branded as an appendix. Finally, I have also outline the prominent place of the justice theme in the DtrH, and its importance in Samuel.

2

# A Survey of the Interpretive History of 1–2 Samuel

CHAPTER 1 LAID OUT the primary concern of this work, the investigation of the fates of Saul's heirs in David's reign. It also situated the books of Samuel in the context of the DtrH, highlighting the connection between the Torah and its important motifs and themes, not the least of which is justice—the undergirding criterion for evaluating David's dealings with the Saulides in the book.

The present chapter is an overview of the history of the critical study of the books of Samuel, beginning from the early nineteenth century. It also highlights pivotal points in Samuel scholarship in the twentieth century, leading up to where we are early in the twenty-first century. The general overview is followed with a narrower focus on a review of selected literature that is centered either on David (2 Samuel) or on Saul (1 Samuel). Additionally, the review also considers the methodological approaches that have been employed, and the presuppositions underlying their assumptions.

## AN OVERVIEW OF THE HISTORY OF THE CRITICAL STUDY OF SAMUEL

J. G. Eichhorn's demonstration of the existence of sources in the book of Samuel in 1823 set the critical study of the book of Samuel on its path.[1] O. Thenius further refined this initial effort.[2] However, Wellhausen's study was a definitive turning point.[3] Wellhausen's criterion for identifying the sources was the attitude toward the monarchy. He read the texts with a favorable disposition toward the monarchy (cf. 1 Sam 9:1—10:17;

---

1. Eissfeldt, *The Old Testament*, 244.
2. Thenius, *Der Bücher Samuels*.
3. Wellhausen, *Der Text de Bücher Samuelis untersucht*.

11:1–11, 15) as early, while those with unfavorable dispositions (1 Sam 7:2—8:22; 10:17–27; 12:1–25) he considered late in origin.[4] A long succession of scholars who found the Pentateuchal sources continuing into the Former Prophets (such as Eduard Meyer and Karl Budde) expanded on these initial efforts.[5]

At the turn of the twentieth century, critics considered the sources of Joshua identical with those of the Pentateuch, hence the practice of referring to the whole as the Hexateuch. Some had even considered extending the range of these sources even beyond Joshua. R. Kittel was the first major voice to limit the scope of the sources to the Hexateuch. For him, it was the fragmentary theory that accounts for the corpus from Judges through Kings.[6] His point was that this corpus "consists in a variety of complexes of larger and smaller sizes: hero stories, royal stories, ark stories, prophet stories, and the like."[7] Building upon the insight of Kittel, Hugo Gressmann argued that the books of Samuel consist of a loose compilation of individual narratives of varying scopes.[8] Gressmann held that this collection eventually underwent a Deuteronomistic redaction at some stage in its history.[9] What is called the "successive block" theory is a modified form of Gressmann's theory. Some of the main suggested blocks include the History of David's Rise (HDR, 1 Sam 16 [or 15]—2 Sam 5); the Ark Narrative (AN, 1 Sam 4–6 and 2 Sam 6); the Succession Narrative (SN, 2 Sam 9–20 and 1 Kgs 1–2); and the Appendix (2 Sam 21–24).

Following the trail blazed by Gressmann, Leonhard Rost began a slightly different strand of fragmentary theory, in which he laid his emphasis more on the traditio-historical approach. In his work, published in 1926 (Eng. 1982), Rost saw the book of Samuel as consisting of a series of independently existing traditions that were crafted together without much intervening material.[10] Rost's work became the bedrock of almost all research in the books of Samuel for the rest of the twentieth

---

4. Klein, *1 Samuel*, xxviii; cf. McCarter, "The Books of Samuel," 260–80.
5. For example, see Budde, *Die Bücher Richter und Samuel*.
6. Kittel, "Das erste Buch Samuel," 407–51; Budde, *Geschichte des Volkes Israel*.
7. Eissfeldt, *Introduction*, 245.
8. Fohrer, *Introduction to the Old Testament*, 217; for more details see Gressmann, *Die älteste Geschichtereibung und Prophetie Israels*.
9. Anderson, *2 Samuel*, xxvi.
10. Rost, *Die Überlieferung von der Thronnachfolge Davids*.

century. To a great degree, it is still the definitive point of departure for contemporary work in Samuel studies.

Another major development along the lines of traditio-historical critical research with similarly significant impact on the study of Samuel is Martin Noth's Deuteronomistic theory of the redaction of the Former Prophets. Noth held that the sources (J, E, and P) never went beyond Numbers, so that there never was a Pentateuch but a Tetrateuch: The books Deuteronomy through Kings are the unified work of an exilic author, reflecting the same Deuteronomic theology. This Deuteronomist compiled the books creatively from independently existing sources.[11] Noth states that 1–2 Samuel was composed from a variety of already existing traditions, which the Deuteronomist stitched together into a unified work using his own compositions—infused with Deuteronomic theology—as the connecting seams.[12]

The previous near unanimity in critical scholarship concerning the high historical reliability of the books of Samuel—considered close to an eyewitness account[13]—began to ebb away with Noth's work, and the weakness only becomes magnified with the multiplication of redactional layers and redactors arising from scholarly responses to Noth's theory of a single exilic redactor. Subsequent to Noth, research in the books of Samuel in general, and in the SN in particular, has focused on either analyzing the text to uncover its different layers and the redactors responsible for them,[14] or considering it as a story or novel,[15] or on outright denial of its historical character and branding it as a fictional creation of the *Golah* community.[16]

---

11. Noth, *The Deuteronomistic History*, 24–26.

12. Noth, *The Deuteronomistic History*, 76–77, 84–91.

13. Cf. Wellhausen, *Prolegomena*, 262; Pfiffer, *Introduction to the Old Testament*, 357–59.

14. As the number of redactors multiply, especially in the method of the Göttingen School, it is easy to characterize the emergent phenomenon as pan-Deuteronomism. In his evaluation of the phenomenon Thomas Römer writes, "This approach risks inflating the number of redactional layers (and sigla), whose precise extent no one has yet to define in the deuteronomistic work; and the descriptions of certain 'layers' often appear quite arbitrary" (Römer, "Deuteronomy in Search of Origins," 116).

15. Eissfeldt, *Introduction*, 141; cf. Whybray, *The Succession Narrative*, 10–11.

16. See Römer, "Deuteronomy in Search of Origins," 117–18. For similar or more strongly stated views see van Seters, *Abraham in History and Tradition*; van Seters, *In Search of History*; Thompson, *Early History of Israelite*; Whitelam, *The Invention of Ancient Israel*; Davis, *In Search of "Ancient Israel"*; and Garbini, *History and Ideology in Ancient Israel*.

Particularly within the last thirty years there has been a shift in the direction of research in Samuel. Two streams of this new direction are noteworthy. One relates to the efforts of historical reconstructionists, which consists of the endeavors of radical minimalists or revisionists (such as K. W. Whitelam, Niels Peter Lemche, John Van Seters, Thomas L. Thompson, and Philip R. Davis), and reconstructionists of the more restrained sort, such as Baruch Halpern. Steven L. McKenzie counts himself in the latter group, but in my estimation, he is more proximate to the former group than the latter. The second major stream relates to the works of critics of the ideological bent. Works in this category include those of deconstruction and reader-response critics and feminists such as David Jobling, David J. A. Clines, David Gunn, Cheryl Exum, Mieke Bal, and to some extent Phyllis Trible.

## A CRITICAL REVIEW OF SALIENT RESEARCH IN SAMUEL

### Hugo Gressmann and Other Early Twentieth-Century German Scholars

W. Lee Humphreys rightly notes that if scholarship often appears to entail looking at old questions from a new perspective, "it is also revealing to consider presumed new questions from older perspectives."[17] The application of literary approaches has flourished to hitherto unheard-of dimensions in the last thirty years, yet it is very telling that these approaches had been broached from the early decades of the last century. It is thus fitting to begin this review with the works of Hugo Gressmann, Wilhelm Caspari, Bernhard Luther, and Alfons Schulz.[18]

Gressmann's essay, "The Oldest History Writing in Israel," sets the stage for his other essays by focusing primarily on historical questions. He demonstrates how the literary products of ancient societies were determined by the constitution of their polity. His proof for this is that where the kings were all-important (as in Egypt, Babylonia, or Assyria), their extant literary products are inscriptions, chronicles, lists, and annals highlighting the great deeds of these all-important figures. On the

---

17. Humphreys, a Review of *Narrative and Novella in Samuel*, 746.

18. Here I refer specifically to Gressmann's *Die älteste Geschichtsschreibung*; Caspari's "Literarische Art und historischer Wert von 2 Sam 15–20"; Luther's "Die Novelle von Juda und Tamar und andere Israelitische Novellen"; and Schulz's *Erzählungskunst in den Samuel-Büchern*, from which selected essays are published in Gunn (ed.), *Narrative and Novella in Samuel*.

other hand, in the polity of the Israelites and the Greeks, where the citizens were free, very little in the way of inscriptions or annals is extant, but their "history writing has reached the highest level of perfection that was granted to ancient times."[19] He then shows the relationship between the development of history writing and that of saga and legend. He thus situates the books of Samuel–Kings within the historical framework furnished by the Deuteronomist as the skeleton on which the flesh and blood of various sagas, historical narratives, anecdotes, annals, and legends were hung. Other sections of Gressmann's book delve more directly into literary issues. In these, he highlights such matters as plot embedding, characterization, scenic composition, and the use of one character to foil another. He concludes that in these narratives, reality is not given a sober description but is rather artistically glorified. This is what he calls a "history-narrative with novella-type depth"—anticipatory of Robert Alter's "*historicized*-fiction" or "*fictionalized*-history" concepts.

The essays of the other scholars, similarly ahead of their times, cast the searchlights on the author's narratorial skills. They likewise take note of such phenomena in the books of Samuel as the embedding of one narrative in another, the anecdotal character of narration (especially as it relates to David), characterization, the combined use of novella and narrative and the distinction between the two, and the use of figures of speech (e.g., parallelism, metaphor, and simile). They also follow the development of the storyline of the narrative and its emplotment around three principal, albeit inseparable, characters, namely Samuel, Saul, and David. These men are "active not only one after the other but also alongside one another. As a result, they are drawn the more clearly into the author's unifying scheme."[20]

While the work of these scholars is remarkable, especially when viewed in the context of the prevailing methodological practices of their time, it is still appropriate to point out where their practice differs from the mainstream literary practice of today. They were still very overtly concerned with the prior sources of the narratives. Gressmann's employment of the source and form-critical literary genres of saga and legend, as well as his effort to discern which part of the text is saga/legend and which is history, does not help the literary analysis of the text but is tantamount to preoccupation with matters that are extraneous to the

---

19. Gunn (ed.), *Narrative and Novella in Samuel*, 12.
20. Gunn (ed.), *Narrative and Novella in Samuel*, 122.

text at hand. Alfons Schulz, in particular, is even more indebted to the source critical method, carrying over wholesale the two-source theory for explaining the conflicting account of origins of the monarchy in 1 Sam 7–12 and the repetitions of reported episodes elsewhere in the book (especially in the HDR).[21] He goes further to divide 2 Sam 1–20 into two parts, assigning chapters 1–8 to the first source and chapters 9–20 to the second source. Needless to say, he offers no justification for this brazen assertion. While Gressmann rightly recognizes the structural framework supplied for these narratives by the Deuteronomist(s), he does not deal with the hermeneutical significance that this holds for these narratives. Besides, these authors did not have their focus on the development of the story with respect to particular characters in it. Thus, our concerns in the present project do not fall within the ambit of their interest.

## *Leonhard Rost*

Following hard on the heels of the above reviewed works was the publication in 1926 of Leonhard Rost's book, *Die Überlieferung von der Thronnachfolge Davids* (ET in 1982, *The Succession to the Throne of David*). Rost makes an impressive, comprehensive, and engaging treatment of the AN, the HDR, 2 Sam 7, and the Ammonite War, in addition to the substantive matter of the SN. His key proposition is that the books of Samuel were composed of these blocks that originally were separate and, perhaps, self-contained narratives. He thinks that the SN was comprised of 2 Sam 9–20 and 1 Kgs 1–2, with the likelihood that 2 Sam 6 (which originally belonged to the AN) and was added to the SN by the means of the Michal episode to form, in conjunction with the Dynastic Oracle, its beginning.

With respect to all the passages that Rost treats, his work is a masterful display of exegetical acumen that reckons with both the literary qualities of the text and its religious import. The attention he pays to style and narrative structure, his observation of the narrator's voice in commentary, and his perspicacity in discerning the function of direct discourse in the narratives[22] place him well ahead of his time.

---

21. See Schultz, *Erzählungskunst in den Samuel-Büchern* from which selected essays are published in Gunn's *Narrative and Novella in Samuel*.

22. A good case in point is what he says about the function of direct speech in the Samuel narratives: "Our investigations so far have shown that the narrator often weaves

Though Rost's work remains a point of departure for all critical work in Samuel, none of his major conclusions has escaped the critical appraisal of contemporary scholarship. The theory of a SN itself has been questioned. His definition of the boundary of the SN has been contested. His conclusion, that the question of who will accede to the throne of David is the climax to which the whole narrative drives, has been found flawed and not entirely persuasive. His proposal of self-contained sources for the narrative falls outside of the realm of contemporary literary analysis. Finally, his perception of the content of the narrative as history that is close to an eyewitness account is trivialized or replaced with an understanding of it as story at best, or otherwise branded as fictional narration. With regard to the Saulides, they feature in Rost's work (necessarily by its nature) only in his argumentation for the nature of the editorial activity in the SN.[23] He does not consider their story *qua* story.

## Rolf A. Carlson

Rolf A. Carlson's book was written as a doctoral dissertation under Ivan Engnell. Conscious of the limited familiarity of biblical scholarship outside of Scandinavian circles with traditio-historical criticism, he begins his work with an elucidation of the method. In the early pages of his book he calls attention to the distinction between what he calls the literary critical approach (i.e., the historical-critical approaches) and the traditio-historical approach. The latter nonetheless shares many features in common with the former, not the least important of which is the concern for contextual comparative analysis of the biblical text (against its ancient Near Eastern context); they both are also concerned with the history of the origins, transmission, and final redaction of the material at hand. In this regard it differs from contemporary literary approaches. However, it shares common territory with the latter when it focuses on such literary issues as motific, thematic, syntactical, and lexical analyses, repetition of concepts or key (or ring) words, formulaic use of phrases, and the use of *anachronies* (either *prolepses* or *analepses*, i.e., what he

---

speeches into his narrative as a means of enlivening his story. He wants his characters not only to act but to speak. He therefore attempts to bring them closer to the listeners. As we have already seen, given the importance allotted to words, to speech, it is no wonder that the spoken word appears at climaxes in the narrative or at important turning points" (Rost, *The Succession to the Throne of David*, 16).

23. Rost, *The Succession to the Throne of David*, 13, 65–66, 85, 92–95.

respectively calls the "foreshadowing and retrospection" aspects) in textual composition. Thus, I believe one should place no wedge between contemporary literary and contextual comparative analyses.

Carlson pays great attention to the editorial activity of the Deuteronomists (he prefers to call them the "D-group," and their work the "D-work") in the books of Samuel. He repudiates the view of previous scholarship (including Noth, Rost, and others) that much of the SN was incorporated into this book by the D-group with little changes to it.[24] On the contrary, he argues convincingly that the D-group reworked the material in such a way as to highlight their Deuteronomic dogma of retributive justice, namely, that obedience to Yahweh's law brings blessings, whereas the curse is visited upon the disobedient. In my estimation, he has given an unsurpassed account for the placement of the story of David within the DtrH by highlighting the Deuteronomic retributive theme of "blessing and cursing." With this theme he divides the book of 2 Samuel under the sub-themes of "David under the blessing" (2 Sam 1–7) and "David under the curse" (2 Sam 10–24). The last section of his book shows that David by repentance earns restoration—by this means the D-group found an occasion for exhortation to repentance. Indeed, in David's repentance the D-group places before their contemporaries a future messianic hope that is bound up with the fate of the Davidic house.

Carlson gives a good deal of attention to 2 Sam 21:1–14. He examines it in the attempt to show its connection to the rest of the SN, contra Rost. He finds this linkage in the commonality (between ch. 21 and chs. 9–20) of such motifs as "blood-guilt brought about by the sword, an

---

24. He says, for example, "With regard to the form of the D-work, however, it must be admitted that criticism of Noth's analysis is justified on at least one important point. In Noth's view the author ('Dtr') of the Deuteronomistic History, describing the period of Saul and David, used a ready-made complex to which he added in 1 Sam 13–1 Kings 3 nothing besides a number of introductory formulae (1 Sam 13:1; 2 Sam 2:10a, 11; 5:4–5) and 'list' material (1 Sam 14:47–51; 2 Sam 8, 20:23–26); he loyally reproduced the rest without comment (Rost, 61). However, it is highly remarkable that this hyper-royalist material, which according to Noth diverges so sharply from the main stream of Deuteronomic ideology, should have been influenced by the 'Dtr' as little as he claims. It is true that Noth considers that the 'Dtr,' having made plain his anti-royalist view in a previous passage (1 Sam 8–12) is able to allow this complex to pass without comment. But as von Rad points out, this accords not at all with the Deuteronomist's ability in composition, as demonstrated, e.g. in Judges and 1–2 Kings" (Carlson, *David, The Chosen King*, 23).

oracle from Yahweh, and finally reconciliation through human sacrifice." That is not all. He also envisages that "the narrative of 'removal' of the presumptive claimants to the throne in 21:1–14 has its thematic continuation in the 'neutralization' of Mephibosheth in 2 Sam 9 and the struggle for the throne which follows."[25] Carlson discusses 2 Sam 6 in particular at length. Here he finds multiple parallels within the ANE. Particularly telling is his understanding of the ark procession scene in the light of a similar cultic procession of the Ugaritic king Keret.[26] Similarly, he takes the David-Michal encounter as having been set in the form of the *heiros gamos* of El and Asherah as found in the Ras Shamra texts.[27] Michal's negative reaction to this Jebusite-Canaanite ritual, therefore, becomes the cause of her childlessness.[28] He reads the attribution of Saul's murdered five grandsons in 2 Sam 21 to Michal by the MT as a mistake.[29]

While there is so much in Carlson's method and conclusions that I find very agreeable, there are still some points I disagree with in the work. If the D-group reworked the material as thoroughly as Carlson argues, why is their hand less obvious in Samuel, as scholars have readily found it in such other books in the DtrH as Joshua, Judges, and Kings? While Carlson makes a case for the existence of "Deuteronomic" traits in Samuel, his demonstration of this fails to be persuasive. I am inclined to believe that Carlson overstressed compositional reworking at the expense of redactional shaping of the material.[30] The use of compositional and shaping strategies need not be opposed to each other, but indeed should be seen as working *pari passu*. It is my belief that such an approach would still lead to conclusions other than those reached by Rost. Others would like to know whether the messianic future noted by Carlson is "actually Deuteronomic, or was it simply present in the

---

25. Carlson, *David, The Chosen King*, 202.
26. Carlson, *David, The Chosen King*, 67.
27. Carlson, *David, The Chosen King*, 87.
28. Carlson, *David, The Chosen King*, 94–95.
29. Carlson, *David, The Chosen King*, 93.

30. Carlson argues, "The bias given the material in its new setting came through compositional technique and association, rather than by reshaping" (*David, The Chosen King*, 22). While it may be argued that taking just one sentence out of its context does not do justice to someone's project, even a casual perusal of the book will persuade the reader of the great capital he invests on the D-group's use of compositional techniques in the reworking of their sources.

tradition?"[31] Naturally, having his focus more on questions of the compositional and redactional nature of the books, rather than on the story they tell, Carlson does not systematically trace the storyline of the narrative of Samuel, especially as it affects the Saulides.

## R. N. Whybray

Whybray in his monograph posits wisdom instruction as the underpinning presupposition for the SN.[32] Indeed, he writes at length to hypothesize on the introduction and development of the wisdom tradition in Israel. He regards the book of Proverbs as serving as an example of the active embrace and use of this innovation in Israel.[33] In making a case for locating the SN in the wisdom tradition, Whybray also allows that it is the product of creative imagination. Furthermore, he writes, this work, along with the Joseph narrative (also thought to have arisen within the wisdom schools), and the Yahwistic history "are to some degree works of imagination, and whether they are to be judged as 'history' or 'fiction' is a matter of degree."[34] This marks the first significant challenge to the consideration of this narrative as a historical work since the publication of Rost's book. In underscoring the novelistic traits in this narrative, Whybray makes a breathtaking assertion, which he takes no time to substantiate, namely, that the SN stands by itself as "a free composition rather than dependent on older sources."[35]

He rightly sees the threat that the surviving Saulides pose to the survival of the Davidic house as the thread that links chapters 9, 16, 19, and 20. These chapters show how the danger was fought until it was elim-

---

31. John Bright, review of *David, The Chosen King*, 247.

32. Whybray's argument is that David, who proved to be an innovator in many regards, was the initiator of what von Rad thought to be a Solomonic "enlightenment." This, he says, David did as he, for the first time, brought Israel "into full and continuous contact with the intellectual tradition, common to all the civilized peoples of the ancient Near East, which we know as wisdom" (Whybray, *The Succession Narrative*, 1).

33. Whybray, *The Succession Narrative*, 5.

34. Whybray, *The Succession Narrative*, 7. Indeed he approvingly quotes Eissfeldt in this vein and says, "Eissfeldt characterized the work as a 'good historical novel.' It is difficult to disagree with this judgment: the theme is historical, the treatment that of the novelist. But the term 'historical novel' is imprecise: its meaning depends upon the degree of emphasis which is placed respectively on the adjective and noun" (*The Succession Narrative*, 10–11).

35. Whybray, *The Succession Narrative*, 19.

inated.[36] Whybray penetratingly notes the innocence of Mephibosheth in the accusation leveled against him by Ziba in that his mourning over the king is reported by the narrator, who elsewhere deliberately avoids directing the reader's thoughts. He also observes that the scheming of this unscrupulous servant was facilitated by the undue advantage Ziba enjoyed, being "free from proper supervision by a lame master who is forced to live away from his estates."[37] Whybray follows the beaten path in understanding Michal's childlessness as being due to barrenness, which we shall show not to be the case.

Whybray stands in agreement with Rost in many respects. These include such issues as the boundaries of the narrative, its central theme, and literary analysis (such as the use of characterization and the function of dialogue). However, his concept of David as the bringer of death shares affinity with R. A. Carlson's theme of David under the curse. With regards to the genre of the SN, Whybray dismisses forthwith the suggestion that it is a national epic, but he is more dubious as to whether it is a tale with a religious moral. He is, however, persuaded of its character as political propaganda and accords it a Solomonic dating.

Furthermore, he argues that the monarchy and its ideals are derivatives of sapiential ideals and proceeds to furnish copious examples of the correlations between these ideals as found in the SN and the book of Proverbs. In fact, Whybray is of the view that the goal of the author of the SN was to outline a vivid illustration of specific proverbial teaching for the instruction of the wisdom school pupils.[38]

While it is hard to deny the influence of wisdom in this narrative, the argument for such direct correlation is rather tenuous. In Walter Brueggemann's view, the process of this connection is certainly obscure.[39] J. L. Crenshaw in particular finds Whybray's work objectionable on many counts. Finding Whybray's rejection of the story as a moral-religious tale unsatisfactory, he writes, "It is difficult to envision a reading of the story without grasping the moral implied about family relations (adultery, sibling rivalry, and sex) and obligations of office and friendship, in spite of (or *because of*) the psychological concerns of the narrative."[40]

36. Whybray, *The Succession Narrative*, 21–23.
37. Whybray, *The Succession Narrative*, 44.
38. Whybray, *The Succession Narrative*, 95.
39. Walter Brueggemann, "On Trust and Freedom," 3–19.
40. J. L. Crenshaw, "Wisdom Influence," 138.

He similarly rejects Whybray's political propaganda hypothesis, on which account the SN is supposedly set to legitimize the Solomonic regime. His reasons for this position include the fact that neither David nor Solomon is portrayed in favorable light; Solomon's accession was the result of the scheming skills of the court prophet Nathan with the connivance of Bathsheba. Besides, he notes that Solomon's first acts upon his accession are unsurpassed in cruelty in the Old Testament.[41]

Fundamentally, Crenshaw shows that Whybray erred in failing to search for stylistic and ideological peculiarities found primarily in wisdom literature. With regard to literary devices, Crenshaw counters that the sages by no means monopolized such devices as simile, comparison, and metaphorical language. Likewise the use of retributive ideology is found in all the sources of the OT (Yahwist, Elohist, and Deuteronomist, as well as the prophets). Besides, since Proverbs covers the whole gamut of human existence, he says, it is hard not to find a story that illustrates its themes. Moreover, he charges that Whybray's argument is deficient because he fails to explain the non-wisdom emphases in the succession document.[42]

## Robert Polzin

Two of Robert Polzin's books, *Samuel and the Deuteronomist: 1 Samuel* and *David and the Deuteronomist: 2 Samuel*, are relevant to the enterprise at hand. The two books are sequels to his *Moses and the Deuteronomist*, in which he laid out his methodological theory. Polzin's approach is based on the literary theory of Mikhail Bakhtin, which he enunciates in *Moses and the Deuteronomist*. In *Samuel and the Deuteronomist*, Polzin sets the tone of the book with a polemic against historical criticism's genetic and fragmenting approach to the biblical text. He deplores its profound "lack of attention to what the entire text might mean in its final shape."[43]

---

41. Crenshaw, "Wisdom Influence," 138.

42. Crenshaw, "Wisdom Influence," 138–39.

43. Polzin, *Samuel and the Deuteronomist*, 2. His frustration with the unproductive nature of this approach surfaces as he asks rhetorically, "What has brought us to the present situation in which we on the one hand recognize in theory and practice the necessity of *establishing the text*, but on the other simply use it to do the kind of excavative scholarship that has dominated our field for well over a century? Why have we chosen to apply our not inconsiderable skills to reconstructing a supposed prior text and to determining its theological intention and probable date of composition, without employing as much sympathetic care and effort in determining the global meaning of the very text that has helped shape Western civilization and the Judeo-Christian culture

In effect, he writes, this approach "denigrates the Bible in many of its esthetic, historiographic, and ideological dimensions, however loudly and often scholars claim the contrary."[44] In his work, therefore, Polzin set out to depart from the situation where lavish focus on the pre-texts and their background denies corresponding attention to the real texts and their interpretation. He then proceeds with the assumption that the text of Samuel makes sense in its present form, its text-critical deficiencies notwithstanding.

Turning to 1 Samuel itself, Polzin sees the first seven chapters as a parabolic representation of the story of the nation itself. In this parable Hannah stands for Israel; her request for a son for Israel's demand for a king; her son for Israel's king; Eli's house for the monarchy. Ultimately he finds the climax of this programmatic parable in 1 Sam 7:3–17, wherein worship of foreign gods is Israel's sin par excellence, while repentance means returning to the Lord. Similarly, Samuel's role as the ideal judge adumbrates the fact that a true return to the Lord involves the removal of the monarchy, which was alien to Israel's fundamental Yahwism in pre-monarchical days.[45] Indeed, for Polzin, the tragic end of Saul formed the basis for the Deuteronomist's message to the *Golah* community that to have demanded a king was not just political but also communal suicide.

He presents Samuel, especially in chapters 3 and 4 of his book, as being a self-interested, self-serving, calculating, and obstructive person. Polzin accuses Samuel of setting Saul (the hapless victim of both Samuel's lust for power and the darkness of God's displeasure) up for disaster.[46] The story of David's rise to power is covered largely in three chapters (5 to 7). In these, Polzin shows that the story, as narrated in 1 Samuel, is contrived as much against David as it is for him. For example, in discussing David's relationship with Achish, he points to David's growing duplicity in character and says, "One continues to wonder whether David's

---

at its core? Why do we typically choose to do what we do, even as we avoid what we choose not to do?" (ibid., 3).

44. Polzin, *Samuel and the Deuteronomist*, 3.

45. Polzin, *Samuel and the Deuteronomist*, 74–79

46. Polzin emphatically says, "Between the two, the reader's sympathies probably lie more with Saul, who appears—so far at least—more sinned against than sinning, more manipulated than manipulating, with Samuel just the opposite" (*Samuel and the Deuteronomist*, 147).

dealings with various Israelites might not conceal similarly self-serving motives."[47]

In the second book (*David and the Deuteronomist*) Polzin commences his discussion of the text of 2 Samuel without an introduction. That notwithstanding, even the way his chapters are titled ("Heroes," "Brothers," "Houses," "Servants," "Messengers," "Women," "Curses," "Counselors," "Crossings," and "Numbers") gives an inkling of his approach, which is focused on characters, motifs, and themes. In this volume, he deliberately keeps minimal his engagement with contemporary commentators. He characterizes his approach as a contemporary reading and acknowledges his conscious backgrounding of methodological and theoretical matters. Yet methodological questions are addressed in the consideration of the content. For example, one literary device that Polzin pays close attention to is repetition, and he brings his insightful, analytical skills to bear on his discussion of duplexes in the text, such as the double accounts of Saul's death.[48] The idea of conceptual refraction looms large in this work; Polzin shows the author's point of view mirrored in that of his characters—as in David's elegy for Saul and Jonathan being the Deuteronomist's prophetic lamentation over fallen Israel.

Polzin follows through the entire book to give a detailed literary analysis of 2 Samuel. For instance, he pays close attention to the use of the Hebrew words for "after," "coming," "going," and "knowing" in 2 Sam 2 and 3.[49] He also paints a vivid picture of the Deuteronomist's use of fratricide (either tribal or familial) through the "smiting" in the "belly," which expression is found only in 2 Samuel (2:22–23; 3:27–30; 4:6; 20:9–10).[50]

In both books, Polzin's commitment to a literary analysis of the text is unflinching. He observes keenly the interplay between narration and reported speech, especially the effectuation of characterization with direct discourse. He is adept at exegetical analysis of key words, phrases, and entire episodes, at the same time not being oblivious to the presence of ambiguity, wordplay, and the multivalency of words in the text. He builds a strong case for the parabolic (almost allegorical) implications of earlier parts of the narratives for their latter ends. He has carried through in an unparalleled fashion the hermeneutical implications of the setting

---

47. Polzin, *Samuel and the Deuteronomist*, 217.
48. Polzin, *David and the Deuteronomist*, 1–10.
49. Polzin, *David and the Deuteronomist*, 29–37.
50. Polzin, *David and the Deuteronomist*, 50–53.

of the books of Samuel within the DtrH. Polzin's avowed commitment to a literary understanding of the text does not deprive his interpretation of historical grounding. Unlike the more *readerly* kinds of literary reading, Polzin anchors his interpretation in the historical context of the Deuteronomist's audience, which he understands to be exilic.

I, however, find troubling his perception of 1–2 Samuel as mimetic story. An example of this is his perception of the war accounts in 2 Sam 2–4 as implausible and his questioning of their credibility. He says, "[R]eaders are struck by the unreality of it all."[51] Which readers does he refer to here? Nevertheless, David Jobling's criticism of Polzin for being intolerant of those who stress ideological conflict in the text and the text's "undecidability" is unfounded, as far as I am concerned.[52] While Polzin is decidedly against reconstructing putative sources (on the basis of the apparent contradictions or duplexes) behind the extant text, his own unconventional interpretation (for example, his portrayal of Saul and Samuel) by itself evinces the "undecidability" of the text ingrained in his hermeneutics, even though he does not personally acknowledge this.

Finally, though Polzin's insightful attention to literary hints and signals in the text are highly commendable, I think his obsession with making connections between prior statements and latter statements that the earlier ones seem to prefigure, hinders him from exploiting such insights and highlighting the troubling ethical or theological issues inherent in such texts.[53]

---

51. Polzin, *David and the Deuteronomist*, 27.

52. Jobling, a review of *Samuel and the Deuteronomist*, 416.

53. A case in point is the way he addresses the encounter between Michal and David in 2 Sam 6. He writes, "Here in 2 Samuel 6, as in 1–2 Samuel generally, a voice extolling the glories of Davidic kingship is counterbalanced by another voice intimating the connection between having children and building a royal house. Whereas the Jebusite women *of* Jerusalem help David build his house (2 Sam 5), Michal *in* Jerusalem does not. And whereas Hannah's asking for a son whom she would give to the LORD all the days of his life (1 Sam 1:11) placed her in the role of a sinful Israel about to ask for a king, here in 2 Samuel 6 Michal's despising of David and her subsequent childlessness to the day of her death (v. 23) may represent an ideal Israel that never was. The royal glory (*kābōd*) about which Michal speaks and which David reaffirms in vv. 20–22 involves the abasement of Israel long ago signified by the birth of Ichabod, whose name means 'No-Glory.' The glory somehow departs from Israel when the ark of God is taken up in the behalf of kingship. Michal's childlessness may represent the Deuteronomist's hope that the glory would one day return to Israel, and that Israel, like Michal, would remain kingless before the LORD to the day of her death" (Polzin, *David and the Deuteronomist*, 70–71).

## Gillian Keys

Gillian Keys's book[54] was first undertaken as a doctoral dissertation project. It consists of two major sections. The first is an appraisal of Leonhard Rost's SN hypothesis. Keys, on the basis of literary style, language, content, and theological outlook, says that there is a discontinuity between the story of David (contained in 2 Sam 10–20) and the chapters in the outer rings of Rost's SN boundaries. She attributes these chapters (2 Sam 10–20) to one author and disavows that they have anything to do with succession. In the second half of the book, she thoroughly studies the text (2 Sam 10–20) for its literary unity, theme, genre, purpose, date, and authorship.

Keys proceeds first to review previous critical studies of the SN, beginning with casual references to nineteenth-century scholars like H. P. Smith and going on to in-depth reviews of the works of Rost, von Rad, Carlson, L. Delekat, T. C. G. Thornton, J. W. Flanagan, David Gunn, and the European *Tendenz* critics (Würthwein, Veijola, and Langlamet), among many others. In her evaluation of Rost's work, she begins with the theme of the work, namely, succession to the throne of David. She refers to other scholars like Carlson, Blenkinsopp and Flanagan, Gunn, and Hagan, who have severally questioned the centrality of this theme to this narrative. Even though she argues against the practice of primogeniture in the Israelite/Judahite monarchy, she contends that David had several children older than Solomon (on the basis of 2 Sam 3:2–5; 5:14–16) who would have succeeded David after the demise of the first three. She writes, "If SN is indeed a narrative of succession it tells an incomplete story, for it only accounts for the elimination of three of the nine possible candidates for the throne who were born before Solomon."[55]

Among several other grounds for rejecting succession as the theme of the narrative, she contends that it rests on assumptions that had not been previously questioned. Keys demonstrates this point by showing that the bulk of the content of the SN (outside of the 1 Kings chapters)

---

Yet, one looks in vain for when Polzin would engage such perturbing questions as why was Michal childless, since the text does not say she was barren? Why did David take her from the husband who treasured her, when she would end up just as another addition (like a piece of property) to his harem? What implications does Michal's situation hold for the house of Saul?

54. Gillian Keys, *The Wages of Sin*.
55. Keys, *The Wages of Sin*, 46.

has little to do with succession. With this assessment she asks, "With SN as a whole (as with 2 Sam 10–20), Rost finds the main theme and pivotal point only at the very end of the narrative. Yet surely, such a major theme should become apparent at a much earlier stage in any work. Undoubtedly 'succession' (or perhaps more accurately, the accession of Solomon) is the overriding theme of the first two chapters of 1 Kings, but is this really true of the rest of the work?"[56]

Keys argues convincingly that 2 Sam 10–20 demonstrates both structural and thematic unity, as well as literary independence from the surrounding texts.[57] She repudiates the theory that the sundering of the SN with the so-called appendix was the (clumsy) work of a later redactor. Instead, she is persuaded of the centrality of chapters 10–20 in 2 Samuel, wherein it forms the core of the book both in terms of structure and of content. She adds, "Chapters 1–9 build up to this central section and the appendix rounds off the book, with its chiastic structure and its reference to the latter years of David's life (21:15–17) and to his death (23:1). It would appear then that 2 Samuel 1–9 and 21–24 are in fact some form of framework for the central section of the book, that is chs. 10–20."[58]

In the further study of the central core of 2 Samuel, Keys assesses its main theme to be "sin and punishment," which is supplemented by a multiplicity of other themes or motifs such as David the man, David's family, his weakness, his humility, and his death. With regard to genre, she rejects all such other suppositions as political propaganda, wisdom literature, or novella. She rather posits that the narrative is a "theological biography." As far as she is concerned, 2 Sam 10–20 consists of the life of David painted on the canvas of divine retribution. She locates its provenance within the prophetic circles and dates it anywhere from the end of David's life to just before the composition of the DtrH.

Daniel Hawk charges Keys of being long on critical review of previous works but short on her own analysis, and the accusation is not without merit. Hawk, for example, writes, "[A]fter a very fine survey of literature dealing with the genre of the text, she devotes slightly more than two pages to her suggestion that the work is best understood as a theological biography. This proposal raises many questions, and the

---

56. Keys, *The Wages of Sin*, 53.
57. Keys, *The Wages of Sin*, 79.
58. Keys, *The Wages of Sin*, 85.

failure to explore them fully seems a missed opportunity."[59] Burke O. Long criticizes Keys for not including in her critique the methodological assumption about literature, authorship, and high art that underlie Rost's 1926 hypothesis.[60] While there may be value in the criticism, I am of the opinion that it cannot be pushed too far, because it is practically impossible to address all the ramifications of every work one critiques in one's own particular writing. If that were to be the case, it would make the enterprise of academic writing an unwieldy and impossible undertaking.

I particularly find Keys's arguments against the SN as set forth by Rost very convincing. Her arguments for taking 2 Sam 10–20 to be thematically unified and literarily independent (with chapters 1–9 and 21–24 functioning as its framework) are equally persuasive. Nevertheless, in terms of the project at hand, Keys's book does not have much to say. Her focus lies elsewhere, and as such, the Saulides feature in her discussions only tangentially as she critiques Rost's SN hypothesis.

## V. Philips Long

Philips Long's book is a publication of his 1987 doctoral dissertation, with little change made to it. The seven chapters are divided into three parts. Part I begins with the survey of the application of the literary method to biblical narrative. Long begins his account of the rise of literary approach with a review of Gerhard von Rad's work. On von Rad's approach to the biblical text, he observes that von Rad had "moved beyond the 'how' of textual origin to the 'what' of textual meaning. In so doing, he heralded a change of direction in OT studies which has become increasingly apparent in recent years."[61] He follows this with a closer discussion of such literary issues as the rise of the synchronic literary approach, the interplay of synchronic and diachronic concerns, as well as poetics and interpretation. He then organizes his discussion of the features of Hebrew narrative style under three rubrics, namely, scenic narration, economy of means, and reticence and indirection. In the second chapter, he considers the text of 1 Sam 13:7b–15, noting the consensus of scholarship since Wellhausen that views it as secondary.

---

59. Hawk, A Review of *The Wages of Sin*, 332–33.
60. Long, A Review of *The Wages of Sin*, 130.
61. Long, *The Reign and Rejection of King Saul*, 8.

He argues to the contrary, seeing that this passage fulfills Saul's double commission of 1 Sam 10:7–8.

Part II consists of three chapters that deal more directly with the matters of Saul's reign and rejection (as found in 1 Sam 13–15). In this section, Long pays careful attention to the numerous critical problems associated with this text, such as the numerals in 13:1. Notwithstanding these problems and the cacophony of scholarly voices that highlight each of them, Long reads chapters 13 and 14 as a connected, coherent, and sequential narrative. Indeed, he holds that the rejection of Saul in ch. 13 and its elucidation and justification in chapter 14 (accomplished via the contrastive characterization of Saul and Jonathan) "form the gravitational center of the story."[62] He divides these chapters into five scenes (1 Sam 13:2–7a; 13:7b–15; 14:1–15; 14:16–23; 14:24–46). Among other things, he elaborates on Saul's sin of incomplete obedience to his commission. Long divides chapter 15 into two scenes: the first focuses on the Amalakite campaign, which he calls "Saul's flawed victory" (15:1–9); while the second dwells on the Samuel–Saul tango, which for Long is a trial that returned the verdict of Saul's ultimate rejection (15:10–35).

In part III, titled "Sense and Significance in the 'Rise of Saul,'" Long first discusses the polyphony of voices in the traditions preserved in the accounts of the rise of the monarchy. The variegated and complex nature of chapters 9–11 (Saul's rise) has posed such an irresistible challenge to scholarly ingenuity that Long borrows A. D. H. Mayes's words to describe it as "a favorite hunting ground for source critics."[63] Long makes a brief survey of various scholarly positions that emphasize that 1 Sam 8:1—12:1 contain largely multiple (or even opposing) traditions of the same matter of Saul's election. Nevertheless, he proceeds to make a case for a synchronic reading of the text. One reason he advances for his stand is that it is "never a good thing when a critical conclusion becomes so entrenched that it is no longer subject to scrutiny."[64] Consequently, on the basis of the advances made in the understanding of the accession process in Israelite ideology and historiography, he concludes that the time has come "to reconsider the possibility that 1 Sam 8–12 present a

---

62. Long, *The Reign and Rejection of King Saul*, 70.

63. Long, *The Reign and Rejection of King Saul*, 173; a citation from Mayes's *The Story of Israel*, 9.

64. Long, *The Reign and Rejection of King Saul*, 175.

more coherent narrative sequence than has commonly been allowed."[65] Additionally, Long examines the issues that constitute tensions and difficulties that might impair the holistic reading of the Saul narrative, if left unaddressed. His study, he says, has uncovered even in these earlier episodes of the Saul narrative various negative elements in Saul's portrayal. These subtle dissonances in Saul's depiction constitute subliminal intimations of things to come. Thus, the hints of passivity, imperceptions, hesitancy, inability to listen, and an excessive concern with externals (to the exclusion of internal concerns) in these early episodes of Saul's life are pointers to the attentive reader that Saul was ill-suited for kingship.[66] Hence, he finds the portrait of Saul in these early chapters consistent with that of 1 Sam 13–15.

Long's study commends itself as a good demonstration of the application of the synchronic literary approach in reading the Bible. It also well illustrates that literary textual readings need not be set in opposition to diachronic readings. Rather, historical perspectives help, not hinder, literary readings.

### Steven L. McKenzie

Steven L. McKenzie conceives of his book, *King David: A Biography*, as his effort to assemble into a comprehensive history of David the myriads of conclusions reached by other scholars who have used the methods of biblical criticism.[67] McKenzie's title seduces one into thinking the book adopts more of a novelistic approach to the study of David. Contrary to such an impression, the book is rather an attempt to paint a portrait[68] of the historical David with the Bible as the paint alongside the tools of archaeological discoveries and comparative social (anthropological and sociological) studies of the ancient Near East (especially, of rulers in the ANE). Not only that, he also compares David to modern Middle Eastern despots such as Ibn Saud, the founding king of Saudi Arabia, and Saddam Hussein.[69] The portrait thus painted by McKenzie shows

---

65. Long, *The Reign and Rejection of King Saul*, 184.
66. Long, *The Reign and Rejection of King Saul*, 233.
67. McKenzie's *King David: A Biography*, 7.
68. McKenzie's own words (*King David: A Biography*, 185).
69. Comparing David with Saddam Hussein he writes, "Both were clever politicians and military commanders. Both led outlaw bands that rivaled the ruling family. Both eventually replaced their rivals, leaving a trail of dead bodies behind. Both gained and

that the story of David we have in the Bible "is not an exact recounting of history but is rather ... a plausible tale."[70]

The book consists of ten chapters. The first chapter examines the two sources for David's life apart from the Bible, namely, inscriptions and archaeology. With these, he seeks to answer two questions: Is there evidence of the existence of the historical David in these sources? If so, what information do they furnish about his life vis-à-vis the biblical material? McKenzie rightly recognizes the falsity of the belief or thought that archaeology produces hard, objective evidence in contrast to the Bible, which must be interpreted: archaeological evidence, just like the Bible, must be interpreted. His conclusion is that archaeology has not yet proven the existence of David, but neither has it disproven it. All that archaeology does is to provide the background and context for the study of the David stories.

In the second chapter the focus shifts to the Bible, describing the different parts of the Bible that have something to say about David (1 Sam 16—2 Sam 24 and 1 Kgs 1–2; 1 Chronicles; and the Psalms), as well as assessing their historical value. Of these biblical sources, McKenzie considers the first (1 Sam 16—1 Kgs 2) to be the most important, containing the longest and most detailed account of David's life. It is also the informing background for the data on David in the other biblical sources (Chronicles and Psalms). In this chapter, he begins to sketch the image of David as a traitor, outlaw, Philistine mercenary, and serial killer (the list of his victims, according to McKenzie, includes Saul, Abner, Ishbaal, Saul's heirs, as well as David's own sons Amnon and Absalom).[71] He regards the biblical account as a vehement protest against David's guilt in these crimes, supplying as it does an alibi for David for each of them. The aim of it all is to legitimate David's accession to the throne of Saul. Thus, this first source has a "ring" of authenticity. McKenzie, however, considers the second source (Chronicles) not to be a reliable source for David's life, as it either merely repeats the first source or introduces changes contrived by the Chronicler to serve his interest. The Psalms, like 1 Chronicles, contain little of significance for a biography of David,

---

retained power through military force. This comparison may seem offensive at first. But it must be remembered that David and Saddam are culturally much closer to each other than either is to Westerners" (*King David: A Biography*, 22).

70. McKenzie, *King David: A Biography*, 186.
71. McKenzie, *King David: A Biography*, 32–34.

## A Survey of the Interpretive History of 1–2 Samuel

since they, too, simply repeat information from the first source. Besides, many of the references to David are not part of the Psalms, but editorial comments.

Chapters 3 through 9 take a closer look at the phenomenon of David's biography. David's life is broken up into time periods. The data concerning him from the biblical text is integrated with extra biblical sources to reconstruct his story in each period. As far as McKenzie is concerned, much of this portion of the Bible is not historical but purely literary creations. One example of this is David's early years, wherein the well-known image of David's youth is that of a shepherd boy. For McKenzie, this is a literary creation, not a historical reality. Similarly, in the Goliath episode, McKenzie holds that the image created of Goliath is legendary and as such merely serves a literary purpose. Other examples of such characterizations include his rejection of the historical nature of the Nob episode, David's double sparing of Saul, and the Abner-Ishbosheth quarrel. In the final chapter, McKenzie sums up his findings as he asserts that the character of David as a Middle Eastern tyrant was refurbished, really subverted, through the success of the Deuteronomist's skillfully crafted apology for him. He writes that the apology "altered David's historical image by legitimating his deeds. Dtr enhanced the apologetic material and used it to convey his own theological principles."[72]

McKenzie's book is both well researched and eloquently argued. He takes the Bible as a source for historical information.[73] However, he does not trust this source and so assumes two critical stances to it, skepticism and analogy. These, apparently, are the correlates of the Troeltschian historical principles of probability and analogy respectively.[74] These two principles lead him to adopt the Davidic apology as criterion for ascertaining the verity of the texts he analyzes: the more forceful the apology for David, the more likely the possibility that he did what he is being defended against. While there may be some occasion where suspicion of a text's affirmations might be healthy, elevating suspicion to the level

---

72. McKenzie, *King David: A Biography*, 189.

73. McKenzie, *King David: A Biography*, 5.

74. Beginning in the late nineteenth but more so at the dawn of the twentieth century, Troeltsch's writings were grappling with the question of the absoluteness of the Christian religion vis-à-vis the historical relativity of existence. It is in that context that he outlined the cardinal principles for historical criticism. These are probability, analogy, and correlativity. For a fuller discussion of these see his *Religion in History*, 11–32; cf. Chapman, *Ernst Troeltsch and Liberal Theology*, 54–55.

of a hermeneutical key, as McKenzie does, is a flawed way of proceeding with research. If such a stance were to be adopted in our law courts, for instance, then anyone who makes a good case before a jury or judge would be the one to be convicted, because the more cogent and spirited your defense, the more likely you are to have committed the offense of which you are accused.

Though McKenzie affirms that there is a historical kernel on which the biblical narrative of David is based, his stance and conclusions engender doubts as to how much such a kernel amounts to, if it amounts to anything at all. This critique is valid because McKenzie reaches a good deal of his conclusions on the basis of self-confessed speculation.[75] Yet, he would want us to believe his speculatively reconstructed story rather than the biblical account. For example, while he repudiates the biblical portrait of David as shepherd boy in days of his youth (cf. 1 Sam 16, 17; 17:15; 2 Sam 7:8; 1 Chr 17:7; Pss 23; 78:70), McKenzie reconstructs his image of David on the basis of a single verse (1 Sam 16:18). He fails to take into account the fact that in more traditional societies, occupational specialization is not as cut and dried as he would like. In such economies, one's job changes with one's age and role in community. Of course, even in modern advanced economies there are far higher (indeed, ever-rising) levels of job mobility than is often realized.

McKenzie, besides, equivocates in the manner of his interaction with the biblical data. A good case in point is his attitude toward David's marriage to Michal, Saul's daughter. He asserts more than once that the story was contrived.[76] Yet, this perception of the data does not stop him from using it in his argument for a negative portrait of David; he makes reference to the marriage more than once to buttress his points. First, in his attempt to conjecture the physical appearance of David, he draws on the story of Michal's use of idols to fool Saul's assassins to surmise that David was short.[77] Second, he brings into play the same marriage to substantiate his allegation that David had attempted a coup against Saul.[78] This is not how to proceed. You cannot discredit a source and yet

---

75. McKenzie makes much of his reading "against the grain." There is no *prima facie* case against such an approach. The problem arises when it is based squarely on speculation (see his pages 87, 108, 109 as succinct examples).

76. McKenzie, *King David*, 88 and 119.

77. McKenzie, *King David: A Biography*, 64.

78. McKenzie, *King David: A Biography*, 87.

turn round to use it as the evidence for constructing an argument, since in the nature of argumentation, any argument at all invariably stands or falls with the evidence adduced for its substantiation.

Another difficulty that attaches to McKenzie's book relates to his great stress on the role the apology for David played in the composition of our text. It is hard to believe that an author concerned with David's reputation, would have taken the trouble to write all the stories that cast doubt over David's image, only to turn around to defend the king's honor. One gaping hole that McKenzie's book leaves is with respect to the iconic place of David in Yahwistic religion. This is where I suspect that McKenzie assumes Troeltsch's third principle for historical research, correlativity, but does not state it. The implementation of the correlative principle (of a closed universe, where all effects have identifiable causes within our world) is seen either in the scanty attention McKenzie gives to texts that contain prophetic messages or his stripping them of their supernatural elements.[79] Overall, though David was such a dismal figure, Yahweh still set his heart on him. Why? McKenzie does not attempt to address this critical question. Perhaps to him it is a non-issue, overshadowed by his "conspiracy" theory. Yet if one takes the Bible not only critically but also seriously, as McKenzie claims he does, then one will have to deal with the question.

## *Baruch Halpern*

Baruch Halpern's book, *David's Secret Demons*, is an attempt to engage the twin issues of the fascination of Western literature and culture with David and the growing scholarly skepticism about the united monarchy epoch of Israel's history. It is Halpern's contention that with a proper understanding of the text, David's achievements would appear more modest than a casual reading of the texts assumes. Those modest achievements, then, become quite credible in the historical context of the tenth century BCE.

In his refutation of "minimalists," Halpern employs literary genre in his argumentation. He sees the history of the united monarchy as an

---

79. He considers Prophet Gad's ascription of the census plague to David's ritual offense in taking the census as evidence of David's waning popularity. He writes, "Even natural disasters such as plagues were blamed on David and viewed as punishment for offensive religious and administrative policies (2 Sam 24). As David's popularity waned, many of his subjects began to seek a change" (*King David: A Biography*, 155).

apology for David—a refutation, by the apologists, of the accusations of complicity against David in the string of murders strewn along the paths of both his rise to power and his reign. Halpern does not see how such an apology would function in any time other than close to David's own time (to be located either late in David's reign or in Solomon's time). On this note, for example, he considers the omissions of portions of the MT from the LXX (which minimalists use as proof of the late composition of the MT) to be the harmonization, on the part of the translators, of apparent contradictions in the MT.[80]

Halpern grants that there is a historical kernel to the stories recorded in this history, only that they were rewritten so as to paint David in a brighter hue. Thus, he writes, for example, "David as we have him is a literary character, and those scholars who claim that the character in the narrative never existed cannot really be blamed for their skepticism. He never did exist precisely and only as the narrative specifies. Indeed, all historical characters have an existence beyond what is recorded about them. Most have lives different from what is recorded about them."[81]

The key to unraveling this history is the understanding of the nature of ancient historiography, especially of the form preserved in the royal propaganda inscribed on monuments, stella, or inscriptions, which has a high tendency to exaggerate the monarch's achievements. He uses the Assyrians to illustrate his point as he writes, "In Assyrian royal inscriptions, then, the touching of a grain field is the conquest of a whole territory beyond it. A looting raid becomes a claim of perpetual sovereignty. But this does not mean that campaigns can be confected. The technique is that of putting extreme spin over real events."[82] His principle for interpreting such literature is what he calls the "Tiglath-Pileser principle."[83] He explains that the important question to ask is, "what is the minimum the king might have done to lay claim to the achievements he publishes?"[84]

---

80. Halpern, *David's Secret Demons*, 6–7.
81. Halpern, *David's Secret Demons*, 14.
82. Halpern, *David's Secret Demons*, 126.

83. The principle is thus named because Tiglath-Pileser typifies the ancient Near Eastern monarch, who was so plagued with megalomania and *amour propre* that his most modest accomplishment would be advertised in the most grandiloquent language.

84. Halpern, *David's Secret Demons*, 126.

Based on this principle, Halpern sets out to ascertain the extent of David's kingdom and to critically reconstruct David's life. He demonstrates the outworking of the principle in the conquest narratives in Joshua. Even though there was limited success in the northern campaigns, the book records that all the territory promised to Israel was conquered as far as the Euphrates (Josh 11:23; 21:43; cf. Josh 1:3–4; Deut 11:24). Yet it sees no contradiction with the land that still remained to be conquered (Josh 13:1–6; Judg 1).[85] When applied to David, for example, he concludes that the record of David's accomplishments in, say, 2 Sam 8 takes the form of a royal inscription, which he considers based on David's royal inscription, which has not been found only due to archaeological accident. He then points to the lack of evidence for David's activity at the Euphrates. Thus, "the river" mentioned in 2 Sam 8:3 should not be read as Euphrates, the usual way it is understood, but as the Jordan River. He vehemently denies that David had conquered Aram Damascus, as the text states. Rather, he posits domination through alliance.

Halpern attends to the issues and characters contained in the history at length. However, his manner of dealing with the text elevates his speculation, anchored in skepticism, over and above what the text states. A few examples of this phenomenon will suffice. In the Absalom revolt, Halpern conjectures that David had set up Absalom as a detour for crushing the opposition of the northern tribes.[86] Indeed, even the murder of Amnon was a Davidic scheme in order to eliminate Amnon. According to Halpern, David orchestrated Amnon's rape of Tamar in order to rid himself of a Saulide. He considers Amnon to be a son of Saul borne by his wife Ahinoam, whom David had snatched.[87] Solomon, he thinks, was Uriah's son, and therefore was a usurper to the throne.[88]

Halpern takes the books of Samuel to be a fictitious narrative that betrays an anxiety to associate David with the house of Saul. With respect to the Saulides, he sees David's preservation of Mephibosheth as calculated to be a fact that could be subpoenaed to support the claim that David was personally allied with Jonathan and to deflate the accusation that he conducted vendetta against the house of Saul.[89] He

---

85. Halpern, *David's Secret Demons*, 128.
86. Halpern, *David's Secret Demons*, 380–81.
87. Halpern, *David's Secret Demons*, 87–90.
88. Halpern, *David's Secret Demons*, 397.
89. Halpern, *David's Secret Demons*, 280–83.

understands David's betrothal to Michal on similar terms. He writes, "[R]egardless of how David laid hands on Michal, it would suit the purpose of the author to insist that the betrothal took place while he was at Saul's court, because that claim shows that he was Saul's lieutenant."[90] The repatriation of the ark, Halpern understands to be an invention of David. Because members of David's dynasty profited from the presence of the ark in Jerusalem, they canvassed that it was an Israelite icon, and later generations are then taken in by this ruse. The murder of Abner ensured the end of the civil war, thus Abner's contretemps with Ishbosheth is contrived to serve the interest of the apology. The presumed return of Michal to David, he reads as marital diplomacy, being Ishbosheth's way of retrieving David from the arms of his Philistine masters and by that act posing a direct threat to the heartland of the Philistines just beyond the Shephelah.

Halpern's book has many helpful insights, especially when he is dealing with historical backgrounds and ancient Near Eastern contextual matters. However, the dominance of his fertile imagination over true exegesis is the book's albatross. While he sets out to answer the "minimalists," his excessive use of skepticism and a superfluity of conspiracy theories (the very stock in trade of minimalists) make the difference between him and them to be rather in rhetoric and of degree, not in essence. He also displays a good ounce of inconsistency, especially regarding arguments based on silence. For example, in one breath he argues that 2 Sam 8 is based on David's royal inscription, which by happenstance has not yet been discovered, and in the next he makes a case for the lack of evidence against David's campaign and conquest as far as the Euphrates on account of the absence of evidence. Yet he gives no clue as to how silence can be used positively and when it can be employed in negative argumentation. The speculative nature of his work diminishes its value, especially when one is considering the text in its present form.

### Israel Finkelstein and Neil Asher Silberman

Israel Finkelstein and Neil Asher Silberman's *David and Solomon* seems to be an expansion of the fifth chapter ("Memories of a Golden Age") of their earlier book, *The Bible Unearthed*. In the earlier volume, they had three major propositions: (1) Israel's sacred traditions from the patri-

---

90. Halpern, *David's Secret Demons*, 284.

archal era to the destruction of Jerusalem are more myth than history; (2) recent archaeological discoveries have unmasked the myth, thereby revealing the true picture of Israel (which to them is just the northern kingdom that was obscured by the tendentious literature of Judah); and (3) the version of the history of Israel (found in the Bible), as told by Judah—a backwater chiefdom dominated by Israel until the latter's Assyrian captivity—is historically unreliable and does not represent the true state of things as they were. They then set out to tell the story of ancient Israel and the rebirth of its sacred scriptures from a new perspective, using the latest archaeological findings. Their goal is to sieve legend out of the history, and by implication produce a corrective to this myth that has been a weapon of mass deception to all until the arrival on the scene of their new breed of scholars.[91] They claim that recent archaeological discoveries have called into question many of the archaeological props that once bolstered the historical basis of the David and Solomon narratives of the Bible. These issues they undertake to address in their newer volume.[92]

While branding the biblical material as fables and tales, they are still interestingly concerned to deny that these tales of the fabled careers of David and Solomon were wholly imaginary myths that evolved from a variety of ancient sources by adding sources, garbling contexts, and shifting its meaning as the centuries rolled on.[93] They begin their enterprise with a characterization of David, whom they brand as being nothing more than a bandit chief. Their conclusion on the Davidic era is that this tale was not composed in the tenth century, but in the eighth century. Yet they still maintain that it seems to preserve some uncannily accurate memories of conditions in the tenth century BCE in the Judean hill country. Archaeological evidence adduced for their conclu-

---

91. Finkelstein and Silberman, *The Bible Unearthed*, 3, 123–24.

92. Expatiating on this in the new book they write, "Our challenge will be to provide a new perspective on the David and Solomon story by presenting the flood of new archaeological information about the rise and development of the ancient society in which the biblical tale was formed. We will attempt to separate history from myth; old memories from later elaboration; facts from royal propaganda to trace the evolution of David and Solomon narrative from its ancient origins to the final compilation of the biblical accounts. By following this path, our search for David and Solomon will reveal the fascinating tension between historical fact and sanctified tradition; in this case, between the reality of Iron Age Judah and the West's still-living legend of ancient Israel's sacred kings" (Finkelstein and Silberman, *David and Solomon*, 3).

93. Finkelstein and Silberman, *David and Solomon*, 22.

sions include environmental surface surveys that show that the northern kingdom had a greater number of high-population centers than Judah. Besides, there is no evidence of widespread literacy in the tenth century, so the stories could not have been written within that century. Rather, the two hundred years of oral retelling of the tall tales of the Apiru-like banditry of David occasioned a stratigraphication process that surely transformed some of the elements, deleted others, and added successive layers of political and theological interpretation that reflected the concerns and realities of the storytellers.

Our authors are piqued at the contradictory way in which Saul is depicted in the Bible as hero, sinner, and tragic, tormented figure—being chosen by God as the savior of Israel and then unforgivingly condemned by God. Like many other readers of the Bible, they are perplexed at the utter rejection of Saul vis-à-vis the unconditional divine promise of eternal rule to David, who perhaps might appear even less deserving than Saul. They have little problem in affirming the historicity of Saul, lack of "archaeological" confirmation notwithstanding. They reach this conclusion based on the description of the tenth-century northern Israelite environment, which is cast in very different terms than those used in later centuries, presumably of the same region. They envisage the possibility of overlap in the reigns of Saul and David and thus posit the possibility of Saul, David, and Solomon living in the tenth century BCE.[94]

The anti-Saul and pro-David stances in the story, they say, reflect a now-silenced argument that has been woven into the overall biblical narrative. However, they consider the dialogue between David and Michal in 2 Sam 6 highly inconceivable in the context of a rustic high-

---

94. Finkelstein and Silberman imaginatively capture the tension and complexity of the polyphony ingrained in the text of Samuel, which is often completely missed because of non-critical application of the apology of David theory to Samuel. They, for instance, write thus of possible arguments amongst the partisans of Saul and David: "The partisans of Saul—the voice of whom can be found only in the background of the stories—would have maintained that David was no more than a bandit, a nobody who was accepted to the circle of the king and then betrayed him, an illegitimate usurper who undermined the throne of Saul and his family. To them, David was a traitor, a Philistine agent, who participated—actively or passively—in the military expedition that resulted in the death of the first great king of the north. The supporters of David had to answer these accusations. David would never have taken up a life of banditry had it not been for the jealous rage of Saul. Moreover, at every opportunity that David had to kill his pursuer, he refrained from taking that action, for the greater good of Israel" (*David and Solomon*, 87).

land chiefdom where social bonds, rather than social differences, needed to be stressed. They are equally dubious about the existence of a woman by the name of Michal, a daughter of Saul, who was married to the historical David. All they can safely assume is "that the story did not take its present form—and certainly its meaning—before the rise of a class-conscious aristocracy in Jerusalem."[95]

They also dispense with the apology of David theory of the provenance of the story. They argue that such a theory would make sense only if the texts were written in the tenth century. It is interesting the way they have turned Halpern's argument for an early dating of the narrative on its head. They further write, "This is highly unlikely: not only is there no evidence of an elaborate royal administration (of the type that might have been expected to possess literary scribes and court bards) in the isolated hilltop village of Jerusalem; there is no sign of extensive literacy or writing in Judah until the end of the eighth century BCE."[96]

Turning to archaeological excavations, they say that nearly a century of excavation at Jerusalem has turned up layers of occupation in the MBA (c. 2000–1550 BCE) and the late Iron Age II (c. 750–586 BCE), but no significant finds for the tenth century. For them, the united monarchy was occasioned only through the marriage of Jehoram (Jehoshaphat's son) to Athaliah (Ahab's daughter), through which the north effectively solidified its hegemony over the province of Judah. They use results of new excavations and re-analysis of old data at sites such as Tell Qasile and Megiddo; they brand previous usage of such sites as proofs of David's conquests as illusory. They contend that archaeologists such as Yigael Yadin and Amihai Mazar were just whirling in the circular reasoning of the Albrightian biblical archaeology movement, in which biblical narratives are used as the basis for archaeological interpretation and then the interpretation of the artifacts are used as proof of the Bible's historical accuracy.[97]

One thing that I find commendable in this book is the trenchant perception of the contest that still raged on between the partisans of Saul and David in the witnesses of the tradition preserved in the books of Samuel. This polyphony is often missed in the multiplicity of theories (either the anti-/pro- theories or the conspiracy theories). The voice

---

95. Finkelstein and Silberman, *David and Solomon*, 107.
96. Finkelstein and Silberman, *David and Solomon*, 86.
97. Finkelstein and Silberman, *David and Solomon*, 94–97.

of the Saulide partisans became muffled subsequent to the triumph of the Davidic house. Nevertheless, it was not silenced. It still engaged the dominant voice of the house of David in counter-testimony, albeit backgrounded, and it deserves a hearing.

The book is, however, fraught with contradictions or inconsistencies or simply an insatiable desire to attach profundity to that which is innately simple. A number of these are enumerated below. First, the authors took a circuitous path (perhaps to sound more professional) to reach the conclusion that the northern kingdom was more populous than Judah. To my mind, you do not need archaeological field surveys to know that. A simple knowledge of geography (especially the geography of the Holy Land) and the theory of human settlement patterns[98] coupled with a close reading of the DtrH will bring you to the same conclusion. Second, they harness the lack of widespread evidence of writing (like inscriptional artifacts) for the period to argue against the writing of these narratives earlier than the seventh century. This argument is tenuous, to say the least. Even if they have proved the case that writing was not *widely* practiced in tenth-century Israel, it does not translate into a successful case against the existence of writing as a whole.[99] Third,

---

98. See, for example, Abler, Adams, and Gould, *Spatial Organisation*.

99. The Bible is replete with intimations that writing was common early in Israel's life. Passages that point in this direction include, Deut 6:4–9; 17:18–19; Deut 27:2–3; Josh 8:32; Judg 8:14; 1 Sam 10:25; 2 Sam 11:15. It may, however, be argued that the Bible, especially the DtrH has theologically (ideological) agenda, and as such its witness must have external attestations, if it is to have validity. Such external attestations are not wanting. The discovery over thirty years ago of the Iron Age I Tel Izbet Sartah Abecedary gives credence to the commonality of writing beyond the palaces much earlier in Palestine. Ron Tappy's discovery of the tenth century BC abecedary at Tell Zeitah/Tel Zayit south of Jerusalem in 2005 further indicates that "Such a find as this adds to a growing body of epigraphic evidence that serves to emphasize the presence of numerous writers and readers of Hebrew, and perhaps other neighboring scripts. The effect is to increase the evidence for the presence of a literacy that could be found in rural areas as well as in state capitals and administrative centers" (Hess, "Writing about Writing," 342–43). This is besides the Iron Age II (esp. eight century) monumental inscriptions with no accompanying art work, which are significant testimonies in their own right to the reading culture of the era. Examples of these include the Tel Dan inscription, Siloam Tunnel inscription, City of David Monument Inscription Fragment, Moabite Stele, and the Neo-Philistine text from Tel Ekron. For fully discussions of these issues see Hess, "Literacy in Iron Age Israel," 82–100; Young, "Israelite Literacy, Part I," 239–53; Young, "Israelite Literacy, Part II," 408–22; Young, "A Response to Richard Hess," 565–67; Niditch, *Oral Word and Written Word*; Jamieson-Drake, *Scribes and Schools in Monarchic Judah*; Cross, "A Fragment of a Monumental Inscription from the City of

in the attempt to establish the dominance of the northern kingdom over Judah, they refer to David Ussishkin's suggestion (on the basis of Aeolic capital blocks found at the Stepped Stone Structure at the City of David) that there may have been a Samaria-like government compound on the Temple mount in Jerusalem.

Finkelstein and Silberman acknowledge the difficulty of archaeologically confirming such a hypothesis because of the massive construction activity that went on in the entire area during the Roman Period. Yet they proceed to cite this same point to buttress their northern dominance theory. They write, "Yet it remains an intriguing possibility that the domination of the royal house of Judah by the northern kingdom was expressed in Jerusalem by architectural imitation—with the construction of an elaborate royal compound on the Temple mount, on the model of the Samarian acropolis."[100] One looks in vain for consistency at this point. The same authors who, on the one hand, reject arguments that evidence for the tenth century may not have been found because of repeated subsequent destruction and construction occurring over the same area, now make a complete about-face to use the same argument to buoy up their position. Ultimately, their project is overly concerned with historical verification and does not have much to say with regard to the biblical material dealing with how Saul's heirs fared in the Davidic era.

## Walter Brueggemann

Walter Brueggemann, in the preface to the second edition of his book *David's Truth in Israel's Imagination and Memory*, states that the David narratives in the books of Samuel "constitute the most powerful and artistic of all of the narratives of ancient Israel."[101] He notes the power of the narratives to draw our attention endlessly as they both offer marvelously detailed characterizations and are not forthcoming on other matters: they both powerfully disclose much and at the same time keep much hidden, thereby providing deep ground for the endless imagination of readers. Brueggemann further reviews the works of such scholars

---

David," 44–47; Cross, "Newly Found Inscriptions," 8–15. Demsky and Bar-Ilan, "Writing in Ancient Israel and Early Judaism," 1–37; Demsky, "A Proto-Canaanite Abecedary," 14–27; Schniedewind, "[T]he Letter of a 'Literatre' Soldier (Lachish 3)," 157–67; Kochavi, "An Ostracon of the Period of the Judges from Izbet Sartah," 1–13;

100. Finkelstein and Silberman, *David and Solomon*, 105.
101. Brueggemann, *David's Truth*, x.

as Robert Polzin, Steven L. McKenzie, and Baruch Halpern that have appeared after the first edition of his book. His interest, however, lies at the conjunction of rhetorical criticism (which focuses on the texts as acts of imaginative construal of a world that the characters of the text inhabit) and social scientific methods (which call attention to the ways in which texts serve the purposes of some socio-political advocacy). He acknowledges that this confluence of imagination and ideology carries the reader toward embracing the text as a vehicle (or realm) of world-making rather than taking it as reportage and description.

Brueggemann points out that in *David's Truth*, he offered rather inchoate ideas of what he further clarified in his *Theology of the Old Testament*, namely, that Israel's textual testimony is an ongoing interaction between "core testimony" and "counter-testimony." Ultimately, for him, the text is about tension and complexity apart from which the truth can never be told. Such complexity is also seen in human experience as "The Truth" engages lived reality in our lives. Thus, the practice of *the text itself in its tensive complexity* is a counterpoint to the practice of *selves in community with a commensurate tensive complexity*.[102]

According to Brueggemann, the tensive complexity ensconced in the story of David makes him out to be a historical figure with a literary future. In Israel's tradition, David generates fascination, attraction, bewilderment, and embarrassment, but he is never disowned. Brueggemann's approach calls for inquiries into questions of truth, not facticity. In the story of David, he says, the truth, being neither obvious nor unambiguous, comes with power and scars; David is found sometimes allied with the truth and at other times the truth moves against him; David is thus inscrutable. Therefore, the truth for Brueggemann is polyvalent. There is then some undecidability with the narratives.

Brueggemann illustrates this point by referring to two extreme characterizations of David as either a "bloodthirsty oversexed bandit,"[103] or the possessor of a pure faith of unnoticed elegant quality.[104] With the truth coming to us relentlessly packaged in ambiguity, inscrutability, and polyvalence, our purpose in exposition, he writes, is never to eliminate

---

102. Brueggemann, *David's Truth*, xv.

103. McKenzie, *The Old Testament without Illusion*, 236; as cited in Brueggemann, *David's Truth*, 4.

104. Terrien, *The Elusive Presence*, 282; cited in Brueggemann, *David's Truth*, 4.

the hiddenness but to wait in that hiddenness for seasons of disclosure as the storyteller intends us never to know for sure.

Brueggemann makes some important hermeneutical points. First, there can be no true historical personage (in the since of a "brute fact") because the "historical" is always constructed. Second, truth is not coterminous with facticity. Even the truth about us is polyvalent, multifaceted, and layered. Methodologically, he is concerned with the convergence of social context, literary articulation, and theological claim. He affirms that none of these three factors can stand on their own without the other two.

In his consideration of the HDR (1 Sam 16:1—2 Sam 5:5) he concludes that this narrative is not disinterested: it is both naively enthusiastic about David and relentlessly polemical against Saul. David, as portrayed here, is cunning, mocking, and self serving; he murders and confiscates women married to other men and is willing to seize holy bread for survival.[105] Thus, the narrative does not censure, but rather trustingly celebrates that which in other contexts might be embarrassing.

In his examination of the SN (2 Sam 9–20 and 1 Kgs 1–2), Brueggemann posits a different storyteller, one who is not so trusting as to be incapable of criticism. He writes, "Now we have a way of truth that looks more closely, if not with suspicion, at least critically and knowingly. It is no longer tribal truth, for this truth is too daring and ambiguous to serve the tribe . . . This literature is neither tribal nor trustful. I suggest that the reason this narrative takes such a different posture is that it is a different narrative with a different agenda, an agenda that had to present a very different David."[106] In this story, the narrator cuts through the red tape of royalty to see the man David as he is, an ambiguous, contradictory, enmeshed man, driven and inept, with a range of emotional possibilities.

While it is not an excessively polemical narrative, it is also not particularly apologetic. Treading upon very dangerous territory, the narrator employs subtlety. Brueggemann contrasts the portrait of David in the HDR with that of the SN. In the former, things work out speedily for him, leading up from triumph to triumph. In the latter, David is a man in whom the clash of personal agenda and public role resulted in anguish and pain. The story of David therefore spotlights the interface of public responsibility and power on the one hand, and personal temptation and

---

105. Brueggemann, *David's Truth*, 10.
106. Brueggemann, *David's Truth*, 36.

self-deception on the other. Thus, the biblical narrator perceptively instructs us that human personhood, in some way or another, necessarily connected with public history, is inevitably a life of anguish.

Brueggemann's approach brings a refreshing touch to textual engagement that will inform what we do in this project. It is an approach that is hermeneutically self-conscious of its service to the community of faith. On this note, it strains to take hold of the theological claims of the text. Yet it is neither oblivious of the context from which the text arose nor negligent of the literary form in which it is communicated. In such an endeavor, methodological approaches (whether rhetorical criticism or sociological approaches) do not becomes ends in themselves, but are rightly seen to be what they are meant to be—means to an end. Brueggemann's concept of tensive complexity pulls the rug from under the insatiable desire for specificity. The willingness to embrace ambiguity opens our eyes to the polyvalence of the text (say in the form of *core testimony* and *counter-testimony*), which is so much an integral part of the text of Samuel. Besides, his other views (especially those on "the historical as a construct" and the non-coincidence of truth and facticity) qualify the renewed search for the "historical David."

## *Sundry Authors*

There are a number of studies about Saul and his reign. Diana Vikander Edelman has published *King Saul in the Historiography of Judah*, an extended analysis of the rise, reign, and wane of Saul recorded in 1 Sam 8—2 Sam 1.[107] In this book, Edelman attempts to bridge the gap between historical and literary criticism through her focus on and analysis of this section of the Samuel books, which she surmises to be a literary unity, the proof of which she fails to furnish. Sarah Nicholson in her book *The Three Faces of Saul* explores the tragedy that is the story of Saul.[108] Her method is a combination of synchronic and intertextual analysis. The texts she engages intertextually are not contemporaneous with the biblical narrative but are modern literary works.[109] She ultimately sees Saul as a victim who is sinned against rather than sinning. Barbara Green employs Mikhail Bakhtin's literary theories (especially his concept of

---

107. Edelman, *King Saul in the Historiography of Judah*.
108. Nicholson, *The Three Faces of Saul*.
109. Lamartine, *Saül, Tragédie*; and Hardy, *The Mayor of Casterbridge*.

"dialogism") in her extended analysis of the characterization of Saul in 1 Samuel.[110] While all these studies, along with several others, have provided different readings of the Saul story in Samuel, none of them has given any account of Saul's progeny, especially after his demise. The only exception to this known to me is Cheryl Exum's work on biblical narrative tragedy.[111] In this book Exum examines the fate of all Saulides that survived into the reign of David. Yet her emphasis on the tragic element in the stories has inhibited her from carrying out a fully orbed study of their story.

Of Saul's descendants who survived into David's reign, only Michal has received more than a casual examination in contemporary biblical studies. Thus, the only book-length study of a Saulides available is David J. A. Clines and Tamara C. Eskenazi's edited volume on Michal.[112] Yet, by the editors's admission, this book does not provide a unified portrait of this biblical character because it is a mosaic-like assemblage of articles and essays from diverse sources and differing temporal settings. There is therefore a gaping hole in the literature that needs to be filled with a more comprehensive and systematic study of what became of the Saulides who survived their father into David's reign.

## Conclusion

This chapter's survey of the relevant literature has focused largely on book-length works and monographs. This is my personal preference stemming from the conviction that books and monographs give fuller treatments of their subject matter than do most journal articles.[113] In these sources, motifs are found that can be said to have been recurrent in scholarship for upward of a hundred years; the emphasis they receive vary in degree with different scholars at different points in time. One of these is the recognition of the role of Deuteronomistic redaction in the composition of our text. In spite of this recognition, not many scholars have carried through the hermeneutical implication of the contextual

---

110. Green, *How Are the Mighty Fallen*.
111. Exum, *Tragedy and Biblical Narrative*, 70–119.
112. Clines and Eskenazi, *Telling Queen Michal's Story*.
113. This should not be taken to mean that I have completely ignored journal articles and essays in the work. As a perusal of the rest of the work shows, I have made extensive use of a diversity of sources.

location of the books of Samuel (in the DtrH) in their critical study of the books.

Another important motif is methodological, namely, the application of literary critical analysis to the study of these texts. It is instructive to note that the application of this approach (even if in nascent form) had begun long before the name itself was formally applied to it. Some of the literary features that have engaged the attention of scholars *ab initio* include plot development, repetition, style, syntactical and lexical analyses, parallelism, metaphor, simile, the use of introductory formulas, ambiguity, wordplay and multivalency, point of view, and the function of dialogue vis-à-vis narration. Similarly, questions as to whether biblical narrative consists of history, fiction, or the artful and imaginative portrayal of reality have been persistent.

Though the move toward the literary approach in biblical studies was initiated early in the twentieth century, its maturation was long in coming. The historical approaches (source, form, tradition-history, and redaction criticism) continued to dominate the scene well into the last half of the last century. Thus, biblical scholars continued to be occupied with the search for sources in the biblical data, isolation of original forms, and the identification of the many and varied redactors and redactional layers in the text.

However, towards the end of the 1970s, the gathering storm of the literary critical movement gained momentum. The eighties and nineties witnessed a flurry of publications of works based on the literary approach, a detailed discussion of which I will offer in chapter three. Most of these works, in their literary analysis, also adopted a stance that simply construed biblical narratives as no more than imaginative fictional creations of their authors. At the turn of the new millennium, there appears to be a new shift in direction. The works of scholars like McKenzie, Halpern, and Finkelstein and Silberman indicate a new wave of a search for historical moorings of the biblical material. This new search attempts to pursue history with a literary mindset. Yet it is plagued with a high dose of skepticism that undermines the ultimate utility of its result. It is in this light that Brueggemann's call for the pursuit of truth rather than facticity is a welcome development.

The next chapter discusses the rise of the contemporary literary approach. It is particularly dedicated to exploring to a greater or lesser extend the narrative critical approach.

# 3

# Narrative Criticism

THE PREVIOUS CHAPTER REVIEWED the history of scholarship in Samuel, beginning from the early nineteenth century to the present (at the dawn of the twenty-first century). The review considered the various methodological approaches used in studying Samuel: historical-criticism, the new criticism, contemporary literary criticism, and the emergent new historicism. Besides methodological questions, the chapter also appraised studies that deal directly with David and Saul. This analysis furnished the needed context for the current endeavor.

The present chapter discusses the methodological approach of the present work—narrative criticism. It explores both the rise of narrative criticism, its elements, how the method facilitates the reader's task of understanding the truth as expressed in the narrative genre—understanding being the preliminary step toward the appropriation of the possibilities of a new self-understanding offered in the world of the narrative text.

John Barton notes that about half of the OT consists of narrative (histories, legends, or stories). He further observes that narrative is necessarily particular—concerned with chains of actions and events that are always about particular people.[1] Making a comparison between overtly didactic biblical literature (Paul's epistles) and narrative, K. L. Noll observes that while the former were explicitly written to persuade an ancient audience toward a particular ideology, the latter addresses no audience

---

1. However, he states, "What is more, Old Testament narrative seldom consists of edifying tales with an obvious moral, like Aesop's fables; usually the stories it tells resist reduction to a simple moral, or 'point.' They are not the kind of stories which we can throw away once we have extracted the meaning. They invite reading and re-reading, pondering over and re-visiting. In short, most of them are literature, not just sermon examples or anecdotes" (Barton, *Ethics and the Old Testament*, 20).

external to its own artificially created story world.² This, however, must not be taken as denial that a narrative's author has the goal of persuading his readers toward a particular course. The only difference is that narrative discourse does not present its agenda of persuasion forthrightly: it skillfully weaves its suasive scheme into its story world. J. L. Palache, for instance, has extensively studied the role of narrative as a didactic tool among the Semites (ancient and modern). Accounting for the important role narrative plays in Semitic cultures, he writes, "Narrative makes up for a person's impotence vis-à-vis the abstract and one's need for visualization, by providing a means to learn all sorts of things and to answer all kinds of questions. Already in the Pentateuch memories from the past must always serve as an admonition for the future (Deut 9:7ff.)."³

After giving a plethora of examples from the *Haggadah*, the *Hadith*, and the writings of the Syrian saints, Palache sets forth the value of narrative as a model for persuasion among the Semites. He pens, "Let these examples from different parts of the Semitic literatures be sufficient proof that narrative, indeed the historical, the semi-historical, the quasi-historical, or the fictitious tale—is the preferred means for expressing a theory or thought and for making it persuasive."⁴ The foregoing shows narrative to be the "preferred" means of presenting "persuasive discourse" among the Semites. In this lies ample justification for the employment of narrative criticism, a theory that studies the structure of persuasive discourses unique to narratives, in the study of biblical narrative texts.

Although within a narrative discourse, the narrator does not often seem to address anyone outside of the story world, there is no gainsaying the ubiquitous orientation of narrative (biblical narrative included) toward an addressee. In the nature of the case, therefore, it is the task of the reader to make purposive sense of it, so as to explain the what's and the how's in terms of the why's of communication.⁵ There is a general tendency to read biblical texts out of communicative context with the attendant result that elements get severed from the very terms of reference that endow them with their role and meaning: parts from wholes, means from ends, forms from function. The starting point of correcting this abnormality, Sternberg says, is the recognition of the biblical storyteller

---

2. Noll, *The Faces of David*, 15.
3. Palache, "The Nature of Old Testament Narrative," 3–22, 10.
4. Palache, "The Nature of Old Testament Narrative," 14.
5. Sternberg, "The Bible's Art of Persuasion," 45.

(like any other locutor) as a persuader in that he wields discourse to shape response and manipulate attitude.[6]

In understanding the biblical storyteller as an ideological communicative persuader, Sternberg posits the most formidable challenges that face him as those deriving from the tensive complexity involving two constraints. The first is his commitment to the divine system of norms (which is both absolute and demanding, and often ruthless in application), while the second relates to his consciousness of the necessity and arduousness of impressing it on a human audience. He hence notes, "Thus suspended between heaven and earth, the narrator must perform feats of tightrope walking in order to maintain his balance and achieve his dual goal."[7] After pointing to the two extremes of Homer, who lashes out at the gods in the *Iliad,* and Jeremiah who excoriates his audience in his prophecies, Sternberg observes, "In the absence of either license, the narrator must establish consensus while observing both the articles of faith and the decorums of communication."[8]

The teaching point of the locutor in biblical narrative is located at the conjunction of ideology (theology or ethics) and literary artistry (aesthetics). To understand adequately the ethical and theological message of biblical narrative, therefore, attention must be paid to its aesthetic qualities as narrative. Failure to grapple with the literary artistry of the Bible accounts for the fanciful interpretations to which some of its genres are subjected, for example, in allegorical interpretations of the Bible or in wooden literalism.

One reason for the neglect of the literary qualities of the biblical text until lately is the tendency to place a wedge between the sacred and secular. Such practice fails to reckon with the fact that such distinctions are alien to the ancient world from which the biblical text arose. Richard G. Moulton argues that extreme reverence for the Holy Writ, divorced from intelligence, seems to mischievously reduce it to the state of inanition.[9] Rather than hamper the efficacy of Scripture's religious utility, the literary approach, on the contrary, vivifies it. Moulton, for instance, reasons that if divine revelation, which might have been made in so many different ways, "has in fact taken the form of literature, this must

6. Sternberg, "The Bible's Art of Persuasion," 46.
7. Sternberg, "The Bible's Art of Persuasion," 47.
8. Sternberg, "The Bible's Art of Persuasion," 47.
9. Moulton, "The Bible as Literature," 3–4.

be warrant sufficient for making such literary form a matter of study."[10] Indeed, he argues further that the literary study of the Bible is not merely permissible, but it is a necessary adjunct to its proper spiritual interpretation. Our contention here is not that the Bible should be treated just like any other book—the traditional staple of historical critical scholarship.[11] Rather, what we advocate is a better appreciation of the Bible's aesthetic qualities for a fuller exploration of its meaning dimensions.

With particular reference to biblical narrative, Erich Auerbach[12] recognized, as far back as the mid-twentieth century, that it could be studied in accordance with the canons of general literary theory. Mark Allan Powell comments, "In choosing narrative discourse as their medium, the biblical writers inevitably selected a form of expression that presents a narrative depiction of reality. This is a feature that biblical texts share with other literary works (including Homer). The representation of reality in narrative form, Auerbach proposed, is a basic element of literature that transcends traditional distinctions between aesthetic and historical purposes. What an author wishes to say about the things reported in a narrative—real or imaginary—may be discerned by observing the style of expression that is used."[13] Since the authors of biblical history choose to employ the narrative form for depicting reality, the explication of reality contained in their works is helped, not hindered, by the use of the narrative critical approach. Thus, I will be utilizing narrative critical analysis as my methodological approach in the present study.

## THE RISE OF CONTEMPORARY LITERARY CRITICISM

Narrative criticism is an outgrowth of the New Literary Criticism that first emerged in literary circles, but was later embraced in biblical studies as well, in the post–World War II era. The key figures associated with this movement at its inception include T. S. Eliot, I. A. Richards, and William Empson. The defining moment of the movement came with the pub-

---

10. Moulton, "The Bible as Literature," 5.

11. The position of historical criticism, which we seek to distinguish from ours here, is well represented in Gunn's comment: "The life-force of modern historical criticism was a determination to deal with the biblical text in the same way as secular texts were treated, even if that should lead to the shaking off some dearly held verities" (Gunn, "New Directions in the Study of Biblical Hebrew Narrative," 65–75).

12. Auerbach, *Mimesis*.

13. Powell, *What is Narrative Criticism?*, 4.

lication of the now-famous article, "The Intentional Fallacy," by W. K. Wimsatt and M. C. Beardsley.[14] Indeed, David Couzens Hoy calls this article "the fundamental manifesto of Anglo-American New Criticism."[15] Barton notes that in this article, Wimsatt and Beardsley explicitly defined what had already been the guiding principle of the New Criticism movement: "This essay clearly enunciated the belief that 'extrinsic' inquiries into what the author intended could be no part of valid literary criticism."[16] Barton also shows that following Eliot, Wimsatt and Brooks argued that a "poem" (the term is used as shorthand for any work of literary art) is not to be understood as the outpouring of the poet's soul, neither should it be seen as a window into his world, but as poihma, i.e., a "thing made," or artifact. A poem, they contend, "is not a vehicle for transferring beautiful thoughts from the poet's mind to the reader's: it is a beautiful object. A poet is not a prophet or a genius, bringing messages from the Muses or from God: he is a maker, a craftsman . . . Literary criticism is criticism of literature, not criticism of the emotions or experiences of writers."[17]

Barton is quick to point out that subsequent readings of Wimsatt and Beardsley, which have banished the author from the interpretive roundtable, have been actually *mis*-readings of their proposition. He writes, "They were not so much concerned to outlaw the author's meaning as the normative meaning, as to rule out certain illicit ways of *establishing* that meaning. It is, on their terms, acceptable to say that the text means what its author meant, provided that 'what that author meant' is understood to be discoverable from the text and only from the text—not from diaries, letters or remarks overheard on the telephone."[18] Hoy even notes that though New Criticism is often understood to completely exclude biographical evidence about the author's intentions, such a conclusion was not envisioned by Wimsatt and Beardsley.[19] Wimsatt, for instance, clearly states, "The use of biographical evidence need not involve intentionalism, because while it may be evidence of what the author intended, it may also be evidence of the meaning of his words and

---

14. Wimsatt and Beardsley, "The Intentional Fallacy," 468–88.
15. Hoy, *The Critical Circle*, 25.
16. Barton, *Reading the Old Testament*, 149.
17. Barton, *Reading the Old Testament*, 145.
18. Barton, *Reading the Old Testament*, 149–50.
19. Wimsatt, *The Verbal Icon*, 11; as quoted in Hoy, *The Critical Circle*, 26.

the dramatic character of his utterance."[20] What constituted the fallacy for them was the confusion of intention with the standard for determining textual meaning. They insisted that in the interpretive enterprise, the evidence inherent in the text is to be preferred over any extrinsic evidence.

Wimsatt and Beardsley were basically reacting against the literary criticism of their time, which was heavily imbued with nineteenth-century romanticism and was overly concerned with the psychological and biographical data of the author as a means for retrieving his meaning. Correctly understood or not, their work inspired a new direction in literary criticism, wherein criticism is understood to be primarily about literature as works of art and not about the authors as individual persons. This tide, ultimately, birthed a flurry of text-centered interpretive approaches such as structuralism, rhetorical criticism, discourse analysis, and narrative criticism. A further development of this movement was not content to pronounce the death of the author but to view the text as mute: the reader remained the only locus for finding meaning, thereby giving rise to such reader-centered reading strategies as reader-response criticism and deconstruction.

Other factors have also facilitated the rise of the contemporary literary criticism in biblical studies. First among these was the growing dissatisfaction with the results of the historical critical approaches. James Muilenberg, for example, in his seminal 1968 SBL Presidential address, while avowing his commitment to form criticism, outlined its shortcomings thus:

> To state our criticism in another way, form criticism by its very nature is bound to generalize because it is concerned with what is common to all the representatives of a genre, and therefore applies an external measure to the individual pericopes. It does not focus sufficient attention upon what is unique and unrepeatable, upon the particularity of the formulation. Moreover, the form and the content are inextricably related. They form an integral whole. The two are one. Exclusive attention to the *Gattung* may actually obscure the thought and intention of the writer or speaker. The passage must be read and heard precisely as it is spoken. It is the creative synthesis of the particular formulation of the pericope with the content that makes it the distinctive composition that it is.[21]

---

20. Hoy, *The Critical Circle*, 26.
21. Muilenberg, "Form Criticism and Beyond," 1–18.

A second source of impetus to literary criticism is the rise of analytical approaches that emphasize the final form of the biblical text. Brevard S. Childs's canonical criticism is in the avant-garde of this movement. Demonstrating the priority of the final form of the text, Childs comments on Isaiah, "[I]n its present canonical context the message of Second Isaiah has already been raised to a new semantic level, which is at least one step removed from Zimmerli's reconstruction in its quality of literal speech."[22] Indeed, in a scathing critique of the purely historical critical exegesis of Deutero-Isaiah, Childs says, "Again, critical exegesis now rests upon a very hypothetical and tentative basis of historical reconstructions. Since it is no longer possible to determine precisely the historical background of large sections of Isaiah, hypotheses increase along with the disagreements among the experts. Finally, the more the book of Isaiah has come into historical focus and has been anchored to its original setting, the more difficult it has become to move from the ancient world into a contemporary religious appropriation of the message."[23] In more specific terms, Childs says that the final form of Second Isaiah "provided a completely new and non-historical framework for the prophetic message which severed the message from its original historical moorings and rendered it accessible to all future generations."[24] Hans W. Frei likewise shows a preference for the final form of the text. In his review of biblical interpretation in the eighteenth and nineteenth centuries, he presents a persuasive case, demonstrating how both historical critics and religious apologists failed "to take proper and serious account of the narrative feature of biblical stories."[25]

The third factor relates to the influences streaming into biblical research from the work of critics in other disciplines. This comes about as a result of the biblical scholar's increasing appreciation of how critics in these other fields handle texts. One such example is, "the importing of structuralist modes of analysis into the study of biblical text (and it was applied mostly on narratives), especially in France and through the pages of *Semeia* in the United States" in the early 1970s.[26] To cite another example, the resurgence of the study of classical rhetorics in the works

22. Childs, *Introduction*, 334.
23. Childs, *Introduction*, 324.
24. Childs, *Introduction*, 337.
25. Frei, *The Eclipse of Biblical Narrative*, 136.
26. Gunn, "Biblical Hebrew Narrative," 67.

of scholars such as Chaim Perelman, Kenneth Burke, I. A. Richards, and Richard Weaver, beginning from mid-twentieth century, bears its influence on the development of rhetorical criticism in the research of George Kennedy and James Muilenberg.[27] The influence of deconstruction (Jacques Derrida) and reader-response criticism (Stanley Fish and Wolfgang Iser) similarly flowed into biblical criticism beginning in the 1980s, through the 1990s, into the new millennium.

## INTRODUCTION TO NARRATIVE CRITICISM

There are varied approaches to narrative criticism. Gunn writes that the term narrative criticism—a loose term found more in NT than in OT studies since the late 1970s—has been used broadly of literary-critical, as opposed to historical-critical, analysis of biblical narrative from a variety of methodological standpoints. That, not infrequently, has meant interpreting the existing text (in its "final form") primarily in terms of its own story world—seen as replete with meaning—rather than understanding the text by attempting to reconstruct its sources and editorial history, its original setting and audience, and its author's or editor's intention in writing.[28] He further notes that the term more specifically has been used of formalist analysis, especially in a New Critical vein, where the critic understands the text to be an interpretable entity, independent of both author and interpreter. From this perspective, "meaning is to be found by close reading that identifies formal and conventional structures of narrative, determines plot, develops characterization, distinguishes point of view, exposes language play, and relates all to some overarching, encapsulating theme. Unlike historical criticism, which in practice has segmented the text, formalist narrative criticism has often been an exercise in holism."[29]

The evidence of the emergence of contemporary narrative criticism is found as early as the mid-twentieth century with the publication of Erich Auerbach's book,[30] but it also includes the works of other

---

27. Tull, "Rhetorical Criticism and Intertextuality, 157–58.
28. Gunn, "Narrative Criticism," 201.
29. Gunn, "Narrative Criticism," 201.
30. Auerbach, *Mimesis*.

scholars like Dan O. Via,[31] William A. Beardsley,[32] Boris Uspensky,[33] and Norman Perry,[34] among many others. Mark Allan Powell, however, states emphatically that secular literary scholarship knows no such movement as *narrative criticism*. Unlike such methodologies as structuralism, rhetorical criticism, and reader-response, he says, narrative criticism "developed within the field of biblical studies without an exact counterpart in the secular world. If classified by secular critics, it might be viewed as a subspecies of the new rhetorical criticism or as a variety of the reader-response movement. Biblical scholars, however, tend to think of narrative criticism as an independent, parallel movement in its own right."[35] He then traces the first use of the term, narrative criticism, to the work of David Rhoads and Donald Michie.[36] Powell may be right in crediting Rhoads and Michie with the term *narrative criticism*. However, the theory that lies behind the nomenclature pre-dates them. Indeed, twenty years earlier, in 1969, Tzvetan Todorov had already proposed the term "narratology" as an umbrella term for the series of theories associated with the works of Gérard Genette, Seymour Chatman, Roland Barthes, and others, including Todorov himself.[37]

The above line of development, sketched by Powell, relates particularly to the advance of the discipline within NT studies. In OT studies, the discipline of narrative criticism has been advanced through the works

---

31. Via, *The Parables*.
32. Beardslee, *Literary Criticism*.
33. Uspensky, *A Poetics of Composition*.
34. Perrin, *Literary Criticism*.
35. Powell, *Narrative Criticism*, 19.
36. Rhoads and Michie, *Mark as Story*. Powell adds an interesting anecdote to the fascinating "discovery" of the duo: "At Carthage College in 1977 a young Bible professor named David Rhoads invited a colleague from the English department to show his students what it would be like to read one of the Gospels the way one would read a short story. The presentation by Don Michie was eye-opening not only for the students, but for Rhoads as well. Ultimately, it led to the publication in 1982 of *Mark as Story*, a collaborative effort by these two scholars that, more than any previously published work, demonstrated the possibilities of reading a Gospel in this way." It is the method used in this collaborative work that Rhoads called "narrative criticism" (Powell, *Narrative Criticism*, 6).
37. Thiselton, *New Horizons in Hermeneutics*, 479.

of David M. Gunn,[38] Robert Alter,[39] Edwin Good,[40] Meir Sternberg,[41] Jan Fokkelmann,[42] Shimeon Bar-Efrat,[43] Mieke Bal,[44] and Tremper Longman,[45] to mention a few of the prominent figures in the discipline. Gunn notes the not-so-subtle distinction between the practice of narrative criticism in OT studies and in NT studies. He observes how by the turn of the new millennium, OT studies, owing to influences from secular criticism, had become more reader-oriented in its approaches to narrative. The influence of secular reading strategies such as deconstruction and ideological criticism on OT narrative approaches makes them face up to "the view that language is infinitely unstable and so meaning always deferrable; they may radically foreground the reader's values as determinative of interpretation; they may argue that criticism is not anchored in fixed texts but in fragile communities of interpreters; and they may recognize explicitly that criticism is social construction, or persuasion, if you will."[46] This is the stream in which the studies like those of David J. A. Clines,[47] Mieke Bal, and Cheryl Exum[48] have flowed. While very approving of these scholars, Gunn is very critical of others, like Sternberg, and Alter and Kermode, whom he considers too conservative and formalistic.[49] Gunn's criticism of Sternberg for the latter's conservative stance is seen in Gunn's other works as well.[50]

---

38. Gunn, *The Story of King David*.
39. Alter, *The Art of Biblical Narrative*.
40. Good, *Irony in the Old Testament*.
41. Sternberg, *The Poetics of Biblical Narrative*.
42. Fokkelman, *Reading Biblical Narrative*.
43. Bar-Efrat, *Narrative Art in the Bible*.
44. Bal, *On Story-Telling*; Bal, *Murder and Difference*; Bal, *Narratology*.
45. Longman, *Literary Approaches*; and Ryken and Longman, *A Complete Literary Guide to the Bible*.
46. Gunn, "Narrative Criticism," 201–2.
47. Clines, *On the Way to the Postmodern*; Clines, *Interested Parties*; Clines, *The New Literary Criticism*.
48. Exum, *Plotted, Shot, and Painted*; Exum, *Fragmented Women*; Exum, *Tragedy and Biblical Narrative*; Exum, *Signs and Wonders*.
49. Gunn, "Narrative Criticism, 206–8.
50. See for instance his "Biblical Hebrew Narrative," 65–75, especially 68–71. For similar bashing of Alter and Sternberg for their more conservative views, also see Long, "The 'New' Biblical Poetics of Alter and Sternberg," 71–84.

The practice of narrative criticism in NT studies, Gunn says, has tended to be "relatively conservative in its methodology, concerned with observing the mechanics or artistry of literary construction, the conventions of ancient rhetoric, and often still haunted by historical criticism's need to know the author's 'intention' and the text's 'original' readership if it is to speak legitimately of the text's meaning."[51] Rather than approach the matter from an ideological perspective, as Gunn does, Powell approaches it from the standpoint of reading strategy. He says that the new literary criticism that has invaded biblical studies in recent times draws upon two broad categories of reading strategies, namely, the text-centered (objective) and reader-centered (pragmatic) approaches.[52]

Overall, Powell identifies four major approaches that enjoy currency in New Testament studies; these are rhetorical criticism, reader-response criticism, structuralism, and narrative criticism. He says there is a sense in which reader-response theory is viewed as a larger category that subsumes both structuralism and narrative criticism (though he acknowledges that in biblical studies these are usually regarded as independent methodologies parallel to reader-response, rather than varieties of it).[53] He has three subcategories of reader-response theories.[54] Powell, however, rightly observes that despite the similarities that structuralism and narrative criticism may share with reader-response approaches, the former differs from the latter "in that the former focus on ways in which the text determines the reader's response rather than on ways in which the reader determines meaning,"[55] as is the case with the latter.

---

51. Gunn, "Narrative Criticism, 202.
52. Powell, *Narrative Criticism*, 12.
53. Powell, *Narrative Criticism*, 16.
54. Powell's first subcategory of reader-response theories is "reader *over* the text," which consists of (1) deconstruction (a reading strategy that emphasizes the reader's dominance over the text, e.g., Derrida); (2) transanctive criticism (describes the process of reading in psychoanalytic terms, e.g., Norman Holland); and (3) interpretive communities (supply accepted reading strategies as means for controlling meaning, e.g., late Fish). The second is "reader *with* the text," and it comprises of (1) affective stylistics (views meaning as a dynamic product of a reader's dialectical interaction with a text, e.g., early Fish); and (2) phenomenological criticism (meaning is produced in dialectical interaction of the text with a reader in an evolving process of anticipation, frustration, retrospection, and reconstruction, e.g., Iser). The third is the "reader *in* the text," where he has both structuralism and narrative criticism (Powell, *Narrative Criticism*, 16–18).
55. Powell, *Narrative Criticism*, 18.

Over the last thirty years, the reader of a text has acquired increasing significance in the hermeneutical critical circle. Every reading strategy, therefore, has to reckon with the identity and place of the reader in its reading scheme. Rhetorical criticism, for example, is interested in the original readers to whom a work was first addressed (the *intended readers*). Structuralism considers the responses of a *competent reader* that masters the codes of a work. The interest of reader-response (of the early Fish and Iser) is in the response of a *first-time reader* of a work, who encounters the text in its sequential order; and the later Fish focuses on the concerns of *reading communities*.[56]

In written communication, a *reader* stands in a certain relationship to two other components in the communicative situation, that is, the *author* and the *text*. Longman writes that in narrative this picture becomes more complex because the "author does not make his or her presence known explicitly, and the reader is not referred to in the text."[57] He therefore calls attention to the distinctions scholars have made with respect to six terms that are helpful in understanding narrative texts. These six terms are author, implied author, narrator, narratee, implied reader, and reader. These six terms are paired up as author/reader, narrator/narratee, and implied author/implied reader.

In explaining these pairs of terms, Longman notes the problems associated with the first pair. In view of editorial or redactional activity in the composition of biblical books, he asks whether we should speak of one author, many authors, or even many editors. Similarly, the identity of the reader is not as easy to descry as one might wish. We have to deal with questions regarding the original readers of the documents vis-à-vis the contemporary reader. Longman acknowledges the difficulty in distinguishing between the actual author/actual reader and the implied author/implied reader. He takes the implied author to be the textual manifestation of the real author. The implied reader, on the other hand, refers to the audience presupposed by the narrative itself.[58] While acknowledging the theoretical validity of these distinctions, Longman despairs of their usefulness, suggesting they could become mere academic exercises in many biblical narrative texts. Powell, however, is more positive. He is convinced that the "goal of narrative criticism is to read the text as the

---

56. Powell, *Narrative Criticism*, 19.
57. Longman, *Literary Approaches*, 145.
58. Longman, *Literary Approaches*, 146.

implied reader."[59] Even then his optimism, however, is not unqualified, as he writes, "To the extent that the implied reader is an idealized abstraction, the goal of reading the text 'as the implied reader' may be somewhat unattainable, but it remains a worthy goal nevertheless."[60] Powell, however makes a valid point: the concept of implied reader serves as a principle that sets criteria for interpretation. Longman, however, is of the opinion that the most fruitful of these pairs for narrative analysis is that of narrator/narratee: "Both narrator and narratee are rhetorical devices and are often explicit in the text, though they both may take different forms from text to text."[61] The narrator is particularly critical because his point of view is pivotal in shaping the reader's reaction to the text.

The importance of this analysis lies in its usefulness in pointing out how these terms serve as gateways to the meaning of narrative texts when they are viewed as literary or rhetorical devices. Other devices that open the meaning dimensions of narrative texts include point of view, characterization, plot, setting, style, repetition, omission (Iser's *aporia*), contrast (or foiling), *inclusio*, irony, dialogue, type-scene, narration, narrative analogy or echo, mirroring, *Leitwort*, motif, and theme. I shall utilize these devices, alongside the usual syntactical and lexical analysis, as heuristic tools for reading the texts selected for close study in this work. However, before returning to consider these compositional devices of narrative in detail, I shall first explore the relationship between narrative and truth referentiality.

## BIBLICAL NARRATIVE AND NARRATIVE ART

The application of literary theory to the Bible understandably raises a number of questions. One such question pertains to how a narrative critical reading of the biblical text affects its truth referentiality. For Long, biblical scholarship has been preoccupied with issues of historicity, which have been addressed from a position of skepticism. Baruch Halpern, to this effect, observes that critical scholars bring the principle of scientific skepticism to bear on biblical texts. Once skepticism is set loose, it acquires a momentum of its own. He adds, "At the extremes it became a juggernaut, generating what amounted to a negative funda-

---

59. Powell, *Narrative Criticism*, 20.
60. Powell, *Narrative Criticism*, 21.
61. Longman, *Literary Approaches*, 146.

mentalism, a denial of any historical value in the text—first in Chronicles and the Pentateuch, and then in such historical books as Judges, Samuel, and Kings, concerning which skepticism has reawakened today."[62] Discussing both the essence and deficiency of previous scholarship's approach on this matter, Gunn states, "For two hundred years Western biblical criticism has been concerned with the question of historicity (the history of Israel) and with the history of biblical literature. The two ran hand in glove, for without the one the other could not be written. Despite some spectacular successes, the major failure of both programs is now becoming obvious . . . It is no exaggeration to say that the truly assured results of historical critical scholarship concerning authorship, date, and provenance would fill but a pamphlet."[63]

Conservative readers of the Bible have always understood the Bible to be historical. This has always been a bone of contention between conservative scholarship and historical critical scholarship, wherein the latter tends to be minimalist in its conception of the historical referential character of the Bible.[64] Many conservative scholars seem, therefore, to have gladly welcomed the literary reading of Scripture because of its preference for the final form of the biblical text. In other words, the literary method's preference for the final form of the text has been seen as a welcome development, as opposed to historical criticism's proclivity for balkanizing the text into different layers, attributable to differing sets of redactors and editors, with the attendant diminishing of the historical value of the text.

As far back as almost a quarter-century ago, Gunn had insightfully cautioned religiously conservative critics, who were finding refuge in literary criticism (especially of "historical" narratives) from the goblin of historicity—that literary criticism did not provide sufficient reason

---

62. Halpern, *The First Historians*, 4.

63. Gunn, "Biblical Hebrew Narrative," 66.

64. Provan, Long, and Longman succinctly put the tension between these two camps this way: "These two trends—the increasing marginalization of the biblical texts and the characterization of previous scholarship as ideologically compromised—are perhaps the main distinguishing features of the newer writing on the history of Israel over against the older, which tended to view biblical narrative texts as essential source material for historiography (albeit that these texts were not *simply* historical) and was not much inclined to introduce into scholarly discussion questions of ideology and motivation" (Provan, Long, and Longman, *A Biblical History of Israel*, 5).

to "roll out the drums."[65] Indeed, he rightly predicted that troubling times lay ahead wherein "the reader theory of the secular critics begins to corrode the edges of normative exegesis and doctrines of biblical authority which insist on viewing the Bible as divine prescription."[66] One area where this corrosion has occurred is with respect to the issue of the biblical text's referential character.

The historicity or otherwise of biblical narrative is not among the least of the concerns of a great many scholars applying narrative critical approaches to the study of the Bible. Characteristically, Adele Berlin, for instance, writing on the poetics of narrative says, "narrative is a *form of representation*. Abraham in Genesis is not a real person any more than a painting of an apple is a real fruit. This is not a judgment on the existence of a historical Abraham any more than it is a statement about the existence of apples. It is just that we should not confuse a historical individual with his narrative representation."[67] Berlin, from her analysis of a diagram of a statue that "guarded" the palace of Ashurnasirpal at Nimrud, concludes, "But the legs of the lion should remind us that *representations of reality do not always correspond in every detail to reality*. This is less troublesome in art than in literature for we are conscious that art is representation, but we forget that literature is, too. When we read narrative, especially biblical narrative, we are constantly tempted to mistake mimesis for reality—to take as real that which is only a representation of reality."[68]

What I fail to find in Berlin's proposition is an elucidation of the distinction that she seeks to make between representation and reality. All historical writing is representational, just as fiction—a novel, play, or movie—is also representational of reality in the form of *mythos* (Chinua Achebe's *Things Fall Apart* is a good example of this). Both representations, however, are of different orders. Two types of representational reference orders are identifiable. Paul Ricoeur refers to them as first-order and second-order reference.[69] First-order reference is a descriptive representation of particular things as they exist or particular events as they

---

65. This is a Nigerian catch phrase for a call for celebration. It stems from the centrality of the drum as a musical instrument in African music.
66. Gunn, "Biblical Hebrew Narrative," 70.
67. Berlin, *Poetics*, 13.
68. Berlin, *Poetics*, 14 (emphasis hers).
69. Ricoeur, "Philosophical Hermeneutics," 14–33.

occurred in the past. It deals with the particular, i.e., the historical. In my estimation, history writing in the tradition of Leopold von Ranke,[70] represents reality in first-order reference. Second-order reference is mimetic in nature and is a more fictive representation of the general state of affairs without any particulars in the cross hairs. It is universal in orientation, in other words. These orders of reference are both concerned with the representation of reality, only at different levels.[71] So, to speak of a distinction between representation and reality, the way Berlin does, only begs the question and obfuscates matters.[72]

---

70. Ranke (1795–1886) began his writing on the historical method around 1824, in which he rejected the prevailing method of reliance on tradition for history writing. He, instead, proposed an objective scientific approach that sought to reconstruct the past as things really were (history as an eyewitness account) without transposing contemporary ethos to former times. His emphasis was on eye witness accounts or documents recorded closest to occurrences of the historical events. He thus laid the foundation not only of modern history writing, but also of the historicism of the modern era which pervaded many other disciplines including biblical studies. See Krieger, *Rankee: The Meaning of History*; Von Ranke, Iggers, and Von Moltke, *The Theory and Practice of History*; Von Ranke and Wines, *The Secret of World History*.

71. With regards to literature that is concerned with second-order reference Ricoeur writes, "It seems to be the function of a great deal of our literature to 'destroy' reality. This is true not only of fictional literature—such as folktales, myths, novels, plays—but also of lyrical literature, in which language seems to celebrate itself at the expense of the referential function such as is achieved in ordinary language.

"In spite of this inwardly directed use of language no discourse is so introverted that it no longer addresses itself at all to reality. Writing such as fiction rejoins reality, however, at another, more fundamental level than the one on which this descriptive, confirmative, didactic form of discourse which we call ordinary language functions. My thesis is that the suspension of a first-order reference, such as is achieved by fiction and poetry, is the condition of the possibility for yielding a second-order reference. This second-order reference no longer touches the world at the level of manipulable objects, but at the deeper level which Husserl designated by the term 'life-world' (*Lebenswelt*) and Heidegger by that of being-in-the-world (*in der Welt-Sein*)" (Ricoeur, "Philosophical Hermeneutics," 25). Ricoeur further explains that literature in the second-order level utilizes metaphorical language to create "the kind of discourse which is most able to generate these imaginative variations and thus to redescribe reality according to the new model created by the poet. Metaphorical—and, more generally—poetic—language aims at a *mimesis* of reality. However this language 'imitates' reality only because it recreates reality by means of a *mythos*, a 'plot,' a 'fable,' which touches upon the very essence of things" ("Philosophical Hermeneutics," 26).

72. One finds the more honest and unambiguous disposition of older scholarship preferable, even if disagreeable. Pfeiffer, for example, saw the bulk of Hebrew narratives as arising "out of some scanty memories of actual events or out of the storehouse of a vivid Oriental imagination" (Pfeiffer, *Introduction to the Old Testament*, 27–28).

Robert Alter does not only propose that biblical narrative be conceived of as prose fiction, but that prose fiction is "the best general rubric for describing biblical narrative."[73] Alter obviously is not unaware of the problematic of his position. This he tries to mollify with a disclaimer that the weight he places on fictionality is meant to discount the history impulse that informs the Hebrew Bible. He insists, "The God of Israel, as so often has been observed, is above all the God of history: the working out of His purposes in history is a process that compels the attention of the Hebrew imagination, which is thus led to the most vital interest in the concrete and differential character of historical events."[74] Such attempts do not go far enough when in the next breath he turns around and writes, "Under scrutiny, biblical narrative generally proves to be either fiction laying claim to a place in the chain of causation and the realm of moral consequentiality that belong to history, as in the primeval history, the tales of the patriarchs and much of the Exodus story, and the account of the early conquest, or history given the imaginative definition of fiction, as in most of the narratives from the period of the Judges onward."[75] Alter adopts an ambiguous stance on the matter, as exemplified in his pair of coupled words, *historicized*-fiction and *fictionalized*-history. Yet, that the balance of his scales tips palpably in favor of fictionality is thinly veiled. Sternberg calls Alter's arguments for the Bible's fictionality a fatal flaw.[76]

According to V. Philips Long, while the Bible may be of vital interest in history, science, law, ethics, theology, literature, or politics, "its essence cannot be reduced to any one of them."[77] He instead calls attention to the distinctive question of truth value and truth claim, which is also recognized by Sternberg as being fundamental.[78] With respect to the issue of truth value, the force of Long's argument, rightly, is to the effect that one's judgment about the macro-genre of the Bible (historiography or fiction) is determined by one's presuppositions regarding its ontological status. Genre decision, on the other hand, is determinative of matters of truth claim. Yet, the Bible consists of a multiplicity of works of diverse liter-

73. Alter, *The Art of Biblical Narrative*, 24.
74. Alter, *The Art of Biblical Narrative*, 32.
75. Alter, *The Art of Biblical Narrative*, 32–33.
76. Sternberg, *The Poetics of Biblical Narrative*, 24.
77. Long, *The Art of Biblical History*, 27.
78. Sternberg, *The Poetics of Biblical Narrative*, 25.

ary genres. Truth claims of any biblical text, therefore, Long concludes, "can be discovered only as each text is read on its own terms, with due recognition of its genre and due attention to its content and wider and narrower contexts."[79]

Furthermore, Long is of the opinion that if properly defined the concept of fiction could be fruitfully employed in the discussion of biblical historiography. In doing this, he sets forth the example of the contradictory positions of Blomberg (for whom historical narrative is the opposite of fiction)[80] and Halpern (for whom all history is fictionalized and yet history),[81] and shows that a clear definition of history and fiction makes it possible to agree with both positions at the same time.[82] Long distinguishes the two senses of fiction as genre and artistry. On the basis of this distinction, he concludes, "fictionality of a certain sort is as likely to be found in the historian's toolbox as in the fiction writer's."[83] Since so much confusion attends the term fiction, and there is lack of perspicuity for its sense as artistry to many readers, as Long himself acknowledges, it is unclear to me as to why anyone would insist on employing it in discussing biblical historiography, when one might as well use the clearer term, artistry.

Artistry, indeed, is the common denominator between historical narration and narrative fiction. The recognition of this shared trait is not sufficient reason to employ terms that seem to efface the distinctions between them. As Sternberg observes both historiography and fiction are genres of writing, and do not in themselves attest to their factuality or otherwise. "What opposes fiction to historiography," Sternberg writes, "is not the writer's breach or avoidance but his independence of factuality: the built-in license to create a world as one thinks fit, which includes the right to bridle or flaunt that license."[84] The bottom line, according to Sternberg, comes down to the rules of the writing game as an affair between writer and audience: what is the writer committed to doing in

---

79. Long, *The Art of Biblical History*, 30.

80. Blomberg, *Historical Reliability of John's Gospel*, xviii, fn. 2; as quoted in Long, *The Art of Biblical History*, 59.

81. Halpern, *The First Historians*, 68; as quoted in Long, *The Art of Biblical History*, 58.

82. Long, *The Art of Biblical History*, 62.

83. Long, *The Art of Biblical History*, 62.

84. Sternberg, *The Poetics of Biblical Narrative*, 26.

his writing, and what is the audience's expectation of him? In such a case, in setting the criteria for the truth-value of a text, caution needs be exercised so that criteria alien to the participants in the first communicative situation are not imported into the discourse.

Sternberg observes that the features of Alter's fiction include invention, individuation, realistic psychology, thematic shaping, play of language, and conscious artistry in general (and all these features either serve as derivative manifestations of or independent markers of fictionality).[85] Sternberg denies that these are sufficient conditions of fictionality, as they could all be encountered in historiography. For his proof, he points to three great historical works, namely, those of Thucydides, Edward Gibbon, and Garret Mattingly. He specifically cites J. H. Hexter's[86] review of Mattingly's *The Defeat of the Spanish Armada*, in which Hexter invokes Alter's measures of fictionality to define Mattingly as a professionally excellent historian.[87] These, being artistic features, are narrative stylistic and compositional tools, and as such they define neither historiography nor fiction; they only show that both fiction and historiography employ narrativity. To put the matter differently, a compendium of facts by itself constitutes no history; there has to be some historiographical presentation to transform it into history. Sternberg holds that such transformation is achieved by the use of invention.[88]

Both genres (historiography and fiction) utilize artistry to fill gaps, as shown above. It can equally be demonstrated that both utilize facts. Thus, genre decisions cannot be made on the basis of form alone, but form has to be correlated with function for a valid decision regarding the

---

85. Sternberg, *The Poetics of Biblical Narrative*, 27. As an example of how this works out in Alter, Sternberg writes, "Due to the 'privilege of invention,' for example, the David cycle transmutes 'history into fiction' through such measures as imaginative dialogue and characterization (pp. 36–37). Whereas the book of Esther's fairy-tale plot and schematic neatness reveals it as a 'comic fantasy' (p. 34)" (ibid., 27).

86. Hexter, *Doing History*, 167–68.

87. Sternberg, *The Poetics of Biblical Narrative*, 28.

88. Sternberg explains: "To develop chronicle into history, after all, the historian must supply a great many missing links—casual connections, national drives, personal motives and characteristics—and the imaginative gap-filling will remain acceptable as long as it operates within the limits of whatever counts as the rules of evidence. Therefore, to demonstrate that the biblical writers allowed themselves some latitude in the treatment of their material is to demonstrate nothing much about their genre, unless that exercise of invention appeals and amounts to the total license of fictionalizing rather than to the constrained license of historicizing" (ibid., 29).

genre of text to be made. Sternberg illustrates this well with the use of the Ewe-lamb parable in 2 Sam 12. His argument is that the transformation of the tale from history to fiction occurred only as the parts took their generic orientation from the coordinates of the whole. He concludes, "To establish either mode, therefore, one must relate the forms of narrative to the functions that govern them in context and assign them their role and meaning. In communication, typology makes no sense unless controlled by teleology. And teleology is a matter of inference from clues planted in and around the writing, extending from title and statements of intent to conventions of representation that signal the appropriate narrative contract in the given milieu."[89] Thus, when all these things are considered—the context of the biblical text, its teleology, its milieu, and its function—to conclude that biblical narrative as a genre is fictional would be a betrayal of its true nature.

The painstaking effort to debunk the fictional characterization of the biblical narrative does not translate to assigning it to the category of Rankian history. Certainly, that is not the purpose of its narratives. While the biblical authors did intend to convey historical truth, they were not writing history *qua* history. The truth given in the biblical narrative, while historical in nature, is oriented toward a theological goal. On this religious bent of the Bible, Ryken and Longman write, "The Bible is pervaded by a consciousness of God. It constantly interprets human experience from a religious perspective. The implied (and sometimes stated) purpose of biblical writers is solidly didactic—revealing God to people, instructing them about how to order their lives, and asserting a religious system of values and morality."[90]

The three streams that feed into the flow of the biblical text thus far identified are literary artistry, history, and theology. The prevailing sentiments have been to adopt one of these characteristics of the biblical text to the exclusion of the others. However, each of these elements is implicated in the other in such a way that attempts to separate and

---

89. Sternberg, *The Poetics of Biblical Narrative*, 30. Long similarly writes, "If, then, historical literature and fictional literature are 'distinguishable only by their overall sense of purpose,' *context* becomes one of the primary means of discovering this purpose. We are reminded of one of the fundamental principles of discourse introduced in the preceding chapter—viz., that 'each successively higher level of textual organization influences all of the lower levels of which it is composed'" (Long, *The Art of Biblical History*, 324).

90. Ryken and Longman, "Introduction," 34.

isolate them tend to obscure rather than clarify the meaning of the biblical text. As seen above, literary artistry is a tool commonly employed in historiographical composition. Every historiography is informed by a particular ideology (which could have theological, political, or ethical dimensions). Besides, it is recognized that the Bible is not history per se, but does contain historiographical materials that serve its didactic purposes.[91] When the matter is construed in this way, then, it ceases to be a matter of whether the Bible is historical or literary, for it has both of these elements. To stress the symbiotic nature of the interplay of these interests, I propose that biblical narrative be seen as being *historary*[92] in nature, with an ideology of the theological kind. Put differently, biblical narrative arises ontologically (at the human compositional level) from the ground and realm of history, existentially inhabits a literary sphere (hence its historarity), and is teleologically driven toward a theological goal (serving divine ends). Its meaning, therefore, can only be properly grasped when all these three axes are held in proper tension.[93] That is to

91. Parry similarly writes, "There is widespread recognition that the biblical story-writers were theologians—their tales are not just accounts of what happened but *theological interpretations of what happened* (Long)" (Parry, "Narrative Criticism," 528).

92. A word of my own coining based on the Bible's historical and literary features. *Historary*, therefore, is the adjectival form, while the noun form would be *historarity*.

93. The need for this comprehensive approach is accented as each scholar tugs in his or her own direction. Emphasizing the literary approach, Alter writes, "The essential and ineluctable fact is that most of the narrative portions of the Hebrew Bible are organized on literary principles, however intent the authors may have been in conveying an account of national origins and cosmic beginnings and a vision of what the Lord God requires of man. We are repeatedly confronted, that is, with shrewdly defined characters, artfully staged scenes, subtle arrangements of dialogue, artifices of significant analogy among episodes, recurrent images and motifs and other aspects of narrative that are formally identical with the means of prose fiction as a general mode of verbal art" (Alter, "How Convention Helps Us Read, 115–30; as cited by Long, *The Art of Biblical History*, 321).

Longman also notes the partial nature of narrative critical analysis. He correctly observes that while narrative critical research does not have historical dimensions of the text as its focus, "still this dimension must in no way be ignored or rejected. Otherwise we would be trifling with the text and not taking seriously its original purpose" (Longman, *Literary Approaches*, 149).

C. S. Lewis, though a literary icon, placed his accent on the theological import of the Bible. He is quoted as having said that the Bible is "through and through, a sacred book. Most of its component parts were written, and all of them were brought together, for a purely religious purpose ... It is ... not only a sacred book but a book so remorselessly and continuously sacred that it does not invite, it excludes or repels, the merely aesthetic approach" (32–33) (Ryken and Longman, "Introduction," 34).

say, the use of a narrative critical approach in reading biblical narrative texts need not be oblivious to the historical and theological interest of the texts. While the method in its own right does not have the goal of engaging in historical or theological interpretation, this tacit acknowledgement does two things. First, it highlights the limited nature of narrative criticism. This way, we avoid making it promise more than it can deliver; it is not a panacea to all interpretive quandaries. Second, while I employ narrative criticism in my analytical procedures, that process will be informed by historical considerations and will by no means be closed to theological implications.

## NARRATIVE CRITICAL READING OF THE BIBLE: SOME REFLECTIONS

I wish to briefly reflect in this section on the payoffs, drawbacks, and essential ingredients that would make narrative criticism a profitable tool in a theologically inclined endeavor. The first benefit of narrative criticism is that its emphasis on the unity of the final form of the text helps the interpreter overcome the impasse of historical criticism, which tends to see a multiplicity of putative sources lying behind the text—a position that consequently problematizes any unified reading of the text. For the community of faith, the final form of the biblical text is what constitutes its Scripture. In the same vein, Parry writes, "For Christians, whatever may be fruitfully said of the prehistory of biblical books, the finished texts we possess are the authoritative source for theological reflection (which is not to say that historicity is unimportant)."[94] The narrative critical method, therefore, is a welcome development because it brings the focus on the text, allowing the reader to immerse him/herself in the

---

The integrative approach is more evident in Powell, who, with regards to the Gospels as narrative, writes, "The recognition that they share certain formal characteristics with fictional works does not in any way prejudge the degree to which they reflect history or the reliability with which they do so." He goes on to add, "The Gospels are not works of fiction but intend to convey historical truth. To the extent that the genres of novel and gospel share a narrative form, however, both are subject to narrative analysis" (Powell, *Narrative Criticism*, 94). Powell's stand approximates Auerbach's. Auerbach writes, "The Bible's claim to truth is not only far more urgent than Homer's, it is tyrannical—it excludes all other claims. The world of Scripture stories is not satisfied with claiming to be a historically true reality—it insists that it is the only real world" (Auerbach, *Mimesis*, 14–15; as quoted in Ryken and Longman, "Introduction," 34).

94. Parry, "Narrative Criticism," 528.

world of the text. This makes the interpretation of the text to be determined by clues ensconced in its narrative context, rather than questions extraneous to the text.

Second, narrative criticism opens the door once again, as in precritical readings, for a transformational reading of the biblical text. Powell observes that while historical critics focus on the referential function of a text, literary critics deal with its poetic function. "This means that literary critics are able to appreciate the story of a narrative apart from consideration of the extent to which it reflects reality. The story world of the narrative is to be entered and experienced, rather than evaluated in terms of historicity."[95] By "reality," I understand Powell to mean historical facticity.

Bruce J. Malina, likewise, highlights a critical problem with the historical-critical method as he notes, "The problem with the historical-critical method as practiced by historians is that as a rule it is entirely insensitive and selectively inattentive to the non-concrete meaning and dimensions of life. From a certain perspective, it is the non-concrete, symbolic meaning–filled dimensions of life that take up most of human concern, energy, and activity."[96] Thus, the concerns of someone reading the biblical text, not just for *information* but more so for *transformation* (for in reality there is no access to the latter without the former),[97] will necessarily penetrate beyond the concrete to the non-concrete meaning and dimensions of life that perfuse the text. Anyone reading the biblical narrative for theological ends ought to aim for its transformational function. Such a reader, therefore, will find the narrative critical reading not to be an end in itself, but a means to an end.

Third, narrative criticism also democratizes Bible reading. For many centuries, the reading of the biblical text was wrested from the laity and vested in ecclesiastical authority. In the wake of the modern era, in the spirit of the Enlightenment, historical critics disavowed submis-

---

95. Powell, *Narrative Criticism*, 8.

96. Malina, "Rhetorical Criticism and Social-Scientific Criticism, 72–101.

97. Combrink, in making the distinction between these two readings of texts, writes, "When one is interested in *information*, the questions asked from the text deal with historical issues, the production of the text, the world of the text and even the theological position of the text. Reading for *transformation* is an existential project in the religious sphere belonging to the field of spirituality. However, when one is interested in transformation, the text cannot be read without getting involved in its informational dimension too" ("The Rhetoric of Sacred Scripture," 102–23).

sion to all forms of authority in the interpretive enterprise. Yet, wittingly or inadvertently, they foist a new hegemony: the episcopacy of the guild of scholars. The skills that were required for being able to decipher either the different *Gattungen* that lay behind the biblical text, for all intents and purposes, practically wrenched the Scripture from the uninitiated. Narrative criticism, therefore, levels the playing field. The publications in the last quarter-century of the work of non-biblical scholars (or non-theologians) such as Northrop Frye, Donald Michie, and several of the contributors to the volume edited by Ryken and Longman as well as that edited by Alter and Kermode testify eloquently to this fact.

One expects that not only would this democratization of biblical reading be the case with the elite in other fields, but that the effect would trickle down to the average person in the pew. This move is made possible because in narrative criticism, textual interpretation is approached from the standpoint of the "implied reader." It is not mandatory for such a reader to "know anything about the history of the text's transmission or to be able to reconstruct the *Sitz im Leben* that passages served before being incorporated into the narrative as a whole."[98] As has been stressed previously, this does not amount to a call for the proscription of historical critical concerns in biblical studies; neither does it in any way whittle down its importance in our trade. It only implies that historical criticism ceases to be the norm for engaging with the text.

Not everyone is an aficionado of narrative criticism. Some critics, for example, charge that the approach foists coherence on what is in actuality an assemblage of disparate material. For instance, some critics argue that it is wrong to categorize the Gospels as "narrative," because they are merely traditional units that have been strung together like "pearls on a string."[99] To such critics the seeming coherence of biblical narrative is an apparition that resulted from an accident of history when these unrelated materials were sequentially juxtaposed. Nothing could be further from the truth. As noted above, biblical narrative has a historiographical dimension as well. All historiography necessarily involves selectivity, collation, and correlation because the facts of chronicles do not constitute history. It is the historian who supplies the connections of causation, furnishes motives, and indicates consequences of actions. This is true of biblical narrative to the degree that it is also historiographical.

98. Powell, *Narrative Criticism*, 87.
99. Schmidt, *Der Rahmen der Geschichte Jesu*; cited in Powell, *Narrative Criticism*, 90.

Powell's response to this criticism is that narrative unity is not something that needs proving; rather, it is assumed. For him, it is the form of narrative itself that grants coherence to the material, its disparateness notwithstanding. He writes, "The presence of inconsistencies in no way undermine the unity of a narrative but simply becomes one of the facets to be interpreted. They may, for instance, signal gaps and ambiguities that must be either explained or held in tension. This is true regardless of whether they are there by design or negligence."[100]

This reflection would be incomplete without the mention of two matters of no mean significance. If literary, historical, and theological elements are woven into the warp and weft of biblical narrative, then, a literary reading of it will of necessity interconnect with the other elements as well. Thus, it is essential that a literary reader of biblical narrative be acquainted with the historical and social milieu in which it arose. On this Powell writes, "Even the perception that narrative criticism is 'nonhistorical' must be mitigated. Narrative criticism demands that the modern reader have the historical information that the text assumes of its implied reader."[101] This implies paying heed to Iser's "reader's repertoire."[102]

Likewise, the theological implications of our readings must not be zoned off from our interpretive terrain, simply because we have adopted a narrative critical approach. This is especially so in view of the Bible's transformational dynamic. The literary explication of the text occasions the unfolding of the world of the text. The convergence of the horizon of the world of the text with that of the reader's self-understanding results in a new self-understanding. Thus, it is this unfolding of the text that "finally forms and transforms the self of the reader according to its

---

100. Powell, *Narrative Criticism*, 92.

101. Powell, *Narrative Criticism*, 97.

102. Wolfgang Iser lists the reader's repertoire as including "familiar literary patterns and recurrent literary themes, together with allusions to familiar social and historical contexts." (Iser, *The Implied*, 288, cf. 32–34, 182–83). Powell explains that the repertoire "comprises practical information that is common knowledge in the world of the story: how much a denarius is worth, what a centurion does, and so forth. It may also include recognition of social and political realities that lie behind the story. It may involve understanding particular social customs and recognizing the meaning of culturally particular social customs and recognizing the meaning of culturally determined symbols or metaphors. Narrative criticism must rely upon historical investigation to provide the reader with this sort of insight" (Powell, *Narrative Criticism*, 97).

intention."[103] However, the potency of the biblical text for this transformation of the self (Ps 19:7–9; Isa 55:10–11; Eph 5:26; Heb 4:12) resides in its character as inspired Scripture.

As inspired Scripture, the Bible has significance not just for people in ancient times, but embodies the very word of God with a dynamic to speak anew to humanity in general, and particularly to communities of faith, in every generation. I do not, however, conceive of this in the same neo-orthodox fashion as Powell, who assumes that revelation "can be an event that happens now, in a present encounter with the text."[104] Such a position fails to reckon with the once-and-for-all character of God's self-disclosure that was given at specific redemptive historical moments (cf. Heb 1:1–4).

God's word continues to speak to his people, not because of unremitting revelatory activity, but rather because of the ongoing work of the Divine Spirit. If we take the apostles as our example, we immediately recognize that they were themselves cognizant of their estate, merely as the fountainhead of the redemptive spring that was gushing into the interminable stream of the eschatological community of the Spirit of God. Thus, unique though the apostles were as receptors of God's revelation, their inimitability stands in tension with the perpetuity of the ongoing work of the Holy Spirit in the redeemed community of the Messiah (cf. John 17:20–21; Acts 2:38–39; Rom 8:9; 1 Cor 12:5–7; Eph 2:13–22).

Therefore, the same Spirit who worked mightily in revealing God's truth for his people through the prophets, sages, and apostles (2 Tim 3:16–17), still works effectually in illumining the understanding of his church so that it is enabled to grasp the reality thus revealed in the text of Scripture (1 Cor 2:13–16; 2 Pet 1:19–21). In view of this, therefore, for the Bible to continue to speak as God's word to faith communities, those communities must continue to accord the Holy Spirit his apposite role in biblical interpretation. The early church demonstrably correlated their kerygma to the tuition of the Holy Spirit (John 14:26; Rom 15:18–19;

---

103. Ricoeur, "Philosophical Hermeneutics," 26.

104. Powell, *Narrative Criticism*, 98. Ditto Riceour, who holds that if the Bible is revealed truth, that revelatory element permeates to the "issue" (i.e., the new being displayed there) of which it speaks. "I would go as far as to say that the Bible is revealed to the extent that the new being unfolded there is itself revelatory with respect to the world, to all reality, including my existence and my history. In other words, revelation, if the expression is meaningful, is a trait of the biblical *world*" (Ricoeur, "Philosophical Hermeneutics," 27).

1 Cor 2:4; 7:40; Eph 2:22; 3:5; 1 Tim 4:1; Rev 2:7). The communities of the Messiah in the twenty-first century, like their first-century forebears, necessarily have to be communities of the Spirit.

## KEY ELEMENTS IN NARRATIVE CRITICISM

The case has already been made above that the biblical narrator is an ideological persuader, albeit one that utilizes techniques that are rather indirect in their suasive rhetoric. It remains for us to enumerate some of the most potent devices of his craftsmanship. A narrative consists of a story (made up of characters, their acts—including inactions—and settings) and discourse (how the story is told). The rhetorical force of a narrative depends on the finesse of its discourse. While not intending to supply an exhaustive survey of all devices employed in narrative composition, we will highlight some of these as a way of underscoring those elements of critical importance in narrative composition, a good grasp of which is imperative for narrative comprehension.

### *Plot*

In narrative, plot is the notional structure that an author employs to give his discourse its macrostructural cohesion. Ryken defines plot as "a coherent sequence of interrelated events, with a beginning, middle, and end."[105] Put differently, plot is the compositional arrangement of narrative components that ultimately gives it its overall shape and thrust. Highlighting the centrality of plot in narrative, Robert Longacre states, "The author by this act of *emplotment* (note the pragmatic implication of this term), draws together disparate elements into a kind of *discordant concordance* (Ricoeur's terms)."[106] Gunn points out that plot is understood through various and incomplete sources such as the voice of the narrator, and the speeches and actions of the characters. In biblical narrative, he continues, the relations between events are not made explicit. For that reason, it is our desire for order that drives us to make connections, in which case plot becomes one dimension of narrative order.[107]

---

105. Ryken, *How to Read the Bible as Literature*, 40.

106. Longacre, *The Grammar of Discourse*, 33. Longacre further points out that while cohesion is provided to the plot by means of surface structure cohesive devices, its coherence is achieved by semantic and lexical binding. This makes lexical studies to have continuing value in the narrative critical studies.

107. Gunn, "Narrative Criticism," 213.

The explication of narrative plot can be as intricate as that of Longacre (based on a text linguistic approach) or as simplified as that of Aristotle (who said that plot consists of a beginning, middle, and ending[108]). For a median position, the key elements of a narrative plot may include exposition, setting, conflict, resolution, and conclusion.

Of the above elements of plot, conflict is the most crucial. Dillard and Longman observe, "As a general rule, plot is thrust forward by conflict. Conflict generates interest in resolution. The beginning of a story, with its introduction of conflict, thus pushes us through the middle toward the end, when conflict is resolved."[109] Laurence Perrine defines conflict as "a clash of actions, ideas, desires, or wills."[110] Narrative conflict may subsist at different planes, or may be brought about by different tensions existing between the narrative characters. For example, it may result from the characters's divergent points of view, irreconcilable personality differences, conflicting desires of different characters, or the strivings of a character against the forces of nature or ineluctable fate or destiny. In studying a narrative, then, its different episodes are questioned with respect to their contribution to the progression or resolution of the conflict in the plot.

## *Characterization*

Plot and character issues are core to narrative critical studies. The two are particularly interrelated. The tendency among critics is to accord one priority over another. Others think the question unnecessary. Such is the view of Longman, who writes, "The debates over whether plot or character is prior seem ill-founded, since they are interdependent and equally important."[111] For him, plot and character are so closely related that they may be separated only for purposes of analysis. The argument of such a position hinges on the understanding that characters are knowable only from their actions and their motivating factors, which are constituent components of plot. Conversely, plot exists only as far as there are characters acting. Gunn seems to place character over plot. However, I am more inclined to agree with him when he concludes, "Plot

---

108. Dillard and Longman III, *An Introduction to the Old Testament*, 32.
109. Dillard and Longman III, *An Introduction to the Old Testament*, 33.
110. Perrine, *Story and Structure*, 44; as cited in Powell, *Narrative Criticism*, 42.
111. Longman, *Literary Approaches*, 152.

and character, on this understanding, are heuristic concepts, having no discrete reality in themselves but useful as starting points for making sense of narrative."[112]

Characterization deals with narrative portrayals of its actors. Characters are known through the narrator's naming, description, and evaluation of them, their actions, their own speech, and the speeches of other characters to and about them (their naming, and description and evaluation) placed on the lips of other characters. The description could focus on appearance (physique, constitution, and overall visage) or inner life, or both. The context of a character's speeches and actions are also very important. Giving keen attention to the state of affairs that a character's speech speaks to, indeed, makes for a better appreciation of what is being said, and what kind of person the speaker is. Gunn correctly observes, "Biblical characters may be seen as bending their speech to their context, speaking obliquely rather than straightforwardly, or simply lying, no less than people in 'real' life. Matching speech and action (as the narrator recounts it), or observing how speech and action are retold by characters, may enable us to see below surface simplicity to underlying complexity."[113]

Another form of characterization is foiling. This occurs when a character's action is cast alongside the action(s) of some other character(s). In this manner, the actions of the character in view are projected in the light of contrasting actions. The contrasting actions usually are those of another character; for instance, Saul is foiled by Jonathan, and David is foiled by Joab.[114] However, the contrast could also be either with the character's own earlier action or with some norm (or even the reader's expectation).[115]

Many critics think biblical narrative is bereft of character description. Ryken and Longman observe a sharp contrast between biblical narrative and the modern novel, with the former lacking the full-fledged portraits of characters as found in the latter.[116] For T. R. Henn, the distinctive elements of characterization are so lacking in biblical narrative that the great figures of biblical characters move in somewhat remote

112. Gunn, "Narrative Criticism," 213.
113. Gunn, "Narrative Criticism," 224.
114. On the latter see Eshelbach, *Has Joab Foiled David?*
115. Berlin, *Poetics*, 40–41.
116. Ryken and Longman, "Introduction," 32.

fashion, being "illuminated as it were from the side by flashes of magnanimity, pity, anger; heroism, deceit, covetousness; suffering and the frequent cry of despair."[117] The reason often offered for this phenomenon is that biblical narrative subordinates characterization to plot, so that details about a character surface only as needed in service to the plot. Berlin repudiates such views emphatically: "No matter what the reason for the description, the reader knows, for instance, that Mephibosheth was lame, that Eli was old and his sight failing, that Saul was tall and David ruddy."[118] She, however, concedes that biblical narrative lacks the kind of physical and psychological description of characters that creates a visual image for a reader. She surmises the possibility that the prohibition on graven images is extended to literary images as well.[119]

The important distinction between the nature of character depiction in biblical narrative and modern narrative is found in their purpose. While in the latter, description is meant to help the reader visualize the character; in the former, it enables him to find the character's social location in society. On this count, Berlin shows that outward description tends to be based on status (king, widow, wise man, wealthy, old, etc.), profession (prophet, prostitute, shepherd, etc.), gentilic designation (Hittite, Amalakite, etc.), or distinctive features (beautiful, lame, etc.).[120] Examples of characters' inner-life portrayals in biblical narrative which she highlights include Amnon's love and hatred for Tamar, the jealousy of Joseph's brothers, Moses's anger (Exod 32:19), and Adonijah's fear (1 Kgs 1:50), among others. All this, she insists, serves "to reduce the 'opaqueness' of characters, and to give the reader insight into their thoughts, emotions, and motivations."[121]

Two types of characters are usually identified. The first is the round (or full-fledged) character, which has the appearance of a "real person," having complex and multifaceted personal idiosyncrasies and character traits. Second, the flat (type) character is usually built on one charac-

---

117. Henn, *The Bible as Literature*, 31; as cited in Ryken and Longman, "Introduction, 15–39. Regarding our book (Samuel), Long suggests that the narrator in Samuel is a master of indirect characterization through comparison and contrast (Long, "First and Second Samuel," 165–81).

118. Berlin, *Poetics*, 34.

119. Berlin, *Poetics*, 34–35.

120. Berlin, *Poetics*, 36.

121. Berlin, *Poetics*, 38.

ter trait or quality. To these two Berlin adds a third, which she calls an agent. The agents are the equivalents of props in drama.[122] Bathsheba is a ready illustration of an agent. She enters the biblical story in 2 Samuel as a passive object, someone espied from a walk on the rooftop, taken, impregnated, and inherited as wife after the murder of her husband. No one reckons with her feelings (whether in the case of her being taken to assuage the king's lust or in her husband's death). She exits the biblical story in 1 Kgs 1, only as one who is used, whether by Nathan or by Adonijah; again, we are not told what she felt about the errands on which she was sent, either by the prophet or the prince.

Overall, however, biblical characters inhabit a messy world and are implicated in its messiness. Neither their world nor they themselves are as spick and span as we would wish them to be. Frederick Buechner characterizes their world as "a Dostoyevskian world of darkness and light commingled, where suffering is sometimes redemptive and sometimes turns the heart to stone. It is a world where, although God is sometimes to be known through his life-giving presence, there are other times when he is known only by his appalling absence."[123] Biblical narrative, therefore, tells the story of what happened to the individuals inhabiting such a world.

Lastly, we ask with Longman, does the study of biblical personages as characters necessarily mean reducing them to fictional beings? His answer is ours as well. He writes, "Indeed some advocates of the literary approach do so and rejoice that they have skirted the historical issue. In my view, however, to analyze David as a literary character in a text is not to deny that he was a historical king or that the events reported in the books of Samuel and Kings are accurate."[124] This affirmative reply does not, however, require a denial of the selective use of sources in the composition of the present biblical text.

## Point of View

Point of view is to narrative what the camera eye is to film; it guides and limits the reader's insight into the plot.[125] Following through on this

---

122. Berlin, *Poetics*, 23–24.
123. Buechner, "The Bible as Literature," 40–48.
124. Longman, *Literary Approaches*, 148.
125. Longman, *Literary Approaches*, 148.

analogy, just as one cannot know the characters in film without the camera, so it is not feasible to know characters in narrative without point of view—they are mediated to the reader by the narrator through point of view. In short, point of view entails a relation between subject and object, perceiving mind and perceived reality.[126] Viewed in this way, the speeches, thoughts, and observations of narrative characters (wherein their point of view is located) are interpretive constructs that betray their unique perspectives of the state of affairs. Point of view, therefore, is not just a baroque folderol in literary textual analysis but a de rigueur condition for articulating the sense of a narrative.

There are four basic perspectives involved in narrative communication: those of the author who fashions the story, the narrator who tells it, the audience or reader who receives it, and the characters who enact it.[127] Where the author and the narrator are coterminous, Sternberg writes, the discourse operates with three basic relationships that constitute the point of view: between narrator and characters, narrator and reader, reader and characters. Of these, he says, the first remains constant "in its inequality, opposing the omniscient and reliable narrator to his essentially fallible agents" while the other two are amenable.[128]

Occasionally, in biblical narrative, one may find the author and narrator to be the same person. A case in point is Nehemiah. Biblical narrative introduces a new dimension to this relationship in equating

---

126. Sternberg, *The Poetics of Biblical Narrative*, 129.

127. Sternberg, *The Poetics of Biblical Narrative*, 130.

128. Sternberg, *The Poetics of Biblical Narrative*, 130. Sternberg further adds, "[W]hat the reader knows and how well he judges, for instance, depend on the narrator's strategy of telling. Whether or not he takes us into his confidence will make an enormous difference to the reading, including our ability to identify or discriminate the perspectives of the dramatized observers and correct their subjective distortions of the implied world and worldview. But regardless of narrative strategy, if we are to make any sense of the text—to distinguish one refracting medium from another, opinion from fact, show from substance, commitment from irony—we must perform these reconstructive operations as best we can" (ibid.).

To perform such reconstructive operations, Sternberg suggests the following set of questions, "Who stands behind this piece of language and what does it project? From what viewpoint does that action or description unfold, and why? Can the perceiver be identified and evaluated by the field of perception? Where does the subject end and the object begin? Is this particular reflector ironic or ironized, reliable or biased or even mendacious, or in short, how does his interpretation stand to the text's and ours? These are among the type of questions arising throughout" (*The Poetics of Biblical Narrative*, 129–30).

the narrator's voice with the divine voice.¹²⁹ Polzin calls our attention to Deuteronomy, where this phenomenon manifests in complexes of "utterance within an utterance within an utterance within an utterance."¹³⁰ Predominantly, it is the voice of Moses and that of God that are heard; and only Moses and the narrator are privy to God's voice. In fact, the narrator brings us God's word more proximately, as the bulk of the book contains God's word mediated through Moses. The book portrays Moses as the only one reporting the authoritative word of God because he is the one who knows God face to face. Yet we know Moses, who knows God, through the narrator, who knows Moses "face to face."¹³¹ By this means, the narrator elevates his speech to the same level as that of Moses, both of which corresponds with God's word; this results in the coincidence of the narrator's point of view with God's.¹³² While Polzin's telling analysis of the complexes of reported speeches in Deuteronomy illustrates well the relationship between the voices of the narrator and God, caution needs be entertained with this position, because it is not every biblical narrator that consciously lays claim to the equation of his voice with the divine voice. Indeed, as the concept of intra-textual consciousness introduced below shows, in certain instances the narrator's perspective may not be necessarily coincident with the divine author's.

There are different ways of considering point of view. As discussed above, it could be from the standpoint of those involved in the communicative situation: the narrator/author, characters, and audience. In considering the point of view of characters, Seymour Chatman has

---

129. Implicit in this is a very complicated divine-human relationship in the communicative situation in biblical narrative. Sternberg comments, "Within an inspirational framework, God himself even becomes the author of the book as well as of its plot, without forfeiting his agent-like status" (*The Poetics of Biblical Narrative*, 130).

130. Polzin, *Moses and the Deuteronomist*, 25.

131. Polzin, *Moses and the Deuteronomist*, 27.

132. Polzin writes, "In our brief introductory remarks to the Deuteronomic History above, we made the assumption that ultimate semantic authority in the work, that is, the implied author's main ideological stance, probably should be looked for both in the words of God and in the words of the narrator. We can apply this assumption to the Book of Deuteronomy itself by stating that the ultimate ideological stance of the book ought to be looked for both in the reporting words of the narrator, its 'author's' spokesman, and in the reported words of Moses, its hero. We may note that in Deuteronomy we find both the narrator and Moses utilizing the formula that is the basic constituent of the whole history: 'God said "such and such"; therefore this event happened precisely to fulfill his word'" (Polzin, *Moses and the Deuteronomist*, 28).

outlined a tri-perspectival approach to point of view. His categories are the perceptual point of view (the perspective through which the events of the narrative are perceived); the conceptual point of view (the perspective of attitudes, conceptions, and worldview); and the interest point of view (the perspective of someone's benefit or disadvantage).[133] For Chatman, point of view may refer to an *action* of some kind—perceiving or conceiving—or to a *passive state*—as in the third sense.[134] Berlin criticizes Chatman for his third category, the interest point of view, which she considers to be too different from the other two.[135] She explains that while perception and conception generally refer to the person doing the seeing, i.e., the subject of the action, interest refers to the person being seen, i.e., the object.

Though in Chatman's articulation, the three categories refer to three perspectives from which a particular character understands (or is understood, in the case of the third category) the relation in which narrative events stand, I envision the possibility of applying these categories to the different parties within the communicative situation of reading. The perceptual point of view, from this perspective, would encompass the points of view of narrative characters; the conceptual point of view would correspond to the narrator's/author's point of view; and the interest point of view would coincide with the reader's point of view. This application is possible because only those whose location transcends that of the story world have the vantage point from which they can assess the various competing interests in the narrative. While the narrator can also do this, the reader is really better positioned to truly evaluate interests. In other words, from the form-content perspective, Chatman's categories are all applicable to people in the narrative discourse (the narrator and characters), while from a functional perspective, they could be applied respectively to narrative characters, the narrator, and the reader. My appropriation of Chatman's first two categories roughly corresponds with Genette's two classes of focalization. The perceptual point of view corresponds to Genette's *internal focalization*, while the conceptual point of view corresponds to his *external focalization*.[136]

---

133. Chatman, *Story and Discourse*, 152–54.
134. Chatman, *Story and Discourse*, 152.
135. Berlin, *Poetics*, 48.
136. Internal focalization means "that the characters, places, and events are presented from thus-and-such a character. That character is the *subject* of the *presentation*.

Two more points need to be made about point of view here. The first is that point of view is accessed through a variety of media found in the narrative. These include the speeches, actions, and thoughts of the characters; the naming of one or more characters by another (whose point of view is being considered); and discursive statements of the narrator. In biblical narrative, however, the manifestations of point of view are much more subtle. Not infrequently, the rhetorical strategy in the stories of the Bible is embodied within the fabric of their discourses.[137] Sternberg refers to these inner textual rhetorical strategies as "the internal premises established by the discourse," which alone determine reliability in interpretation, on the basis of which the reader can never go wrong. I call this textual inner premise intra-textual consciousness, because it is a product of an author's conscious but subtle strategies for endowing his text with a given philosophical, ideological, or theological bent with the goal of orienting the reader toward a given direction. Similarly, it is undergird by a particular set of fundamental assumptions. Every literary work has its own intra-textual consciousness, which permeates its fabric and is constitutive of its mindset, though it is rarely foregrounded (except in consciously ideological or tendentious texts). Therefore, the reader's acuity is critical in picking up the interpretive signals contained in the intra-textual consciousness. The second is that though we have identified different types of points of view, they need not result in the atomizing of the text. Ultimately, the tenor of the intra-textual consciousness of the discourse becomes the fulcrum upon which the entire spectrum of points of view turns.

The concept of intra-textual consciousness is very important, especially for biblical narrative, because of its divine-authorship implications. The divine author identifies with but is never subsumed by the narrator, as he retains his distinct roles of both super-perceiver and super-agent. Thus, intra-textual consciousness is the textual manifestation of his super-perception. This concept is akin to what Powell calls the *evaluative point of view*, in that it governs the work in general. The evaluative point of view refers to, Powell explains, "the norms, values, and general worldview that the implied author establishes as operative for the story.

---

If the story is 'told in *external focalization*,' it is told from the narrator, and the latter has a point of view (in the radical, pictorial sense) on the characters, the places, the events" (Bal, *On Story-Telling*, 91–92). For details see Genette's *Narrative Discourse*.

137. Sternberg, *Poetics of Biblical Narrative*, 51.

To put it another way, evaluative point of view may be defined as the standard of judgment by which readers are led to evaluate the events, characters, and settings that comprise the story."[138] For the narratives in the Former Prophets, the narrator's norm or worldview inhales the air of the Torah, and particularly Deuteronomic ideology, hence our desire to evaluate the relations of King David to King Saul's progeny from a Deuteronomic perspective.

## Narration

Narration is about the narrator's voice. It is heard in a given story, either in the form of formulaic phrases introducing direct discourse, or in extended reports containing expositions, chronicles, sequences of events, or summarizing statements. It is customary for a story to open with a narrated summary, or background, and then proceed to the scenic section, generally marked by the beginning of dialogue.[139] Appearing at the beginning of a narrative, the narrator's voice is heard throughout the entire discourse.

Narration has multifunctional roles in narrative. First, it is the first port of call when determining the narrator's point of view. This is one of the places where the author is wont to drop hints of his rhetorical strategy through which he intends to influence (control) the reader's understanding of the narrative. Thus, it also becomes a good indicator of how to contour the interpretive framework for the story. Second, narration serves as a bridge between larger units of direct speech. According to Alter, this is a particularly important function of narration in biblical narrative because third-person "restatement of what has been said in dialogue directs our attention back to the speakers, to the emphases they choose, the ways their statements may diverge from the narrator's authoritative report of what occurs."[140] Third, the most general use of narration is to furnish a chronicle of public events in summarizing overview. This explains why extended sections of the books of Kings consist of more or less uninterrupted narration because they are meant to offer accounts of wars and political intrigues, as well as national cultic tres-

---

138. Powell, *Narrative Criticism*, 23–24.
139. Berlin, *Poetics*, 57.
140. Alter, *The Art of Biblical Narrative*, 65.

passes and their consequences.[141] Overall, narration supplies both vital and ancillary information to the budding narrative plot. Thus, the reader who wishes to grasp the sense of a narrative will do well to pay heed to the often-subtle voice of the narrator.

## *Dialogue*

Having a propensity for the dramatic, biblical narrative is soused in dialogue. This proclivity is driven by the desire for picturesque presentation of ideas prevalent amongst Hebrew writers. Such dramatic presentations are not uncommon in oral cultures, and it is useful in effectuating immediacy in generating shared experience. Due to this avid predilection to achieve vividness in their discourses, most biblical stories "depend heavily on dialogue rather than summarized narrative as a way of describing the action."[142] Ryken associates the primacy of direct discourse in biblical narrative to the biblical view of man and God. Full meaning for man in the Bible is found in relationship—both to God and to the human community. Relationships are nurtured in communication. Ryken therefore writes, "Dialogue is the natural and inevitable rhetorical mode for this view of man and God, for dialogue is the language of relationship and encounter. It is small wonder, therefore, that biblical literature is full of voices speaking and replying."[143]

Long sees this character of scenic narration[144] to be one of three cardinal traits that affords the narratives in Samuel their sophistication

---

141. Alter, *The Art of Biblical narrative*, 75.

142. Ryken, *The Literature of the Bible*, 20. Illustrating this point, Ryken writes, "The book of Job, although it is a narrative told by a narrator, is structured like a play. And many lyric poems in the Bible are dramatic in structure, with the speaker addressing a mute but implied reader" (Ryken, *The Literature of the Bible*, 20).

Ryken and Longman similarly write, "The dramatic impulse permeates the Bible. Everywhere we turn we find an abundance of quoted speeches, snatches of dialogue, and stationing of characters in a setting. To read the Bible is to become an implied listener of the spoken voice. Of the four means by which a story can be told—direct narrative, dramatic narrative, description, and commentary—dramatic narrative dominates in the stories in the Bible (Licht 24–50), where direct quotation of speeches is a staple." (Ryken and Longman, "Introduction," 15–39). In this quote, Ryken and Longman are referring to Licht's *Storytelling in the Bible*.

143. Ryken, *The Literature of the Bible*, 21.

144. This term derives from Licht, who outlines four modes of narration that all narratives can be classified into, namely, straight narrative, scenic narrative, description, and commentary. He sets scenic narrative in opposition to straight narrative as he

and appeal. He says that these narratives tend to communicate more by "showing" than by "telling." In comparison with stage play, where the viewers are called upon to exercise intellectual and moral judgment in making sense of the words and actions of the dramatis personae, so scenic narration keeps explicit commentary to a minimum and calls on the reader's powers of discernment and evaluation.[145]

Dialogue in biblical narrative performs a number of functions. First, it is intricately connected with scenic narration in advancing the storyline. In this setting, narration often assumes a subsidiary role to direct discourse. Indeed, the ultimacy of dialogue is so pronounced that in many places narration is dialogue-bound and is often relegated to the role of "verbally mirroring elements of dialogue which precede them or which introduce them."[146] Second, dialogue is the author's means for achieving individuation of the narrative characters, as well as focalizing their interactions and dealings with each other. Owing to this, Alter urges that special attention be paid, especially at the beginning of a new story, to the first emergence of dialogue and the initial words spoken by a personage, as they prove to be revelatory and are important in the exposition of character.[147] Berlin, similarly, observes how dialogue constitutes a form of "showing," where a character's own speeches (and actions) serve to reveal his character.[148] Third, it is the place to find points of view of the different characters and, perhaps, of the narrator as well. The access to point of view that scenic narration affords derives from the unmediated entrée it gives the reader to the words and thoughts of the character(s) in question.[149] Lastly, scenic representation is the author's

---

writes, "In straight narrative the author simply reports a series of events, telling his audience that this and this happened ... In scenic narrative, by contrast, the action is broken up into a sequence of scenes. Each scene presents happenings of a particular place and time, concentrating the attention of the audience on the deeds and the words spoken. Conflicts, direct statements of single acts, and direct speech are preeminent. The narrative moves jumpily from scene to scene; to avoid confusion there are unimportant bits of straight narrative linking the scenes or introducing them, where necessary" (Licht, *Storytelling in the Bible*, 29).

145. Long, "First and Second Samuel," 165–81.
146. Alter, *The Art of Biblical Narrative*, 65.
147. Alter, *The Art of Biblical narrative*, 74.
148. Berlin, *Poetics*, 38.
149. The above statement is not unqualified, for we do not intend to deny that the characters' speech reach us through the author's mediation (cf. Bar-Efrat, *Narrative Art in the Bible*, 65).

way of weaving ambiguity into his narration. A quality of unreliability attaches to the speeches of narrative characters when their words are not corroborated by the narrator's voice.[150]

## Narrative Gaps

It is normal that anyone reading a work of art should desire to understand it. In striving toward understanding, the reader seeks to know what is happening in the narrative and the reasons that account for it. S/he also strives to make connections between the different scenes or episodes of the work, as well as to know the characters and what motivates their actions or what informs their perspectives and relations to other characters. The hard fact is that no literary work of worth makes all of these connections for the reader. Berlin likens the situation to painting a picture. Narratives generally provide only partially drawn figure, she says. It is the reader who, guided by the surrounding information, fills and completes the picture.[151] The incompleteness of the picture is what narrative critics call gaps.[152]

The system of gaps in narrative has to be filled in the process of reading. The act of gap-filling in the reading process "ranges from simple linkages of elements, which the reader performs automatically, to intricate networks that are figured out consciously, laboriously, hesitantly, and with constant modifications in the light of additional information disclosed in later stages of the reading."[153] Sternberg, however, denies that gap-filling is an arbitrary act. Rather, he affirms the remarkable powers literature has for controlling and validating its reading; and for that reason, any theory of textual gap filling must receive its legitimation

---

150. For a fuller discussion and illustration of this see Alter, *The Art of Biblical narrative*, 67; and Berlin, *Poetics*, 97.

151. Berlin, *Poetics*, 135. Berlin reminds us that there are many actions and reactions throughout the Bible that are suggested rather than recounted. Yet, "with a few deft strokes the biblical author, together with the imagination of his reader, constructs a picture that is more 'real' than if he had drawn it in detail" (ibid., 137).

152. Stern, defining narrative gaps, writes, "A gap is a deliberately withheld piece of information in a narrative—(1) a missing link in a series of events; (2) an absent cause or motive; (3) a failure to offer satisfactory explanations for an occurrence in a story; (4) a contradiction in the text that challenges the audience's understanding of the narrative; (5) an unexplained departure from norms" (Stern, *Parables in Midrash*, 74; as quoted in Iser, *The Range of Interpretation*, 24).

153. Sternberg, *The Poetics of Biblical Narrative*, 186.

from the text itself.[154] Positions such as these make critics of the more *readerly* sort very critical of Sternberg's project. Bal, for instance, accuses him of erasing "the basic advantage of recent reader-response criticism," and leaving us with "a study in the New Critical mode, interspersed with needless anger at every critic who views the Bible differently."[155] What I find deficient in such criticism is that they focus on the ideological disparities without addressing the theoretical issues at stake.

For Iser, the gaps in the text are reflective of discontinuities (contingencies) in human experiences that occasion and govern communication in general (say, in the dyadic setting). These contingencies also create the need for interpretation as a way of closing the gap.[156] Asymmetry between the text and the reader, just like one's inability to experience how others experience oneself among dyadic communicative partners, is constitutive of the nature of communication in the reading process. In both situations, Iser insists, balance can only be attained if the gaps are filled, and hence the constitutive textual gap is continually bombarded with the reader's projections. However, he says, interaction fails when the mutual projections of the social partners do not change, or if the reader's projections superimpose themselves unimpeded upon the text.[157] This is why Iser sees the text as having the control; it remains constant and

154. Sternberg, *The Poetics of Biblical Narrative*, 188. On the primacy of the text in guiding how it is read, Wolfgang Iser similarly writes, "Reading is an activity that is guided by the text; this must be processed by the reader, who is then, in turn, affected by what he has processed" (Iser, *The Act of Reading*, 165).

155. Bal, *On Story-Telling*, 62.

156. Iser, *The Act of Reading*, 163–66. Iser defines contingency psychoanalytically as the non-coincidence of behavioral plans and people's inability to experience how others experience them (ibid., 166). He relies on the work of Edward E. Jones and Harold B. Gerard (*Foundations of Social Psychology*) for his four categories of contingencies, which are (1) pseudocontingency (when both partners know each other's "behavioral plan" so well and try to put up apposite responses in such a way that their conduct becomes predictable and eventually cancels out contingency); (2) asymmetrical contingency (where Partner A abdicates the drive to implement his own behavioral plan and without resistance tags along that of Partner B—Partner A adapts to and is absorbed by the behavioral strategy of B); (3) reactive contingency (where the respective behavioral plans of the partners are constantly eclipsed by the momentary reaction to what has just been said or transpired—contingency dominates and hinders the partners from implementing their plans); (4) mutual contingency (which involves orienting one's reactions in accordance with one's behavioral plan *and* with the momentary reactions of the other partner—the result could be that interaction is either a triumph of social creativity or a spiraling debacle of increasing mutual hostility) (ibid., 164).

157. Iser, *The Act of Reading*, 167.

constantly provokes the reader to change his views and hence projections. Yet, the reader does not have a passive role. The text draws him into the events it records and makes him supply what is meant from what is not said. Consequently, *the said* takes on significance in reference to *the unsaid*. In other words, "it is implications and not the statements that give shape and weight to the meaning. But as the unsaid comes to life in the reader's imagination, so the said 'expands' to take on greater significance than might have been supposed: even trial scenes can seem surprisingly profound."[158]

All this goes to summon the reader to a close reading of the text. The reader is summoned to embrace the seductive suggestiveness of the gaps in the texts. The biblical author's deft parsimony with words requires imaginative projections on the part of the reader in order to fill the missing part of the picture the author has sketched. The books of Samuel, renowned for their literary quality, are richly ensconced with gaps. Thus, a faithful reading of these books must not shirk the demand for gap filling. Nevertheless, one needs to do this with the awareness that the biblical authors had also intentionally embedded ambiguities in their texts. Therefore, caution needs be exercised so as not to trivialize the profundity of the narrative text by attempting to fill all gaps and thereby leave the text bereft of all ambiguity. This is a delicate balancing act that calls upon the reader's discernment and skill, which are developed only through experience.

## *Repetition and* Leitwort

In the old literary (or historical) criticism all seeming textual superfluity were thought to be the result of a conflation of disparate sources. The rise of contemporary literary criticism is changing this manner of approaching texts. Ever-increasing numbers of critics are open to the idea that repetition is part of the fabric of narrative discourse. In literary critical theory in general, repetition has been recognized to be both a constitutive element of narrative and a concept with significant thematic implications.[159] The principle of repetition has been recognized as the

---

158. Iser, *The Act of Reading* 168.

159 . Lothe, "Repetition and Narrative Method," 117–32. Indeed, Miller, writing of repetition in the novel says that any novel is "a complex tissue of repetitions linked in chain fashion to other repetitions" (Miller, *Fiction and Repetition*, 2–3); as cited in Lothe, "Repetition and Narrative Method," 118.

most reliable guide to what a story is about. Invariably, what keeps being repeated in a story points to its central focus.[160]

Underlining the critical place of repetition in narrative composition, and hence interpretation as well, Gilles Deleuze writes, "*'seul ce qui se ressemble diffère,' 'seules les différences se ressemblent'*"[161] Deleuze's statement repudiates the banality with which repetitions were attended. It bids the reader pay closer attention in his readings, which alone would enable him to spot the subtle meaning differentials in the interrelations of apparent similarities and discern commonalities in seeming differences. The strength of this point is skillfully illustrated in Licht's discussion of several Bible stories. A ready example is his discussion of Samuel's call narrative (1 Sam 3:3–10). The account of the call is repeated four times. Yet Licht shows that there is development, omission, and the substitution of elements for those omitted. He writes, "The device produces both compactness and variety. Some of the variations are used to convey minor subtleties of meanings."[162]

Repetitions take different manifestations: they range from the repetition of form and stylistic elements such as words, figures of speech, sounds, and even syntactic forms to content elements such as repeated actions, events, episodes, dialogues, or perspectives. Another way of considering repetition is its reportage both in the narrative world and in narrative discourse. Genette has set forth four possible relationships between frequency in discourse time and story time.[163] Three of these consist of aspects of repetition. The first is repetitive narration, where an event that happened once is reported more than once (e.g., Paul's Damascus Road encounter with the risen Son of God, cf. Acts 9:1–2; 22:4–16; 26:9–18). Second, multiple-singular narration, where an event that happened repeatedly is also reported repeatedly (e.g., the Sign of Jonah in Jesus' confrontation with the religious authorities of his time, cf. Matt 12:38–45; 16:1–4). Third, iterative narration, where an event that happened iteratively is reported only once (e.g., some of the common practices of Jesus, cf. Luke 4:16; 22:39; Mark 10:1). Each of these forms of repetition (whether in the narrative world or narrative discourse) is indicative of where the narrator places emphasis in the narrative. This

---

160. Ryken, *How to Read the Bible as Literature*, 59.
161. Deleuze, *Logique du sens*, 119.
162. Licht, *Storytelling in the Bible*, 52–54.
163. Genette, *Narrative Discourse*, 113–60; as cited in Powell, *Narrative Criticism*, 39.

requires the reader to discreetly consider each of the forms of repetition in a narrative, noting their nuances and their attendant significations.

Repetition of lexemes, morphemes, or the semantic range of word roots in their varied forms (e.g., verbs in different tenses, voices, and moods; nouns; and adjectives) assumes new heights of significance. Such diversity of repetition is often borne in phonetic tallies (giving rise to puns and word-plays), synonyms, and antonyms.[164] Martin Buber and Franz Rosenzweig have identified the phenomenon and given a good explication of it as a distinctive artistic convention of biblical narrative, which they christened *Leitwort*. The style that employs *Leitwort,* they called *Leitwortstil*.[165] They explain that the key word establishes a relationship between different stages of the narrative, thereby making its essential point. Often that point comes out in the slightly altered form of the recurrent key word.[166]

Among several examples, Buber uses the account of the golden calf apostasy to illustrate the intricate working of *Leitwortstil* in narrative discourse. The two key-words (*Leitworter*) he identified are *'ām* ("people") and *'ālāh* ("to go up"). Buber shows that within the space of three chapters (Exod 32–34) these terms occur about thirty and a dozen times respectively. He skillfully lays out the meaning implications of, say, the back and forth exchange between Moses and Yahweh on whose "people" Israel is, and on who brought them up from Egypt.[167] The depth of meaning unfolded by the various nuanced ways in which those two terms have been used is very revealing. Such observed repeated words or key words identified in a narrative can become buoys, marking anchors to which textual interpretations can be trussed.

In a reader-response fashion, Gunn is of the opinion that another way of engaging *Leitwort* is to recognize that words often participate in more than one pattern of concatenation; words are always potentially on the move along a spectrum from literal to metaphorical. Such multivalence of language can be exploited for a subversive reading of the

---

164. Bar-Efrat illustrates the recurrence of a key word with an antonymic sense with the sixfold occurrence of the verb *bārēk* with two opposing meanings, bless and curse, in the Job 1:5–2:10 (Bar-Efrat, *Narrative Art in the Bible*, 212).

165. Buber and Rosenzweig (eds.), *Scripture and Translation*.

166. Bar-Efrat, *Narrative Art in the Bible*, 213.

167. Martin Buber, "Leitwort and Discourse Type," 143–50.

text.[168] One cannot deny that variation in the concatenation of words has high potential for yielding semantic differential in textual reading. I believe this is the essence of the proposition of *Leitwortstil* as set forth by Buber and Rosenzweig. Its proper use unveils the ambivalence, ambiguity, and irony ingrained in biblical narrative. However, I do not believe that Buber and Rosenzweig's project supplies the reader with a ticket to the fantasyland of textual indeterminacy. It is beyond the scope of the present project to fully engage the debate as to whether there is just a single determinate meaning of a text or a total textual undecidability. Phyllis Trible's position on the issue is worth a more sympathetic review. She holds that the articulation of meaning implies many possibilities for author, text, and reader. She, then, allows that a text has "more than a single meaning and fewer than unlimited meanings. In addition, it works at the boundary of text and reader, with emphasis on the former."[169]

## *Type Scene and Narrative Analogy*

The type-scene is an episodic literary convention consisting of a determined set of motifs that recur in a recognizable and ordered fashion. Ryken cautions that type-scene should not be confused with either types or typology.[170] Alter, the chief proponent of the use of type-scene in biblical narrative analysis, enumerates the two sources of influence on his application of type-scene to biblical narrative.[171] The first comes from Robert C. Culley's influential monograph on Hebrew narrative published over thirty years ago.[172] The second is the analysis of type-scene in Homeric studies. The confluence of these two influences resulted in his awareness of the analogous functioning of type-scenes in Homeric literature and biblical narrative. He makes a distinction, however, between the two in this way: type-scenes in Homeric studies are located in quotidian situations of the heroes concerned, whereas those in biblical narratives are found at critical junctures in the careers of biblical heroes.[173] The central motifs of the betrothal type-scene, for example,

---

168. Gunn, "Narrative Criticism," 225.
169. Trible, *Rhetorical Criticism*, 99.
170. Ryken, *How to Read the Bible as Literature*, 192.
171. Alter, *The Art of Biblical Narrative*, 49–51.
172. Culley, *Studies in the Structure of Hebrew Narrative*.
173. Alter, *The Art of Biblical narrative*, 51.

*mutatis mutandis*, include the journey of the groom or his surrogate to a foreign land; his encounter of girl(s) at a well; the drawing of water from the well (by the man or girl); the girl's flight to herald the news of the stranger; the welcoming of the stranger (customarily with a festive meal); and finally the betrothal.[174]

Repetition, omission, and informational gaps are some of the key elements in the structuring and orchestration of the motifs of a type-scene.[175] The hermeneutical dividend of type-scenes derives from the effective understanding of the deployment of these elements in a narrative's compositional artistry. This fact is well demonstrated in the variation of the central motifs of the betrothal type-scene. Fuchs shows, for instance, how the drawn-out orchestration of the first betrothal type-scene affords the opportunity for a fuller characterization of the actants in it. This proleptically gives the reader a window into both the quiet dominance that Rebekah will exercise in her home and Laban's greed, which will become fully manifested in his encounter with Jacob. On the other hand, she argues that the terse presentation of the third betrothal type-scene both shows the diminished status of the bride as well as the betrothal scene in general and makes its accent fall on the groom's (Moses') character as the deliverer of the underdogs.[176]

Narrative analogy shines its light on given narrative discourses (focusing on either characters or chains of actions, for instance), whereby the fabric of one discourse is woven with the same yarn and loom as that of another. Richard Levin, writing on English Renaissance drama, offers a fitting illustration of how narrative analogy (very prevalent in Renaissance literary art) works: "In almost all the plays, the formal analogy joins two or more actions concerned with the same area of human experience ... love, marriage, friendship, manners, war, class conflict ... or a 'nuclear parallel'—two fathers misjudging their children, two wives tempted to commit adultery ... pairs of lovers thwarted by parental opposition ... the basis of connection is immediately apparent in the common subject matter."[177]

---

174. Alter, *The Art of Biblical narrative*, 52.
175. Fuchs, "Biblical Betrothal Type-Scene," 7–13 [13].
176. Fuchs, "Biblical Betrothal Type-Scene," 11–12.
177. Levin, *English Renaissance*, 148; as cited in Berman, *Narrative Analogy*, 3). For a detailed study of narrative analogy in the Hebrew Bible, see Garsiel, *The First Book of Samuel*.

We reason, from the foregoing, that it is not just the plot outlines, but also the inner interlacing of elements within the plots that signal the existence of narrative analogy. Thus, from the example, it is not just that both stories have fathers and children, but also that both fathers misjudge their children; neither is it that both stories have wives in them, but that both wives are tempted to commit adultery. The elements of analogy are not limited to plot components or subject matter. They may also include correspondences in language, sound, imagery, and style.[178]

Narrative analogies serve the interpretive agenda by inviting "the reader to read one story in terms of another."[179] In this way, the one discourse provides oblique commentary on the other.[180] The operational facility of narrative analogy derives from the fact that the analogous narratives usually contain some points of similarity and dissimilarity. The similarity furnishes the basis for the linkage and confrontation of the analogical elements, whereas the dissimilarity occasions their mutual illumination, qualification, or simply concretization.[181]

Examples of narrative analogies abound in Scripture. The book of Judges, for instance, is replete with narrative analogies.[182] The well-celebrated case is that of the analogies between Gibeah (Judg 19) and Sodom (Gen 19),[183] which has been recognized as such from the time of Pseudo-Philo (*L. A. B.* 45.2). The similarities are so numerous and stretch from motific issues to syntactic patterns that the analogy being drawn is not lost on a keen reader. These include the number of travelers (two angels; the Levite and his wife); the travelers being detained (by Abraham's hospitality and intercession; by the father-in-law's merry making); arriving late in the evening (Gen 19:1; Judg 19:15); staying in the public square (Gen 19:1; Judg 19:16–17); being seen by a man who insists on hosting the strangers (Gen 19:1–3; Judg 19:17–21); the knock on the door and the nefarious demand of the bawdy men of the city (Gen 19:4–5; Judg 19:22); the ardent entreaty of the host (Gen 19:7–8; Judg 19:23–24); the intransigence of the men at the door (Gen 19:9; Judg 19:25); and the destruction of the city (Gen 19:18ff; Judg 20:1ff). However, there are

---

178. Berman, *Narrative Analogy*, 8; cf. Garsiel, *The First Book of Samuel*, 22–23.
179. Berlin, *Poetics*, 136.
180. Alter, *The Art of Biblical Narrative*, 21.
181. Sternberg, *The Poetics*, 365; cf. Garsiel, *The First Book of Samuel*, 27.
182. For more on this see O'Connell, *The Rhetoric of the Book of Judges*, 281–304.
183. Block, "Echo Narrative Technique," 325–41.

divergences between the two accounts as well. One, in the Genesis account the travelers started out three in number (Gen 18:2) but only two arrived in Sodom; in Judges the three initial travelers from Bethlehem arrived in Gibeah, except that the servant is more or less backgrounded. Two, in Genesis Lot offered his two virgin daughters to spare the guests (Gen 19:8), though neither of them was sexually assaulted; in Judges, the host offered his virgin daughter with the female guest (the concubine) to spare the male guests (Judg19:24), and yet it is only the female guest (the concubine) who is thrust out to the sexual perverts.[184] Three, in Genesis the host (Lot) is pulled in by the guests (Gen 19:19); in Judges one guest (the concubine) is pushed out by another guest (the Levite) (Judg 19:25). Four, the consequences of the actions in the preceding point is that Lot's daughters were saved while the concubine was lost. The sum effect of this is to show the wickedness of the Benjaminites (particularly those at Gibeah). Within the context of the DtrH, therefore, this narrative analogy functions as an anti-Benjaminite polemic. The dismemberment of the concubine obliquely adumbrates, first, the nearly obliteration of Benjamin (dismemberment of Israel), but more so, Saul's butchering of his oxen, thereby subtly equating him with the worthless men of Gibeah and ultimately disqualifying him from the Israelite throne.

## CONCLUSION

In this chapter, I have reviewed scholarly approaches to biblical narrative, and paid especial attention to the rise and growth of narrative criticism in biblical interpretation. I have also shown narrative to be a preferred form of communication among Semites. While it does not seem to address anyone outside of its story world, narrative by its nature, tantalizingly draws its reader into the rhetoric of its persuasion. I have also demonstrated how both historical and fictional narrations are concerned with the representation of reality, though from different perspectives. I, then, showed how biblical narrative, in its *historarity*, employs historical data, literary artistry, and theological goals in its representation of truths

---

184. Brettler sees this dissimilarity as a good support for the literary dependence of Judges on Genesis. He characterizes the addition of the host's daughter in the offer as *blind motif*, which refers to a story element that seems to be intrusive or leads nowhere and thus shows that its inclusion in that story is explained by a parallel in the source story where that same motif or plot element has an integral narrative function ("The Book of Judges," 395–418).

that have concerns of ultimate reality. Without doubt, then, to properly explicate the meaning of a biblical narrative text, one must reckon with the literary conventions or artistry that informed the text's composition vis-à-vis the historical and theological dimensions of the text as well. All the foregoing is preparatory to our study of the narratives in Samuel dealing with David's relationship with the surviving Saulides in the next three chapters.

# 4

# The Contest for the Succession to the Throne of Saul
# (2 Samuel 2–4)

IN CHAPTER 3, I outlined the methodology of the present study, namely, narrative criticism. In discussing the narrative critical method, I pointed out the centrality of the final form of the text in its analysis, not the text's prehistory. Additionally, I noted the *history*[1] nature of biblical narrative, which ontologically arises from the ground of history, existentially inhabits a literary sphere, and teleologically drives towards a theological goal; and I also noted how all of these trajectories have to be kept in tension for a proper explication of the world of the biblical narrative text. I also explored the various aspects or literary devices of narrative criticism, which, together with the traditional grammatical tools of exegesis, would constitute the exegetical paraphernalia for the present chapter and the next two in which I will be embarking upon close readings of the narratives of David's dealings with the heirs of Saul after the his death.

The story of David's rise, which begins in 1 Sam 16, finds its conclusion in the first five chapters of 2 Samuel. The entire HDR narrative can be divided into three main parts (David as a favored courtier at Saul's court, 1 Sam 16:1—18:30; David as a fugitive and a mercenary, 1 Sam 19:1—2 Sam 1:27; and David's final ascent to the throne, 2 Sam 2–5). We find David taking a very active, indeed, a proactive role in the first two sections of the HDR. However, in the concluding section of the HDR, David is surprisingly portrayed as being passive; all the key actions that finally thrust him upon the throne of Israel are reportedly taken by others. This passive depiction of the man who is otherwise not content to be the flaccid object of the action of others in this riveting

---

1. See footnote 92 in chapter 3 of this work.

story stimulates a desire for a closer scrutiny of the text. Such scrutiny, James C. VanderKam observes, will lead the keen critic to a different conclusion than a surface reading of the text may suggest.²

The purpose of the HDR as a whole has been identified as an apology for David.³ Niels Peter Lemche observes, "Without doubt the motivation for the author of this narrative was—and here the dating is of no consequence—(a) to legitimize David's succession to the throne which rightly belonged to the house of Saul, and (b) to acquit David of charges brought against him for complicity in the disaster which ruined Saul's family."⁴ From this perspective, the narrator goes to great lengths to show that it was Yahweh who was at work, charting David's path to the throne. Thus, whether it was during his days of service at Saul's court, or during his wilderness wandering days as a fugitive (or rebel leader, freedom fighter, perhaps a terrorist in today's parlance—all depends on whose point of view is under consideration),⁵ or during his service as leader of a mercenary cartel at the court of the Philistine Achish of Gath, or in the final reach for the throne, Yahweh is shown to be with David, thereby guaranteeing his success (cf. 1 Sam 16:18; 18:12, 14, 28; 23:2, 4, 9–12, 14; 30:7–8; 2 Sam 2:1; 5:10). Additionally, the narrator employs several alibis to absolve David of blame or guilt for the murders of Saul, Jonathan (and his brothers), Abner, and Ishbosheth. To this last point we

---

2. VanderKam, "Davidic Complicity in the Deaths of Abner and Eshbaal," 521–39 (esp. 521–24).

3. Apology is a literary genre of political legitimization literature, which ancient Near Eastern usurpers (or their supporters) employed to validate and authenticate their accession to the throne, and to canvass for the acceptance of their reign (cf. Finkelstein and Silberman, *David and Solomon*, 86).

4. Lemche, "David's Rise," 2–25 [2].

5. Lemche takes the idea of a rebel militia seriously and prefers to label it in terms of the diction of the ancient Near East. He calls David and his band *habiru*. He writes, "Otherwise the author describes David's behavior during this period as if David was another *habiru* . . . It is generally accepted today that the *habiru* were a class of outlaws in exile, who had run away from unbearable social conditions in their own country (city-state) and now appeared as marauders and troublemakers all over the Fertile Crescent in the second millennium B.C." And he adds, "In all respects David lives up to the conception of the *habiru*/Hebrews as a troublesome, parasocial element, which had broken away from the establishment. According to the expressive statement in 1 Sam 22:1–4, undoubtedly an old, authentic source, David was no ordinary outlaw, but very soon became the standard-bearer of the malcontents in Southern Palestine, as is seen from v. 2:" (Lemche, "David's Rise," 11).

## The Contest for the Succession to the Throne of Saul (2 Samuel 2–4)

shall give greater attention shortly. Presently, we will briefly consider the plot of this concluding part of the HDR narrative.

The first chapter of 2 Samuel, as the foreground of this sub-narrative, signals the beginning of the end of the story of David's rise with the death of Saul. Now that Saul is out of the picture, the throne of Israel is vacant. The big question now is who is going to fill that vacancy: There was a lingering question as to whether someone from the Saulide dynasty or the usurper from the south will seize the opportunity. This story is developed in an intriguing plot from chapter 2 until it reaches its crescendo in chapter 5 with David's accession to Israel's throne. It consists of four episodes, which are aligned according to our present chapter divisions of the book: (1) the rise of conflict, the beginning of the civil war (ch. 2); (2) the climax, the death of the key opposition figure, Abner (ch. 3); (3) the anti-climax or denouement, the death of Ishbosheth (ch. 4); and (4) the conclusion, David's ascendency (ch. 5).

This turn of events begins with David's advance on Hebron which he took and made his operational base. Subsequently, as a first step toward his ultimate goal of becoming the king of Israel, he was, for the time being, content to be anointed the king of the southern tribes of Judah. With his eye on the kingship of all Israel, David commenced his maneuver towards his goal by dispatching a diplomatic mission to the seemingly most valiant community of Transjordanian Israel (Jabesh-gilead). Meanwhile, with David in his neck of the woods, Abner tactically relocated the capital of the faltering Saulide dynasty of Israel to Transjordan, where he also anoints the lesser-known son of Saul, Ishbosheth, as king. Having carted the puppet king away to safety, Abner returned to Benjaminite territory to meet head-on the burgeoning menace from the south. Civil war broke out, and at the end of the first major encounter, the scales tilted indubitably against the northerners.

The decisive moment in this plot comes in 2 Sam 3:1, where the narrator announces, "There was a protracted war between the dynasty of Saul and the dynasty of David; and David was waxing stronger continually, but Saul's dynasty was waning unremittingly" (author's translation). The rest of chapters 3 and 4, therefore, are a detailed recounting of the dwindling fortunes of Saul's dynasty and the gains of David, who profits from the misfortunes of Saul's house. With the key figures of the northern dynasty (Abner and Ishbosheth) decimated and Israel in need of a deliverer from the prevailing Philistine threat, the humbled elders of Israel bowed at David's feet in Hebron, hailing him as their king.

The outworking of the plot is not as straightforward as its outline above would suggest. We referenced in our first chapter Brueggemann's distinction between the narrator of the HDR and that of the SN. The former, he said, is both naively enthusiastic about David and relentlessly polemical against Saul and trustingly celebrates that which in other contexts might be embarrassing. The author of the latter, he notes, is not so trusting as to be incapable of criticism. The juxtaposition of these narratives side-by-side in the biblical canon, therefore, alters how they are to be read. Put differently, the stitching together of these narratives by the final redactors creates a new dynamic for how they are to be read. It amounts to a kind of disorientation for reorientation.[6] It is therefore a legitimate literary undertaking to read the HDR in the light of the SN and vice versa.

To sum it all up, then, 2 Sam 2–5 constitute a sub-plot within the larger narrative plot of the HDR. The focus of this concluding sub-plot of the HDR is the death throes of the Saulide dynasty and the final forward thrust of David to grasp the throne of Israel. It consists of an intertwined web of conflicts, the resolution of which leads to the emergence of David as the victor, who finally receives the crown as the king of Israel in the last episode of the HDR (2 Sam 5). In other words, this sub-narrative contains several streams of conflict that are fed by the deep aquifer of human desire and ambition. These conflicts include the larger dynastic struggle between the house of David against the house of Saul (David vs. Ishbosheth), the conflict within the divided house of Saul (Abner vs. Ishbosheth), the clash of the generals on both sides (Joab vs. Abner), and finally the conflict of interest of fortune-seekers (the two sons of Rimmon vs. Ishbosheth). It is absolutely remarkable that in the midst of these ferociously ambitious and avaricious men, is trapped a hapless, helpless, and witless individual, Ishbosheth, who manifests no ounce of ambition, not even a drive for survival. It is a sad turn of events that he becomes the sacrificial lamb to service the ambitions of these others, especially David. It is with this perspective that we proceed to examine the contest for the succession to Israel's vacant throne that has been preserved in this concluding part of the HDR.

---

6. Ricoeur's terminology.

## THE BEGINNING OF CIVIL WAR (2 SAM 2:1-32)

2 SAMUEL 2:1-11

1 After this, David inquired of the Lord, saying, "Shall I go up against one of the cities of Judah?"[7] And the Lord replied to him, "Go up." And he asked, "Whither shall I go up?" And he replied, "To Hebron." 2 So David marched up there; along also tagged his two wives: Ahinoam, the Jezreelitess, and Abigail, the wife of Nabal—the Carmelite. 3 David also brought along with him his militia;[8] each one with his family—they lived in the settlements of Hebron.

4 Now the men of Judah came, and anointed David king over the house of Judah. Then it was told David, saying,[9] "*It was*[10] the men of Jabesh-gilead who buried Saul." 5 So David sent messengers to the men of Jabesh-gilead. He said to them, "Blessed are you of Yahweh because you have done this *act of* loyal love with your lord, with Saul—you have buried him. 6 Now then, may Yahweh show you loyal love and faithfulness; and I also will show you this loyal love, because you have done this thing. 7 Now

---

7. I have chosen to translate this clause this way because of the contextual and literary factors. There are five places in the narratives in Samuel in which David inquires of the Lord (two in 1 Samuel and three in 2 Samuel; cf. 1 Sam 23:2; 30:8; 2 Sam 2:1; 5:19; 5:23). Of these verses, both pairs that come before and after our verse concern "going up against for conquest." Out of these five occurrences of David's inquiry of the Lord, four are in connection with a military expedition. Other notices of people inquiring of the Lord in the DtrH similarly have clearly military connotations (cf. Judg 1:1; 20:18, 28; see also Num 27:21). It is, therefore, a good inference to conclude that on this one occasion also, David moved on Hebron to seize it militarily so as to make it his operational base for his impending onslaught on Israel. The action of the elders who anointed him as their king is comparable to similar action taken by the elders of Israel (2 Sam 5:1-3) after the demise of Abner—the strong man of Israelite politics: It was basic surrender, in view of David's superior war machine.

8. Lit. "The men who were with him." For a fuller characterization of this group as a militia and its achievements see VanderKam, "Davidic Complicity," 524-26.

9. The Lucian recession of the LXX has the demonstrative "that" (ὅτι). The Hebrew direct discourse marker (לֵאמֹר), makes the need of "that" rather redundant. McCarter considers the position of the Hebrew אֲשֶׁר to be displaced and that it is the Greek ὅτι that reflects its rightful place (McCarter, *II Samuel*, 81). He fails, however, to substantiate this claim. When we reckoned with the MT's presentation of this sentence in direct speech, then, the אֲשֶׁר would make perfect sense, as per our translation here. This difference is not significant.

10. Here, as with all my translations of the Hebrew Text, italicized words are indicative of what is not stated explicitly, but is understood from text's construction.

therefore, brace up yourselves, and be courageous; for your lord, Saul, is dead. Moreover,[11] the house of Judah has anointed me king over them."

8 Now Abner, son of Ner, commander of Saul's army, took Ishbosheth,[12] Saul's son, brought him across to Mahanaim, 9 and made him king over the Asherites,[13] and over Jezreel, and over Ephraim, and over Benjamin, and over all Israel.

---

11. This is more like our modern-day use of "P.S." In this case David places his main agenda in the P.S. section of his communication with the men of Jabesh-gilead.

12. There are different renditions of this name in different manuscripts. 4QSam$^a$ has the definite article prefixed to it (which makes it to be an epithet rather than a proper name, i.e., "the man of shame"). The Aquila, Symmachus, and Theodotion manuscripts of the LXX render it as *eisbaal*, which differs from the MT's איש בשת. Henry Preserved Smith reasons that the MT's Ishbosheth (echoed in Qumran's "the man of shame") "would be no name to give a son, especially a king's son. There can be no doubt that the original name is preserved to us in the form אשבעל, 1 Chr 8:33; 9:39." He anchors his supposition in the renditions of the ancient translations of the LXX, in which, he says, the traces of the original form of the name are preserved. He concludes therefore that it is the reluctance of later Jews to pronounce the name Baal that led to the substitution of בשת for בעל, even where the latter appears in proper names (Smith, *Samuel*, 269). I find Smith's argument convincing because evidence exists to show that in Iron Age Israel, Baal was used as a synonym of Adonai in reference to Yahweh. A case in point is the tradition concerning David's wars with the Philistine, in which the etiological explanation for the origin of the name of the site of David's defeat of the Philistines—Baalperazim—the epithet Baal is used in reference to Yahweh. The naming of the place is attributed to David, and yet no connotation of Baal as a pagan deity is attached to it (cf. 2 Sam 5:20; 1 Chron 14:11; 12:6; 14:7). For further discussion of the meaning of the name Ishbosheth, see Matitiahu Tsevat "Ishbosheth and Congeners, 77- 85; Anderson, *2 Samuel*, 32; and McCarter, *II Samuel*, 85-87.

13. The Syriac and Vulgate versions translate האשורי as "Geshurite," while the Targums have "*bet Asher*" (i.e., "house of Asher"). There is no simple solution to the enigma of this word, of which Keil and Delitzsch write, "In the Septuagint we find Θασιρι or Θασουρ, an equally mistaken form. The Chaldee has 'over the tribe of Asher,' which is also unsuitable, unless we include the whole of the northern portion of Canaan, including the territory of Zebulun and Naphtali. But there is no proof that the name *Asher* was ever extended to the territory of the three northern tribes" (K & D 2, 565, n. 1). McCarter translates as "Geshurite" (McCarter, *2 Samuel*, 87), while Anderson notes that the Targumic redition of "Asherites" "is often regarded as the best reading, indicating האשרי 'Asherite' or simply אשר as 'Asher'" (Anderson, *2 Samuel*, 31, translation note on verse 9a). He is however not oblivious of the considerable uncertainty associated with determining what the right reading of the word is. He writes, "The two possibilities are the reading suggested by Tg אשר 'Asher' or that provided by Syr and Vg, namely, אשור 'Geshur.' Yet Geshur must have had its own king quite early in David's reign (cf. 2 Sam 3:3) and therefore it could hardly have been annexed by the Israelites at this point in time. Furthermore, David's marriage with the daughter of the king of Geshur could be seen as part of an attempt to isolate Ishbosheth's kingdom. Unfortunately, also the

10 Ishbosheth was forty years old when he began to reign over Israel, and he ruled two years. Only the house of Judah followed David. 11 The period of time that David was king in Hebron over the house of Judah was seven years and six months.

The last section of the HDR begins in 2 Sam 2. It is clearly marked by the circumstantial phrase ויהי אחרי־כן ("After this," or as the KJV has it, "It came to pass after this").[14] It ends in 2 Sam 5:25 with David obeying Yahweh's commands and completely routing the Philistines (the two things that Saul is shown in 1 Samuel to have been incapable of doing). By this means, the succession is shown to have been completed. With our focus on Saulides, our discussion will terminate with chapter 4. Each of the three chapters that will be engaging our attention constitutes an

---

other alternative, 'Asher,' has its problems. It could not very well be controlled without the possession of Zebulun, Issachar, and Naphtali. A doubtful solution is to regard the above list of territories as giving administrative districts (cf. 1 Kgs 4:1–19) rather than tribal possessions (see Schunck, *Benjamin*, 129); it may be questioned whether Saul had already established such an administrative system" (*2 Samuel*, 35).

In arguing for the propriety of translating האשורי as "Geshur," John Mauchline notes that while "Assyria" is completely out of the question, "Asher" will require the inclusion of Naphtali, Zebulun, and Issachar, but these areas would have been dominated by the Philistines after their victory at Gilboa (Mauchline, *1 and 2 Samuel*, 204). A close reading of the list of place names included in the verse indicates that the narrator is here listing the major regions that constitute his Israel, not necessarily the areas that Ishbosheth had effective control over. If we are to follow through on the problem of Philistine control postulated by Mauchline, then even Jezreel should not be mentioned in verse 9 because that was the very gateway through which the Philistines poured into northern Israel. However, when understood as regions of the narrator's Israel, it makes perfect sense. In this regard Gilead refers to the Tranjordanian two and half tribes; Jezreel can be understood as a reference to the two tribes of Issachar and Zebulun, whose tribal allotment included the Jezreel valley; Ephraim refers to the Cisjordanian Joseph tribes of Ephraim and Manasseh; while Asher(ites) could have been an abbreviated name for the Upper Galilee tribes of Asher, Naphtali and Dan (though this is not attested elsewhere). Besides, Asher is the furthest westward reach of northern Iron Age Israel. In this sense the mention of the furthest extremity of the land presupposes the inclusion of all that comes before it, not necessarily because that entire region was called by this particular name. This line of argumentation is supported by the narrator's effort to emphasize that Ishbosheth's realm covered all Israel save Judah: at the end of the list he writes, ועל־ישראל כלה ("and over Israel, all of it").

Na'aman has argued recently for the emendation of the text so that it reads "to the boundary of the Geshurites" (Na'aman, *Ancient Israel's History and Historiography*, 20–21).

14. Anderson observes that it "is a recurrent transition-marker, and it is fairly characteristic of 2 Samuel (see 8:1; 10:1; 13:1; 21:18; cf. also 15:1)" (Anderson, *2 Samuel*, 22).

episode of its own. Chapter 2 focuses on the beginning of hostilities between the two houses contending for the throne. Chapter 3 has two parts to it: the first section is brief but showcases the rising profile of the Davidic house, while the lengthier second section launches a two-part narration of the downward spiraling of Saul's house. The first part of that narration concludes at the end of the chapter with Abner's death. Chapter 4, an episode that focuses on Ishbosheth's death, continues and completes the story of the downward spiral of Saul's house in the HDR. We shall presently focus on the first episode (i.e., the commencement of the civil war).

The first step that David took was to shift base from Philistine territory, in Ziklag, to Judahite Hebron, reportedly at divine instigation (2 Sam 2:1–4). In his characteristic pro-David and anti-Saul polemic tone, the narrator begins to "show" the reader that the rightful monarch has arrived. Unlike Saul, who is never recorded to have successfully sought Yahweh's face,[15] David's first action in the post-Saul era is to determine the divine will for his next step. There are a number of issues that need to be addressed with regard to this first episode: The nature of David's rise in Hebron, the identity of the person who carried out the anointing, and the attitude of the Philistines toward David's rise in Hebron.

Contemporary scholars have attributed David's uneventful rise in Calebite Hebron to the marriages he contracted with women of the southern tribes (Abigail and Ahinoam, esp. Abigail).[16] Levenson and Halpern make a strong argument by raking through the genealogies of the Hebrew Bible. They pay special attention to those recorded in Ruth 4:18–22, 1 Chr 2:9–17; and 1 Chr 2:50–51. The first two of these references agree that David's foremost ancestor was Nahson (in which line Caleb is a distant collateral relative of David). However, in the third passage, Caleb becomes David's most prominent ancestor. They account for this by assuming the priority of 1 Chr 2:9–17 over 1 Chr 2:50–51. On this account, they explicate the grafting of David directly into the Calebite line thus: "It is difficult to resist the idea that the text here re-

---

15. This statement has to be qualified in that Saul's first venture into this endeavor of inquiring of the seer was at the instigation of his servant (cf. 1 Sam 9:5–10). In the two attempts he initiated on his own, the first was aborted midway (1 Sam 14:18–19), while the second ends in disaster (1 Sam 28:5–19).

16. See Levenson, "1 Samuel 25 as Literature and as History," 11–28; and Levenson and Halpern, "The Political Import of David's Marriages, 507–18; and Mauchline, *1 and 2 Samuel*, 171.

flects David's assumption of kingship in the very capital of the Calebite patrimony, Hebron. More specifically, 1 Chr 2:50–51 reflect a process by which the Calebites came to see David as one of theirs, a process which his assumption of their chieftain's lady would surely have facilitated, and probably necessitated."[17]

Supplying the motivation for David's marriage to the nobility of the south, Bill T. Arnold observes, "The political significance of his marriage should not be missed. David's exile from Saul's court means he has lost his power base in Gibeah, where he was hailed as a military hero (18:6–7)."[18] Furthermore, Saul, by marrying Michal to Paltiel, truncates David's claim to royal lineage (1 Sam 25:44). His marriages to Abigail and Ahinoam "give him ties to the Hebron and Jezreel areas, perhaps giving him a new power base among the inhabitants of Judah."[19] Additionally, the gifts that David had sent to the elders of Judah constitute another factor that may have helped to pave the way for his coronation in Hebron.[20]

Anderson notes the diversity of opinions regarding who had anointed David, ranging from the priests, suggested by Martin Noth, to the people and their representatives, proposed by Kutsch.[21] Evidently, there is no mention of any religious personality at this anointing ceremony; neither is there any such mentioned at David's coronation as king of all Israel. This creates the need for a sacral authentication of his kingship (as was the expectation of the era), which David sought to meet in his removal of the Ark to Jerusalem, his new capital city in 2 Sam 6 (to which issue we shall return in our next chapter). Suffice it now to

---

17. Levenson and Halpern, "The Political Import of David's Marriages," 509.

18. Arnold, *1 & 2 Samuel*, 345.

19. Arnold, *1 & 2 Samuel*, 345. While these marriages may have played a very significant role in the rise of David in Hebron, his superior military power is another factor that cannot be overlooked. This factor was highlighted in footnote 7 above. If the Calebites were normal human beings, as we expect them to be, there would have been both those who would have warmed up to David, on account of his marriage to Abigail, as well as those who would have loathed him for snatching their inheritance. This made a military advance, as demonstrated by the consultation of the divine oracle, necessary.

20. McCarter identifies the "men of Judah," in 2 Sam 2:4a with the "elders of Judah" who were the recipients of David's gratuitous gifts in 1 Sam 30:26–31. In fact, on this incidence Lemche plainly writes, "In this instance the author passes in silence over the fact that David had already paved his way through bribery" (McCarter, "David's Rise," 15).

21. Anderson, *2 Samuel*, 24.

merely say that we are not persuaded by Tryggve N. D. Mittinger's supposition that prior to Solomon, the anointing of leaders was wholly a secular affair.[22]

The Philistine elimination of Saul at the Mt. Gilboa confrontation is what made possible David's return to Israelite territory. The question to be answered is what was the attitude of the Philistines toward David's return to Hebron and his coronation as the king of Judah? In other words, since David as ruler of Ziklag was a vassal of the Philistine king of Gath, Achish, what circumstances made it possible for him to relocate to Hebron without incurring Philistine wrath and repercussions? Anderson is of the view that his return was done with the express permission of the Philistines, and that David's rule in Judah could have been seen as an extension of Philistine control.[23] In all probability David had remained a Philistine vassal until the latter's principle of divide-and-conquer[24] was breached when David emerged as a unifying factor for Israel in his anointing as the king of all Israel in 2 Sam 5:1–3. Only then did hostilities break out between David and the Philistines.[25]

After his relocation to and his subsequent coronation in Hebron in the first scene of this first episode, the second scene narrates that David received intelligence that the most vibrant force to be reckoned with amongst the northerners was the men of Jabesh-gilead. Their valor

---

22. Mittinger, *King and Messiah*, 198–208; as cited in Anderson, 2 Samuel, 24.

23. Indeed, Anderson goes further to write, "likewise David's hostilities with Israel may have served the Philistine interest because this could have been one of the means whereby the Philistines kept Israel in check" (Anderson, *2 Samuel*, 22–23).

24. If such an arrangement existed then, while David harassed the south, the Philistines directed their energies northward in the Jezreel valley region (cf. 1 Sam 28:1–4; 29–30). Grappling with the question of the Philistine position on David in Hebron, Lemche comments, "We can only note that this problem did not interest the author. Most probably the Philistines still regarded David as their client king who guaranteed the Philistine position in Southern Palestine. If so, they were able to concentrate their own efforts on stemming the Israelite expansion to the north" (Lemche, "David's Rise," 16).

25. For a similar position see VanderKam, "Davidic Complicity," 528. On the other hand, while David's move to Hebron may have been tolerated, it may not have required the express permission of the Philistines. Mauchline suggests that so long as David did not go beyond the area of Hebron, the Philistines "could keep watch on him. Further, David had reported to Achish that he had waged war against peoples in the Hebron area so that there must have been no *prima facie* case to make the Philistines suspect that he would make an aggressive alliance with these peoples now (1 Sam 27:10)" (Mauchline, *1 and 2 Samuel*, 202).

*The Contest for the Succession to the Throne of Saul (2 Samuel 2–4)*

and their unflinching loyalty to Saul were demonstrated in their determination to give Saul a fitting burial. With this determination they had broken through the ranks of the Philistines in order to recover the mutilated corpses of Saul and his sons for burial in Jabesh-gilead. With this information, David wasted no time in dispatching a diplomatic mission to court the allegiance of the Jabesh-gileadites. The author of this narrative records this communication with very telling artistry.

The skillful crafting of David's message to the men of Jabesh-gilead is designed to have great rhetorical effect. This message, as shown below, is set to a threefold parallelism of ABC, A′C′B′, and A″B″C″ in verses 5, 6, and 7 respectively.

5    וישלח דוד מלאכים אל־אנשי יביש גלעד
David sent messengers to the men of Jabesh-gilead.

    ויאמר אליהם
    He said to them,

A    ברכים אתם ליהוה
    "Blessed are you of Yahweh,

  B    אשר עשיתם החסד הזה עם־אדניכם עם־שאול
    "because you have done this *act of* loyal love with your lord, with Saul;

    C    ותקברו אתו
    since you have buried him.

A′    6    ועתה יעש־יהוה עמכם חסד ואמת
Now then, may Yahweh show you loyal love and faithfulness;

  C′    וגם אנכי אעשה אתכם הטובה הזאת
    And I also will show you this loyal love,

  B′    אשר עשיתם הדבר הזה
    because you have done this thing.

A″    7    ועתה תחזקנה ידיכם והיו לבני־חיל
Now therefore, brace up yourselves, and be courageous;

  B″    כי־מת אדניכם שאול
    Because your lord, Saul, is dead.

    C″    וגם־אתי משחו בית־יהודה למלך עליהם
    Moreover, the house of Judah has anointed me king over them."

In this structure, we find a marshaling of lexical, grammatical, and syntactic forms for maximum effect. In verse 5, there is the dominance of the preterite verb form in all three clauses. In A, the verb form is a passive participle, which though carrying the idea of continued activity (their blessed state), that continuity only flows from an activity which is essentially completed (the show of loyalty to Saul).[26] Both clauses B and C contain finite verbs dealing with past action: the former in the perfect tense and the latter a *waw*-consecutive imperfect, which essentially has a perfective import. In this way, David seeks to align himself with his addressees as he highlights their blessed state, which he shows to be a consequence of their deed (of showing their loyalty to Saul by burying him). Yet, the accent of this sentence falls squarely on the past. David subtly points out to the Jabesh-gileadites that all that had transpired belongs to a passing era.

The first two clauses (A' and C') of verse 6 have imperfect verbs (pointing to Yahweh's pending or ongoing work of covenant faithfulness and David's pledge to do the same for the Jabesh-gileadites). The third clause (B') again anchors both future actions on the past deed of the addressees. The significance of this is that the deed of loyalty and faithfulness of the Jabesh-gileadite has been recognized and they will be rewarded for it. Nevertheless, they are made to realize that their destiny lies in the future (with the new work of Yahweh and David), and not in the past with the dead.

While verses 5 and 6 serve as the "indicative" of David's locution, verse 7 forms its "imperative." Thus, the first line of verse 7 (A") consists of two imperatival clauses. The next line (B") supplies the premise for the action called for in A". The third line (C") provides a basis for the action demanded in the first line (A"), which further supports the premise in B". In essence, David calls upon the Jabesh-gileadites to wake up to the reality that the man to whom they have shown so much loyalty is actually dead. A new reality and era is dawning in David's ascendency.[27]

---

26. Cf. Waltke and O'Connor, *Biblical Hebrew* Syntax, 612–14; Lambdin, *Introduction to Biblcial Hebrew*, 158.

27. Conveying the same sentiments Anderson writes, "David encourages Saul's faithful compatriots by pointing out that although their king is dead, there is a ray of hope because he, David, has been made king of Judah. We do not know whether at this point David was already aware of the crowning of Ishbosheth, but, in any case, the main reason for the encouragement was David's own rise to effective power" (Anderson, *2 Samuel*, 29).

They must, as valiant men, act with courage on the basis of fact, not sentiments.

At the semantic and syntactical levels, the "Blessed are you of Yahweh" (which is more like a prayer, with a passive participle) of verse 5 (A) corresponds to both the jussive of verse 6 (A′) and the imperatives of verse 7 (A″). In other words, the double blessings invoked in Yahweh's name eventuate to a double demand (חזקנה ידיכם and והיו לבני־חיל) on the recipients of such blessings. The reason for the blessings pronounced on the Jabesh-gileadites—their loyal love to Saul in burying him—is twice indicated by being marked off with the deictic particle אשר (which in these sentences means "because") both in verses 5 (B) and 6 (B′). The reason for their blessing (in vv. 5 & 6) correspond to the reason why they must now change course in pitching their tent with David, i.e., because their lord is dead (verse 7 [B″]).[28] Similarly, the action of the Jabesh-gileadites on behalf of Saul in verse 5 (C), calls up David's pledge of *ḥesed* (i.e., David's future action) on their behalf in verse 6 (C′), likewise the action of the men of Judah on David's behalf in proclaiming him king in verse 7 (C″) should stimulate an appropriate response from the men of Jabesh-gilead.

In the next four verses (2 Sam 2:8–11), the author, using a *waw-disjunctive* (*we-X-qatal* form), provides the necessary background information before giving a full report of the first military encounter on the battlefield. Abner, Saul's commander, took Ishbosheth, Saul's son, across the Jordan to Mahanaim and there anointed him king. He ends the unit with the regnal formula summary statement (a DtrH trademark) on the reign of Ishbosheth and David's reign in Hebron (vv. 10–11). When viewed in the light of similar regnal summary statements in the rest of the DtrH, especially the books of Kings, our attention is immediately drawn to the absence of any achievement for both kings for the period covered (vv. 1–11). Ishbosheth's achievement was simply being anointed king, while David's efforts were consumed in seeking to unseat the Saulide dynasty.

A number of pertinent issues arise from vv. 8–11. The first is Ishbosheth's age of forty at the beginning of his reign. If he was that old, was he in the war that claimed the other older male members of his family? If not, why not? Bergen suggests that his absence from the battle at

---

28. Note that David does not call Saul his own lord—he does not use the first person plural, which would have included himself, but the third person plural.

Gilboa was a tactical plan to ensure a male member of the family would remain to take up the reins of power.²⁹ While this is entirely reasonably possible, it is not wholly convincing, since there is no clue from the text in this direction. We cannot be certain of any answer, but we can take cues from the text. Anderson painstakingly addresses the matter on the basis of textual analysis. His conclusion that Ishbosheth may have been younger than indicated here is plausible.³⁰ While Anderson's proposal cannot be proven, it is supported by textual indicators. First, he points out the statements that Abner "took" (לקח) and "brought him [Ishbosheth]" (ויעברהו) across to Mahanaim (2:8); these statements fit more the profile of a youngster than of a forty-year-old man. Secondly, Ishbosheth's failure to inherit his father's concubine Rizpah is just another piece of datum that supports this proposal.³¹ Thus, the forty years could be a scribal error, which is not uncommon to find in the Samuel manuscripts (cf. 1 Sam 13:1).³²

Another thorny issue is the synchrony of the overlapping reigns of David and Ishbosheth. David reigned in Hebron for seven and half years while Ishbosheth reigned in Mahanaim for two years before being murdered: at what period did their reigns overlap? Addressing this question Ronald F. Youngblood places the overlap towards the end of David's reign in Hebron, i.e., his last two years in Hebron. He writes, "[I]t must have been several years after Saul's death before Ish-Bosheth had gained enough support to become king over the northern tribes.

---

29. Bergen, *1, 2 Samuel*, 300.

30. Anderson's position can be summarized as follows: From the camaraderie between David and Jonathan displayed in the text, it stands to reason that they might have been within the same age bracket, i.e., they did not belong to two different generations. From the cultural anthropology of the era it is known that marriages took place quite early. Yet at his death Jonathan (apparently the older of Saul's children, cf. 1 Sam 14:49; 31:2; 1 Chr 8:33) had only a five-year-old son (2 Sam 4:4); an indication that he himself was very young, perhaps slightly younger than David, who was thirty at the beginning of his reign (2 Sam 5:4). There is no record that any of Jonathan's other brothers that perished in that war along with him were either married or had children; the obvious conclusion is that they were too young to be married. From this flows the conclusion that Ishbosheth was a youngster, perhaps too young to go to war, when kingship was thrust upon him (Anderson, *2 Samuel*, 34–35).

31. Anderson writes, "Furthermore, Ishbosheth speaks of Rizpah as his father's concubine and not as his own, when he accuses Abner of having intercourse with her (2 Sam 3:7). Hence it is possible that either Ishbosheth had not made use of this practice or he was still too young to marry his father's concubine" (*2 Samuel*, 35).

32. For a different suggestion see McCarter, *II Samuel*, 88.

# The Contest for the Succession to the Throne of Saul (2 Samuel 2–4)

Thus Ish-Bosheth's two-year reign would have coincided with the last two years of David's seven-and-one-half-year reign over Judah."[33] The problem with the suggestion is that there is no indication of any revolt against Saul. He had died fighting against foreign aggressors, and his zeal for Israel is well attested in the biblical narrative (1 Sam 11:5–7; 2 Sam 21:2). Besides, Abner was the uncontested *de facto* leader of Israel, not only militarily but also politically. With him still alive, it is hard to see how there would have been any challenge to the house of Saul arising within northern Israel.

Anderson, on the other hand, considers the whole idea of an interregnum, before Ishbosheth's accession, unlikely; since the dynastic principle was Ishbosheth's only claim to the throne, it would make more sense if he were to have acceded to the throne immediately after Saul's demise.[34] Anderson attributes the gap in the text with regard to this matter to the fact that "the author did not think it relevant to give an account of the events in Israel between the death of Ishbosheth and the anointing of David as king over Israel (2 Sam 5:3)."[35] He explains the narrative gap of five and half years, from Ishbosheth's death to David's accession over Israel, on the possibility that "the remnant of Ishbosheth's kingdom continued hostilities with David since the prolonged war mentioned in 2 Sam 3:1 may indicate a period lasting more than two years."[36] The effort that David put into dramatizing his innocence with respect to the murders of Saulides does indicate that suspicions were rife. Be that as it may, then, it is more likely that there would have been some northern resistance to David immediately after these murders, before prolonged combat would have weakened the leaderless north into surrender. Taking a different view on the biblical data, VanderKam holds that Ishbosheth's reign commenced immediately after Saul's death and coincides with David's last

---

33. Youngblood, "1, 2 Samuel," 553–1104, esp. 824. For similar argumentation for the existence of a five-year interregnum before the ascendency of Ishbosheth see McCarter, *II Samuel*, 88–89; and Soggin, *Old Testament and Oriental Studies*, 34–36.

34. On the same note Arnold writes, "David's offer to become king in the north (2:4b–7) is no match for a genuine son of Saul in the light of Israel's new impulse toward dynastic succession. Events in the north quickly move against David, and his hopes for a peaceful transition of power over a unified Israel are not to be realized. This paragraph leaves us with competing royal houses and illustrates that union between north and south was always a tenuous proposition in ancient Israel" (Arnold, *1 & 2 Samuel*, 433).

35. Anderson, *2 Samuel*, 36.

36. Anderson, *2 Samuel*, 36. See also Gordon, *I & II Samuel*, 214.

two years at Hebron.³⁷ "Tantalizing bits of evidence raise the possibility (and it is no more than that) that David assumed his Hebronite throne prior to Saul's death and did so in conscious opposition to Saul, indeed, at his personal expense."³⁸

2 Samuel 2:12–32 affords the reader a battlefield snapshot of the bitter prolonged civil war. In the context of the HDR, however, this battlefield account serves to furnish a motive for Joab's slaying of Abner (cf. 2 Sam 3:27, 30). The goal clearly is to shine the spotlight on Joab's guilt and David's innocence. Abner is shown to have been unwilling to engage Asahel: Asahel is cast as the unrelenting aggressor (2 Sam 2:19); twice he was implored by Abner to turn aside and engage a less experienced foot soldier, but he would not listen (vv. 20–23).³⁹ Indeed, Abner's second address to Asahel in verse 22⁴⁰ already anticipates the animosity and blood feud that Asahel's death would engender between Joab and Abner. The narrator implies that, all this notwithstanding, Abner merely extended the butt of his spear, perhaps in self-defense, but it was Asahel's reckless rush on Abner that led to Asahel's unfortunate death (v. 23). This scene, therefore, supplies the motive for Joab's killing of Abner in the next epi-

---

37. VanderKam, "Davidic Complicity," 527–28.

38. VanderKam, "Davidic Complicity," 527. He adds further, "The final form of the Story of David's Rise, in line with its theme of a politically unsullied David, presents Saul's death before David's assumption of office (1 Sam 31:4–6; 2 Sam 2:1–4a), but the following details favor, historically speaking, a reversal of that sequence" (ibid.).

39. The words used of Asahel's unwillingness to heed Abner's warnings are ולא אבה (literally, "he was not willing"). This phrase is used in an almost special sense that suggests that anytime someone is "not willing" to do something that is asked of him, he endangers either himself or those precious or close to him. This is the basic sense of the phrase here and in most of its other appearances in Samuel (cf. 1 Sam 31:4; 2 Sam 2:21; 13:14, 16, 25; 14:29), but the same sense surfaces in other places in the Bible as well (cf. Exod 10:27; Deut 2:30; Judg 19:10; 2 Kgs 24:4; 1 Chr 10:4; Ps 81:12). In opposition to the human situation, when Yahweh is "not willing" to do something, often it is because he wants to avert harm or danger for his people (Deut 23:6; 2 Kgs 8:19; 13:23; 2 Chr 21:7). On the other hand, there are a few instances where someone is "not willing" to do something because of the fear of dire consequences (2 Sam 6:10; 12:17; 1 Chr 19:19). Overall then, it is seen that in one way or the other, the use of the phrase "not willing" is associated with danger. Having said that, we still note that there are very few exceptions where its use directly portends or averts no danger (Judg 11:17; 2 Sam 23:16, 17 [and its parallel 1 Chr 11:18, 19]).

40. סור לך מאחרי למה אככה ארצה ואיך אשא פני אל־יואב אחיך, "Turn aside from pursuing me. Why should I strike you to the ground? For how shall I lift up my face to Joab, your brother?" (author's translation).

sode, which from the narrator's point of view is plain murder (avenging wartime killing in the time of peace, cf. 1 Kgs 2:5).

## ABNER: CONFLICT, COMPACT, AND CATASTROPHE (2 SAM 3:1–39)

### 2 Samuel 3

1 There was a protracted war, between the dynasty of Saul and the dynasty of David. And David was waxing stronger continually, but Saul's dynasty was waning unremittingly. 2 Now sons were born to David in Hebron. His firstborn was Amnon, son of Ahinoam—the Jezreelitess; 3 the second was Chileab, of Abigail—the wife of Nabal the Carmelite; the third was Absalom, the son of Maacah—the daughter of Talmai, king of Geshur; 4 the fourth, Adonijah, the son of Haggith; the fifth, Shephatiah, the son of Abital; 5 the sixth, Jithream, of Eglah—David's wife. All these were born to David in Hebron.

6 While the war raged on between the dynasty of Saul and the dynasty of David, Abner was strengthening his position in the house of Saul. 7 Now Saul had a concubine; her name was Rizpah.[41] *Ishbosheth*[42] said to Abner, "Why have you gone into my father's concubine?" 8 Abner became exceedingly angry because of the words of Ishbosheth. So he said, "Am I a dog's

---

41. Some of the versions (e.g., Lucian's LXX and 4QSam$^a$) have additional information here; they insert the words: "and Abner took her." This explains Ishbosheth's accusation that follows. While this addition conveniently supplies the ground of Ishbosheth's complaint against Abner, it is hard to tell if it is no more than the translators' gloss.

42. This clause does not contain an independent identification (subject) in the MT (lit. it says, "and he said to Abner"). However, a number of LXX manuscripts (including those of Aquila, Symmachus, and Theodotion), as well as the Vulgate, have "Ishbosheth." The Qumran text (4QSam$^a$), though defective, has "Saul" with the immediately preceding words missing. Presumably the missing words are "*Ishbosheth son of*," which would stand in construct relationship to "Saul"). Other ancient versions, like the LXX$^L$, instead have "Mephibosheth, son of Saul" (see McCarter, *2 Samuel*, 106–7).

head which belongs to Judah?⁴³ This day I continue to⁴⁴ show loyalty to the house of Saul, your father, and to his brothers, and to his friends; and have not delivered you into David's hand, and you are this day accusing me of iniquity *on account of* this⁴⁵ woman?" 9 "May God do so to Abner, and more so to Abner unless, as Yahweh has sworn to David, even so I shall do for him,⁴⁶ 10 to turn over the kingship from the house of Saul; and to establish the throne of David over Israel and over Judah: from Dan to Beersheba." 11 And he was not able to reply Abner a word anymore; for he feared him.

12 Then Abner sent messengers to David on his behalf, saying, "To whom does the land belong?" He said further,⁴⁷ "Make

---

43. This prepositional phrase (ליהודה) is rendered in the Vulgate as "against Judah." The entire sentence is very difficult to translate. This difficulty is evident in the divergence of the English renditions: "Am I a dog's head of Judah?" (ESV); "Am I a dog's head, which against Judah do shew kindness this day unto the house of Saul thy father ... ?" (KJV); "Am I a dog's head that belongs to Judah?" (NASB); and "Am I a dog's head—on Judah's side?" (NIV). The entire relative phrase (אשר ליהודה) is omitted in the LXX and the Old Latin versions. There is a wide range of opinion among scholars on how to take this phrase. Smith regards it as a gloss, and as such when omitted the text makes better sense (Smith, *2 Samuel*, 276). Youngblood observes, "Early Jewish commentators (e.g., Rashi, Kimchi) frequently understood the phrase 'dog's head' to mean 'head/commander over dogs.' Abner thus accuses Ish-Bosheth of treating, 'the commander of Saul's army' (2:8), as though he were merely the captain of a pack of dogs" (Youngblood, *1, 2 Samuel*, 836). McCarter considers it a gloss. He opines that Abner's protest, הראש כלב אנכי (lit. "Am I a dog's head"), is understood in the MT tradition as "the Chief of Caleb." From this perspective he deems אשר ליהודה to be a gloss "in the sense of 'one who is on the side of Judah.'" He surmises that this addition arose based on the glossator's conclusion that Abner was objecting to being treated like an enemy (McCarter, *II Samuel*, 106).

44. The idea of the continuation of the action derives from the grammatical meaning of the imperfect tense, i.e., the progressive aspect (*Aspekt*) of the imperfective form (cf. Waltke and O'Connor, *Biblical Hebrew Syntax*, 347).

45. The article prefix to האשה serves as a demonstrative as it functions similarly in the case of היום.

46. The LXX versions (except LXX⁰) add the prepositional phrase, εν τη ημερα ταυτη.

47. The MT text here is uncertain, with the double use of לאמר. A number of the Greek versions understand the MT's למי־ארץ לאמר [תחתיו] (תחתו) as indicating David's location (cf. LXX εις θαειλαμου ην; LXXᴬ θενλαμου γην παραημα λεγων; LXXᴸ conceives of David's location, but goes ahead to name the place, Hebron, εις Χεβρων). McCarter explains that most of the Greek translations had merely transliterated the problematic Hebrew rendition of this text. For him, it is LXXᴸ's εις Χεβρων λεγων that "apparently reflects the shorter, original text *thtw* understood in reference to David ('where he was') and rendered interpretively as 'in Hebron'" (McCarter, *II Samuel*, 107). Yet this proposal does not address the difficulty even to McCarter's satisfaction, as he admits,

# The Contest for the Succession to the Throne of Saul (2 Samuel 2–4) 129

a covenant with me; and behold, my hand will be with you, to turn over to you all Israel." 13 Then he replied, "It is good for me to make a covenant with you; but one thing do I require of you." Then he said, "You shall not see my face, unless you bring before me[48] Michal, Saul's daughter, when you come to see me.[49]

14 Now David sent messengers to Ishbosheth, Saul's son, saying, "Give me my wife, Michal, whom I betrothed with a hundred foreskins of the Philistines." 15 So Ishbosheth sent, and took her from her husband, from Paltiel, son of Laish. 16 Her husband went along with her, weeping continually as he went, as far as Bahurim. Then Abner commanded him, "Go *back*, and return *home*." So he returned.

17 Meanwhile Abner spoke with the elders of Israel, saying, "*All this while* you have been desiring David for a king over you. Now therefore do it. For Yahweh had spoken to David, saying, 'By the hand of David, my servant, I shall save my people Israel from the hand of the Philistines, and from the hand of all their enemies.'" 19 Abner also went to recount in David's hearing in Hebron all that is good in the eyes of Israel, and in the eyes of all the house of Benjamin. 20 So Abner came to David in Hebron, and with him were twenty men. And David made a feast for Abner and the men who were with him. 21 Then Abner said to David, "Let me arise, and let me go, and assemble to my lord the king all Israel; that they may make a covenant with you; that you

---

"The source of the intrusive *lmy/w'rs (l'mr)* is as difficult to surmise as its meaning" (ibid., 107). Anderson holds that LXX[L]'s addition of "to Hebron" "makes good sense, but its authenticity is questionable" (Anderson, *2 Samuel*, 53). I therefore opt to take the text as it has been handed down in the MT. Therefore, the second לאמר is to be taken as an intrusion of the narrator's voice; it is not part of Abner's voice. That is why I translate it as "He further said." By this intrusion the narrator is spotlighting the first statement as a way of highlighting Abner's conceit and hubris. A similar structure is found in David's response to Abner (verse 13). Even though there is no doubling of לאמר, the only one found in David's reply occurs in the middle of his speech; in which case it corresponds to the second one in Abner's speech. We also find it in the direct discourse of the Jebusites in 2 Sam 5:6 (for exactly the same format of construction, see 1 Kgs 2:4). This kind of construction is modeled on the format of a quoted speech within a direct discourse, where the speaker quotes another speaker or his earlier thought (cf. 2 Sam 14:15, 17, 32; 19:12; 20:18; 1 Kgs 1:51; 12:10). The key idea is the separation of one idea from another for the sake of emphasis.

48. The LXX, Syriac, and Vulgate translations do not have the prepositional phrase לפני, I suppose, because of the פני at the end of the sentence. However, I consider the deletion of either of these unnecessary because they are in sync with the general use of resumptive deictic particles so preponderant in biblical Hebrew literature.

49. This entire clause is absent in the Syriac version.

may reign over all that your soul desires." So David sent Abner away, and he went in peace.

22 Behold! The servants of David and Joab arrived from a raiding expedition. They brought much plunder with them. Now Abner was not with David in Hebron, for he had sent him away, and he went in peace. 23 Then Joab and all the army, which was with him, arrived. And it was told Joab, saying, "Abner, son of Ner, came to the king;[50] and he sent him away, and he went in peace." 24 Then Joab came to the king, and said, "What have you done? Behold! Abner came to you; why did you let him go, and he indeed went[51] *away*. 25 You know Abner, the son of Ner—for to deceive you he came, and to spy out your going out and your coming;[52] and to know all that you do. 26 Then Joab marched forth from David; and sent messengers after Abner, and they brought him back from the well of Sirah. But David did not know *about it*. 27 So Abner returned to Hebron. Joab steered him aside into the chamber of the gate, for a tête-à-tête. And he smote him there, in the stomach, and he died because of the blood of Asahel his brother. 28 When David heard about this, he said, "I and my kingdom are forever innocent before Yahweh, of the blood of Abner, the son of Ner. 29 May it rest upon the head of Joab, and upon[53] all his father's house. May there never cease from Joab's house one who has an issue, or one who has leprosy, or one who leans on a staff, or one who falls by a sword or one who lacks bread." 30 So Joab and Abishai, his brother, killed Abner, because he killed Asahel, their brother, at Gibeon in war.

31 Then David said to Joab, and all the people who were with him, "Rend your garments, gird sackcloth, and wail before Abner." The king himself followed behind the bier. 32 They buried Abner in Hebron; and the king lifted up his voice, and wept at Abner's grave. *Likewise* all the people wept. 33 Then the king chanted a dirge over Abner, he said, "Should Abner die a fool's death? 34 your hands were not bound; neither were your feet put in fetters. As one falls before unjust men, you have fallen." And all the people again wept over him.

---

50. Qumran and LXX versions have "David" here.

51. LXX translations have an additional prepositional phrase εν ειρηνη ("in peace").

52. Here we follow the Qere just like many medieval manuscripts.

53. The MT has אל, but here we follow the Qumran text's על, which makes more sense.

35 Then all the people came, to persuade David to eat bread while it was still day. But David swore, saying, "May God do so to me, and more so if I eat bread or anything before the sun sets." 36 And all the people noticed it; and it was good in their eyes. Similarly all that the king did was good in the eyes of all the people. 37 So all the people and all Israel knew in that day that it was not from the king to kill Abner, son of Ner. 38 Then the king said to his servants, "Do you not know that a prince, a great man has fallen this day in Israel? 39 I am this day weak, *even though* I am anointed king; for these men, the sons of Zeruiah are too hard for me. May Yahweh requite the evil doer according his evil deed."

Mauchline considers the opening statement of our present episode (3:1) to be the work of a later redactor who was giving a summary statement on the whole course of events between the death of Saul and the recognition of David as king of Israel and Judah.[54] As if in direct contradiction to Mauchline's statement, McCarter holds that 2 Sam 3:1 belongs to the original narrative. He sees it as leading directly into the story that begins in 3:6. It is rather the list of David's sons that intervenes between verses 1 and 6, which he attributes to a Deuteronomistic redactor.[55] Both Mauchline and McCarter approach the passage from a historical critical perspective. However, when viewed from a literary perspective, the entire chapter makes perfect sense as it is. Bergen rightly sees the narrator as characterizing the general course of hostilities between the two contending royal houses.[56]

In 2 Sam 2 the narrator had given an example of the nature, pattern, and course of the conflict between the houses of Saul and David. In this new episode he goes on to show the state of the two houses in the course of the conflict. He therefore has two catchy captions for his narration of the fate of both houses at the head of each of their accounts. The first

---

54. Mauchline, *1 and 2 Samuel*, 207. He even suggests that the statement would fit more conveniently at the end of chapter 3.

55. McCarter, *II Samuel*, 101–2.

56. Commenting on 2 Sam 3:1, Bergen observes that though the previous incident was the only one that gave the ongoing conflict in detail, "many more took place, for 'the war between the house of Saul and the house of David lasted a long time.' Nevertheless, the incident characterized the general course of the hostilities because throughout the two-year conflict 'David grew stronger and stronger, while the house of Saul grew weaker and weaker.' As characterized by the writer, the conflict was fundamentally between two families vying for undisputed control over one nation, not two nations at war with each other" (Bergen, *1, 2 Samuel*, 305).

caption (3:1) relates to David's house and its progress (3:2–5), while the second (3:6) relates to the regression and disintegration of Saul's house (3:7–4:12).

The first segment of this episode is an episodic narration, more in the fashion of a genealogical record, of the progress of David's house. David has advanced from being a fugitive to someone with a blossoming family. Within the short span of seven and a half years, David has proven to be so fruitful as to have six sons. Indeed, it is doubtful if these were the only children or even sons that David had from six wives during this period. Anderson, while commenting on the two lists of David's sons (2 Sam 3:2–5 and 5:13–16), observes that it is unlikely that each wife had only one son, and as such it seems rather "that the list names only the firstborn son of each wife."[57] That being the case the list sets in bold relief the contrast between the growing house of David and the dwindling house of Saul.

Besides, the multiplication and diversity of David's wives also show him broadening his power base through alliances consummated with marriages with the daughters of the chieftains of the various nationalities around Israel. Most telling of these is his marriage to Maacah, daughter of Talmai king of Geshur. The practical effect of such alliances would be to double the total of potential menace that would pose challenges to the territorial integrity of Ish-Bosheth's shaky kingdom. In the example of the alliance with Talmai, Ish-Bosheth would now have to be concerned not simply with David but also with a northern ally of David. This added pressure would have helped to destabilize the Saulide regime.[58] In other words, with such alliances, David was tactically tightening the noose of subversion and sabotage around the neck of the moribund kingdom.

The next scene commences with the narration of the decline of Saul's house. It begins with an expansion of the second part of the statement first made in verse 1 ("And David was waxing stronger continually, but Saul's dynasty was waning unremittingly"). The waning of Saul's house is shown to be accruing to the personal advantage of Abner, who "was strengthening his position in the house of Saul" (3:6; author's translation).[59] The amassing of military and political clout prompts

---

57. Anderson, *2 Samuel*, 50.
58. Bergen. *1, 2 Samuel*, 306.
59. Anderson is of the opinion that the portrayal of Abner in 3:6 is positive, in view of his positive portrayal in the rest of the chapter. He therefore suggests מתחזק (a parti-

Abner to overreach into Saul's harem (a clear indication of royal pretensions in the ancient Near East).⁶⁰ The situation where a contender to a throne reaches for the king's harem, like Abner's dabbling into Saul's harem, is attested in the ancient Near East. It is this extent of Abner's assault on Saulide honor that prompts even the otherwise biddable Ishbosheth to raise a voice in protest (מדוע באתה אל־פילגש אבי, "Why have you gone into my father's concubine?").

Rather than address Ishbosheth's niggle, Abner, livid with rage, showed no compunction but resorted to an irate outburst. Thus, rather than deal frontally with the matter, Abner slantingly referred to it as a trifle; he considers it a dent on his dignity and loyalty to be charged with a matter on a count of "a woman" (note the MT's definite article, functioning as a demonstrative, "this woman," i.e., Rizpah, v. 8).⁶¹ Having been reminded that he owes both his throne and life to Abner, Ishbosheth became too crippled with fear to reply to Abner. Abner, then, stormed out and began hatching the plot of how to reconcile with David and secure a future for himself in the emerging Davidic kingdom of Israel.

The vehemence of Abner's response trumps Ishbosheth's feeble accusation. Abner's excessive response makes one wonder if it derived from genuine provocation or if it was simply a reasoned ready riddance of the unenviable burden of propping up an ineffectual monarch of a doomed kingdom. Doubtful of Abner's sincerity, John Goldingay reads Abner's reaction to Ishbosheth as being said with a straight face but adds that it is hard to read it with a straight face.⁶² Gordon, on the one hand, writes that notwithstanding Abner's seeming sudden conversion to David's

---

ciple) should be translated as "kept faithful to" (Anderson, *2 Samuel*, 55). Without engaging in an evaluation of Abner at this point, I think the crucial issue is that of Abner's growing stature at the expense of the fading Saulide dynasty. Contra Anderson, I agree with Arnold's position that while Saul's dynasty wane in power, Abner was increasing in political influence and became the real power behind the throne in Israel and had the wherewithal to influence things in whichever way he wanted (Arnold, *1 & 2 Samuel*, 437).

60. Cf. Tsevat, "Marriage and Monarchical Legitimacy," 237–43; Levenson and Halpern, "The Political Import of David's Marriages," 508.

61. Gordon writes on this episode, "Abner, white-hot with indignation, attacks Ishbosheth for petty-mindedness. There is no admission of wrongdoing, since he reckons that he has been scolded for a trifle (*a woman*). At the same time, the indebtedness of Ish-bosheth to Abner is evident to the extent that the latter stands between him and capitulation to David" (Gordon, *I & II Samuel*, 217–18).

62. Goldingay, *Men Behaving Badly*, 201.

cause, "he must have realized for some time that David's progress was irresistible. In that case the squabble with Ish-bosheth over Saul's concubine was merely the pretext for breaking with the feckless monarch. In particular, Abner was aware of certain pro-Davidic sympathies that were gaining ground among the tribal heads of Israel."[63] On the other hand, he finds Ishbosheth's accusation of royal pretensions against Abner to be a reflection of the late Saul in his son.[64] Taking the kind of proposition Gordon makes a step further, Bergen demonizes Ishbosheth and makes Abner out to be the saint that he was not. He writes, "Like Saul, Ish-Bosheth falsely accused his most loyal and capable soldier of treason ... Ish-Bosheth was exhibiting his father's insane tendencies, and Abner did not wish to inflict a second Saul on the nation. From now on he would redirect his efforts to 'do for David what the Lord promised him' (v. 9). Rather than contest David's claim for the divine right to rule Israel, he would vigorously support it."[65] Such a position cannot be sustained from the text. The paucity of the textual data on Ishbosheth notwithstanding, one can say with confidence that there is nothing in it that portrays him as insane, while there is a lot in it that hints at Abner's ambition and survivalist instincts.

Whatever his motivation, Abner proceeded to initiate reconciliation talks with David aimed at securing a compact with the latter. This scene as whole (vv. 12–16) centers on the proposal for covenant and the conditions for it. In the scene, the contest for and display of power or authority is made manifest in the author's use of שלח ("to send") as a *leitwort*. Abner *sends* messengers to David; David *sends* a message to Ishbosheth; and Ishbosheth *sends* someone to go fetch Michal from her husband. In each of the three "sending" sentences, some leverage of power is either outrightly claimed or presupposed by the sender. Abner's claim to power before David lies in his control of the northern tribes of Israel as he asks rhetorically, למי־ארץ ("To whom does the land belong?" i.e., who really

---

63. Gordon, *1 & 2 Samuel*, 216.

64. Gordon writes, "Abner, who was consolidating his own position all the while that Ish-bosheth's rickety kingdom was in decline (cf. 1), allegedly makes use of one of Saul's concubines. While it is disputed whether such an act might amount to a formal claim to the throne in Israelite palace politics, it is likely that Ish-bosheth's suspicions tended in that direction anyway. He was a true son of Saul (cf. 1 Sam 22:7ff.)" (*1 & 2 Samuel*, 217).

65. Bergen, *1, 2 Samuel*, 308.

controls this land that David desires other than Abner?).⁶⁶ That Abner laid claim to power over the northern lands is evident in his following statement to David: "Make your covenant with me, and my alliance will be with you"; the result of that alliance will be להסב אליך את־כל־ישראל ("to turn to you [David] all [the land of] Israel"). In other words, while David may have all the prospects of being a monarch over all of Israel, the kingdom for now is Abner's to give to whomever he wills.

David on his part asserted his power in two ways, first in his response to Abner, and second by the message he sent to Ishbosheth. The narrator skillfully sets Abner and David's speeches in an interesting pattern. Each of the two speeches after the initial introductory formula (I.F.) begins with a preliminary statement or a preamble, which is followed with the main focus of the speech. The preamble and main thrust of the speech (in both the speeches of Abner and David) is separated by an infinitive construct form of the verb "to say" (אמר) in the qal stem. To Abner's boast of "possessing the land," David's response is something like, "I will play along" ("It is good to me to make a covenant with you"); yet that is not on Abner's terms but David's ("but I am requiring one thing from you"). To Abner's request that David enter into a covenant with him as a person (accompanied with his personal promise of delivering the whole of Israel to David),⁶⁷ David responds with an imposition of a condition: "You shall not see my face unless you bring Michal, Saul's daughter, along when you come to see me."⁶⁸

---

66. Anderson argues, "It is possible that the rhetorical question, 'To whom does the land really belong?' is a later addition, suggesting that Abner is not committing a high treason but is simply instrumental in helping to bring about the fulfillment of Yahweh's promise to David; in other words, the land *already* belongs to David because of the above oath." He buttresses his argument by a reference to Yahweh's oath in verse 9 (Anderson, *2 Samuel*, 57). Anderson's position does not take the totality of Abner's speech into consideration. Abner's claim to be able to turn all Israel over to David clearly demonstrates what he meant by his question: he, Abner, has the land.

67. Commenting on the clause *Make your covenant with me* (3:12), Gordon observes that it "suggests that he [Abner] wanted to exclude all possible rivals from making a deal with David (cf. v. 7). He is concerned about his safety and his status in the reunified kingdom. Not unjustifiably, he claims the ability to be able to divert Israelite loyalties in David's direction." (Gordon, *1 & 2 Samuel*, p. 218).

68. McCarter observes that David had required the return of Michal as proof of his good faith. He compares David's demand here with Gen 43:3, 5, where Joseph makes a similar requirement of his brothers—that they will never see his face unless they had Benjamin with them (McCarter, *II Samuel*, 114). In Genesis, Joseph had uncontested superiority over his brothers. The use of the same literary form here makes a case for David's claim to superiority in power over Abner.

## 2 Sam 3:12–13

### Abner's speech

| | |
|---|---|
| | ¹² וישלח אבנר מלאכים אל־דוד (תחתו) [תחתיו] |
| | Then Abner sent messengers to David on his behalf, |
| 1st Introductory formula (I.F.) | לאמר |
| | saying, |
| The Preamble | למי־ארץ |
| | "To whom does the land belong?" |
| The 2nd I.F. | לאמר |
| | He said further, |
| The main | כרתה בריתך אתי |
| | "Make your covenant with me; |
| thrust of the | והנה ידי עמך |
| | and behold, my hand will be with you, |
| speech | להסב אליך את־כל־ישראל |
| | to turn over to you all Israel." |

### David's speech

| | |
|---|---|
| The 1st I.F. | ¹³ ויאמר |
| | Then he replied, |
| The Preamble | טוב אני אכרת אתך ברית |
| | "It is good for me to make a covenant with you; |
| | אך דבר אחד אנכי שאל מאתך |
| | but one thing do I require of you." |
| The 2nd I.F. | לאמר |
| | He said further, |
| The main | לא־תראה את־פני |
| | "You shall not see my face, |
| thrust of the | כי אם־לפני הביאך את מיכל בת־שאול |
| | unless you bring before me Michal, Saul's daughter, |
| speech | בבאך לראות את־פני |
| | when you come to see me. |

By this, David makes it plain to Abner that he (David) calls the shots, not any other person, when he is involved in a deal. Having thus dealt decisively with the *de facto* ruler of Israel, David now turned his attention to the *de jure* leader, to whom he "sent" a message, demanding the return of Michal to him.

Ishbosheth, who trembled with fear before Abner and seemed incapable of contending with David, here, at last, finds someone over whom he could exercise authority. That person he finds in Michal—the common pawn in the men's power game; we shall give a fuller treatment to this aspect of the text in the next chapter. Reading between the lines, however, suggests that Ishbosheth may have done this under duress— under the overbearing hand of Abner. While both Abner and David send messages to specific individuals, Ishbosheth sends for Michal to be collected like a piece of property. Michal is the central figure in this scene (though speechless, neither is any action of hers reported), because all the named men in the scene take one action or the other that directly impact her. Yet the most humane action towards her comes from her husband, Paltiel, who mourns her departure right up to the borders of Judah, where Abner drives him away with the wave of the hand.

At the end of this scene (vv. 12–16) only David stands as the man with real power.[69] He reduces Abner (in the anticipated covenant) to vassal status by imposing the conditions for the covenant. Similarly, he addresses Ishbosheth more like a vanquished rival king, whereby the victorious king imposes a levy upon the former. The tribute David demands is none other than the very daughter of the late king. The *leitwort* of שלח ("to send") functions in this text to bolster David's preeminence over the house of Saul. Both Abner and Ishbosheth, from Saul's house, send messages or messengers that serve David's interest. David sends two messages to both men: the message to Abner trims him to size from his overweening self-conceits; and to Ishbosheth, David sends a message

---

69. Our position here directly contradicts that of Mauchline, who opines that the fact that Abner's emissaries could come to Hebron "gives us warrant to infer that David in Hebron was politically much weaker than Ishbosheth in Mahanaim, who had inherited, even if he did not effectively rule, Saul's kingdom centered in Benjamin" (Mauchline, *1 and 2 Samuel*, 209). Such a reading finds no support from the text. Both David's action and demands on the one hand, and Abner's actions (in both this scene and the one that follows, where he is portrayed more like David's errand boy) evinces David's strength not weakness.

that not only asserts his superiority but the result of which reestablishes his claim on Saul's throne.[70]

The next scene (vv. 17-21) is full of Abner's scurrying maneuvers between the northern elders and David. In his outburst against Ishbosheth, Abner had made a stunning reference to Yahweh's oath to give David the kingdom of Saul, the fulfillment of which he was now going to work towards (3:9-10). In his communication with the northern elders, he refers to this oath again. To this Yahwistic promise, he adds the elders' own longing for David to be their king. To cajole them to go along with him he reminds them of the Philistine threat that hung over them like the sword of Damocles. After securing their consent, Abner heads to Hebron to galvanize his position in the emerging political order. His desertion of the Saulide is complete as he unreservedly submits to David's hegemony, evinced by his reference to David as "my lord the king" (3:21). In the narrative world, then, Abner has succeeded in making David king, because it is only after he calls David king that that title is subsequently applied to David in the narrative, both in direct discourse and in narration. David, on the other hand, furnishes a lavish (treaty) meal for Abner and his twenty companions. When Abner sets out to go, David gives him free passage.

A few salient points at this juncture need closer consideration. First, if Abner was aware of both Yahweh's oath to give David the kingdom and the desire of the northern elders to have David as their king, why was he all that while propping up Ishbosheth as Israel's king? If this were the situation as Abner paints it here, one suggestion could be that, being aware of Ishbosheth's weakness, Abner only used him (in anointing him as a rival king to David) as a bargaining chip so he could secure for himself a good station in David's kingdom, most likely the position of שׂר־צבא (commander of the army). That is to say, personal ambition and self preservation, rather than loyalty to the house of Saul, undergirded his motivation from the beginning. Second, when Abner got to Hebron, he was bringing to David the terms of the northern elders, that is, "all that is good in the eyes" of all Israel and the whole house of Benjamin (v. 19).

---

70. Bowman penetrates to David's intentions in his demand for the return of Michal: "By means of this condition, David makes yet another attempt to establish ties with the house of Saul. In seeking to regain Michal, Saul's daughter, he is attempting to legitimate his monarchical claims" (Bowman, "The Fortune of King David/The Fate of Queen Michal, 97-121). On a similar position see Bergen, *1, 2 Samuel*, 309.

The motif of "what is good in the eyes of" a person features prominently in the whole of this episode (cf. 3:13;⁷¹ 3:36; see also v. 21). By this means of narrative echo, the author makes this era of Israelite history comparable to the Judges era wherein "everyone did what was right in his own eyes" (cf. Judg 17:6; 21:25). As in the times of the judges, there was no "king" in Israel, but war and chaos. Whenever anyone does what is right in his or her own eyes, rather than what is right in the sight of Yahweh, the end result is war, fratricide, or death: as it obtained in the Judges era so it was in this early monarchical period of Israel's history. Third, while Abner had announced his covenant terms and the benefits David was to obtain from it, we hear only of David's condition for dealing with Abner, but not the benefit that would accrue to the latter from this covenant. This is one of the gaps that are frequent in the Samuel narrative. One is inclined to surmise that this particular gap is reflective of David's duplicity in his dealings with Abner. This omission is comparable to the non-inclusion of David's response to Joab's challenge to David's sagacity in letting Abner go in peace, discussed below.

Verse 22 begins the scene that leads up to Abner's death at Joab's hands. Shortly after Abner's "peaceful" departure, Joab and his troops arrived from a raiding expedition. He is informed of Abner's visit and departure. There is more than a hint in the report that the Judean courtiers were more than dissatisfied with the way David had carried on with Abner: they apparently thought things ought to have gone differently and now they found a ready ally in Joab. They complained, "Abner, son of Ner, came to the king; and he sent him away, and he went in peace," (v. 23). Joab wasted no time in confronting the king with the latter's ineptitude.⁷² Just like in the previous scene, where we did not find David's

---

71. Though in this verse only the adjective טוב ("good") appears, the personalization in David's statement טוב אני ("It is good to me," or "I am pleased") carries the same force as that which is "good in the eyes of David."

72. Bodner considers Joab to be a reader-response critic of David's speech and non-speech. Comparing Joab's action here with the one he took with regard to the murder of Uriah, he writes, "Joab appears to exercise a hermeneutic of suspicion toward both the actions of Abner and the silence of David. David's very public avowal of innocence does not lack melodrama as he elaborately calls down curses and composes lyrics to distance himself from this heinous deed and its perpetrators, but makes no move to rid himself of Joab and his brother Abishai; in fact 'he continues to depend on their activity as strongmen.' In addition to the display of creative hermeneutics, another crucial similarity between the Abner episode (2 Sam 3:22–39) and the Uriah affair (2 Sam 11:14–25) is that in both, Joab censures David for inferior political judgment" (Bodner, "Is Joab a Reader-Response Critic?" 19–35).

response to Abner, David's response is wanting.[73] Did he agree with Joab that he had made a mistake (and hence Joab's marching forth for "war" against Abner)? Did he object to Joab's innuendos? Did Joab proceed with his plan in stubbornness in spite of David's objections? We are not told any of these, neither here nor even at the point of Solomon's execution of Joab, where such objections could have surfaced to buttress the innocence of the Davidic house with regard to Abner's murder. We can never know the truth, which is lost in narrative gaps. However, from the apology of David stance of the HDR, one is inclined to think that if David had objected to Joab's suggestion, the author would have readily cited that in his spirited defense of David. This is an argument from silence, but it has warrant from a close reading of the text. Furthermore, in view of Joab's direct confrontation of David on the Abner question (vv. 24–25), the narrator's comment that David did not know of Joab's action (v. 26) becomes suspect.

There are other textual data here that evince the complexity of this narrative. First, David is depicted in the HDR as a defender of Saul and members of his court: he twice refused to slay Saul when he had good occasion and was urged on by his associates (1 Sam 24:6; 26:11); he exacted vengeance on Saul's alleged killer (2 Sam 1:14–15), and also avenged Ishbosheth's death by executing the murderous pair of brothers (2 Sam 4:12). We observe that there were three occurrences of deaths in the house of Saul within the last phase of the HDR, and David kills those immediately connected with a couple of the deaths (2 Sam 1, 4). Sandwiched between these two incidents is Joab's execution of Abner; in this case David claims he is powerless to do anything. While it is true that those whom David killed to avenge Saulide blood were aliens and less powerful figures than Joab, it is doubtful that David could not do anything about Joab if the former was truly innocent.

There are possible explanations for this policy difference regarding murderers of Saulides. One possibility is that the selectivity in David's administration of justice may be due to nepotism (which is in itself wrong), since the sons of Zeruiah were his nephews: the weakness of

---

73. Anderson comments, "It seems somewhat strange that David, apparently, did not reply to Joab's complaint and that neither Joab nor his informants seemed to be fully aware of the real purpose of Abner's meeting with David. One may also note that Joab accused Abner of treachery (v. 25) and that he did not charge David with the failure to avenge Asahel, unless this is implied in Joab's word" (Anderson, *2 Samuel*, 60).

David as far as family members are concerned is attested with respect to his sons. Besides, the narrator intimates that Joab and his raiding band had brought back a lot of loot. David is also known to be soft anytime he stands to gain materially from any situation. One example of this is the success of Ziba in besmirching Mephibosheth after he had lavishly supplied the fleeing king with victuals, which story we shall be giving more attention to in chapter 5 (cf. 2 Sam 16). Also to be noted is his planned attacked on Nabal for supplies and how the attack was averted only by the provision of such supplies by Abigail (1 Sam 25).

Another possibility is that David had a hand in Abner's death. David has been suspected of complicity in Abner's murder because he protested too much.[74] What attracts me to such accusations is David's conduct in the other cases of killings (both with regard to the Amalekite and the two sons of Rimmon). In both cases David made no reference to himself but squarely addressed the murderers. In Abner's case, the first recorded response of David was to assert the innocence of both himself and his line of succession (vv. 28–29). Besides, even though David knew the Amalekite had not killed Saul as he [the Amalekite] had claimed (as David's own later boast indicates, cf. 2 Sam 4:10), he [David] went ahead and had him executed. Yet, here was a clear case of murder committed right under his nose, and all he could do was to assert his innocence and resort to the pronouncement of invectives on Joab. It is also highly unusual that a sovereign would keep the chief of defense staff of his military oblivious of a treaty as significant as the one David was supposedly pursuing with Abner.[75] If Joab was ignorant of the whole deal, as the

74. VanderKam, on this note, writes, "Several notes in the text do reveal David's fear that his contemporaries would draw what seems to be the correct conclusion regarding his engineering Abner's assassination ... In other words, precisely the zeal of the editor to exonerate David, the fact that he protests too much, leads one to suspect him as a conspirator in Abner's death" (VanderKam, "Davidic Complicity," 533). Steussy similarly considers David to be protesting a little too much. He observes, "Some Christians, seeing such misgivings as an example of modern skepticism, might call for a return to more 'innocent' interpretations. But if the stories were indeed composed to defend David, we can conclude that even the original audience entertained suspicions. Otherwise, pro-David propaganda would not have been needed" (Steussy, "David, God, and the Word," 365–73).

75. The possibility of David's complicity in Abner's murder is strengthened by the fact Joab did not attack Abner without first consulting David. It is only after the deafening silence of David that Joab marches forth to silence Abner. Bodner sees this as part of Joab's reader-response critique of David. He writes, "David's silence on the crucial matter of Abner's reliability is unexpected. Until this juncture in the narrative, David

text seems to suggest, then his suspicion of Abner would not have been unwarranted.[76] The Moabite courtiers' suspicion of David's motive when he sent emissaries to commiserate with their new king on the death of his father Nahash is a case in point (2 Sam 10:1–3). Similarly, the emissaries sent by Babylon to commiserate with Hezekiah were actually spies (2 Kgs 20:12–18). Our case, then, is argued not merely on the basis of an *a priori* speculatively presumed guilt of David, but rather on the basis of strong circumstantial evidence embedded in the fabric of the text.

The last scene of this episode contains David's histrionic display of his innocence and grief over Abner, which is aimed at winning hearts for political gain. Bodner is correct in characterizing it as a melodrama (see footnote 72 above). The scene begins in verse 31 with David's address to Joab and "all the people who were with him." A certain ambiguity attaches to the second part of the object of David's address: are "all the people," referred to here, with Joab or with David? The pronominal suffix attached to the preposition את can have either David or Joab as its antecedent. Contextually, considering the repetition and significance of the phrase "all the people" (כל העם, the phrase occurs 7 times within the

---

has taken a multitude of opportunities to unleash his political rhetoric. The reader may have anticipated that David would defend Abner's newly found loyalty to him. David's silence—especially considering Joab's personal sense of affront with respect to Abner—indicates yet another contour of their 'entangled and stratified' relationship" (Bodner, "Is Joab a Reader-Response Critic?" 26, footnote 21). From another perspective, if David had kept Joab in the dark on his dealings with Abner, there could have been no motivation for such secrecy and equanimity (when life was at stake) other than it being a calculated act aimed at setting Abner up so that Joab would finish him off (Joab being a man who would not fold his arms while he is being displaced by his brother's killer).

76. Bodner rightly observes, as he elaborates further on his theme of Joab as reader-response critic, "According to Joab's interpretation, Abner is a dangerous dissembler, and the audience may well concede that he has a point. First, according to 2 Sam 3:6 Abner's powerbase in the north is 'growing in strength.' Second, since Abner has defected once, there is the continual risk that he may turn again. Third, Abner shows all the signs of having royal ambitions, especially (as Ish-Bosheth alleges) he appropriates Saul's concubine (2 Sam 3:7)" (Bodner, "Is Joab a Reader-Response Critic?" 27). Bergen similarly notes that Joab may have distrusted Abner as Saulide, but that Abner's acceptance constituted a threat to Joab's job (Bergen, *1, 2 Samuel*, 311). One thing that Joab cannot be faulted for is his singular loyalty to David. It is fair to say that all his actions were always guided, first and foremost, by the goal of protecting David's best interest. It is rather an irony that at the end of the day, David is said to have called for the execution of Joab (1 Kgs 2:5–6). Be that as it may, Joab certainly read David correctly when he said of the latter, "you love those who hate you and hate those who love you" (2 Sam 19:6).

space of seven verses), it becomes clear that it is referring to the people who were with David. This, in my view, refers to the elders of Judah and the twenty (elders) from Israel who had come with Abner, in view of the context of the covenant feast David had just made for Abner. The narrator skillfully weaves each statement in this scene with the next by the re-echo of the phrase כל העם ("all the people"). The phrase assumes the dimension of a stitch-word or stitch-words.[77] Viewed in this way, then, it becomes obvious that from the very beginning, David's actions are targeted to impinge upon, not just the cognition of the people who were with him, but more so their affective core. From this seemingly innocent first occurrence of כל העם, the narrator dexterously develops the melodramatic performance of David with his focalizing of the people and their action becoming more apparent as the stitch-words also begin to occur with greater frequency. The sum effect of all this is that the narrator makes manifest the process by which David stirred up the people's emotions until they were moved into a frenzied empathy and began to weep for Abner alongside of him. By this means David was able to draw them into a sphere of shared sentiments with him. This, then, became a shortcut to the hearts of the populace, as they became deeply affected towards him, thereby making them more acquiescent to his royal aspirations as well.

One literary feature that is used with great relish—particularly in this episode, but also in the book as a whole—is repetition. Indeed,

---

77. My concept of stitch-words is analogous to but different from the *wiederaufnahme* concept. The latter entails a recall of antecedent narrative material at a later stage in a narrative, with disparate narrative material intervening between this resumptive recall and its antecedent. A good example of this is the first reportage of Samuel's death in 1 Sam 25:1 and its recall in 1 Sam 28:3 (see Niccacci, "Biblical Hebrew Verb System in Prose," 167–202). Stitch-word(s), as conceived here, occurs within the same narrative space and functions as a way of linking the narrator's thoughts like the way the quilt maker's seams join pieces of a quilt together. Thus, in the use of stitch-word(s), a key word or a key phrase recurs from sentence to sentence or with only a few sentences intervening between one occurrence and the next. In our text, for instance, כל העם first occurs in verse 31, and is repeated in verse 32. There is a brief gap in verse 33 and part of verse 34 (direct speech), but as soon as historical narration resumes we again find כל העם, by which means the proceeding thoughts are joined to the preceding sentences (the earlier verses) and then stitched back to back with the next sentence in verse 35. This pattern continues to verse 37. See also verses 26 and 27, which are stitched with the word שוב. The narrator also uses the same stich-word technique in stressing the innocence of David in verses 21 to 24, the stitch-words being the pair of key phrases "he sent him away" (√שלח) and "he went away in peace" (בשלום וילך).

even the device of stitch-word we have just discussed above, at core, is a form of repetition. The narrator employs repetition in diverse ways in this discourse to produce the desired effect in very subtle ways. For example, we observe the use of divine oaths both at the beginning and towards the end of the Abner episode. At the beginning Abner swears by Yahweh not to live unless he has turned the kingdom over to David (כה־יעשה אלהים לאבנר וכה יסיף לו, vv. 9–10). There is a sense of irony here, in that Abner did not get to live but David got the kingdom. Towards the end of the episode, David makes a similar oath in honor of Abner (כה יעשה־לי אלהים וכה יסיף, v. 35). By this echo of the oath, the narrative inseparably intertwines the destinies of the two men, in which the one has to die for the other to continue; and this is the subject matter of the intervening material. We also find iterative repetition in verse 36, which indicates that David, in his melodramatic performance, did many other things to impress his audience. Lastly, the narrator uses repetition as a bracketing device for focalization purposes. In verse 27 the narrator says that Joab smote and killed Abner to avenge the latter's slaying of his brother Asahel; he repeats this basic idea, with some nuance, in verse 30. Thus verses 27 and 30 form a bracket that focalizes verses 28 and 29, thereby underscoring David's innocence, from the narrator's point of view.

## *Ishbosheth's Death (2 Sam 4:1–12)*

### 2 SAMUEL 4

1 When Saul's son[78] heard that Abner had died in Hebron, he became dispirited, and all Israel was disturbed. 2 Now Saul's son had two men, captains of raiding bands; the name of the one was Baanah, the name of the second was Rechab—sons of Rimmon the Beerothite from the Benjaminites, because Beeroth is reckoned *as belonging* to Benjamin, 3 though the Beerothites had fled to Gittaim; and they are *still* there to this day.

---

78. Corruption in the text at this point is evinced by the divergence of the witnesses. The MT (followed by the Targumim) has no name for Saul's son; 4QSam[a] and the LXX versions have Mephibosheth; the Syriac has Eshbashol. McCarter notes that LXX[MN] have Ishbosheth (McCarter, *II Samuel*, 124). I agree with Anderson that the context clearly requires Ishbosheth (Anderson, *2 Samuel*, 66).

4 Now Jonathan, Saul's son, had a son *who was* crippled in both feet. He was five years old, when the news of Saul and Jonathan's death in Jezreel came; so his nurse took him, and fled. But as she hurried to flee, he fell, and he became lame. His name was Mephibosheth.[79]

5 The sons of Rimmon the Beerothite, Rechab and Baanah, departed; and they arrived at Ishbosheth's house by the heat of the day, while he was sleeping at the midday nap time. 6 And behold! They came into the house, *as if* they were conveying wheat; and they smote him in the stomach. Then Rechab and Baanah, his brother, escaped.[80] 7 They had come to the house, while he was sleeping upon his bed in his bedchamber; and they smote him; and they killed him. Then they cut off his head, and they took the head;[81] and they went by the way of the Arabah all that night.

8 They brought the head of Ishbosheth to David *in*[82] Hebron. Then they said to the king, "Behold! The head of Ishbosheth, the son of Saul—your enemy, who sought *to destroy* your life. Yahweh has exacted vengeance this day for my lord the king from Saul and his progeny." 9 David replied Rechab and Baanah, his brother, the sons of Rimmon the Beerothite—and he said to them, "By the living Yahweh, who redeemed my life from all distress, 10 when one told me saying, 'Behold! Saul is dead.' Now he had thought himself a bearer of glad tidings,[83] But I seized him, and slaughtered him in Ziklag; which was the *prize* I awarded him for *his* glad tidings. 11 How much more *when* wicked men slaughter a righteous man in his house—upon his bed. Now therefore shall I not require his blood from your hand, and extirpate you from the earth?" 12 So David commanded his militia, and they slaughtered them. Then

---

79. LXX$^L$ has "Mephibaal" instead.

80. The text of the LXX is markedly different here; it has καὶ ἰδοὺ ἡ θυρωρὸς τοῦ οἴκου ἐκάθαιρεν πυροὺς καὶ ἐνύσταξεν καὶ ἐκάθευδεν καὶ Ρεκχα καὶ Βαανα οἱ ἀδελφοὶ διέλαθον ("And, behold, the portress of the house winnowed wheat, and she dozed off and slept, so Rechab and Baana, the brothers, sneaked into the house"). The LXX here witnesses to the poor state of Ishbosheth's security. It is hard to imagine that the man who laid claim to royalty would have had a woman porter doubling as his security detail. This compares poorly with Joab, who as David's chief of defense staff, for instance, had ten aide-de-camp (2 Sam 18:15). It is very possible that after Ishbosheth's quarrel with Abner, the latter withdrew whatever security detail he had posted to the former, leaving him very vulnerable.

81. This entire clause is lacking in LXX$^L$.

82. A few medieval manuscripts have בחברון ("in Hebron").

83. The LXX versions have additionally ενωπιον μου ("before me," i.e., to me)

they cut off their hands and feet, and hung them by the pool of Hebron. But the head of Ishbosheth[84] they took,[85] and buried it in Abner's grave in Hebron.

2 Samuel 4 contains the last episode of the civil war period of the HDR. While it is a separate discourse unit (within this narrative) from the previous chapter, both chapters are inseparably subsumed under the heading of the misfortunes of the house of Saul announced in 2 Sam 3:6. The first verse of this chapter stands at the head of the exposition (vv. 1–4) that foregrounds the two scenes of the episode of which the chapter consists.[86] The transitional character of the first verse, however, is not lost on any keen reader. Jean-Claude Haelewyck in recognition of this fact writes, "Le *v*. 1 assure la transition entre le récit de l'assasinat d'Abner et celui de l'assasinat d'Ishbaal. La mort d'Abner, 'homme fort du régime,' constitute une veritable catastrophe tant pour Ishbaal, qui se voit privé de son plus fort soutien, que pour tout Israël. Ce verset fait déjà presenter au lecteur qu'il approche du dénouemount."[87]

The foregrounding exposition contains disparate data, which are necessary for grasping the subsequent account. In verse 1 the reader is confronted with the disheveled state of Ishbosheth and his realm of the northern tribes of Israel following the death of Abner.[88] Abner's

---

84. The LXX and probably 4QSam[a] have "Mephibosheth," consistent with what obtained previously in 2 Sam 3:7; 4:1, 2.

85. The clause "they took," does not exist in the LXX and Latin versions. In the MT, it takes on the plural form like all the other preceding verbs. However, in 4QSam[a] the verb for "take" (לקח), unlike in the MT, is in the singular form. The MT's plural refers to David's retainers, while the singular of 4QSam[a] would refer to David himself. However, it is unlikely that David would have buried Ishbosheth's head himself. I therefore follow the MT.

86. In this we differ from Anderson, who writes, "V. 1 links the events of the previous chapter with those of the present narrative, without being an integral part of either chapter" (Anderson, *2 Samuel*, 67).

87. Haelewyck, "L'Assassinat d'Ishbaal (2 Samuel IV 1–12)," 145–53.

88. Commenting on the phrase וַיִּרְפּוּ יָדָיו Jeremy Schipper writes, "This idiom of 'enfeebled hands' communicates Ishbosheth's lack of courage and military leadership." He further demonstrates the depth of its meaning from its use with regard to David as he writes, "This idiom for discouragement occurs only one other time in the Books of Samuel: 2 Sam 17:2 uses it in reference to David's discouraged state while in exile from Jerusalem. Here Ahithophel reports that David is 'weary and feeble-handed' (יגע ורפה ידים). The imagery used to characterize non-Davidic groups during David's solidification of power now emphasizes the extent of David's collapse" (Schipper, "Disability in 2 Samuel 5:8b," 422–34).

death portended doom for Saul's tottering kingdom because Ishbosheth showed no ability to hold on to the throne (without a strong military commander like Abner, upon whom he had relied completely heretofore), neither was there any other figure that could marshal the military levy of the north to form a formidable match for David's skillful band of rebel and mercenary fighters. By this, the narrator supplies the reader with the requisite background against which to read the events surrounding Ishbosheth's tragic end, which automatically led to the end of Saul's kingdom. In the next two verses the narrator volunteers the names, as well as the family, clan, and tribal affiliations, of the would-be murders of the last Saulide monarch. The fourth verse offers the introduction of Mephibosheth, Jonathan's son. The first scene of the episode (vv. 5–7) narrates the actual murder itself, while the second scene (vv. 8–12) deals with the aftermath of the murder.

Some ambiguity attaches to the stated tribal background of the pair of the regicide brothers (Rechab and Baanah). They are said to be the "sons of Rimmon the Beerothite from the Benjaminites, because Beeroth is reckoned *as belonging* to Benjamin" (בני רמון הבארתי מבני בנימן כי גם־בארות תחשב על־בנימן, v. 2). A good number of scholars take it to mean that they were ethnic Israelite Benjaminites.[89] However, there are others who take the sons of Rimmon to be who the text says they were, Beerothites.[90] A number of the rea-

---

89. Concerning the city of Beeroth, Bergen writes that it was "a former Gibeonite settlement located approximately four miles northwest of Jerusalem." But of its inhabitants at the time of David he writes, "They were descended from a family of Benjaminites that had helped to resettle Beeroth (cf. Josh 9:16–18) after the original inhabitants were forced to move to Gittaim, a less desirable location." Indeed, in footnote 21, he comments further, "Noth's hypothesis that Recab and Baanah were vengeance-seeking Gibeonites serving in Ish-Bosheth's army is without merit, since the explicit claim of the text is that they were 'sons of Rimmon ... from the tribe of Benjamin' (v. 2). Cf. M. Noth, *The History of Israel*, trans. P. R. Ackroyd (New York: Harper & Row, 1960), 186" (*1, 2 Samuel* 315–16).

In the same vein Gordon writes, "In continuation of his father's policy (1 Sam 22:7), Ish-bosheth (or Abner?) appears to have favored Benjaminites for command positions in his army. *Be-eroth also is reckoned* (2): originally Be-eroth was a member of the Gibeonite league (Josh 9:17) ... At some point, possibly in the period of the Israelite settlement (cf. Josh 18:25), the Amorite inhabitants of Be-eroth were driven from their city and found refuge in *Gittaim* ..." (*1 & 2 Samuel*, 222).

90. Mauchline, for instance, observes, "According to Jos 9:17 Beeroth was one of the four towns of the Gibeonite league which made a covenant with Joshua during the period of the Israelite occupation of Palestine. They constituted an Amorite enclave in Benjamin; this explains why the parenthesis at the end of 2 states that Beeroth was

sons that are advanced for taking the Beerothites as bona fide ethnic Benjaminites are based on faulty reasoning. Gordon's argument (see footnote 89) is basically circular in nature. Based on 1 Sam 22:7, he syllogistically argues something like this: Saul and his dynasty appointed only Benjaminites to command positions in their military; Rechab and Baanah, were commanders in Ishbosheth's army, therefore they were Benjaminites. However, such an argument finds no warrant in the text. There is no indication in the text that Ishbosheth (or Abner) followed all of Saul's policies. It is true that with the prevalence of gaps in the narrative, gap-filling necessarily has to be done by the reader. However, such gap-fillings must be based on textual cues, not purely on the reader's creativity or ingenuity. Bergen, on the other hand, cites Josh 9:16–18 to assert that members of a Benjaminite clan had repopulated Beeroth after they had driven its original inhabitants to the less favorable Gittaim. To speak as he does is a disingenuous subversion of the text, which clearly states that the Israelites did not attack the Gibeonites (Beeroth is listed among the Gibeonite cites) because of the oath of Yahweh that the elders of the congregation of Israel had sworn with the Gibeonites (Josh 9:18).

The supposition of the preceding position is that because the text says Beeroth was also "reckoned" to belong to the sons of Benjamin, therefore its dwellers were Benjaminites. Two things are missed in such thinking. First, the word (√חשב) used here would rather suggest that the people were not Benjaminites but were "thought" or "assumed" now to be Benjaminites. The basic semantic domain of the verb חשב is the idea of "to think, account, regard, esteem, and consider" (cf. Hos 8:12; Isa 29:16, 17; 40:15; Ps 44:23 [ET 44:22]; Job 18:3; 41:21 [ET 41:29]; Lam 4:2). And when it is found in the niphal stem it carries the essential idea of to "be accounted, thought, reckoned" (cf. the following passages for the imputation of righteousness or sin Lev 7:18; 17:4; Num 18:27, 30; Ps 106:30–31).[91] In the passages cited above, the idea invariably is of what does not obtain but is considered or thought to be the case. Seen in this way then, the Beerothites were not Benjaminite Israelites ethnically, but now, because of the Yahwistic oath, were reckoned as Benjaminites, within whose tribal allotment they belonged. This is analogous to several of the other non-Israelites tribes in the south, like the Calebites—originally

---

reckoned to Benjamin" (*1 and 2 Samuel*, 212). See also Ackroyd, *The Second Book of Samuel*, 48; Soggin, *Old Testament and Oriental Studies*, 46–48.

91. BDB, 363.

Kenizzites, possibly of Edomite extraction—who were now reckoned as belonging to Judah.[92]

Second, some of the association of the Beerothite displacement to Gittaim with Saul's activity mentioned in 2 Sam 21:1 seems to imply that because of the sour relations between Saul and the Gibeonites, Saul's son could not have given Gibeonite Beerothites command positions in his military. An alternative argument is that on the basis of 1 Sam 22:7, if the Beerothites are proven to be Gibeonites, then, they would not have been officers in Ishbosheth's army because he, like his father Saul, appointed only Benjaminites to positions of influence. Such thinking is oblivious of the fact that things were never as cut and dried as that. For example, that David had fought against (and was renowned for that very fact among) the more alien Philistines stopped neither David from lending himself as a mercenary to the Philistine king of Gath (1 Sam 27–29) nor Philistine mercenaries from working for David later (2 Sam 16:18–22; 18:2–12). Besides, it cannot be considered to be abnormal for non-Israelites to attain such high ranks when there is a longstanding history of such phenomenon right from the exodus days (when Caleb was the representative of Judah), through the judges era (when Othniel was the first judge),[93] into the early monarchy (when Doeg was something like the agriculture secretary to king Saul, 1 Sam 21–22)—not to mention the large contingent of foreign mercenaries that worked for David both before and after his accession to the throne of Israel. Our conclusion then is that Rechab and Baanah were Gibeonite Beerothites.

The mention of Mephibosheth amongst the disparate data of the exposition section of this episode is seen an intrusion that is disruptive of the narrative flow.[94] The pertinent matter for us, however, is the

---

92. See Hubbard, "Caleb, Calebites," 120–22.

93. Although Caleb and his younger brother Othniel are reckoned under the tribe of Judah, they are also unambiguously said to be Kenizzites, descendants of Kenaz, one of Esau's grandsons (Num 32:12; Jos 14:6, 14; Judg 1:13; 3:9–11; cf. Gen 36:10–15, 42). Thus, while the Kenizzites were among the peoples that the Israelites were supposed to annihilate in the Promised Land (Gen 15:19), because of the exemplary faith and commitment of Caleb and his brother Othniel to Yahweh they ended up not only being adopted into the assembly of Israel, but even became chieftains therein. For similar positions see Hasel, "Caleb, Calebites," 573–74; Noth, *History of Israel*, 56–58; and Mauchline, *1 and 2 Samuel*, 204–5.

94. Arnold, *1 & 2 Samuel*, 439. Indeed, Haelewyck avers that since this verse meets the apologetic goal of the author of the HDR, he must have been the one that inserted it into the composition. He writes, "Puisque la pointe de ce verset rejoint l'objectif apolo-

purpose it serves in the present text. A few suggestions have been made, most of which at the core relate to the question of the fate of Saul's progeny. Anderson has suggested that the insertion was to make clear the unfitness of Mephibosheth as a successor to Ishbosheth due to his physical disability and his youth, being only five years old at Saul's death.[95] Going on the same tangent Haelewyck further explains that the verse thus prepares the reader for David's anointing in 2 Sam 5:3. He explains that the author of the HDR (in his apology for David) was by this showing that in being anointed as king over Israel, David was not depriving anyone of rights. He writes, "Le *v.* 4 joue un rôle particulier dans le contexte. Certes, il n'appartient pas originellement au récit sur l'assassinat d'Ishbaal. Toutefois cette notice sur le fils boiteux de Jonathan, qui en raison de son handicap ne peut succéder à Saül, prépare 2 Sam. V 3: David, en étant choisi comme roi sur Israël, n'a privé personne de son droit; c'est en toute légitimité qu'il a pu accepter d'être oint roi sur tout Israël."[96]

The record of the actual murder of Ishbosheth (vv. 5–7) is contained in a text that has been considered corrupted.[97] It is on this ground that

---

gétique de l'auteur de l'HAD, il faut attribuer à ce dernier, non pas la composition, mais l'insertion de ce *v.* 4 dans le récit de l'assassinat d'Ishbaal qui précède de peu l'onction de David comme roi sur Israël" (Haelewyck, "L'Assassinat D'Ishbaal 145–53).

95. Anderson, *2 Samuel*, 67.

96. Haelewyck, "L'Assassinat D'Ishbaal," 148–49. Arnold, similarly, writes, "Although it is true that this verse disrupts the flow of the present narrative, its inclusion highlights the pitiable end of Saul's progeny. In addition to Ish-Bosheth (whose life is about to end), there remains another descendant of Saul—but he is crippled. Just as impressive physical features confirmed the right of Saul and David to rule (1 Sam 9:2; 10:23; 16:12), so Mephibosheth's disability makes him an unlikely candidate in a time of political uncertainty" (Arnold, *1 & 2 Samuel*, 439). On the same note Segal writes, "The original place of the parenthesis iv 4 is between iv 1 and iv 2, and is intended (as already observed by Rashi) to emphasize the helplessness of the house of Saul" (Segal, "The Composition of the Books of Samuel," 318–39)

McCarter adds another dimension to this discussion. For him this insertion is intended to make the reader aware that the line of Saul will not be brought to an end by the impending assassination of Ishbosheth. He suggests further that the insertion may have been occasioned by the confusion over the identity of the "son of Saul" in vv. 1, 2, and elsewhere in the passage. To buttress his argument he points to the fact that in Josephus (*Ant.* 7.46–47), where such confusion was absent, this insertion is also not found at this point in the narrative; rather Josephus offers this information about Mephbosheth at a place in his narration that corresponds to 2 Samuel 9:3 (McCarter, *II Samuel*, 128).

97. The LXX text, for instance, diverges significantly from the MT (see the translation above). Most historical critical studies see different redactional layers or a confla-

O. Thenius referred to the repetition of the murder of Ishbosheth and the flight of the pair of brothers in this unit as "nonsense."[98] Keil believes that such conclusions are erroneous judgments of ancient discourse on contemporary standards. He makes a case for the understanding of the peculiarities of Hebrew historical narratives, where repetitions are not only common but are also made with the aim of adding something new.[99] It is interesting to note how in these verses the author varies his expansion of the major key words, phrases, or clauses that are repeated, and how these varied repetitions function in the scene. The whole unit consists of a parallelism as shown below.

A  5 וילכו בני־רמון הבארתי רכב ובענה
The sons of Rimmon the Beerothite, Rechab and Baanah, departed;
ויבאו כחם היום אל־בית איש בשת
and they arrived at Ishbosheth's house by the heat of the day,

B  והוא שכב את משכב הצהרים
while he was sleeping at the midday nap time.
6 והנה באו עד־תוך הבית לקחי חטים
And behold! They came into the house, *as if* they were conveying wheat;

C  ויכהו אל־החמש
and they smote him in the stomach.

D  ורכב ובענה אחיו נמלטו
Then Rechab and Baanah, his brother, escaped.

A'  7 ויבאו הבית
They had come to the house,

B'  והוא־שכב על־מטתו בחדר משכבו
while he was sleeping upon his bed in his bedchamber;

---

tion of alternative accounts lying behind the present text (so Anderson, *2 Samuel*, 70; and Haelewyck, "L'Assassinat d'Ishbaal," 146–50).

98. K & D 2, 576 n. 1.
99. K & D 2, 576 n. 1.

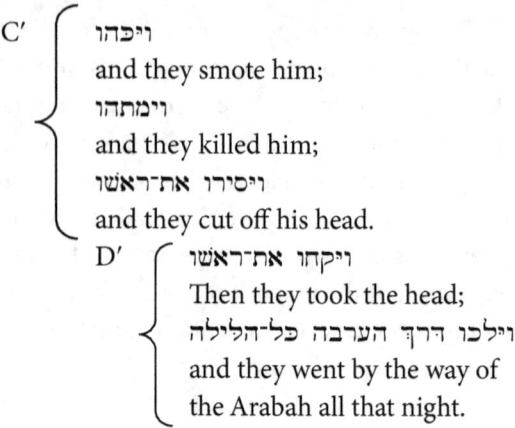

First, we observe how the phrase "they departed/went" (וילכו), or its analogous counterpart "escape" (מלט) in verse 6, occurs in both the opening and closing clauses of each of the parallel unit above, thereby forming an *inclusio* around the murder itself. In the first occurrence, Rechab and Baanah are said to have left (without an indication of their place of origin), while in the second occurrence they are said to have departed (without the mention of their destination within the verse). By this means, the narrator makes palpable for the reader the befuddlement, perplexity, and uncertainty felt by those who were the first responders on the crime scene: not knowing where the regicide brothers came from nor where they departed to.

Second, between the first mention of their coming (ויבאו, "and they came," *qal* 3mp *waw*-consecutive) in verse 5 and the second occurrence is one element that is not found in data repeated in verse 7, namely, the pretext by which the Rimmon brothers gained entrance into Ishbosheth's bed chamber: pretending to be carrying or fetching wheat. This is another example of the repetition device we have called bracketing, which serves the purpose of focalizing an element. The narrator's voice, comparable to the eye of the camera, focuses on the double treachery of the Rimmon brothers, who not only turned against their master but also employed deceit to beat whatever scanty security detail Ishbosheth may have had left after Abner's defection and subsequent demise.

Third, the narrator uses repetition in this unit for emphasis. Twice the narrator refers to Ishbosheth being killed upon his bed. While this may be viewed as weakness on Ishbosheth's part, it may also undergird the villainy and cowardice involved in the crime: villainy because the murderers were taking an unwarranted advantage of a defenseless man, and cowardice because they did not so much as offer Ishbosheth an opportunity to defend himself, such as challenging him to a combat (what even the Philistine Goliath offered Israel).

Finally, as the author repeats some elements, he chooses to prioritize some of the occurrences by expansion. In comparing the parallelistic display of the unit above, the lines expanded are A and B (which relate to the arrival and initial actions of the Rimmon brothers), and then C' and D' (which relates to their last actions and departure from the scene). Whereas in A' the reader is simply reminded that they came (without the mention of even their personal names), the lines in A begin with the regicide brothers setting forth (wherever they were coming from) to Ishbosheth's house: they are not just suddenly found in the house. Similarly, the reader is informed of the time of the day and the weather condition at the time; it was midday and it was hot. The lines in B similarly expand matters not addressed in the repetition in B': justifiably Ishbosheth is taking his afternoon nap, and the pair of brothers sneak in on the pretext of fetching wheat (even then, B' enriches B—in order to scandalize the reader—by indicating that Ishbosheth was sleeping on his bed in his bed chamber). On the other hand, the issues that C and D do not stress receive expansion in C' and D'. Where C merely reports that they smote him in the stomach, C' brings the macabre goriness of the dastardly act by piling up short verbal sentences: "they smote him and they killed him, and they cut off his head." Similarly where D simply reports that Baanah and his brother escaped, D' tells us a lot more: they took the head, and headed out in the direction of the Arabah and journeyed all night.[100] Through this skillful artistry, the author affords the reader the vividness that is comparable to motion pictures.

---

100. The entire report of Ishbosheth's death, his dismemberment, and the burial bears striking similarities to Saul's end. Just like his father, Ishbosheth died at the hands of foreigners: Saul at the hands of the Philistines (and an Amalekite?), Ishbosheth at the hands of the Gibeonites. Just as Saul's head was severed and carried as a war trophy through Philistia, Ishbosheth's head was carried as vengeful trophy through Israel to Judah. Just as Saul's head ended in a foreign land and his body was buried outside of his homestead in Transjordan (Jabesh-Gilead), Ishbosheth's head ends up being buried in "foreign" Judah and his body most likely buried in Transjordanian Mahanaim, away from his home in Benjaminite territory. Just as Saul's death ended his reign and signaled the end of his dynasty, Ishbosheth's death was the deathblow that snuffed out the last survival gasps of the Saulide dynasty. The event not only brings closure to the fate of Saul's dynasty, but also displays the Saulides' shared tragic destiny of ineluctable doom.

The setting of the second scene (vv. 8–12) shifts from Mahanaim to Hebron. There, with Ishbosheth's head in hand like a trophy, the Rimmon brothers arrive to proudly announce their cold-blooded murder of Ishbosheth to David as Yahweh's vengeance on the son of David's archenemy, who had sought David's life. David recounted his execution of the Amalekite, who brought him the tidings of Saul's death in Ziklag and subsequently ordered the execution of the Rimmon brothers. David's men did not only execute the Rimmon brothers and dismembered their corpses (as they had done to Ishbosheth), but also made a spectacle of them.

One thing that scholars try to fathom from this scene is the motive for the murder. As noted above, some like Noth have suggested a revenge motive (in view of 2 Sam 21:1).[101] As demonstrated above, there is a lack of textual evidence in the DtrH supporting the allegation that Saul had broken faith with the Gibeonites, which would have made revenge a candidate for possible motives for the murder. Moreover, even if that were the case, there is precedence for members of sworn perpetual enemy ethnicities (the Philistines and Israelites) crossing over into what would ordinarily be enemy territory to work for an overlord on the other side (David for Achish, and Ittai for David). That scenario diminishes the probability of revenge being the motive even if we grant the possibility that Saul may have persecuted the Gibeonites. Nevertheless, cues from the text seem to point in a different direction.

Anderson suggests the possibility that the Rimmon brothers belonged to the same disaffected Benjaminite circles as Abner (cf. 2 Sam 3:19) and as such were simply bringing about the implementation of Yahweh's promise to David (cf. 2 Sam 3:17–18).[102] The whole suggestion of a person working to bring about Yahweh's will (as per Abner) out of being disgruntled with his boss raises severe doubts about the integrity of such service. Thus, to take up Yahweh's name upon one's lips as a cloak to conceal self-seeking treachery ought not to be whitewashed. It would be a better reading of the text to understand the perspective of the Rimmon brothers as mirrored in David's perspective on the event. David took it that this pair of brothers were fortune diggers, seeking to obtain a reward from him—i.e., to profit from their criminal murder of a helpless innocent fellow. This view is reinforced by David's correlation of their action

---

101. Noth, *The History of Israel*, 186.
102. Anderson, *2 Samuel*, 70–71.

to that of the Amalekite (v. 10, cf. 1:14). It is interesting to note that David, at this time, does not attribute the death of Saul to the Amalekite as he did in chapter 1, where he murdered the Amalekite to exhibit his innocence with regard to the blood of Saul and his sons. There, David accused the Amalekite of stretching out his hand to exterminate Yahweh's anointed (לשלח ידך לשחת את־משיח יהוה); here he has come full circle to admit that the Amalekite was merely looking for reward as a bearer of glad tidings (והוא־היה כמבשר בעיניו ואחזה בו ואהרגהו בצקלג אשר לתתי־לו בשרה).[103] David's equation of the action of the Rimmon brothers and the Amalekite therefore show their real motivation: to seize the opportunity and ingratiate themselves with David, the favored contender for the throne, so they may profit thereby at his ascendency. In this sense, their motivation is not too distinct from that of Abner's defection; and it is very telling that they share the same fate as Abner—death at the hands of David's retainers.

In comparing David's treatment of the Rimmon brothers to the Amalekite, Bergen points to the former as David's consistency in following the Torah's demands for just retribution for a murder (cf. Gen 9:6; Exod 21:12; Lev 24:17; Num 35:31).[104] But this pious projection of David falls flat on its face in view of his barefaced failure to apply the same retributive justice to his henchman, Joab, for the brazen execution of Abner. Evidently, such selective enforcement of justice evinces a manipulative use of the powerless in David's melodramatic performance aimed at winning the hearts and minds of the northerners in order to realize his desire of ruling over all Israel (which desire is rightly recognized by Abner, cf. 3:21).

There is a desire among readers of this narrative to ascertain if the Rimmon brothers had acted independently or in concert with some other persons or as hired assassins. Haelewyck, for instance, believes that they were contracted to carry out the assassination by Joab. He finds

---

103. Anderson does not think the difference between 2 Sam 1:14–16 and 2 Sam 4:10 are significant. He takes the latter passage to be an abbreviation of the former (Anderson, *2 Samuel*, 71). This proposition fails to grapple with the seriousness of the charge that David slammed on the Amalekite, who even in his white lie had projected himself as merely offering mercy-killing not unlike the contemporary physician assisted suicide for the king who was going to die anyway. Such mercy-killing at the time was not looked upon as murder (cf. Judg 9:54; 1 Sam 31:4–5), even though we would shudder at it from the morality of our own times.

104. Bergen, *1, 2 Samuel*, 317.

this connection in the similarity of language describing the murder method of stabbing the victim in the stomach, which Joab himself had employed twice against prominent leaders in Israel (הַחֹמֶשׁ, or the form with the preposition, אֶל־הַחֹמֶשׁ, 2 Sam 3:27; 20:9–10; cf. 2 Sam 18:14).[105] While Haelewyck has made a valid observation regarding some striking similarities between the end of Abner and Ishbosheth, it is our belief that these similarities lead in a different direction than that which he has put forward. If we follow the tangent suggested by Haelewyck then, even Abner's slaying of Asahel would be attributed to Joab because of the use of the same phrase to describe how Abner killed Asahel. More than just this singular phrase, other similarities between the death of Abner and Ishbosheth include: (1) Both were killed by a pair of brothers; (2) both were struck in the stomach; (3) both (at least, parts of their bodies) were buried in the same grave; (4) both pairs of murderous brothers commanded raiding bands; and (5) both pairs of brothers had pretexts by which to camouflage their intentions (a tête-à-tête for one; and carrying wheat for the other). But also note the difference: one pair of brothers is killed—execution style— the other receives only verbal diatribes. By means of these similarities the author reminds the reader that Ishbosheth, as king of Israel, was Abner's creation—his "son," so to speak. Thus, just as Ishbosheth shared the same destiny with his biological father, he in this case now shares the same fate (including the same grave) with his political godfather, Abner.

Others place the murder of Ishbosheth squarely on David, for whom the Rimmon brothers were mere agents. We have already noted, in our chapter 1 that McKenzie, for instance, holds David responsible for all the strings of murders that trail his rise to power.[106] In David's defense, Mauchline writes that while it can be assumed that David did

---

105. Haelewyck writes, "Toutefois la mention du 'bas-ventre' dans le contexte de l'assassinat d'Ishbaal n'est pas fortuite. Il est hors de doute que l'auteur du récit ancien a voulu par ce moyen livrer un indice permettant d'identifier le veritable commanditaire de l'assassinat. Tant le rapprochement de tonalité entre iii 26–27 et iv 5–6 que l'utilisation d'un même terme rarement employé dans l'Ancien Testament indiquent que Rékab et Ba'ana ont agi sur l'order de Joab. Celui-ci, après qu'il s'est débarrassé d'Abner, achève—plus exactment fait achever par deux hommes de main—le travail commencé. Cette conclusion est plausible, car elle correspond à l'image qui a été dégagée de Joab en 2 Sam iii et à celle que ferait apparaître une analyse de chapitres rapportant la mort d'Absalom et celle d'Amasa" (Haelewyck, "L'Assassinat D'Ishbaal, 151–52).

106. McKenzie, *King David*, 32–34. For similar view also see Halpern, *David's Secret Demons*, also discussed in chapter 1.

not fail to perceive that the death of Ishbosheth opened up the way for him to rule a kingdom extending from Dan to Beersheba, in fairness to him "we must assume that that thought was not uppermost in his mind. He himself had, on one occasion, resisted the urgent demands of his own supporters to take advantage of a God-given opportunity to kill the Lord's anointed, king Saul (cf. [1 Sam] 24:4; cf. 26:8)."[107] While Mauchline's goal of fairness is a noble one, he assumes too much, and ends up psychologizing David rather than analyzing the text before us. David's attitudes to Saul and Ishbosheth were too ambivalent for one to make such sweeping conclusions *a priori*. Mauchline himself notes that while David had recognized Saul as a bona fide king of Israel (Yahweh's anointed), he did not accord the same recognition to Ishbosheth.[108] Our point here is not to prove David's complicity in Ishbosheth's death, but that his innocence has to be argued on other grounds, not by extrapolations from how he had acted toward Saul. Questions concerning David's guilt regarding Ishbosheth may have been raised then as they are nowadays[109] without any certain answer.

My conclusion on this question rests on two basic conditions. First and foremost, from the suggestions of the text, we assume that the Rimmon brothers, like the Amalekite in Saul's case, were a pair of opportunists seeking to exact some reward (material or political position or military command positions) from David. More tentatively, my second assumption hinges on whether Saul had violently sought to eliminate the Gibeonites (of which I am rather dubious) and whether the Rimmon brothers were ethnic Gibeonites (as our argumentation above suggests). Given these two conditions, then, there would have been reasonable and sufficient motive for them to have acted independently in their murder of Ishbosheth, and as such there is no compelling need to look for an external accomplice.

---

107. Mauchline, *1 and 2 Samuel*, 214.

108. Mauchline, *1 and 2 Samuel*, 214.

109. On this Gordon writes, "The death of Ish-bosheth was merely the *coup de grâce* for his ailing kingdom. Nevertheless, the suggestion that it was in any sense engineered by David could have had a disruptive effect on his attempt to secure the allegiance of the northern tribes. Acting with full regal authority on this occasion (cf. 1:15ff.), he has the self-confessed murderers executed and their mutilated bodies put on display, in testimony to his own revulsion at what had befallen Ish-bosheth" (Gordon, *1 & 2 Samuel*, 222).

## CONCLUSION

This chapter has focused on the two year-long civil war that forms the last segment of the HDR. Particularly, we examined the events immediately following Saul's demise: David's relocation to Hebron vis-à-vis Abner's tactical relocation of the capital of the Saulide dynasty from Gibeah to Mahanaim in Transjordan. I explored the confrontation between the forces loyal to the Saulides and David's highly mobile band of rebel fighters, which encounter is an exemplar of the fortunes of the two contending dynasties. I also examined Abner's conflict with his sovereign, Ishbosheth, Abner's defection and switching of allegiances from Ishbosheth to David, and the subsequent catastrophe that terminated his drive for a covenant with David. Finally, we also considered the circumstances surrounding Ishbosheth's murder and how David avenged his murder as well as the possibilities of David's complicity in both murders.

Alongside of these more substantial matters, we also discussed the key literary devices employed by the author in narrating these stories, and their impact in communicating the ethos and pathos of the stories. In the next chapter, we shall be considering the stories of the most prominent woman from the house of Saul and her fate in her association with David.

# 5

# David and Michal

THE FOCUS OF THIS endeavor as a whole is to investigate the fortunes of King Saul's progeny during David's reign. My goal is to ascertain, if possible, the factors that account for the great ills that visited the Saulides after the demise of their father, and especially to determine if there had been any Davidic complicity in any of these misfortunes. In the previous chapter, the analysis of the civil war years, reached a few tentative conclusions. First, with respect to the murder of Abner by Joab, David, by his actions and especially his inactions, was at the least blameworthy, but textual circumstantial evidence would actually implicate David in the murder. Second, regarding Ishbosheth's murder, however, the study produced no implicating evidence against David. Rather, the text shows that the murderous Rimmon brothers were driven more by greed and ambition (which was rife among all the men mentioned in the concluding section of the HDR) than by anything else. Nevertheless, the conditions that created a suitable environment for this reckless opportunism were brought about, in the first place, by the civil war that David and his forces instigated against Saul's kingdom (the aim of which, of course, was to vanquish the Saulide dynasty), and secondarily by the murder of Abner in David's capital.

The relationship between David and Michal, the daughter of Saul, is the concern of the present chapter. I will be examining this relationship first within the HDR—considering Michal's love for David and her overall investment in their relationship vis-à-vis her flagrant exploitation by the men who were closest to her, namely, Saul and David (in 1 Sam 18:17–19:1–17; 25:39–44; 2 Sam 3:12–16). Secondly, I will examine her fate in the early days of David's ascendency, giving consideration to her estrangement in David's palace (2 Sam 6). Lastly, we will study the gruesome murder of her five sons and two half-brothers in the context of a religious sacrifice (2 Sam 21:1-14).

A glance at the passages we will be studying in this chapter, as listed above, shows that we do not have "a story of Michal" *per se*. Her tragic destiny, nevertheless, is fatefully intertwined with the fortunes of David. Thus, her name surfaces at critical points in David's life story. It is only by gleaning through the story of David that we are able to pick bits and pieces of the hard life which was dealt to Michal.

## MICHAL IN THE HISTORY OF DAVID'S RISE

This section of the chapter is the most extensive, spanning three chapters in 1 Samuel and one in 2 Samuel. To make the discussion more manageable I have divided this section into three subheadings, namely, Michal: David's Lover, Trap, or Savior? (1 Sam 18:17—19:17); David as Michal's Loss (1 Sam 25:39-44); and Michal as David's Victory Trophy (2 Sam 3:12-16).

### *Michal: David's Lover, Trap, Or Savior? (1 Sam 18:17—19:17)*

1 SAMUEL 18:17—19:17

**Chapter 18**

> 17 ¹Then Saul said to David, "Behold my elder daughter, Merab; I will give her to you for a wife. Only be a valiant man for me and fight Yahweh's battles." Now Saul had said, "Let not my hand be against him, but let the hand of the Philistines be against him." But David replied, "Who am I? And who are my kinsfolk,² my

---

1. Just like the beginning of this chapter or even slightly earlier (1 Sam 17:55—18:5, 10-11), verses 17-19 are not found in some ancient translations like LXX[BWOL]. McCarter considers LXX[B] the most direct witness to the Old Greek in 1 Samuel, and he concludes that the absence of these verses in LXX[B] mean that they were not found in the Old Greek and by implication they were also absent in the Hebrew *Vorlage* behind the LXX. He acknowledges, however, that many critics have followed Wellhausen to suppose that the LXX was a later editorial shortening of the primitive text for harmonistic purposes of economy, story balance, and elimination of contradictory elements in the text. He nevertheless is not persuaded by such arguments (McCarter, *1 Samuel*, 306-7).

2. Driver notes that the word חי is rare in the Hebrew (hence the appositional explanatory gloss, "my father's clan," אבי משפחת), and thus explains it from an Arabic cognate word. He believes that the word denotes "'a group of families united by blood-ties,' moving and acting together, and forming a unity smaller than the tribe, but larger than that of a single family" (Driver, *Samuel*, 153).

father's clan, that I should become the king's son-in-law?" 19 So when it was time to give Merab, Saul's daughter, to David, she was given to Adriel the Meholathite as wife.

20 Now Michal,[3] Saul's daughter, loved David; and they told Saul, and the thing was right in his eyes.[4] 21 And Saul had said, "Let me give her to him, and let her be a trap[5] to him, and let the hand of the Philistines be against him." [6]So Saul said to David, "This second time be my son-in-law today." 22 Then Saul commanded his servants,[7] "Speak to David secretly saying, 'Behold! The king delights in you, so do all his servants. Now therefore, become the king's son-in-law.'" 23 And the servants of Saul spoke these words in David's hearing. David replied, "Is it *a light matter* in your eyes to be son-in-law to the king? For I am a poor man and lightly esteemed." 24 Saul's servants reported to him saying, "According to these words has David spoken." 25 And Saul replied, "Thus shall you say to David, 'The king has no delight for dowry save a hundred foreskins of the Philistines, to be avenged of the king's enemies.'" Now Saul had thought to make David fall by the hand of the Philistines. 26 Then Saul's servants told David these words; and it was right in David's eyes[8] to become the king's son-in-law.

---

3. Smith observes that Michal's name appears in the LXX as Μελχολ and in the Syriac version as מלכיאל. "It is possible therefore that the form is contracted (or mutilated) from מכיאל" (Smith, *Samuel*, 174). This is significant because it goes to indicate the religious sentiments of Saul as he gives theophoric names to his children.

4. This phrase ישר בעיני ("right in the eyes of") or its synonym טוב בעיני ("good in the eyes of") is often used to indicate a personal preference and has the connotation of choosing one's way rather than God's way (cf. Deut 12:8; Judg 17:6; 21:25; Prov 21:2). The same expression is used later in 1 Sam 29:6, 9 and 2 Sam 3:19, 36 (cf. Num 24:1; Prov 3:4; Mal 2:17, where the reference is directly to what is pleasing to God). The emphasis is on the personal delight that a person takes in another person or thing.

5. Most modern translations use "snare" for the Hebrew מוקש (cf. ESV, NASB, KJV, and NIV). I have elected to use "trap" instead, following the nuance put forward by Driver. He points out that a snare has the idea of a noose whereas the basic idea in מוקש is that of "a trigger trap with a bait laid upon it ... Hence it is often used metaphorically of that which allures a person to destruction, as here, Ex 23:33; Dt 7:16" (Driver, *Samuel*, 153).

6. The entire sentence is lacking in LXX[OLW] manuscripts.

7. Though the MT *Ketiv* has the singular (עבדו, "his servant"), its *Qere*, along with many medieval manuscripts and the ancient versions, has the plural form. Besides, the imperatival verbal form has the plural masculine form, and subsequent references to this referent are all in the plural form (cf. vv. 23, 24, 26); hence we translate it here also as plural.

8. See my comments in footnote 4 above.

So while the appointed days were not yet fulfilled,[9] 27 David arose and went, he and his troops, and smote the Philistines, two hundred men.[10] David brought their foreskins: They stacked[11] them for the king, in order *for David* to become the king's son-in-law; and Saul gave to him Michal, his daughter, for a wife. 28 Saul saw and realized that Yahweh was with David and that Michal, Saul's daughter,[12] loved him. 29 Saul continued still to be afraid of David; so Saul was David's enemy perpetually.

30 Now the lords of the Philistines marched forth *for battle*; whenever they marched forth, David succeeded more than all of Saul's servants; and his name was highly esteemed.

## Chapter 19

1 Saul told Jonathan his son and all his servants to kill David. Now Jonathan Saul's son delighted exceedingly in David. 2 Jonathan told David, saying, "Saul, my father, is seeking to kill you. Now therefore, be on your guard in the morning. Sit in a secret place and hide. 3 I will go forth, and stand by my father's hand in the field where you are and I will speak to my father concerning you; and I will see the outcome and report it to you.

---

9. LXX[BOL] manuscripts do not contain this clause.

10. Many ancient translations (LXX, Syriac, Targumim, and Latin) have 100 here instead of 200. This seems to be more harmonistic in view of 1 Sam 18:25; and 2 Sam 3:14. Josephus, because of his context in the Roman world, where circumcision was considered a barbaric act, had changed this dowry to 600 heads of the Philistines (Josephus, *A.J.* 6.10.2–3 [201–3]).

11. The verb used here, וַיְמַלְאוּם ("they filled them"; piel, waw-consecutive, masculine plural with masculine plural pronominal suffix), is plural in meaning, though its focus obviously is David, in whose behalf the action was being executed. I understand this to mean that David's lieutenants carried out the stacking of the foreskins before Saul for David. This is very similar to other such odd services David's retainers carried out for him with regard to the matters of both the Amalekite and the Rimmon brothers (2 Sam 1:15; 4:12). In this verse this difficult construction aims to vividly paint for the reader the grotesque picture of David's retainers counting the Philistine foreskins and stacking them up before Saul. This is what the modern English translations miss in their attempt to smooth out the difficult phrase by adding a different verb of their own (for "to give") and changing the original verb into a noun (cf. "they gave them in full number to the king," NASB; "which were given in full number to the king," KJV; "presented the full number to the king," NIV; the ESV even goes so far afield as to render it in the passive voice, when the piel stem has a very strong active voice, "which were given in full number to the king").

12. LXX manuscripts have καὶ πᾶς Ισραηλ ("and all Israel"), while LXX[L] largely agrees with the MT.

## David and Michal

4 So Jonathan spoke well to his father about David. He said, "Let not the king sin against his servant, against David, for he has not sinned against you; indeed, his work *has been* exceedingly beneficial to you. 5 He hazarded his life, and smote the Philistine, and Yahweh wrought a great deliverance for all Israel. You saw it and celebrated. Why, then, will you sin against innocent blood? 6 Saul hearkened to the voice of Jonathan. So Saul swore, "By the Living Yahweh he will not be killed.[13]" 7 Then Jonathan called David, and Jonathan told him all these words. And Jonathan brought David to Saul; and he was before him as previously.[14]

8 The war persisted, so David marched forth and fought against the Philistines; and he smote them with a great slaughter, and they fled before him. 9 Now the evil spirit of Yahweh was upon Saul while he was sitting in his house with his spear in his hand and David was making music with his[15] hand. 10 Then Saul sought to pin David to the wall with the spear; however, David broke away from Saul's presence. The spear struck the wall, but David fled and escaped that[16] night.

11 Now Saul sent messengers to David's house to guard him and to kill him by the morning. Nevertheless, Michal told David saying, "If you do not escape with your soul this night, tomorrow you will be killed." 12 Then Michal lowered David through a window;[17] and he walked away; he fled; and he escaped. 13 Then Michal took an idol, and placed it on[18] the bed, while she placed a quilt of goat's hair at its head, she covered it with a garment. 14 Saul sent messengers to take David away; but she said, "He is sick."

---

13. The MT has a hofal stem (יומת), which possesses a passive twist to the causative element of the stem, while two medieval manuscripts have qal stem. The difference ultimately does not have much implication for meaning.

14. Driver notes that in this verse alone, Jonathan's name is mentioned three times. This, he suggests, "shows the desire of the author (or perhaps the desire of a scribe) to call especial attention to Jonathan's nobility of character" (Driver, *Samuel*, 177).

15. Here we are following the overwhelming witnesses that include this possessive pronominal element. Examples include many medieval Hebrew manuscripts that have בידו ("his hand"), many LXX medieval manuscripts that have ταις χερσιν αυτους ("his hand"), and the Syraic version that also has the third person pronominal suffix.

16. The MT has הוא; the normal form is that contained in many medieval manuscripts, i.e., ההוא.

17. The MT has a determinative ה prefix; however, in English it is better to translate it as non-determinative, since we do not have an antecedent reference to the window.

18. The Targumic rendition על ("on," or "upon") is here preferred to the MT's אל (which lit. means "to," or "toward").

> 15 Saul sent messengers to see David saying, "Bring him upon the bed to me, that he might be killed." 16 The messengers arrived: and behold—an idol upon the bed with the quilt of goat's hair upon its head! 17 The Saul said to Michal, "Why have you thus deceived me, and sent away my enemy, and he has escaped?" Michal replied Saul, "He had said to me, 'Send me away. Why should I kill you?'" 18 But David fled and escaped and came to Samuel, to Ramah; and he reported to him everything which Saul had done to him. And he went, he and Samuel, and dwelt in Naioth.[19]

The interactions between David on the one hand and Saul and his house on the other are enmeshed in complexes of maneuverings that display intriguing and unfathomable binary operations of power and perfidy, appeal and peril, altruism and ambiguity. First Samuel 17–19 manifests these trends in a multiplicity of ways and levels. For example, David's altruism in confronting the Philistine giant who had defied the armies of Yahweh Sabaoth is hailed by all who are familiar with the narrative (1 Sam 17:36–37, 45–47). Yet the keen reader does not fail to notice the ambiguity ensconced in the text with David's repeated question as to what will be done to the person who defeats the giant (1 Sam 17:25–30). Similarly, we are told that Saul and his entire household were enamored by David's appeal (1 Sam 16:22; 18:1, 3, 5, 16, 20, 22; 20:17). Yet there was a lurking peril for both David and Saul: for David because Saul would attempt to entrap him through the former's involvement with the latter's house (1 Sam 18:10, 21; 19:10), while David's rise to prominence within Saul's house spelled doom for that house (1 Sam 20:31; 2 Sam 6:21). The Samuel narrative is so replete with intrigues, power plays and treachery that I forbear recounting them here (refer to chapter three above for some aspect of this).

This entire intertwined web of relations is skillfully woven around our passage (1 Sam 18:17—19:18) in an interesting chiasm that begins at the end of chapter 17 and goes into chapter 20 (see the chiastic structure below). Each item in the first part of the chiastic structure finds its direct counterpart (often the opposite, or the intensified form of the same phenomenon) in the second part of the chiasm.[20]

---

19. We are following the *Qere* (בניות) rather than the *Ketiv* (בניית); cf. 1 Sam 20:1.

20. Notice that all the actions recorded in the first half of the chiastic structure receive some form of intensification in the second. These are demonstrated as follows: (1) while the interaction of Jonathan with David in A is brief, that reported in A' is elaborate; (2) whereas the praise singing of the women celebrating the victory over the

A  Saul and a lieutenant seek after David while Jonathan bonds with David (17:55–18:4)
  B  Women's action stirs up jealous rage in Saul against David (18:6-9)
    C  Saul attempts to kill David but David escapes (18:9-11)
      D  Saul dreads David for Yahweh is with him (18:12-15)
        E  Saul's subjects love David (18:16)
          F  Saul promises Merab to David but gives her to another man (18:17-19)
          F'  Michal loves David but Saul sees it as an opportunity to entrap David (18:20-21)
        E'  Saul's servants love David (18:22, cf. 18:5)
      D'  Saul dreads David for Yahweh is with him (18:28-29)
    C'  Saul attempts to kill David but David escapes (19:1-10)
  B'  A woman's action saves David from Saul's jealous rage (19:11-18)
A'  Saul and lieutenants seek for David while Jonathan bonds with David (19:19-20:23)

The outer boundaries of the chiasm consist of the interaction between Saul and his retainers on the one hand and David and Jonathan on the other. Saul and his lieutenant (Abner) seek David to honor him; secondly, Saul and his unnamed servants seek David to kill him (A, A').

---

Philistines aroused passionate hatred in Saul enough for him to seek to kill David (B), it was Saul's own daughter's (i.e., a woman's) witty action that delivered David from certain death (B'); (3) in C Saul covertly (in the secrecy of his palace) makes one attempt to kill David, however in C' there are three more public murder attempts on David's life from all of which he escapes largely with the help of Saul's children; (4) in D Saul's fear of David stems from Yahweh's presence with David, whereas in D' Saul's fear of David is exacerbated by his daughter's (Michal's) love for David in addition to Yahweh's presence with the latter; (5) in E Saul's subjects (Israel and Judah at large) love David, however, in E' it is Saul himself who acknowledges the love of his inner caucus for David; and (6) lastly, in F Saul promised Merab to David, but no one knows where Merab's loyalties would have been, whether with her father or with her husband had she married David, but the indication that Michal loved David (F') clearly showed where her allegiance would be.

However, in both instances the narrator skips over David's interaction with those seeking him (even in first instance where David was found and brought to Saul there is no account of their interaction). Yet there is a detailed account of his bonding with Jonathan, and in both cases that bonding works to David's advantage. In the next layer, after the outer boundaries, we find, first of all, the women's celebratory praise song stirs up Saul's jealous rage against David and spurs him to seek to kill David, while in its counterpart in the second half of the chiasm Michal's wits and scheming delivered David from certain death (B, and B'). In the next concentric layers Saul makes several attempts to kill David, but on each occasion David escapes unscathed (C, and C'). Saul's unsuccessful attempts on David's life are either succeeded (D) or preceded (D') by his dread of David. Before we reach the core of the chiasm, we find disclosures of the love that Saul's subordinates (both Israel at large—Judah inclusive—and Saul's immediate retinue of staff) had for David (E, and E'). Walter Brueggemann notes that the word "love" as used in this chapter has a special rhetorical import beyond just a personal attachment; it also includes the idea of public commitment.[21] What is interesting about this is that no such affection has been reported as having been shown toward Saul. Thus, the text possibly insinuates that the divided loyalty of both Saul's subjects and his court officials was becoming apparent to even Saul himself.

At the hub of the chiasm, the three pairs of complexes operative in the narrative come together in the persons of Saul, Merab, Michal, and David (F, and F'). We can characterize Merab as an agent (no word, thought, or action of hers is recorded); we are not told what she felt about either David or Adriel. She was a woman of her times who moved at the behest of her man (whether it was her father or husband). Michal, on the other hand, is more than an agent. Perhaps we can say she is a flat character, as there is no full development of her complex personality at this point, indeed, in the whole narrative. She is shown to have lived ahead of her times: she is portrayed as one woman who would not fold her arms and let others determine her fate. Thus, she tried, albeit in futility, to take her destiny into her own hands; as the story of David unfolds, she is shown to be racing against the ineluctable, which makes her story tragic. Yet her bane (and indeed, that of the house of Saul) was the love

---

21. Brueggemann, *First and Second Samuel*, 140. For a different perspective on this see Miscall, *Old Testament Narrative*, 84.

she (and her brother Jonathan) had and demonstrated for David, on which account she who was meant to be a trap for David became his escape route.

The report that Michal loved David (1 Sam 18:20) is very remarkable, as she is the only woman in the entire Hebrew Bible of whom it is said that she loved a man.[22] The tragic twist in the narrative is the reaction of the two key men in her life, each of them viewing her love as an opportunity to advance his political ends. The interplay of this game of wits between Saul and David is crafted in an interesting chiasm in this unit that has Michal's love for David (the only constant in the equation) at the outer frames of the chiastic structure (A and A').[23] The next concentric layer contains the opposing perspectives of Saul (B) and David (B'), with each viewing the matter at hand as being to his own advantage. Thus, for each of them, it is reported that the matter was right in his eyes. Enclosing the inner core of the chiasm is Saul's determined purpose to have David die at the hand of the Philistines (C, and C'). The inner core itself consists of the maneuvering messages the duo sent back and forth to each other (D).

A   Michal's love for David reported (18:20a)
    B   The thing was right in Saul's eyes (18:20b)
        C   Saul contrived to have David die at the Philistines' hands (18:21)
            D   Saul's servants convey messages back and forth between Saul and David (18:22–25a)
        C'   Saul contrived to have David die at the Philistines' hands (18:25b)
    B'   The thing was right in David's eyes (18:26–27)
A'   Michal's love for David reported (18:28)

---

22. See Sakenfeld, *Just Wives?*, 79.

23. David Toshio Tsumura, while observing how Michal's love for David forms an inclusio around this text, writes, "Once again, Saul's strategy has backfired. Instead of killing David, his attempt has given David honor in the eyes of all the people as the king's son-in-law (as in 22:14), has given him someone who will protect him against Saul (19:11–17), and has strengthened his claim as Saul's successor (2 Sam 3:13–16)" (Tsumura, *The First Book of Samuel*, 488).

Saul, we are told, saw Michal's love for David as an opportunity to set up a trap for David.[24] David, on the other hand, took it as a chance to elevate his social and political standing to the coveted status of the king's son-in-law.[25] The absence of the mention of any reciprocal love David had for Michal sets in bold relief his underhanded dealings with Saul's house and political motivation for getting into the marriage. This implication helps to unveil how David took advantage of a sincere and unsuspecting Saulide within Saul's lifetime and reign.[26] The author's word

---

24. In his discussion of what the trap would have meant Bergen suggests, "As Saul envisioned it, David would be facing a double threat: 'the hand of the Philistines' (v. 21) and Michal herself, who would be a 'snare to him.' Michal could be a snare in two ways: first she could motivate David to place his life at extreme risk in battle with the Philistines; second, she could corrupt David spiritually" (Bergen, *1, 2 Samuel*, 204). While his first suggestion of what the trap was is on target, nothing could be farther from the truth than his second suggestion. Even the narrator, with his anti-Saul stance, does not portray Saul as a religious pervert (cf. 1 Sam 13:8–12; 20:24–26; 28:6–9; 2 Sam 21:2). To the contrary, Saul is shown to be a Yahwistic loyalist. It is even less likely that Saul would have seen himself or anyone in his house as a religiously perverse instrument for the spiritual corruption of anyone in Israel.

From my explanation of the Hebrew term for trap (מוֹקֵשׁ) in footnote 6 above, it is apparent that Bergen's error comes from his rendering it as "snare." When understood properly as trap, then the accent falls on Michal being a bait that allures David into his death either at hands of the Philistines, or, as events will show in Saul's attempted vigil to slay David, at the hands of Saul's retainers (in the worst-case scenario). From the account of the narrative it is clear that David was living within the precincts of Saul's property—perhaps it may have been part of the conditions for his marrying Michal.

25. The deafening silence of the narrator on David's love for Michal speaks volumes to the political motivation of his marriage to her. Friedmann comments, "The biblical text does not say that David loved Michal but that the offer originated with Saul and that considerable persuasion was needed until David agreed. Equally clearly, David was not forced into the marriage. His standing enabled him to refuse Merab, though he was willing to marry Michal. The text indicates that he saw advantage in marrying into the king's family, rather than any love for his bride-to-be" (Friedmann, *To Kill and Take Possession*, 275). While agreeing with Friedmann that David's marriage to Michal was a grasping after political advantage, I fail to see the narrator as making any statement about considerable persuasion dealt to David to get into the marriage. Rather, by relating how messages were sent back and forth between Saul and David, the narrator lays bare before the reader the shrewd scheming between these two men.

26. Lawton paints a lucid picture of David's duplicitous dealings with Saul's house by drawing attention to the parallels between the David-Merab-Michal narrative and that of Jacob-Leah-Rachel in Genesis. He writes, "The story parallels in some ways the other biblical account of an elder and a younger sister offered in marriage, the story of Leah and Rachel in Genesis 29. Why the parallel? Why should the 'author' want the reader to think about Jacob, Leah, and Rachel? Is there, in fact, a parallel? After all, Jacob loves Rachel. But that is the point. Aware of the parallel, the reader expects to learn

choice and pragmatic use of repetition unveils David's machinations. On this note, David's pretended reluctance on account of his unworthiness to be the king's son-in-law (התחתן, 1 Sam 18:23a) contrasts sharply with the alacrity with which he met the king's demanded bloody bride-price in order to be the king's son-in-law (להתחתן, 1 Sam 18:27). The author also employs contrasting viewpoints in his portrait of David's character. Compare David's pretentious claim to being lightly esteemed (1 Sam 18:23b) with the renown and high esteem he enjoyed both in Israel and beyond (1 Sam 18:5–7, 30; 21:11). Such a depiction can be read as illustrative of either David's humility or his dissimulation.

The love that all who were around Saul (his servants, his crown prince, and his daughter) seemed to have had for David made Saul and his whole house so transparent to David that it is hard to imagine that David did not have access to the most secret council in the palace. Thus Saul's intention to allure David into marriage with one of his daughters as a trap for his elimination may not have been a secret to David. This may have informed his refusal to marry Merab; seeing that she was a woman of her times, it would have been a lot easier for her father to have influence over her and so get David killed. Since he also obviously loved the opportunity to ascend to the position of the king's son-in-law, he still cherished the idea of marrying a Saulide. Michal's assertion of independence coupled with her naïve love for David made it more palatable for David to accede to marrying her than Merab. Her love and independent disposition made it possible and easy for her to switch her loyalty from her father to her husband. This created the possibility for David to have his cake and eat it too (become the king's son-in-law and yet not be killed).

Thus, Michal, whom her father had hoped would be the occasion for David's fall, became the channel of his escape. This again relates to her passion for independence, a desire to take her destiny in her hands: she would not sit idly by and lose her husband through the murderous schemes of her father. Yet fate was not on her side: dead or alive, David was a loss to her anyway. Michal's role in David's escape is better appreciated when seen in the context of the Saul's attempts on David's life on four occasions in 1 Sam 18–19. Saul increasingly intensified

---

that David 'loves' Michal. And yet that is what the reader does not hear ... Mentioning Merob sets up a parallel which underscores what David lacks in his relationship with Michal: love." (Lawton, "1 Samuel 18: David, Merab and Michal," 423–25).

his efforts with each attempt, while David's chances of escape became progressively narrower. In 1 Sam 18:10–11, Saul tried to strike David with his spear but missed. As a follow up on this first attempt he then met with his kitchen cabinet, in David's absence, to plot David's demise. But Saul's son Jonathan came to the rescue of David through persuasive rhetoric (1 Sam 19:1–6). The third attempt on David's life, like the first, is an incident in which Saul, though acting alone, was in a position of advantage (with spear in hand) and David in a position of weakness (playing a musical instrument: the text stresses that David was making music with his hand, 1 Sam 19:9). In addition, it appears as if while the first incident happened in the daytime, the third happened at night (with all the difficulties that would come with a night flight) (1 Sam 19:9–10). In the fourth attempt, like the second, Saul acts in concert with others (excluding Jonathan from the plot this time around; cf. 1 Sam 20:1–2), but this time, rather than merely deliberate, he takes the decisive action to first post a sentinel at David's house to prevent his escape (1 Sam 19:11). David was hemmed in; there was no way of escape.

Thus far the ploy of the trap has worked. Then love threw a wrench into Saul's works. Michal's swift action checkmated Saul's move (1 Sam 19:11–17). When she received intelligence concerning the advance of Saul retainers, she promptly swung into action. Warning David of the impending danger (v. 11), she let him out through a window (v. 12), devised a decoy to allow David time to escape (v. 13–16), and when her ruse was discovered, she instantly invents a cover-up (v. 17).[27] As one reads the story, one cannot miss being struck by the sense of irony and ambiguity engrained therein. Michal loved David, but her love is never reciprocated. At David's escape Michal spoke to David, but we hear no word from David. As the story progresses, David would have time to confer with Jonathan on two separate occasions (1 Sam 20:1–42; 23:16–18), but would not seek Michal out.[28] Michal was very disposable to David,

---

27. David Jobling suspects that the plausibility of Michal's concocted Davidic threat might have arisen from David's lackluster relationship with Michal even when they were together. He writes, "When she invents David's threat to kill her (v. 17) she obviously does so to get herself out of a jam. Nonetheless, Saul accepts the idea as plausible. If David had gone about the court behaving like an ecstatic newlywed would Saul have been prepared to believe that David would threaten Michal's life under any circumstances? The story Michal invents has to be one that she thinks Saul will find believable, and this is the story she chooses" (Jobling, *1 Samuel*, 152).

28. My inference from all this is that if David had wanted Michal, he would have

unfortunately. While David had gained the title of the king's son-in-law and with that closer access to the throne, he was now a loss to Michal, who had fought losing him to death.

At this juncture we make some observations on matters of literary interest in this section of the narrative. The first relates to the pragmatic use of repetition (with respect to the words "escape," מלט, and "send," שלח). "Escape" is used by the narrator (1 Sam 19:10, 12), Michal (1 Sam 19:11), and Saul (1 Sam 19:17), and each time with the increasing sense of finality. Observe that the first time David escaped from Saul's spear the author only uses the word "fled," נוס (1 Sam 18:11)—he fled only from Saul's presence. There is no finality in his escape or separation from Saul. However, in 1 Sam 19:10, the narrator uses both "fled" (נוּס, a synonym of ברח) and "escape" (מלט) with no such limiting phrase as "from Saul's presence." This means the increasing distance and the finality of separation are being made more palpable. In Michal's warning to David she again used the word "escape" (v. 11) and the accompanying risk of death if escape is not embarked upon requires us to see this as the major point of severance with the palace and hence the expectation that David should have arranged to get Michal out as well. After David was hurled out of the window, the narrator piles up verbs: "walked" off, "fled," and "escaped." This invokes vivid imageries of David scurrying away from the palace wall on tiptoe, then sprinting away when he has gained some good yardage, and finally being lost in the night's darkness and the shadows of the woody hills of Israel's hill country. Lastly, the despondency of Saul's question (v. 17) drives home the finality of David's escape.

In all this, the emphasis falls squarely on Michal's role in David's escape. We observe how the narrator's double use of מלט in the narration (vv. 10 and 12) forms an inclusio around both Michal's use of the same word in her speech to David and her role in letting him down through the window. If we consider its first use in this scene by the narrator (v. 10) and the last use in Saul's speech (v. 17), we again see both uses forming an inclusio around Michal's flurry of activities to secure David's safe passage out of the tight corner into which he had been boxed. Herein lies the reason for the befuddlement and wonder as to why David would expurgate from his life and memory someone who had risked so much for him as soon as he was out in safe quarters.

---

sent people to ferret her out of the palace, or even Jonathan would have arranged safe passage for her.

Similarly, we observe the ironic employment of the word for "send," שלח, which also can mean to "let go," or "set free"[29] and therefore can also be rendered as "to release." While Saul sent his retainers to seize David (vv. 11, 14–15), Michal released him (vv. 11, 17). The ironic twist to the story arises because Michal, the supposed trap in whose firm grip David was to remain, instead of tightening her grip on David (the prey) for Saul's retainers to pounce on him like the Philistines did to Samson (cf. Judg 16:8–21), released him (שלח) and he indeed escaped (מלט).[30]

Furthermore, the author's use of the literary motif of "the woman at the window" both in the earlier part of the HDR (1 Sam 19:12) and at the end of the HDR (or more properly, at the beginning of the SN, cf. 2 Sam 6:16) is significant.[31] At the beginning of their narrative David

---

29. BDB, 1019.

30. There are narrative echoes from the book of Judges here. First, the fact that David was married to Michal but remained within the precincts of Saul's property corresponds to Samson's first Philistine betrothed being married to Samson's best man but still remaining in her father's house (Judg 15:1). Second, Saul's use of his daughters as bait for David corresponds to the Philistines use of Delilah as a trap for Samson (Judg 16:5). Third, Saul's sentry being sent to catch David and kill him by morning corresponds to the same kind of sentinel posted by the Philistines to catch Samson (Judg 16:1–2). With all the similarities there are also striking differences and that is where the rhetorical force lies. By making Saul's tactics similar to those of the Philistines the narrator makes him out to be another Philistine fighting David, and as such he like them was guaranteed to lose to David. On the other hand, David's comparison with Samson is also striking. Samson loved those who hated him, while David showed no love to (and by implication, hated) those who loved him (cf. 2 Sam 19:5–6). And like Samson, David is Yahweh's instrument, though an imperfect one, for Israel's deliverance from the Philistines.

31. The literary motif of the woman at the window is commonly attested in the ancient Near East (cf. King, *Amos, Hosea, Micah*, 100, 146–48; and Cartledge, *1 & 2 Samuel*, 439). In biblical narrative, standing at the window is often ominous of impending ill-fate. Examples of women who stood at the window in biblical literature as they faced an uncertain but perilous time include Rahab (Josh 2:15–21), who faced the danger of her people being annihilated by the Israelites. Like Michal, she let down through a window those who would decimate her people. And like Michal she was spared alive. Unlike Rahab, Michal's immediate family was decimated, but her people faced no danger of extinction, whereas for Rahab her immediate family was spared, but her people perished. Similarly, the mother of Sisera (Judg 5:28) faced the likelihood that her son may have perished in the conflict with Israel. Jezebel (2 Kgs 9:32) faced the danger of dying with her family in Jehu's revolt. The use of this motif on two occasions with respect to Michal, hints at the ill-fate that awaits her.

There are biblical examples of men in danger at the window as well, though theirs may not be as drastic or as tragic as those of the women. Examples include Noah (Gen 8:6), who faced the danger of the receding water of the flood; Abimelech (Gen 26:8),

exited Michal's life with her standing at the window (1 Sam 19:11–12). At the end of the story of their togetherness Michal exited David's narrative at a window scene as well (2 Sam 6:16). David remained outside as if to show how since his exit through the window the previous time, he had not come back into Michal's life. Michal ventured to meet David outside, but they would never be seen retiring to her bedchamber together.[32] The intervening years between the first window and the second window episodes had brought about radical transformation in Michal: from a Michal once oozing with such affection for David that she could not endure to see any harm come to him, even defying her own father, thereby jeopardizing her father's house, to a Michal cold with such resentment that she had nothing for David but cynicism. We shall return to this theme later; in the meantime we turn to consider what Michal lost when she released David.

---

who faced the danger that he and his subjects would be plagued for taking Rebecca to be wife (cf. Gen 12:17; 20:17–18); King Joash before Elisha (2 Kgs 13:17), who faced the threat of the Arameans; the wise man of Proverbs (Prov 7:6), who faced the danger of corruption from the wayward wife out on the loose; and Euthycus (Acts 20:9), who faced physical death out of his own recklessness. Of all the biblical characters facing precarious predicaments, the window portends good fortune, namely the escape from death, for only two men—David and Saul of Tarsus. Paul, also a Benjaminite like King Saul, faced certain death in Damascus if he were found (Acts 11:33). He like David (unlike all the other biblical characters) found the window as an instrument of deliverance, not of death. Both men did nothing but let themselves be lowered down (or be released) through the window. It is interesting that both men occupy very central positions in the New and Old covenants respectively. Both men were murderers. Both men did not deserve the kind of roles they have played in the biblical narrative. Both men received extraordinary grace. Thus both men became great instruments in God's hands out of sovereign elective grace.

32. Jobling describing how Michal helped David escape from Saul, writes: "The means she uses is to 'let David down through the window,' that is, to enable his passage from inside to outside, from the dangerous confinement of Saul's court to his life as a separate agent. The symbolic connection to the birth process is easy to see" (Jobling, *1 Samuel*, 229; Jobling is here borrowing from Exum, *Fragmented Women*, 47). When "the woman at the window" motif is construed in this way, it reinforces the fact that just as a child once birthed never returns to a mother's womb, David was never again going to return into the bosom of Michal.

## Michal Loses David (1 Sam 25:39–44)

### 1 SAMUEL 25:39–44

> 39 Now, David heard that Nabal died. He said, "Blessed be Yahweh who pleaded my case, my reproach from the hand of Nabal, but his servant he has withheld from evil. Indeed, the evil of Nabal Yahweh has returned upon his head."
>
> Then David sent and he spoke to Abigail to take her to himself for a wife. 40 David's servants came to Abigail, to Carmel; and they spoke to her saying, "David sent us to you, to take you to him for a wife." 41 Then she arose and bowed her face to the ground and said, "Behold your handmaid, for a servant, to wash the feet of the servants of my lord." 42 So Abigail hastened and arose and mounted upon a donkey, with the five maidens who attended her,[33] and she went after David's messengers; and she became a wife to him. 43 David had taken Ahinoam from Jezreel,[34] and the two of them became wives to him.
>
> 44 Now Saul gave Michal, his daughter, David's wife, to Palti son of Laish who is from Gallim.[35]

David's wilderness wandering years had passed on with no mention of Michal, his wife who loved him and rescued him from imminent death. Her mention resurfaces only as an appendage to the story of David's burgeoning harem. After the narration of how David had acquired Abigail as his wife (1 Sam 25:1–42), the narrator, in two consecutive

---

33. A first reading of this clause would seem as if Abigail and her five maidens rode on one donkey. This is not the case. Driver explains, "לרגלה is not quite the same as ברגלי v. 27; the ל is the so-called ל of norm, 'going *according to* her *foot*,' i.e. *guided by her foot*=attending to her. Comp. for this sense of לרגל Gen 30:30 hath blessed thee לרגלי *at my foot*=whithersoever I turned (RV.); 33:14 and I will lead on softly לרגל המלאכה *according to the pace* of the cattle (*Lex.*516b)" (Driver, *Samuel*, 204). Smith simply writes that Abigail and her maids "did not ride—she rode and they *walked by her side*" (Smith, *Samuel*, 229).

34. Driver notes, "Ahino'am is mentioned before Abigail in 27:2; 30:5; she was also the mother of David's firstborn, Amnon (II, 3:2); so probably he married her shortly before Abigail, as the Heb. here permits (not ויקח ד, but . . . ואת אחינעם לקח)." (Driver, *Samuel*, 204)

35. Smith makes two very interesting observations here: first, that the narrator does not indict Saul for resuming responsibility over his daughter; two, that the only other Gallim mentioned in the Bible (Isa 10:30) is apparently located in Benjamin (Smith, *Samuel*, 229). Driver similarly notes, "The situation of Gallim is not known; but it was plainly (Isa 10:30) a little N. of Jerusalem" (Driver, *Samuel*, 204). Driver also writes, "V. 44 hints at the reason why David took now these two wives; he had been deprived of Michal (18:27)" (ibid., 204).

*waw*-disjunctive sentences, offers snippets about two of David's other wives, Ahinoam and Michal (1 Sam 25:43–44). Verse 43 reveals that prior to his "taking" of Abigail, David had previously taken Ahinoam of Jezreel in marriage.

Because of the *we-X-qatal* construction found in both verses 43 and 44, John Kessler understands them both to have a pluperfect value, meaning that David's marriage to Ahinoam took place before his "taking" Abigail and that Saul's giving of Michal to Paltiel preceded David's marriage to Ahinoam.[36] For support, Kessler cites GKC, §106f.[37] This citation is not a sufficient support for Kessler's conclusion, because the use of GKC to substantiate the pluperfect value of *we-X-qatal* is problematized by GKC (§106d) assigning a simple perfect value to the same syntactical form elsewhere (cf. Gen 4:4; 7:19; Job 1:1; see also Gen 2:5, 6; 3:1; 4:5). What we need to note is that the *we-X-qatal* form primarily functions as a sign of a hiatus from the main storyline in Hebrew narrative in order to mark background information or a secondary storyline, and to accentuate a contrast between phenomena. In other words, it pragmatically serves to mark thematic discontinuity in narration.

Niccacci observes that the *we-X-qatal* form is a dependent verb form and when it is encountered, one should look for the *wayyiqtol* form upon which it depends. He outlines its twofold function in discourse grammar relative to the *wayyiqtol* text that it may precede or follow: "If it [the *wayyiqtol* form] precedes, the text shows a tense shift from foreground to background. If it follows, the tense shift is from antecedent information to degree zero, or main level of communication."[38] In our passage the *wayyiqtol* form precedes the *we-X-qatal* forms, the implication of this being that the narrator is supplying backgrounded information that is off the main storyline (which in this case is David's acquisition of Abigail). Therefore, the choice of the event time is a matter of interpretation; it is not native to the form of the construction itself. On this basis Kessler's suggestion that David married Ahinoam only after Saul had given Michal to Paltiel[39] is flawed and has no basis in the text. One may at best say that the text is ambiguous. It may be easier to accommodate the possibility that David's marriage to Abigail is subse-

---

36. Kessler, "Sexuality and Politics," 409–23.
37. Kessler, "Sexuality and Politics," 414 (footnote 24).
38. Niccacci, "Analysis of Biblical Narrative," 178.
39. Kessler, "Sexuality and Politics," 414.

quent to his marriage to Ahinoam because of the proximity of these two sentences to each other. The text gives no clue whatsoever as to which preceded which as far as the marriages of Ahinoam and Michal are concerned. The possibility that Saul may have found ground for giving Michal away to Paltiel only after David had taken other wives, therefore, should not be left out of the equation. Besides, Michal's ruse (that David threatened to kill her, if she did not let him go) would have been enough proof to any father of a husband's hatred for his wife.

The narration of David's "taking" of Abigail raises a lot of questions on his conduct during his days as the leader of a roving rebel band, if not his character as whole. In Israel, as was the case in other cultures of the ANE, a woman was never just free to act at will: she was always either under her father as a youngster or under her husband or his kinsfolk as a married woman (see Num 30:4–17 [ET 3–16]; cf. Num 5:29–30). Thus, no one could just go take a woman as a wife on the basis of mutual consent between two adults. She had to be given to the suitor either by her father with his kinsfolk (cf. Gen 24:49–52; 29:21–28; 34:11–17; Judg 14:1–20) or her husband's kinsfolk, in the case of a widow (Deut 25:5–10; Ruth 3:9–13; 4:1–11). David obviously was no kinsman of Nabal. There is no record of David negotiating either with her parents or her deceased husband's kinsfolk: he just sent his servants and they went and took her. This is an attitude typical of marauding bands in all times.

A man with such scruples would have no qualms about expurgating the memory of a former wife, for whom he showed no affection, and moving on with his life. Thus, though Michal had saved him from her father's henchmen, David remained a loss to her anyhow. David had entered into the marriage with Michal for the political advantage it offered, and once he was out of favor with Saul's court, he appears to have been done with the marriage as well. It remains for us to see how the same political motivations would lead David to pluck Michal from the home of Paltiel, where she had found comfort in the arms of a loving and caring husband, and relegate her finally to misery in what essentially amounts to imprisonment in David's palace.[40]

40. Commenting on the question of political advantage that the marriage to Saul's daughter offered David before and after Saul's death, McCarter writes, "It must also be pointed out that David's marriage to Michal, though at one level just another example of Saul's machinations turned to David's advantage, has a special significance of its own. Marriage to the king's daughter gives David a certain claim to membership in the royal house of Israel, which he will later, when already king of Judah, use to justify his suc-

## Michal as David's Victory Tribute (2 Sam 3:12–16)

2 SAMUEL 3:12–16[41]

> 12 Then Abner sent messengers to David, saying, "To whom does the land belong?" He said further, "Make a covenant with me; and behold, my hand will be with you, to turn over to you all Israel." 13 Then he replied, "It is good to me to make a covenant with you; but one thing do I require of you." He said further, "You shall not see my face, unless you bring before me Michal, Saul's daughter, when you come to see me."
> 14 Now David sent messengers to Ishbosheth, Saul's son, saying, "Give me my wife, Michal, whom I betrothed with a hundred foreskins of the Philistines." 15 So Ishbosheth sent, and took her from her husband, from Paltiel, son of Laish. 16 Her husband went along with her, weeping continually as he went, as far as Bahurim. Then Abner commanded him, "Go *back*, return *home*." So he returned.

Very surprisingly, in this scene, the narrator characterizes Michal as an agent (prop) and displays neither a word nor an action nor an emotion of hers. One wonders whether this was not the author's way of showing her powerlessness. One who otherwise would take her destiny in her hand is here bound, not just existentially but also literally—completely deprived of voice and act—and taken captive to be delivered to the usurper from the south as a tribute pledge for the north's submission and loyalty.

After Abner's heated exchange with Ishbosheth, he made conciliatory advances to David (see chapter 4 above). Now David's precondition for this alliance was the return of Michal, Saul's daughter, who was presently married to Paltiel. Tomoo Ishida has demonstrated that with the importance of the dynastic hereditary principle in the ancient Near East, it was customary for usurpers to marry a princess of the previous royal house to secure their legitimacy.[42] The HDR has relied upon di-

---

cession to the northern throne as well (cf. II Sam 3:12ff). In other words there is great political significance to this little episode, and in reporting it our narrator is looking ahead to David's assumption of kingship over Israel and the question of legitimacy that will arise. It has even been supposed that a formal rule of son-in-law succession is assumed to be in effect here" (McCarter, Jr., *I Samuel*, 318).

41. For a translation of this passage with the relevant notes, see chapter four above.

42. He shows that even in a society like Egypt where divine election was the theoretical basis of royal authority, in practice the dynastic principle of heredity still under-

vine election for the authentication of David's rise. Yet in his demand for Michal's return one sees a convergence of the ideological perspective of divine election and the praxis of legitimation through connection with royal blood. The use of marriages to solidify alliances, so common in the ANE, was not unknown in Israel (cf. 1 Kgs 3:1; 16:31; 2 Kgs 8:26). Thus, Michal served two purposes: she was a token of the northerners's submission to David's sovereignty, and at the same time she provided for David the affiliation with the previous dynasty he so much needed for his legitimation.

David's equivocation about who Michal was to him is evidence that his relationship to the Saulides as a whole was duplicitous. Indeed, his ambiguity toward the Saulides manifests itself in his discordant communications with them. In such cases, his communication with Abner (whom he treats with a patronizing and condescending attitude) reflects his true perspective on the Saulides, whereas in his address to the Saulides (who, at least in a formal sense, are his overlords) there is equivocation and concealment of his true contempt for them. In 1 Sam 26:15, while talking to Abner he refers to Saul as "your lord": David shows his true opinion of Saul—Saul is Abner's lord, not David's. He refers to Saul this way twice in this short interlocution. But in his dialogue with Saul he prevaricates, addressing Saul as "my lord" (1 Sam 26:17–19). In the same way, when talking to Abner he simply refers to Michal as "Michal, Saul's daughter"—again reflecting his true value for her—a purely utilitarian value as the king's daughter (2 Sam 3:13). But in his message to the puppet king, Ishbosheth, the same dissimulation resurfaces as he now refers to her as "my wife, Michal, whom I betrothed with a hundred foreskins of the Philistines" (2 Sam 3:14).

Many reasons motivating David's demand for the return of Michal have been proffered. J. J. von Glück, for instance, suggests that David "wished to be reunited with her perhaps because he *still* loved her and probably also to strengthen his position with the supporters of Saul's House"[43] (emphasis added). It is hard to agree with Glück, especially as he does not demonstrate where he finds David's love for Michal in the first instance, whereupon one could speak of him as *still* loving her. Glück's

---

girded all succession. So strong was the hereditary principle that it was not uncommon for a usurper to marry his half-sister (Ishida, *The Royal Dynasties in Ancient Israel*, 12–19, and 73).

43. Glück, "Merab or Michal?" 72–81.

viewpoint, I believe, comes more from a pietistic reading of David by the church and the synagogue than from the text. Besides the main reason of political legitimation advanced above, I am inclined to agree with Daniel Friedmann, who writes, "One explanation, deriving from the text, is that he considered her to be 'his property,' having purchased her with the Philistine foreskins."[44] David made no appeal to anything other than what he had paid to acquire this piece of "property." The truth, however, is that there is no precedence in Israel's traditions or law providing for the return of the bride-price when a marriage fails: there was no "cash-back guarantee," contrary to Anderson's view.[45] The bride-price, instead, was a payment for the bride's virginity: since a woman's virginity could never be restored, her bride-price was also never returned even when the marriage failed. This is why a rapist had to pay the bride-price even if the victim's father would not marry her out to the rapist (Exod 22:15-16 [ET 22:16-17]; cf. Deut 22:28-29). There is also the possibility that David wanted Michal sequestered in his palace as way of ensuring that no challenge or upset to his firm grip on Israel arose from the house of Saul.[46] We will return to this theme later in the chapter.

Pertinent at this point is the need to consider the status of Michal's marriage to Paltiel and her "remarriage" to David. There is some dissonance between the two perspectives on Michal in this text: the narrator's perspective and David's perspective. From the narrator's perspective Michal was Paltiel's wife (vv. 15, 16), but in some way David claimed that she was his own wife. The guide to whose is the right position here is the lack of consistency in David's perspective: on the one hand Michal was only Saul's daughter, and on the other she was "my wife." The absence of a unified position in David's locutions raises a cloud of doubt over the authenticity of his claim.

44. Friedmann, To Kill and Take Possession, 162-63.

45. Anderson, *2 Samuel*, 58. Firth also erroneously harps upon this issue of the dowry David paid to question the legality of Michal's Marriage to Paltiel and dismisses the relevance of Deut 24:1-4 this matter without even engaging the text (*1 & 2 Samuel*, 272, 348).

46. Friedmann on this writes, "But David may have had another motive, connected to his ambition to eradicate Saul's dynasty. He wanted to prevent Michal from bearing children to Palti son of Laish and preferred to have her in his harem, under his watchful eye. Michal had no children. Perhaps she was barren, but it is also possible that David had no intimate relations with her because he did not want her to bear children . . . Michal remained childless, alone and abandoned in David's court" (Friedmann, *To Kill and Take Possession*, 163).

Approaching the matter with a legal slant, Zafrira Ben-Barak gives detailed consideration to the laws of Eshunna, Babylon, and Assyria regarding the phenomenon of the missing husband, who may have been taken captive to a foreign land during a siege, had gone on a voyage abroad, or had gone hunting and never returned and was never heard from for an extended time period. In all these three cases the wife was free to legally remarry. However, upon the return of her first husband, her second marriage was immediately and incontestably invalided, and she would be returned to her first husband.[47] Ben-Barak, then, concludes that the "comparison of the Mesopotamian law and the biblical narrative thus shows that identical principles were involved. We may therefore conclude that the same practice that was widespread in Mesopotamia was known and followed in Israel, at least at the beginning of the monarchic period."[48] However, this position assumes David's demand to be the norm on the basis of what was obtainable in Mesopotamia without any anchorage in any other part of the traditions of Israel. Although I shall be returning to this issue and giving particular attention to Deut 24:1–4 later in chapter 6, suffice to mention at this point that this passage only highlights the fact that the people were divorcing their wives without the formality that should go with it. Therefore, to argue, as do Anderson (who leans heavily of on Ben-Barak's work) and Friedmann that because David did not serve Michal formal divorce papers they were not divorced only begs the question.[49]

Rather than go to Mesopotamian culture to understand this text, paying attention to the DtrH will provide the needed clues to unraveling this enigma. The DtrH clearly shows that paramount on the mind of the final redactors of these documents, like their Early Iron Age counterparts, was the impact of the cultures of the surrounding nations. Thus, DtrH shows that in his pre-conquest final address Moses had warned the people against intermingling with the surrounding nations; Joshua initiated the first failure by enacting a covenant with the Gibeonites; the Judges era was a massive sellout to the surrounding cultures; and in the Monarchic era Solomon entrenched the sellout (Deut 7:1–4; Josh 9:18; Judg 2:2–4, 11–14, 20–23; 3:1–6; 1 Kgs 11:1–5). Given this background, then, the parallel passage of one man's wife being married off to another

---

47. Ben-Barak, "The Legal Background," 74–90.
48. Ben-Barak, "The Legal Background," 88.
49. Anderson, *2 Samuel*, 58; and Friedmann, *To Kill and Take Possession*, 279.

on his absconding is found in Judg 15:1–2. We need to keep in mind the other parallels already highlighted above between Judges and Samuel. Just like Samson, David had absconded; and just like Samson's Philistine father-in-law, Saul concluded on that basis that David had "utterly hated her."[50] The refusal of the girl's father, coupled with Samson's failure to seek legal redress and his resort to jungle justice, does show that Samson no longer had any valid claim on that particular girl once she was married to another man;[51] hence his father-in-law offered him another of his daughters. Because the Philistines were the overlords of Israel, their culture, as the passages above does denote, would have impacted Israel much more than distant Mesopotamia. Our conclusion therefore is that David not only lacked moral ground for reclaiming Michal, he had no legal ground for it either.

When we keep in mind that in narrative, the narrator is wont to "show" rather than to "tell," Anderson's claim that the author of Samuel did not censor David for reclaiming Michal becomes opaque.[52] On the contrary, the critique of David is first hinted at in the narrator's reference to Paltiel twice as Michal's husband. Secondly, Paltiel's deep grief and open mourning for his wife in itself constitute a critique of David, who had showed no ounce of love for Michal even from the beginning of

50. As pointed out above, Saul, through the narrative echoes of themes and motifs from the book of Judges, has been cast in the mold of a Philistine.

51. It is interesting that Friedmann uses this passage in the diametrically opposite direction to argue against the validity of Michal's marriage to Paltiel (Friedmann, *To Kill and Take Possession*, 279). However, Friedman would have been consistent only if he held that the giving of Samson's wife to his best man was wrong. But as it is now, the second husband of the woman is the direct parallel of Paltiel: the two situations share quite a number of commonalities along side with differences as well.

52. After his reference to Ben-Barak's "Legal Background" Anderson concludes, "In view of this, it seems that David acted strictly within the legal rights; he had not divorced Michal nor had the equivalent of the bride-price (מהר) been returned to him. Therefore he was entitled to reclaim his wife. This may also account for the uncritical viewpoint of the editor and the passive attitude of Michal's second husband. The latter was obviously upset but he did not, apparently, raise any objections because legally no injustice had been done to him" (Anderson, *2 Samuel*, 58). It is rather surprising that Anderson fails to see how powerful David's war machinery was. So powerful it was that, as the narrative shows, even the Philistines could not withstand it. What then could one man in Israel do against David when even Abner, the strong man of Israelite polity, had capitulated to David? As we have shown above, it was with the same brute force that he could "send and take" Abigail; it was with the same powerful war machine that he overwhelmed the Hebronites and made their city his capital. Anderson, by his comments, rubs salt into the injury of a brutally victimized man.

their marriage. In addition, Paltiel's weeping for his only wife is set in the context of the list of David's many wives and hence adumbrates Nathan's critique of David's later overreaching to "take" another man's wife (2 Sam 12:1–6). The story of how David reclaimed Michal has to be read in the context of all the other stories of how David acquired his wives (only three of these are recorded). In this context, one espies the vivid picture the narrator paints of David's progressive moral degeneracy, which is invariably proportionate to the power, authority, and influence he amassed in the process of his rise to prominence. The more power he wielded, the more brazen he was in his act of "taking" over other men's wives (1 Sam 25; 2 Sam 3; and 2 Sam 11).[53]

The figure of David looms large not only in the memories of the Hebrew as inscripturated in the Hebrew Bible, but also in the traditions of the synagogue and church. One who is accustomed to a more pious reading of David (in the church and synagogue) and embarks upon a close reading of the text of Samuel cannot help but be afflicted with cognitive dissonance. It is my belief that the church has tended to either acquiesce in the face of oppression or even sided with oppressors because of this kind of one-sided reading of the biblical text without paying attention to counter-testimonies that are also constitutive of it. God, like any good parent, does not instruct his people only through positive reinforcement of the character he desires but also through the negative disaffirmation of that which he loathes. Our evaluation of the Davidic engagement with the Saulides through Deuteronomistic lenses in chapter 6 will afford us an opportunity to listen to the voice of God afresh, especially in the area of being a justice community.

---

53. On this note Kessler writes, "When one compares these three texts, a clear progression emerges. At the outset, David, a victim of Saul's murderous plots, flees for his life. He refuses to exact culturally acceptable personal vengeance. Yahweh intervenes and gives David his enemy's wife. At the midpoint, David uses his political prerogatives to deprive an individual Israelite of his only spouse, to whom he is deeply attached. At the conclusion, David, like Saul, is guilty of treachery against those who are loyal to him. It is only because of the mercy of Yahweh that he does not share the fate of Nabal or Saul" (Kessler, "Sexuality and Politics," 420–21).

## Michal at David's Triumph (2 Sam 6:1-23)

2 SAMUEL 6:1-23

1 David again gathered[54] all the warriors in[55] Israel, 30,000. 2 Then David arose and went with all the people that were with him from Baalah Judah[56]—to bring up from there the ark of God, who is called the name: The name of Yahweh Sabaoth dwelling upon its cherubim. 3 They rode the ark of God[57] upon[58] a new cart. They took it from the house of Abinadab which was on the

---

54. McCarter points out that the MT's "*wysp* is a defective spelling of *wy'sp* (*wayye'ĕsōp*), but it is vocalized *wayyōsep*." (McCarter, *II Samuel*, 162), *pace* Driver, who cites Ps 104:29, and GK. §68b. Driver also suggests that this verse "may form a sequel to 5:17-24 (in its original position: see on 5:17)." (Driver, *Samuel*, 265).

55. The Syriac and the Targumim have no prepositional prefix making ישראל ("Israel") to be in absolute-construct relationship with בחור ("warriors"). The LXX has ἐξ ("out of").

56. Driver equates Baalah Judah with Kiriath Jearim and cites 1 Chr 13:6 and Jos 15:9, 10; its other form is Kiriath Baal (Josh 15:60; 18:14). The name of Judah accompanying Baalah distinguishes it from other towns of the same name of Baal (cf. Josh 19:8—Simeon; Josh 19:44—Dan). He further writes, "The partitive was prefixed, in order to produce some sort of connexion with the preceding clause. The place must have been originally sacred to Ba'al" (Driver, *Samuel*, 266). Gnana Robinson writes similarly on the identity of Baale-Judah, "Baale-judah (2 Sam 6:2) is probably another name for Kiriath-jearim. In Josh 15:9 a place called Baalah is identified with Kiriath-jearim. In Josh 18:14 Kiriath-jearim is identified with Kiriath-baal. Kiriath simply means 'city' in the OT sense of 'settlement' or even 'village.' Baalah is feminine from of Baal. A Baal sanctuary was probably located in Kiriath-jearim, and the ark was kept in it and not in any common place. In early times the Israelites had no hesitation about using Canaanite cultic places and altars such as high places for their worship of Yahweh (cf. 1 Sam 9:14; 1 Kgs 18:19ff.)" (Robinson, *Let Us Be Like the Nations*, 180).

McCarter observes that 4QSam[a] renders it (when translated) as "to Baalah, that is, Kiriath jearim, which belongs to Judah" (Josh 15:9). He states that the MT's defective writing of miḇbaʿălê yəhûḏā[h] can be read as "'(all the people who were with him) from the lords of Judah'; but this is probably a corrupt remnant of a reading like that of 4QSam[a]. We hear of the 'lords of Judah' nowhere else, and the reading leaves the subsequent *miššām*, 'from there,' without antecedent, unless it refers back to 'from Gibeon to Gezer' in 5:25 (cf. Blenkinsopp, 1969a: 152) or, assuming an original connection with the ark narrative of I Samuel (see the COMMENT), to 'the house of Abinadab on the Hill' in 1 Sam 7:1 or 'Kiriath' in in 7:2 (Campbell 1975: 169-71)" (McCarter, *II Samuel*, 162).

57. Here and in verse 4 LXX[L] and the Targumim both retain κυριου (i.e., the equivalent of "Yahweh").

58. Lit. "toward," but many medieval manuscripts and 4QSam[a] have על ("on," "upon"). These latter make more grammatical sense, hence I have followed them in my rendition.

hill, while Uzzah and Ahio sons of Abinadab were driving the new cart. 4 They took it from the house of Abinadab which was on the hill with the ark of God, and Ahio was going in front of the ark.

5 Now David and the entire house Israel were carnivalizing[59] before Yahweh with all the instruments of cypress wood, lyres, harps, tambourines, castanets, and cymbals. 6 When they came to the threshing floor of Nacon, Uzzah reached out toward the ark of God and grabbed it because the oxen fell.[60] 7 Then the anger of Yahweh burned against Uzzah, and God smote him

---

59. I have decided to translate משחקים (√שחק, with the basic idea of to play, make sport, or carefree play) as carnivalizing because in most of the places that the word is used in the Hebrew Bible the dominant idea is that of mockery, derision, jesting, or other forms of non-serious (or even derisive) fun-making. Examples of this include (1) derisive laughter—2 Chr 30:10; Prov 29:9; Lam 1:7; Psa 52:8 [ET v. 6]; Job 30:1; Ps 37:13; Jer 48:26, 27, 39; Lam 3:14; (2) entertainment that borders on jesting—Judg 16:25, 27; Eccl 3:4; 2 Sam 2:14; Prov 26:19; and (3) music making as a form of jesting or clowning (fun-making carnival) Jer 15:17; 30:19; 31: 4; Zech 8:5; (4) the use of such carnivalizing at pagan shrines (Amos 7:9) (cf. BDB, 966). It is in this light, I believe, that the uses of the word in the Samuel narratives (1 Sam 18:7; 2 Sam 6:5, 21) should be understood as well.

I borrowed the idea of using the word *carnivalized* from Bruce Rosenstock, although I attach a meaning different from his to the way I have used the word here. I use the word with the more mundane sense of the meaning that derives first of all from the root of "carnival" as a "season or festival of merrymaking," or "an instance of merrymaking, feasting, or masquerading," or "an instance of riotous excess," or "an organized program of entertainment or exhibition" (see *Merriam-Wesbster's Collegiate Dictionary*, 174), but also secondarily from my reference above to the usage of the word שחק in the Hebrew Bible. Rosenstock employs it as jargon that refers to the phenomenon of role reversal in a fertility cult setting. For instance, he writes, "In bringing the ark and, therefore, the throne of YHWH into Jerusalem, David was enacting the divine analog of his own enthronement, and Michal points to this with her address to him as 'king of Israel.' But unlike YHWH, whose glory remains hidden, David uncovered his nakedness. Thus, Michal's taunt is precisely directed at David's pretension to bring the divine glory into Jerusalem by the very reversal of YHWH's self-concealment. Her words highlight what might be called David's play as a form of *carnivalization* . . . Michal's words make this self-carnivalization apparent by comparing the king's glory to that of the 'worthless fellows' who expose themselves" (Bruce Rosenstock, "David's Play: Fertility Rituals and the Glory of God in 2 Samuel 6," *JSOT* 31.1 (Sep 2006): 63–80 [70]. The fertility cultic implication of David's carnivalizing cannot be ruled out, but we will return to this later.

60. The basic meaning of שמט is "to let drop," or "fall" (BDB, 1030); see similar usages elsewhere in the Hebrew Bible: 2 Kgs 9:33; Ps 141:6. Even the non-literal sense (not connected with a physical fall) still retain the idea of letting go of something; cf. Deut 15:1–3; Exod 23:11; Jer 17:4. In this case the subject of the verb is the oxen, and if they fell then the cart that bore the ark would also be out of balance, hence the need to steady the ark—what Uzzah tried to do.

there on account of his error; and he died there beside the ark of God. 8 And David became angry because Yahweh had burst forth wrath against Uzzah; and he called the name of[61] that place Perez-Uzzah *and so it is called* to this day. 9 And David dreaded Yahweh that day, so he said, "How shall the ark of Yahweh come to me?" 10 And David was not willing to take the ark of Yahweh into[62] the city of David. So David turned it aside to the house of Obed-Edom the Gittite.

11 Now the ark of Yahweh dwelt in the house of Obed-Edom the Gittite for three months. And Yahweh blessed Obed-Edom and his entire house. 12 And it was reported to David saying, "Yahweh has blessed the house of Obed-Edom and all who belong to him on account of the ark of God." And David went and brought up the ark of God from the house of Obed-Edom to the city of David with pomp and pageantry. 13 When the bearers of the ark of Yahweh had taken six steps, he sacrificed a herd of cattle and a fatted calf. 14 And David was dancing *vigorously* with all his strength before Yahweh. 15 Now David and all the house of Israel were bringing up the ark of Yahweh with shouting and with trumpet sound.

16 [63]When the ark of Yahweh was entering the city of David, Michal, Saul's daughter, looked down from behind a window; and

---

61. Many medieval manuscripts insert the "the name of" here. The insertion only brings out what is implicit in the MT.

62. Many medieval manuscripts have אל ("toward," or "to") and the Syriac and Targumim have the prepositional prefix ל ("to"). I have followed these other witnesses instead of the MT's על ("upon," "on").

63. The verse begins not in the usual Hebrew narrative tense: it has והיה instead of ויהי. I have followed the witnesses of the Chronicler (1 Chr 15:29), 4QSam\ua, and the LXX (και εγενετο, the Greek equivalent of ויהי), which all have ויהי. McCarter, however, calls attention to the work of de Boer (1974), in which the latter sees the perfect-plus-*waw* construction as a feature in Samuel that is used as a means for a brief resumption of an event whose detail narration had been going on previously (McCarter, *II Samuel*, 166–67). In our case, the event being narrated is the bringing up of the ark to Jerusalem. The other verses he refers to are 1 Sam 1:12; 10:9; 17:48; 25:20.

Contrary to the above, a close study of these passages reveals a unique phenomenon but not the one that McCarter is referring to. Rather than a resumption of an earlier event, what I have observed is that at each of these points where the narrator in Samuel departs from the usual Hebrew narrative tense, he is also making a turn in (perhaps an interruption of) the narrative itself. That is to say what follows the והיה form is in some way different from what precedes it. Put differently, this unusual form functions like a *we-X-qatal* construction, to highlight a thematic discontinuity. For instance, immediately preceding 1 Sam 1:12 is the narration of Hannah's prayer, but the והיה of verse 12 introduces Eli's rude interruption of Hannah's prayer. Similarly, prior to 1 Sam 10:9 we have Samuel's instruction to Saul, but the והיה of verse 9 prefixes Saul's turn

she saw the king, David, gamboling and cavorting before Yahweh, and she disdained him in her heart. 17 And they brought the ark of Yahweh, and they placed it in its place, in the midst of the tent which David pitched for it. And David sacrificed burnt offerings and peace offerings before Yahweh. 18 When David finished offering the burnt offering and peace offerings, he blessed the people in the name of Yahweh Sabaoth. 19 Then he apportioned to all the people and all the multitude of Israel, to every man and woman, to each one cake of bread, one cake of date, and one cake of raisin. Then all the people departed, each to his house.

20 When David returned to bless his house, Michal Saul's daughter went forth to meet David. And she said, "How the king of Israel honored himself today when he uncovered himself this day to the eyes of the maids of servants: in the manner that one of the worthless fellows[64] would *dishabilledly*[65] uncover himself.[66]"

---

from Samuel to depart, with the focus turning squarely to the changed heart that Saul received. In the verse before 1 Sam 17:48 David was speaking to Goliath, but with the ויהי the narrator turns the reader's attention away from David's defiant *speech* to the *action* of the approaching giant and David's *counter-reaction*, the focus having moved from speech to action. In the same way, 1 Sam 25:20 turns the focus away from Abigail's journey to David's advance. Indeed, exactly the same ויהי construction with the same implication is found elsewhere in the Hebrew Bible as well (cf. 2 Kgs 3:15; Jer 37:11; Amos 7:2). Applied to the situation in 2 Sam 6, the ויהי in verse 16 the narrator turns the focus, albeit momentarily, from the exuberance and pageantry of the crowd of carnivalizers before the ark to the lonely daughter of Israel's first king behind the window and her pent-up feelings against David.

64. The LXX softens this to "one of the dancers" (εἰς τῶν ὀρχουμένων). This is unnecessary and obscures the scandalous manner in which David carried himself, as portrayed, certainly, in the perspective of Michal and possibly the narrator's (if our translation of שחק as "to carnivalized" is accepted, note also his gamboling and cavorting).

65. The word "dishabille" exists in English in the noun form only. However, in the French language, the source of the English word, it has verb forms as well. I have carried over the verbal form into English so as to derive an adverb corresponding to the Hebrew construction of this clause as explained in footnote 66 below.

66. The Hebrew כהגלות נגלות is a difficult construction. Smith notes, "No other case of the *inf. c.* being strengthened by the *inf. abs.* seems to occur" (Smith, *Samuel*, 272; *pace* Anderson, *2 Samuel*, 98). Others consider נגלות to be an erroneous repetition of כהגלות (cf. GKC. § 75y). However, an understanding of the general workings of the infinitive absolute and infinitive construct will lead to a different conclusion about this clause. The infinitive absolute is much more versatile, with respect to functioning as a finite verb, than the infinitive construct. The situations where it is found (excluding numerous other places where it is closely bound to a finite verb by *waw*-conjunctive) include serving as an imperative (Deut 5:12), a cohortative (1 Kgs 22:30; Isa 22:13), and a jussive (Prov 17:12). The occurrence of the infinitive absolute as a finite (perfective and non-perfective) verb in narrative texts is often in direct discourse (2 Chr 31:10; 2

21 David replied to Michal, "Before Yahweh,[67] who chose me over your father and over all his house and commanded me to be leader over Yahweh's people—over Israel, before Yahweh have I carnivalized.[68] 22 And I will yet make myself lightly esteemed more than this, and I will be base in my own eyes, but the maids of whom you have spoken, I will be honored among them."

23 Now to Michal the daughter of Saul were no children to the day of her death.

This chapter has a sub-plot that is interesting, to say the least. It has the main plot concerning the movement of the ark from Gibeonite territory to Jerusalem. The anecdotal story of the conflict between Michal and David is piggy-backed onto this main plot. Put differently, there is an embedded sub-plot (perhaps we may call it a *plotlet*[69]) about the conflict between Michal and David (undeveloped, though) stitched onto the main sub-plot of the movement of the ark.

Verses 1–2 constitute the stage of the episode; since the movement of the ark makes up the major focus of the episode, all of the initial actions of David are just the staging platform for the removal of the ark. Verses 3–5 comprise the preliminary action stage, the first steps in the ark removal, with David and all Israel carnivalizing in the procession.

---

Kgs 4:43). It is also used as a finite verb in cases of emotionally charged or animated speech (Jer 7:9; Hag 1:9). These last two uses are directly related to our verse. On the other hand, the most common use of the infinitive construct as a finite verb tends to be in result or consequence clauses (Gen 31:28; Num 20:4; 35:6; 1 Sam 19:1), or in circumstantial clauses (Gen 2:4; Num 35:19; 1 Sam 11:6), or in poetic passages. Where it is prefixed with both a *waw* and ל, the infinitive construct is used as finite verb to continue the thought of the immediately preceding finite verb (Job 34:8; Jer 9:12; Ezra 3:12) (for a further discussion of these see Waltke and O'Connor, *Biblical Hebrew Syntax*, 597–610). From the foregoing, my conclusion is that in this intriguing subordinate clause, in an emotionally charged direct discourse, lacking a finite verb but having two infinitives, the infinitive absolute functions as a finite verb in the modal sense, while the infinitive construct serves an adverbial function.

67. LXX$^A$ inserts a verb here (ὀρχήσομαι, "I will dance"). But to do this is to miss the tenseness of the situation with the almost jumbled tirade that the angry David spews out against the daughter of Saul. Likewise, LXX$^O$ adds εὐλογητὸς κύριος ("Blessed be the Lord") here. Again this seems to be an editorial addition to the original statement.

68. See footnote 59 above. The LXX again inserts καὶ ὀρχήσομαι here. It does stress the difference of perspective between David and Michal (and perhaps the narrator), but it is doubtful if it is original.

69. My own coinage using the diminutive "*let*" (as in playlet or piglet) to indicate the undeveloped character of this embedded plot. As a piglet rides piggy-back, so the plotlet is piggy-backed on this sub-plot.

The inciting moment comes in verses 6–7, where Yahweh strikes Uzzah dead, thereby initiating a conflict (of perspectives) between himself and David. The conflict develops further in verses 8–10, where it leaves the reader wondering whether the ark would ever reach its destination. The climax comes in verses 10–15, where out of jealousy, arising from the prosperity that Yahweh bestows on Obed-Edom, David resumed the removal of the ark. It is at this climactic stage that the setting of the *plotlet* is introduced in verse 16, following which is the denouement that announces the placement of the ark in its tent and the sacrifices that followed (v. 17). The closure of the ark removal comes up in verses 18–19, with the benediction and the parting gifts. The closure of the ark removal plot is followed by the climactic conflict of David and Michal in the *plotlet* (vv. 20–22). Verse 23, then, is used pragmatically as the closure to the *plotlet*.

The primary verses of interest in 2 Sam 6 are verses 16 and 20–23, since the focus of this study is on the relationships between David and Saul's progeny vis-à-vis the unenviable fate of the latter. However, to do justice to these verses one has to read them in their literary context. Historical critical scholarship has classified 2 Sam 6 along with 1 Sam 4:1–7:1 as the Ark Narrative (AN). The natural historical critical approach, therefore, is to seek to isolate the strands of traditions found within the chapter and/or to identify the redactional layers found therein. While it falls outside the scope of the present endeavor to enter upon such matters, suffice it to say that this chapter (2 Sam 6), which sews together cultic materials from the ark tradition with matters of the dynastic struggle from court sources, furnishes a useful starting point for transiting from a rising David to a reigning David. 2 Sam 6–8 stands in this unique relationship both to the HDR and the SN. While the HDR deals with David's murky rise to power, the SN chronicles the ineptitude, nepotism, and power abuse that characterized his declining years, which eventually led to some stirrings of revolution in the twilight years of his reign. In between these trouble-ridden annals, 2 Sam 6–8 stand as the jewel of David's story.[70] In this section we shall consider the movement of the ark, Michal from the window, Michal's encounter with David, and the question of Michal's childlessness.

---

70. Römer and Pury have characterized these chapters as "the apex of David's reign" (Römer and Pury, *The So-Called Deuteronomistic History*, 9).

## The Return of the Ark

The ark had not featured in the national life of Israel for a very long time. Very little was heard of the ark in Saul's reign (1 Sam 14:18); nothing at all in the time of Samuel, except for the account of its loss to the Philistines in Samuel's days of apprenticeship under Eli. On a major scale, the last that was heard of the ark was in the waning days of Eli, when after the resounding defeat of Israel, the Philistines took the ark captive (1 Sam 4). The subsequent woes visited upon the Philistines and their gods (1 Sam 5) led to the return of the ark to Beth-shemesh (1 Sam 6:1–18). However, due to their irreverence toward the ark, the Beth-shemeshites were also smitten (1 Sam 6:19). Consequently, the ark was sent to the people of Kiriath-jearim (1 Sam 6:20—7:1) and it remained there for a very long time.

A possible reconstruction of the narration of these events surrounding the ark is that after their encounter with the ark as recorded in 1 Sam 5–6, the Philistines did not want a repeat of that nasty experience. However, it does seem that the Philistines still sought some other way of holding the ark captive thereby denying the Israelites unhindered access to it, a palpable manifestation of the latter's subjugation. This would be a good explanation for the presence of the Philistine garrison within Gibeonite territory within the land of Benjamin. It is this garrison that Jonathan had defied (1 Sam 13:3), which event then sparked off the confrontation reported in 1 Sam 13–14. Because of that initial defeat of the garrison, Israel now had a brief season of access to the ark (1 Sam 14:18).[71] If our proposal is correct then, it would explain why through-

---

71. Some critics prefer the LXX rendition (which has it as the "ephod" instead of the "ark") over the MT. The major reason often advanced is that the ephod, not the ark, was the means of obtaining oracles (cf. Campbell, *2 Samuel*, 486; and Payne, *I & II Samuel*, 69). The additional reasons Alter gives for his preference of the LXX over the MT are the statements that the ark was left at Kiriath-jearim for a long time without being moved, and the unusual construction in the verse in the MT, "for the ark of God on that day was, and the Israelites," as opposed to the LXX's smoother "for on that day he was bearing the ephod before the Israelites" (Alter, *The David Story*, 79). But seen from another perspective, the difficult construction seems more authentic (pace Firth, *1 & 2 Samuel*, 160) because it stands to reason that someone would like to smoothen out a difficult construction but not vice versa. Besides, the Hebrew conjunction *waw* is too diverse in its sphere of meaning for it to be limited in an English translation to "and"; it can very well be translated in the context of this verse as "with." Thus, the subordinate clause would mean "for the ark of God on that day was with the sons of Israel" (כי היה ארון האלהים ביום ההוא ובני ישראל). In fact, after noting that the LXX substitutes "the ephod of God" for the MT's "ark of God," Bergen observes, "The fact that the phrase

out Samuel's reign there is no single reference to the ark, even though he grew up sleeping before the ark (1 Sam 3:1–3), and in spite of "the return" of the ark from Philistine territory earlier in his youth.

This brings into perspective one of the possible reasons for which the people were asking for a king because, if our postulation here is correct, it does appear as if Samuel's success over the Philistines is either exaggerated or was only for a limited time, after which there was a resurgence of Philistine hegemony. Unfortunately, after the defeat of Israel at Mt. Gilboa, things returned to the status quo: the Philistines took the ark captive within Israelite territory again by posting a garrison around the ark's location. David's decisive victory over the Philistines (2 Sam 5:17–25), provided the occasion to remove the ark from Gibeonite territory. The close connection between the ark's captivity in 1 Samuel and its return here in 2 Sam 6 is highlighted by the recurrence of themes from the former passage in the latter. This is demonstrated by table 4 below.

---

'ephod of God' is absent from the entire Hebrew Bible, whereas the phrase 'ark of God' occurs thirteen times, suggests the MT reading is superior" (Bergen, *I, II Samuel*, 157, note 66). If our rendition here is correct, it further highlights the temporal lacuna within which the Israelites once again had access to the ark. The Philistine internment of the ark came to a brief end, with the offset brought about by Jonathan's success against the Philistines in ch. 13 such that someone who was well acquainted with the captivity of the ark on account of the Philistine garrison could report that on this particular day the ark was with the Israelites.

I, indeed, am also inclined to disagree with the position of scholars—like Payne, Philips, and Alter—who plead the non-oracular use of the ark as outlined above. While the ephod may have been the immediate tool for divining the deity's will, it is presumed that under normal circumstances, such activity was to be carried out before Yahweh (cf. Num 27:21). The priests' service before the ark, for instance, is equated with standing before Yahweh, and similarly the place that Yahweh chooses to place his name refers to where the ark is found (Deut 10:8; 17:8–10; 18:5–7). We find this Torah instruction of inquiring before Yahweh (i.e., before the ark) followed in the judges era (Judg 20:18, 23, 27–28). Thus the close association of the ark with divining the will of God, as Saul sought to do here, cannot be denied.

**TABLE 4:** The Comparison of Ark Motif Occurrence in both First and Second Samuel

| Ark Motif in 1 Samuel | Ark Motif in 2 Samuel |
|---|---|
| The Ark departs Israelite territory (1 Sam 4) | The Ark departs Gibeonite Kirjath-jearim (2 Sam 6:1–5) |
| The Ark on a Seven-month sojourn in Philistine territory (1 Sam 6:1) | The Ark on a three-month sojourn in Philistine home (3 Sam 6:11) |
| The Ark brings curses to the Philistines who captured the Ark (1 Sam 5) | The Ark brings bountiful blessing to a Philistine who accommodates the Ark (2 Sam 6:12a). |
| The Ark returns to Israelite territory (1 Sam 6:1–16) | The Ark returns to Israelite "captured" Jerusalem (2 Sam 6:12b–16) |
| Israelite city which desecrates the Ark is severely punished (1 Sam 6:19). | [Gibeonite] Israelite who desecrates the Ark is severely punished (2 Sam 6:6–7) |
| Israel rejects the Ark (1 Sam 6:20) | Israel's king rejects the Ark (2 Sam 6:8–10) |
| The Ark sojourns in "alien" Gibeonite Kirjath-jearim for 20 years (1 Sam 7:1–2). | The Ark tabernacles in "alien" Jerusalem permanently (2 Sam 6:17). |

Because of Samuel's inability to secure access to the ark, the people had good cause to seek for a king; and David emerged as the king par excellence.[72] Another motif that links these narratives is that at the beginning of the ark's journey, when the Philistines had routed Israel, 30,000 Israelites were slain (1 Sam 4:10), whereas in David's resounding defeat of the Philistines he has 30,000 Israelites (a kind of national resurrection). With these 30,000 Israelites David had pursued the Philistines from Geba to Gezer (2 Sam 5:25)—the very axis wherein the ark sojourned in Gibeonite territory under the surveillance of a Philistine garrison. It is upon their return from this pursuit of the Philistines that they assembled at Baalah-Judah to bring from there the ark of Yahweh

---

72. Another motif that powerfully connects this narrative with those in 1 Samuel is the number of soldiers with David—which works to highlight David as Yahweh's chosen king. Just like the songs of the celebratory women had portrayed David to be ten times better than Saul through the number of their slain (1 Sam 18:7), the narrator here demonstrates the same point by the number of fighting men they were able to levy. While Saul could garner only 3,000 (cf. 1 Sam 13:2; 24:3; 26:2), David marshaled 30,000 chosen men (for a similar position see Carlson, *David, The Chosen King*, 64).

(2 Sam 6:1–2).[73] Indeed, there is a discernable compositional pattern in 1 Samuel that is mirrored (either in the same way or with an opposite idea) in the composition of 2 Samuel, and the ark seems to be pivotal in both cases. This pattern is illustrated by the table below:

**TABLE 5**: Compositional Motific Similarities between 1 & 2 Samuel

| Major motifs/themes in 1 Samuel | Major motifs/themes in 2 Samuel |
| --- | --- |
| A hymn in praise of Yahweh, 2:1–10 | An ode to Saul and Jonathan, 1:17–27 |
| Leadership change (from Eli to Samuel) that included the decimation of the previous leader's family, 2:27—4:22 | Leadership change (from Saulide dynasty to David) that involved the decimation of previous king's family, 2:1—5:3 |
| The movement of the ark to captivity, 5:1—7:1 | The movement of the ark to its permanent abode, ch. 6 |
| The mediation of God's presence to Israel by the new leader and his subsequent defeat of the Philistines, 7:1—14 | The mediation of God's word to the new leader and his subsequent defeat of the Philistines and the surrounding nations, chs. 7—8 |
| The story of Saul's rise, ch. 8—12 | The story of the rehabilitation of a Saulide, ch. 9 |
| The rejection of Saul, chs. 13—15 | The censorship of David, chs. 11—12 |
| Saul pursues David (his anointed successor), chs. 18—26 | Absalom (David's pretended successor) pursues David, chs. 15—18 |
| Saul's death clears coast for David, ch. 31 | The murder of the Saulides clears coast for David's house, 21:1–14 |

David's enterprise of bringing the ark to his new capital was a powerful fusion of matters sacral and political. In this singular act, the place of Yahweh's choosing and the house (dynasty) of Yahweh's choosing are fused into one, permanently ensconcing this unity in Israel's memory. This then becomes the foundation upon which the invincibility of Zion and the eternal commitment of the deity to the house of David in an

---

73. This understanding of the text completely eliminates the difficulty associated with 2 Sam 6:1-2. The "again" of verse 1 relates to rallying the troops after their pursuit of their enemies. Similarly, the suddenness of verse 2 ("he arose to bring from there . . ." when there is no previous mention of "going" there in the first instance) becomes meaningful when the events of chapter 5 are seen as intricately connected with the beginning of chapter 6.

inviolable covenant would be built. It is by the means of this integration of the sacred and secular that Saul's house was permanently dislodged from the reins of power.

There are several reasons that account for this ingenious move by David. With the popularity of Saul, David struggled for years after his ascendency to claim legitimacy to his kingship. The ark represented the old order that celebrated Yahweh as Israel's ruler and as the one that led Israel's troops out in the "holy war" tradition. The monarchy represents a new order with all its concomitant crutches of bureaucracy and taxation, harem, military levy, and foreign mercenary elements. Those who were in the vanguard of the old order may have been suspicious of the new order, if not downright opposed to it. David's appropriation of the ark not only served to legitimate his reign but also to bind the people to himself.[74]

The motive of using the ark for power legitimation became even more imperative for David in view of the absence of any religious figure at his public acclamation during his anointing both by Judah (2 Sam 2:4) and by all Israel (2 Sam 5:1–3). Power legitimation on the basis of divine election was fundamental to the institution of the monarchy in the ANE, and this is evident in the history of Israelite monarchy itself. Ishida illustrates this with examples from both Egypt and Mesopotamia: "Although there was a great difference between the Egyptians and the Mesopotamians in their conception of the nature of kingship, these two great civilizations in the ancient Near East were of one mind on the basic idea that a monarchy originating in the divine realm was the fundamental institution of their society."[75] If this was the case in Israel as well, then, David had to persuade the Israelite populace of his divine election. With

---

74. On this Brueggemann writes, "By his appropriation of the ark, David has placed the old conservatives in a difficult bind. They have not forgotten the significance of the ark, which referred to the raw presence of Yahweh, the power of Yahweh, and the conventional implications of Yahweh's sovereignty. Now, under David, in order to have access to the ark and its old significance, even conservative Israelites with long memories and keen theological sensitivity must make their pilgrimage to Jerusalem, the new city with David's new power and new ideology. They have nowhere else to go. To make contact with the ancient symbol, they must give tacit assent to the new royal apparatus" (Brueggemann, *First and Second Samuel*, 248). It is in the recognition of the potency of religion in politics that Jeroboam (who had lived as political refugee in Egypt) likewise embarked up another ingenious act of inventing new gods and new traditions so as to secure permanently the loyalty of the northern tribes to himself (1 Kgs 12:26–29).

75. Ishida, *The Royal Dynasties in Ancient Israel*, 71.

the absence of the involvement of any religious figure of prominence in David's public installation,[76] David, in his striving for his power legitimation, found for himself the best imprimatur any Israelite could find in Israel's most sacred cultic object—the ark, which symbolized the very embodiment of the deity amongst his people.

The influence and power of priests in the polities of the ANE are well documented and need no repetition here.[77] Political figures ensured the security of their reigns by either appeasement or pacification and containment: a political lesson Saul never learned and hence the transience of his dynasty. David was too shrewd to fall into the same pit. Obviously, as demonstrated by the Philistines whom he had just defeated, the best way to hold a people captive to one's power was to possess their sacred estate. Aware of this (perhaps from his days of service to the Philistines), David eliminates the uncertainty and unpredictability associated with the mobility of the ark by radically doing away with its variable location at differing cult centers, as it was hosted at various times at Gilgal (Josh 9:6; 7:6), Bethel (Judg 20:26–27), and Shiloh (1 Sam 4:3–4). Instead he devised the establishment of permanency through the institution of state-controlled temple religion.[78]

David extended state control of religion by appropriating to himself the power of determining who became the chief priests, thereby curtailing their powers as well (2 Sam 8:16–18; 20:23–25; cf. 1 Kgs 2:26–27, 35; 12:31–33). By this means David took the sting (and whatever threat

---

76. Samuel's anointing of David was a private affair (1 Sam 16:1–13), the veracity of which was most likely to be questioned by those who were wont to contest his legitimacy

77. Cf. David, *The Ancient Egyptians*; Grabbe, *Priests, Prophets, Diviners, Sages*; Holloway, *Aššur is King! Aššur is King!*; Berlin, *Religion and Politics in the Ancient Near East*; Bottéro, *Religion in Ancient Mesopotamia*; and Sayce, *The Religions of Ancient Egypt and Babylon*.

78. On the same note Rosenstock writes, "One can hardly imagine a more powerful legitimation of his claim to the throne. The return of YHWH's glory and 'throne' to the city of David is at the same time an occasion for David to 'get himself glory.' It is hardly accidental that the next step David contemplates is the transformation of the cult from one centered on a moveable tent to one involving all the regalia of a state-controlled temple" (Rosenstock, "David's Play," 65–66). Robinson similarly observes, "By bringing the ark (which earlier had been kept in the 'temple' at Shiloh) to Jerusalem, David displays his reverence for the traditions connected with Shiloh and at the same time asserts his claim over the cult in Jerusalem. Thus the northern tribes are made to move toward Jerusalem, not only politically but also cultically (Robinson, *Let Us Be Like the Nations*, 180).

it may have posed to his rule) out of Yahwistic religion, the kind that sought to subsume kingship under the priesthood (Deut 17:14–20; cf. 2 Kgs 11:4–12:3; ET 12:2), as demonstrated in Samuel's relationship to Saul. That David had seized the cult is further affirmed by three features of this ceremony. First, sacrifice is offered (2 Sam 6:13), but no mention is made of any priest making the offering. The obvious conclusion is that David executed the sacrifices himself.[79] Later the text states plainly that David offered burnt offerings as well (vv. 17–18). In Israel's traditions, such a cultic service was an exclusive preserve of the priesthood, with dire consequences for anyone who otherwise ventured upon it (1 Sam 13:10–14; cf. 2 Chr 26:16–21). The priesthood, with its previous sole power of presiding over the cult, was therefore the threat in Yahwistic religion to whoever was king, if kingship was subservient to the priesthood. This threat (which doomed Saul), David eliminated by seizing upon the cult itself. Secondly, David wore the priestly garb of a linen ephod (אפוד בד, 2 Sam 6:14). In the context of the movement of a religious icon of the highest significance, there is nothing else David would be doing wearing a priestly attire other than performing priestly service of officiating the sacrifice. Thirdly, David's blessing of the people (6:18) is apparently a usurpation of the Levitical benedictory role of the Aaronic priesthood (Num 6:23–26).

## Michal at the Window

While all the carnivalizing, with its religious and dynastic implications, was going on with the involvement of "all the house of Israel," Michal, Saul's daughter, was kept out (or did she keep herself in?).[80] J. Cheryl

---

79. We note that the expression for "offer sacrifice" is a waw-consecutive piel 3ms pronominalized phrase (וַיְזַבַּח). The only antecedent for the masculine singular pronoun is David. It could be argued that the sacrifice may have been done vicariously for David by priests. However, David's sporting of the priestly apparel contradicts such an argument. Robinson similarly writes, "That David was 'girded with a linen ephod' suggests that he was performing a priestly function (cf. 1 Sam 2:18)" (Robinson, *Let Us Be like the Nations*, 182). Firth also notes the conjoining of the secular and the sacral in David's action here (*1 & 2 Samuel*, 377–78).

80. We refuse to be as categorical about this as Campbell, who writes, "Verse 16, on the other hand, brings out Michal's self-imposed exclusion; she despised David in her heart (6:16). The note prepares for the exchange in vv. 20–23, to be discussed below. It signals from the outset, however, as the ark of YHWH was entering David's city, that the last significant representative of the old era held herself apart from the inauguration of a momentous new epoch in the story of Israel" (Campbell, *2 Samuel*, 67). The text does not grant us the latitude for such sweeping conclusions.

Exum, in a picturesque word-play conveys the irony of Michal's situation: "The text provides our window on Michal, offering us only a glimpse, the kind of view a window gives, limited in range and perspective. We are, as it were, outside, watching her, inside, watching David."[81] The limited perspective the window on Michal provides leaves us groping in the dark as to what triggered the deep-seated resentment that she here harbors against David. In a manner characteristic of the Samuel narratives, the narrator leaves his readers with an epistemological gap,[82] not affording them the luxury of volunteering the reasons why Michal despised David in her heart.

Though we may never unravel the enigma (perhaps it was not meant to be unraveled), we may grapple with it by paying attention to the fabric of the text. One way of doing this is to consider the viewpoints contained in the text. In 2 Sam 6:16, two points of view are shown: that of the narrator and that of Michal. It is significant that after 1 Sam 25 the narrator never calls Michal David's wife: in 2 Sam 3:15–16 she is Paltiel's wife, and even here in 2 Sam 6:16, when she had already been reclaimed by David, the narrator still calls her Saul's daughter. Michal, on the other hand, sees David as the king—not her husband. By the means of these points of view the narrator "shows" that the encounter between Michal and David in this chapter is not a mere difference of perspectives between husband and wife but actually a vestige of the conflict between David and the vanquished house of Saul.

There are several possible explanations for this turn of events. Perhaps, as a Saulide having witnessed how David wormed his way into the confidences of the Saulides only to work for their decimation, she was piqued at the hypocrisy of this flamboyant display of religiosity. Plausibly she was scandalized by David's undignified manner of behavior, which she considered unfit for royalty. Possibly she was horrified at this element of cultic practice that from every indication seems to have been alien to Israel's religious practice.[83] It may be recalled that Saul's first problem

---

81. Exum, *Tragedy and Biblical Narrative*, 89.

82. Ackerman's term for narrative gap, a concept he also sees to be a germane characteristic of the Court History (Ackerman, "Knowing Good and Evil," 41–64).

83. Several scholars find many parallels between this procession and processions of similar type within the ancient Near Eastern milieu. In the ancient Near Eastern context, such processions were an integral part of fertility cultic practices involving phallic display that should eventuate into a *hieros gamos* with the *gebirah* (cf. Rosenstock, "David's Play," 67–74; Carlson, *David, The Chosen King*, 87–95). From such perspective, then, it is to such pagan practice that Michal was adamantly opposed.

with Samuel arose from his performance of the priestly function of officiating at the sacral altar. Here David not only performs sacrifice, he also sports priestly garb. Besides, the kind of wild dance that David engages in here is unreported of any other previous leader of Israel. The orthodoxy of Michal's religious sentiments is not lost on the rabbis, who in the literature of midrashic traditions have shown a remarkably impressive and positive appreciation of Michal. Tamara C. Eskenazi shows that while rabbinic literature thrives on debate, it is surprisingly consistent in its praise of Michal and its sympathy for her second husband Paltiel. She writes, "They describe her as both beautiful and accomplished. Indeed, Michal has been able to wear tefillin (phylacteries), as men do in prayer. Such a privileged obligation normally belongs to those who study Torah. By inference, the rabbis credit Michal with study of sacred texts. It is especially fascinating that the rabbis, in a literature famous for its love for debate, do not disagree as to whether Michal wore tefillin. They only argue whether or not some sages protested against her wearing them (Pesiqta Rabbati 29.11)."[84] To further explore the issues involved we now turn to Michal's encounter with David.

## Michal's Encounter with David

At the end of the ark procession, David, having dismissed the people with gifts and blessings, returned to bless his family as well.[85] It is at this

---

84. Eskenazi, "Michal in Hebrew Sources," 157–74.

85. The scholars who believe the ark procession to be a Canaanite cultic practice see that very fact to be the immediate source of conflict between Michal and David at this point. Rosenstock in this vein writes, "The ark and David are sources of blessing for corporate Israel and for each 'house' within Israel. The narrative makes a point of stating how each person, after receiving the foodstuffs, went back to 'his house.' David, too, 'returned to bless his house' and encounters Michal who comes out to greet him with abusive speech. Given the ritual nature of the events thus far depicted, it is not implausible to believe that the blessing of the house was also of a ritual nature, involving the participation of the wife. What we have in the case of David and Michal is an upsetting of ritual expectations, ending not in reproduction but in the report that 'Michal the daughter of Saul had no child to the day of her death'" (Rosenstock, "David's Play," 68).

However, there are also those who view the matter differently. Brueggemann, for instance, sees in this narrative some abnormality, not only in terms of liturgy but also both social extravagance and royal extravagance. On the cultic nature of the dance he writes, "There has been much speculation about David's dance. At the negative extreme, it is suggested that David participated in a Canaanite ecstatic dance that became something of an orgy, and that is why he is rebuked by Michal. At the positive extreme, the dance is taken as legitimate liturgic dance, the bodily expression as proper worship. The narrative invites such probes, but it gives us little clue about David's intention" (Brueggemann, *First and Second Samuel*, 250).

point that Michal ventures to encounter David "outside."[86] There is so much irony in this encounter. It has the intimate feel of familial affairs, yet it is out in the open. It is seemingly a matter between "husband and wife," yet undoubtedly it is a conflict between representatives of feuding factions (the house of Saul and the house David).

In the only dialogue ever recorded between Michal and David, she began with a reference to the impropriety of his self-exposure to the basest of women in the realm. Commentators often get hung up, and perhaps understandably so, on David's dressing or lack thereof in Michal's locution. Some see Michal's gibe at David as a result of sexual jealousy on account of David's phallic display. This, they explain, is because what used to be Michal's exclusive right now belongs to other women, and is even shared with servant girls.[87] Brueggemann, on the other hand, thinks that David's behavior reminds Michal of her own father's self-exposure when he ran amok (1 Sam 10:9–13; 19:20–24). She is therefore not prepared to have "a husband who is out of control in public."[88]

We are bound to miss the rhetoric of Michal's locution when we pay less attention to her simile of the "worthless fellows." The word (√ריק) I translated as "worthless fellows" is a substantive adjective given in the masculine plural form. It is used literally of physical objects to show that they are empty of content (cf. Gen 37:24; 41:27; Judg 7:16; 2 Kgs 4:3; Ezek

---

86. Exum, drawing upon the well-attested ancient Near Eastern motif of the woman at the window, observes that only from the window could the woman look out upon the world to see what men have accomplished. To venture outside was to invite trouble, so to speak. She writes, "Whereas Michal was able to exercise power 'inside' in 1 Samuel 19, David has the power 'outside,' in society—reflecting the conventional notion that women hold sway over domestic matters but men rule the world. Michal has stepped outside her 'place'; she has seen fit to criticize the king, and she does so not as the king's wife but, what is worse, as the representative of the rejected house, as 'Saul's daughter'" (Exum, *Tragedy and Biblical Narrative*).

87. See Rosenstock, "David's Play," 71; Alter, *The David Story*, 229; Exum, *Tragedy and Biblical Narrative*, 87; and Tidwell, "The Linen Ephod." In fairness to Alter, it is necessary to note that elsewhere he highlights more than just the sexual jealousy factor. He writes, "The scorn for David welling up in Michal's heart is thus plausibly attributable in some degree to all of the following: the undignified public spectacle which David just now is making of himself; Michal's jealousy over the moment of glory David is enjoying while she sits alone, a neglected co-wife, back at the provisional palace; Michal's resentment over David's indifference to her all these years, over the other wives he has taken, over being torn away from the devoted Palti; David's dynastic ambitions—now clearly revealed in his establishing the Ark in the 'City of David'—which will irrevocably displace the house of Saul" (Alter, *The Art of Biblical Narrative*, 123).

88. Brueggemann, *First and Second Samuel*, 251.

24:11; Jer 14:3). On another level it is used, in a sense more metaphorical than literal, to refer to vanity or vain pursuit (Prov 12:11; 28:19). It is in this latter sense that it is used substantively of humans to mean worthless persons. However, in this latter sense it has acquired a specialized meaning in the Hebrew Bible by referring to a band of social misfits who attach themselves to a rebel leader to disrupt established social order or to rise up against established authority (see Judg 9:1–6; 11:3; 2 Chr 13:6–7, cf. 1 Sam 22:1–2). The illocutionary force of Michal's use of this word then is to evoke this connotation, bringing to light who David really is. It is only such base fellows who rise up against their lords who will have no qualms about the display of easy virtues, such as David's exposure while gamboling and cavorting in dishabille. This, then, is the explanation for David's explosive response.

In his response to Michal, David vehemently contests Michal's point of view: he is not a rebel; the kingdom rightly belongs to him as a fief from Yahweh, who chose him over Michal's father and the latter's house (v. 21). Before such a suzerain (Yahweh), to whose beneficence he owes his rise to power, David will take no shame in being debased for the former's glory. Indeed, Yahweh is to get honor and glory from those who draw near him to offer sacrifices (Lev 10:3), as David was doing at this historic moment. Yet they were not to uncover themselves, as David did; they were to be properly clad (Lev 6:10; 16:4; Ezek 44:18; cf. Rev 3:18). It is to avoid indecent exposure of the officiating priest that there even was a strict provision with regard to the construction of the altar— it was to have an access ramp rather than steps (Exod 20:26).[89]

David, having dislodged the priesthood from presiding over the cult at this critical historic moment, was the one calling the shots and hence the sole determinant of what gave Yahweh glory. His scornful rebuttal of Michal seems to have signaled the end of his tenuous and exploitative relationship with her, now that he had achieved his ultimate goal. David is in his true elements in his subversion of Michal's words. While she had thought him to have dishonored himself in his self uncovering (we note her use of sarcasm to this effect in v. 20) before the servant girls, he

---

89. It is in the light of all this that some commentators readily see Michal as a loyal Yahwist who was appalled at "the king's participation in a ritual no doubt associated with the Jebusite cultus of Jerusalem. Clearly it was not normal Israelite practice for a person acting as a priest to appear clad only in a linen ephod" (Phillips, "David's Linen Ephod," 485–87).

replies that his debasing of himself will result in his glory (v. 22).[90] It may be recalled that at the beginning of his relationship with the house of Saul (especially with Michal) in 1 Samuel, David had "lightly esteemed" himself (1 Sam 18:23) while he was in reality "highly esteemed" by both Israel and the Philistines (1 Sam 18:30; 21:11; 22:14). David has now come full circle—terminating his relationship with Michal with the dishonor-honor motif with which he had initiated it.

## Michal's Childlessness

At the end of the sour encounter between Michal and David, the narrator reports that Michal had no children at the time of her death (v. 23). Alter lays his finger on the thorny issue in the verse when he asks rhetorically, "The whole story of David and Michal concludes on a poised ambiguity through the suppression of causal explanation: Is this a punishment from God, or simply a refusal by David to share her bed, or is the latter to be understood as the agency for the former?"[91] The ambiguous nature of this verse has given rise to a variety of interpretations from commentators. To some Michal's childlessness is the consequence of divine retribution for her faithlessness, disobedience, uncooperativeness, and/or disrespect for Yahweh's anointed.[92] To others it is not divine retribution but rather David's refusal to fulfill his conjugal duty to her.[93] To feminist interpreters, it is also possible that Michal had no child because she refused to have sexual relations with David.[94]

Others make a connection between Michal's childlessness and the question of succession. Rost, for example, is of the opinion that Michal's childlessness threatened the Davidic dynasty, since all the sons he has to this point were born in Hebron and as such were Judahites and hence

---

90. It is a self-fulfilling prophecy to realize that David would later uncover his nakedness to a handmaid of one of his servants (Bathsheba, Uriah's wife), and get humiliation (both in Nathan's rebuke and Absalom's open use of his father's concubines) and glory (the glory of Solomon's kingdom).

91. Alter, *The David Story*, 230. While Gordon holds a similar view concerning the ambiguity of the verse, he is inevitably caught in the web of seeing Michal as in some way suffering some divine judgment (Gordon, *I & II Samuel*, 235).

92. Bergen, *1, 2 Samuel*, 335; Payne, *I & II Samuel*, 185. Carlson is largely in agreement with those who see Michal's fate as divine retribution. He differs only slightly, in the sense that he conceives of Michal's fault in terms of her attitude toward the Ark (Carlson, *David, The Chosen King*, 93).

93. Ishida, *The Royal Dynasties in Ancient*, 73; and Lemche, "David's Rise," 7.

94. Exum, *Tragedy and Biblical Narrative*, 88.

not heirs to the throne of all Israel. It is in response to this threat, comparable to Sarah's barrenness, that Yahweh assured David with the eternal promise in chapter 7.[95] However, Rost fails to demonstrate that one's place of birth rather than one's pedigree (and, more importantly, divine election) was the determinant factor in royal succession. Besides, his analogy to Abraham and Sarah fails to make the point precisely because, unlike these latter, Michal at her death had no children. A more pertinent implication of Michal's childlessness is the fact that it ensured that no claimant to the Davidic throne had Saulide blood flowing through his veins. This then guaranteed the irrevocability of the divine rejection of the Saulide line forever.

Some uneasiness still attaches to this curious report of Michal's childlessness. As pointed out above, the primary function of the *waw*-disjunctive is to spotlight thematic discontinuity. Therefore, without the narrator's clear statement of causality, conclusions in one direction or the other are interpretations at best and (baseless) speculations at worst. While in some instances of the epistemological gaps in Samuel it may suffice to accept ambiguity on account of our insufficient knowledge, in this case there are sufficient clues in the text (if taken in its canonical context) that lead to an informed conclusion. The first thing to note is that our text (2 Sam 6:23) does not say that Michal, Saul's daughter, was barren. All it says is, "Now to Michal the daughter of Saul were no children to the day of her death" (ולמיכל בת־שאול לא־היה לה ילד עד יום מותה). The typical expressions for barrenness in the Hebrew Bible are "she was barren" (עקרה), "and Yahweh shut her womb" (ויהוה סגר רחמה),[96] or something similar; none of which is used of Michal. 2 Samuel 6:23, therefore, is not to be interpreted as meaning she was barren, but it simply means that beginning at a certain point to the time of her death she had no children.

There is also the need to pay close attention to word usage with regard to this matter. There are two ways in which the phrase לא־היה is used in the Hebrew Bible. The first is the case where the occurrence or presence of the thing that לא־היה negates is contemporaneous with the action of the focus of the sentence. For example, in Josh 8:35 the focus is on Joshua's reading of the words of Moses, and לא־היה is used to negate the existence of a word commanded by Moses that Joshua failed to read, "There was not a word of all that Moses had commanded which

---

95. Rost, *The Succession to the Throne of David*, 86–87.
96. Cf. Gen 11:30; 20:18; 25:21; 29:31; Judg 13:2–3; 1 Sam 1:5–6.

Joshua did not read before all the assembly of Israel with the women and the little ones and the strangers who were living among them" (לא־היה דבר מכל אשר־צוה משה לא־קרא יהושע נגד כל־קהל ישראל). This use of לא־היה does not refer to the presence of the thing referred to in antecedent time but at the time contemporaneous with the focus of the sentence (cf. Num 26:64; 27:3; Deut 10:9; 1 Sam 21:7 [ET 21:6]; 1 Sam 28:20; 2 Sam 14:25; 1 Kgs 3:13, 21; 10:3; 12:20; 2 Kgs 18:5; 20:13, 15; 2 Chr 18:32; Ezek 29:18).[97]

The second use of לא־היה is the one where it does refer to time outside of the contemporaneous moment (either anterior time, posterior time, or both). In any of these three cases, the text would make the reference to antecedent or precedent time explicit by incorporating time-defining phrases. Such time-defining phrases or clauses may be a specific time (לא־היה על־כל־מלך לפניו על־ישראל) "which had not been on any king before him in Israel" 1 Chr 29:25 NASB);[98] or it may have a non-determinate time reference, past or future (...לא־היה לפניך ואחריך לא־יקום כמוך) "so that there has been no one like you before you, nor shall one like you arise after you," (1 Kgs 3:12 NASB). For further examples of this use of (לא־היה) see Exod 9:18, 24; 10:14; 2 Kgs 23:25; 2 Chr 1:12; Neh 13:2.

From the foregoing linguistic analysis, the conclusions with regard to the use of לא־היה in the Hebrew Bible are twofold: one, it is usually concerned with time contemporaneous with the focal point of the sentence in which it occurs; two, where the concern goes beyond the contemporaneous moment there are time-defining phrases or clauses to indicate the extent of the time frame—either back (in the past), forward (in the future), or both. When we consider our text (2 Sam 6:23) from this standpoint, then, we find only a forward time reference point (עד יום מותה, "to the day of her death"). Clearly there is no reference to antecedent time. We can only assume, from the above analysis that

---

97. A similar construction can be found in the phrase ולא־יסף; in most of the cases where it is used it deals with time from the current moment of speaking and forward (Gen 38:26; Deut 5:22; Judg 13:21; 1 Sam 15:35). In poetic literature, likewise, the occurrences of לא־היה very often can be translated with the present tense (Ps 53:6 [ET v. 5]; Jer 14:4, 5), or even with a prophetic perfect—a future event prophetically viewed as having taken place already. The emphasis in all these situations is not on the past, but on the current state of affairs.

98. This is specific time because there is a definite beginning point of monarchial leadership in Israel.

the beginning point of the time reference would be the contemporaneous moment. What we are left to find, then, is the focal event which is contemporaneous with the beginning point of this time frame. There are two possible candidates for this focal event: the ark procession or the Gibeonite sacrifice of the Saulide Seven in chapter 21. The latter is mostly like the focal event.

The murder of the Saulide Seven in all likelihood is the point from which Michal had no children to the day of her death due to both positive and negative factors. Positively, MT (ch. 21) mentions that the mother of the five Saulides was Michal (we shall give fuller consideration of the text in the next section). The possibility that Michal had five sons explains why there is no reference to antecedent time in the statement because these are the sons who were murdered along with Saul's two sons from his concubine Rizpah. Negatively, there are several factors, not the least of which is the absence of a direct linkage between the Michal-David confrontation and Michal's childlessness. Admittedly, ours is an argument from silence but as the saying goes, the absence of evidence is not evidence of absence. One factor that buttresses our position is the fact that the dominant voice of testimony in the Samuel narratives has an anti-Saul tenor. Thus, there would be no satisfactory explanation for the failure of the dominant voice to appropriate such theological capital to draw the reader's attention to Yahweh's retributive visitation on Michal as a vindication of his anointed servant David. This fact becomes more glaring in the face of the statement made elsewhere (of women who were perhaps less "deserving" of such a statement than Michal, granting the veracity of the suggestion of divine retribution against Michal for despising David during his self-debasing show of piety) that Yahweh had closed their wombs (1 Sam 1:5; Gen 30:1–2). One looks in vain for such a statement concerning Michal. It is therefore preposterous to directly attribute her childlessness either to her confrontation with David or to divine retribution.

Additionally, a close study of the biblical text shows that לֹא־הָיָה is never used with respect to barren women. In reference to the women in the Bible who are said to have had no children, the expression used is never (לֹא־הָיָה לָהּ יֶלֶד) but (עֲקָרָה וְלֹא יָלְדָה). Where the former expression is used of someone not having children, the reference always is to a man, and particularly his not having sons, as the Bible has never called any man barren (e.g., Num 27:3; 2 Kgs 1:17). The only exception to this would be the reference to Hannah, even though a different construction is used (ולחנה אין ילדים, "But Hannah had no children," 1 Sam 1:2). However, it is immediately explained that it was Yahweh who had shut her womb (ויהוה סגר חמה, 1 Sam 1:5).

Furthermore, the Bible has no record of any barren women. The Lord eventually blesses with a child or children all those called barren (cf. Gen 11:30; 21:1–3; 25:21–26; 29:31; 30:22–25; Judg 13:2–3; 1 Sam 1:5–8, 19–21; 2:21; Luke 1:7, 36). This state of affairs is in consonance with the Deuteronomic theology of the blessedness of the covenant people, among whom none will be barren—the fates of their barren are always reversed (Deut 7:14; cf. Exod 23:26; 1 Sam 2:5; Ps 113:9; Isa 54:1). It is pertinent at this point to consider Carlson's application of 1 Sam 2:5 to Michal. He writes,

> The episode of Michal concludes in v. 23 with a statement of her barrenness. It seems likely that this is to be interpreted as a punishment sent by Yahweh on account of her attitude to the Ark. This was probably the view of the D-group at least, remembering their incorporation of "Hannah's song of praise" in 1 Sam 2:1–10 as a statement of the theme of 1 and 2 Sam. The antithesis in v. 5b, "The barren bears seven, but she who has many children withers," is followed in vv. 6ff. by an ideological interpretation along the lines "Yahweh kills and brings to life . . . he humiliates but he also exalts (*mašpîl' af měrōmēm*)." This theme applied in a "disintegrated" form to the description of the birth of Samuel in 1 Sam 1 is also relevant to the events of 2 Sam 6:20–23. This is emphasized by the associative linking of the episode of Michal, via the thrice-repeated *bat-šā'ûl* in vv. 16, 20 and 23, to the *šā'al* passage in 1 Sam 1–2: Hannah, who was barren, gives birth to three sons and two daughters after Samuel; Michal, the proud daughter of a king, is dishonored by being left childless.[99]

To buttress his above quoted statement further Carlson asks rhetorically, "Was the thematic penetration too strong for the later exponents of these traditions, since Michal—quite mistakenly—is accorded five sons in 2 Sam 21:8?"[100] It is to be argued, on the contrary, that it is to Carlson (not the D-group) that the thematic penetration is too strong in that he fails to see the rational conclusion of the motific parallel he rightly sees in these narratives. Carlson here fails to notice the inconsistency

---

99. Carlson, David, *The Chosen King*, 93.
100. Carlson, David, *The Chosen King*, 93.

of his conclusion on 1 Sam 2:5–6 vis-à-vis its analogous relationship to Michal's situation. His argument pursued to its logical end shows that while the humble Hannah, the barren, bore children, "the proud" Michal, the mother of many children, withers away consequent upon the loss of her five sons in the Gibeonite episode. This then places Michal's childlessness (not barrenness) at David's doorstep.

## MICHAL'S SONS AND BROTHERS: PAWNS IN THE DYNASTIC STRUGGLE (2 SAM 21:1–14)

### 2 SAMUEL 21:1–14

1 Now there was a famine in the reign of David for three years from year to year. And David resorted to Yahweh; and Yahweh said, "To Saul and to *his*[101] bloody house *belongs the blame*, because he killed the Gibeonites." 2 So David called the Gibeonites and he said to them, (now the Gibeonites were not of the sons of Israel; they were indeed from the remnants of the Amorites, but the sons of Israel had sworn to them, but Saul sought to smite them in his zeal for the sons of Israel and Judah), 3 and David said to the Gibeonites, "What shall I do for you? And by what *means* shall I atone that you may bless Yahweh's heritage?" 4 The Gibeonites replied him, "We[102] have no money matter with Saul and his house. And there is no one in Israel for us to kill." So he said, "What do you want? Name it and I will do it for you." 5 Then they replied to the king, "The man who plotted against us, who was intent on having us wiped out of existence in all the territory of Israel, 6 let seven men from his descendents be given to us,[103] that we may execute them in Gibeon on the mountain of Yahweh." [104] And the king said, "I will give."

101. We follow the LXX, which has αὐτοῦ ("his") here.

102. We follow the Qere here, which has the plural first person pronominal suffix, instead of the singular of the Ketiv.

103. The Ketiv is niphal 3ms verb form while the Qere is qal 3ms passive verb form, both with understood jussive force without any unique jussive form. Even if we accept Driver's understanding of the Qere as being of the hofal stem (Driver, *Samuel*, 351), the meaning would still remain the same as that of a qal passive. The meaning in either case (whether niphal or qal/hofal) would be the same as we have adopted above. Many medieval manuscripts follow the LXX and 4QSamª, which have imperative forms. However, understanding the social conventions of the time, where the royalty was addressed in the third person, the MT rendition is preferred.

104. Contrary to the MT's בגבעת שאול בחיר יהוה "in Gibeah of Saul, the chosen of Yahweh," LXX manuscripts have Γαβαων ("Gibeon"). Driver (*Samuel*, 351), McCarter

7 And the king spared Mephibosheth the son of Jonathan the son of Saul because of the oath of Yahweh which was between them—between David and Jonathan son of Saul. 8 And the king took the two sons of Rizpah daughter of Ayyah, whom she bore to Saul, Armoni and Mephibosheth; and the five sons of Michal[105] daughter of Saul, whom she bore to Adriel son of Barzillai the Meholathite. 9 And he delivered them into the hand of the Gibeonites, and they hanged them on the Mountain before Yahweh; and they fell seven of them[106] together in the early days of the beginning of the barley harvest.

10 Then Rizpah daughter of Ayyah took sackcloth and spread it out for herself upon the rock from the beginning of harvest until it rained on them from heaven upon the rock. She allowed neither the birds of the sky to rest upon them by day nor the beasts of the field by night. 11 When David was told what Rizpah the daughter of Ayyah, Saul's concubine, had done; 12 David went and took the bones of Saul and the bones of Jonathan his son from the lords of Jabesh-gilead, who had stolen them from the square[107] of Bethshan, where the Philistines had hung them,

---

(*II Samuel*, 438), and Anderson (*2 Samuel*, 247) understand this phrase to be "in Gibeon on the mountain of Yahweh." In the same vein Smith writes, "The narrative is favorable to Gibeon as the site of the expiation. Saul has come in by mistake.—בהיר יהוה] in v. 9 we find that the men were exposed בהר לפני יהוה. It is therefore probable that בהר יהוה was original" (Smith, *Samuel*, 376). All these inform our rendition above (*pace* NLT) against other modern translations, which overwhelmingly follow the MT (cf. KJV, NASB, ESV, and NIV).

105. Two medieval Hebrew manuscripts, like medieval LXX, have Merab instead of Michal. The Targumim have Merob. The LXX[B], however, agrees with the MT. McCarter considers it a later recension and argues that from 2 Sam 6:23 it is known that Michal was childless (McCarter, *II Samuel*, 439). Whether we retain Michal or substitute her with Merab, one aspect of the text or the other (either the name of the woman or the name of the husband) will have to be altered. We have elected to follow the MT for many reasons, not the least of which is that the MT never says Michal was barren. In fact, the abrupt manner in which 2 Sam 6:23 is introduced without any direct attribution of Michal's childlessness to any direct cause is a veiled pointer to this incidence in which she lost all her children. For further details on this refer to our discussion of 2 Sam 6:23 above; and for a further discussion of whether it is Michal or Merab that should be translated here see our main argument below.

106. We follow the Qere (and the versions); the Ketiv means "seven times," which could mean that the seven of them were killed one at a time.

107. Some medieval LXX manuscripts have απο του τειχους ("from the wall," cf. 1 Sam 31:12) instead of the MT's מרחב ("from the square"). The focus is primarily on the action of the Jabesh-gileadites. In terms of location, Bethshan is more important than the specific spot of where the corpses were. Besides, there need be no conflict between the two locations; the corpses may have been hung on the wall in front of the public

on the day the Philistines smote Saul in Gilboa. 13 He brought from there the bones of Saul and the bones of Jonathan his son; and he gathered the bones of those who were hung. 14 And they buried the bones of Saul and Jonathan his son[108] in the land of Benjamin in Zela in the grave of Kish his father. They did all that the king had commanded; and after this God was entreated for the land.

The episode narrated here has a self-contained sub-plot, though it is not elaborately developed. Verses 1 and 2 contain the stage, exposition, and inciting moment. The stage, though not clearly defined, is set in the reign of David over a three-year period—most likely early in his rule over all Israel. The exposition consists in the explanation of who the Gibeonites were, while the initiation of conflict comes in the oracle that sets the Gibeonites up against the house of Saul. Verses 3–6 consist of the stage of developing conflict, as David guides the Gibeonites to demand seven Saulides for sacrifice before Yahweh, to which demand he accedes with alacrity. The climax comes in verses 7–9, where David hand picks the Saulides he wants dispatched, and hands them over to the Gibeonites, who waste no time in executing them. The denouement is found in verses 10–13, in which Rizpah seeks dignity for the deceased. Her action leads to the repatriation of the remains of Saul and Jonathan from Transjordan for burial in their own ancestral land. Finally, the closure comes up in verse 14, where Yahweh is reported to have been supplicated only after the burial of the bones of Saul and his progeny.

The text at hand (2 Sam 21:1–14) is fraught with many difficulties ranging from literary composition (in terms of its location within the stream of narration in Samuel), ethical dilemmas (did Yahweh really order human sacrifice, or did David plan the execution of his stepsons and other Saulides?), to textual issues (was the mother of Saul's five grandsons Michal or Merab?). We shall only broach some of these difficulties due to the limited scope of the present endeavor. Our goal ultimately is to

---

square. Keil justifies this harmonistic approach by pointing out that the market-place (*rechob*) in eastern towns is not in the middle of the town but is an open place against or in front of the gate (cf. 2 Chr 32:6; Neh 8:1, 3, 16)" (K & D 2, 679).

108. Some LXX and Syriac versions do not have the phrase "his son" (בנו). It is possibly a gloss based on verse 12. Some LXX manuscripts rather have added the phrase και (τα οστα) (παντων) των ηλιασθεντων ("and the bones of all those who were crucified"). This only makes obvious what is implied in the MT.

ascertain the fate of the Saulide Seven: For whom were they sacrificed—Yahweh or David?

Compositionally many scholars recognize that this text has been severed from its original setting. For example, Carlson correctly, in my view, writes that the evidence apparently shows "beyond question that the generally accepted view (following Budde) that 21:1–14 forms an original prelude to 2 Samuel 9 is correct."[109] As already pointed out in the first chapter, there is a sense in which 2 Sam 21–24 (the so-called appendix) has been structured into a unity. That, nonetheless, is not to say that the events recorded therein have direct chronological linkage in the sense that they all come from one time period. Keys points out that the episodes of the appendix derive from different times during David's reign. She writes, "21:1–14 may record events that took place relatively soon after David assumed control of all Israel. Certainly the complaint of the Gibeonites refers to the period of Saul's rule, therefore it seems most likely that their demands were made not long after David assumed control of all Israel."[110] While it is not possible to locate this passage precisely to an exact point in David's earlier years, I suggest the possibility that 2 Sam 6:23 may have been the conclusion to this episode such that from this time thence to Michal's death she no longer had children; and that the events of 2 Sam 21:1–14 took place before those of ch. 9.[111]

---

109. Carlson, *David, The Chosen King*, 198–99.

110. Keys, *The Wages of Sin*, 83. Cartledge supplying the evidence to support an early time for the events of 2 Sam 21:1–14 writes, "There is no chronological referent for the story, except for three possible lines of evidence. First, seven Saulide scions are known to exist, which is no longer the case at the beginning of chapter 9. Thus, it is likely that this event preceded the story of David's kindness to Mephibosheth in 9:1–13, which would have occurred early in David's reign over the united kingdom. Second, David responded to a time of crisis by seeking Yahweh's guidance, which is quite characteristic of his early years, but not of the period following the Bathsheba incident (2 Sam 11). Third, Shimei's vitriolic rage in 16:5–14 accuses David of wantonly shedding Saulide blood, which has no known referent aside from the Gibeonite incident" (Cartledge, *1 & 2 Samuel*, 636)

111. Other scholars consider the mention of Mephibosheth in 2 Sam 21:7 to have assumed the events of chapter 9 (cf. Gordon, *I & II Samuel*, 248; and Bergen, *1, 2 Samuel*, 444). While it is hard to be categorical in establishing priority between these two passages, the possibility of editorial harmonization should not be left out of the equation. I surmise that ch. 21, just like ch. 24, was originally a strong counter-testimony to the dominant testimony about David. However, in order to incorporate this tradition into their grand narrative the final redactors in some way sought to mitigate the voice of the counter-testimony so as to bring the text into some symphonic harmony with the dominant testimony.

A great many scholars consider the so-called appendix to be a dumping ground for any material the author did not know what to do with or could not easily fit into the other sections of the book.[112] One of the best outlooks on the unit is that of Campbell, who sees it as constituting a third wave of Davidic tradition, which assumes the air of neutrality toward David, excluding the songs.[113] But beyond this, these chapters perform the compositional function of shaping the books of Samuel, a theme that is treated in our first chapter. There are several themes that are found almost exclusively in the earlier chapters (chs. 1-9) and the concluding chapters of 2 Samuel (21-24) but do not surface in the middle section of the book. These include stories about Saul (chs. 1 and 21), the demise of male Saulides at the hands of Gibeonites (chs. 4 and 21), war with the Philistines (chs. 5, 8, and 21), significant interactions between foreigners and David during calamities in Israel (chs. 1 and 24); the threshing floor as a place of judgment (2 Sam 6:6-7) and a place of mercy (2 Sam 24:16, 25), and David's donations for sacral use of what he plundered or acquired from Gentiles (2 Sam 8:11-12; and 24:22-25; cf. 1 Chr 22:1-2). Thus, we can see compositional purposefulness and deliberateness in the placement of these materials where they are.

The ethical dilemma relates to the issue of Davidic complicity in the extermination of the Saulide Seven, five of whom were probably David's stepsons. The surface reading of the text indicates that in the midst of a famine crisis David sought the Lord: What does this mean in light of similar phenomena elsewhere in Samuel (and the Hebrew Bible)? Did Yahweh indeed require human sacrifice? Did the Gibeonites indeed exact Saulide blood, or were they just marionettes of which David pulled the strings? Certainly, there are those who see David's anxiety over the survival of his house vis-à-vis the popularity of Saul even long after the latter's death. This inexorably gave room to political machination for the

---

112. Bergen calls this unit an "aside" even though he considers 1 Samuel–2 Kings to be a literary unity (Bergen, *1, 2 Samuel*, 444); cf. Robinson, *1 & 2 Samuel*, 264. Jobling similarly writes, "I have suggested that this passage is a dumping ground for material that belongs in 1 Samuel but that if put there would upset the theological world" (Jobling, *1 Samuel*, 183).

113. Campbell says the first wave is found in the stories of David's rise with their strong pro-Davidic stance while the second wave is found in David's middle years, where the emphasis is on the exploration of human behavioral motivations. The third way, he posits, neither has a stance toward David nor does it inquire into human motives (Campbell, *2 Samuel*, 185).

elimination of the Saulides so the house of David might stand.[114] It is on this note that Brueggemann writes, "This narrative is a jolt to our expectations. In the preceding account of David, we have come to expect that David is a man of *ḥesed* who will keep his vows of loyalty, especially to Saul and Jonathan. Here David is cast in a very different role. I suggest that this narrative is deliberately intended as a protest against the preceding 'official' portrayal of David. This is, the narrative is presented with high irony, to suggest that David in fact is not as we had first thought him to be."[115] It is ironic that David broke his personal Yahwistic oath to Saul (1 Sam 24:17–23 [ET 24:16–22]), which he made with both eyes open, in order to "fulfill" a Yahwistic oath of several generations before his own time to which he was no party (an oath that was forged under deceptive circumstances).[116]

The hardest of the textual difficulties here relates to whether Saul's five grandsons belong to Michal (MT) or Merab (the ancient translations). There is no easy way around this: whichever position one takes, one aspect of the text will have to be compromised or accounted for in some way or another. If one follows the MT, one will need to account for the wrong name for the husband; on the other hand, if one follows the LXX, one will have to account for the wrong name for the mother. We will however allow the text to guide the conclusion we make in this respect.

## *The Famine, the Oracle, and Its Outcome*

The context of this whole episode is set in a three year period of famine during David's reign. We are not told, however, when in David's reign this famine occurred. Glück suggests that the unfortunate events "may well have their beginning during the time when David was king in Hebron."[117] Glück's statement has its own ambiguity; what he means by

---

114. To explore this further, see Ishida, *The Royal Dynasties in Ancient Israel*, 77; and Glück, "Merab or Michal," 74.

115. Brueggemann, *First and Second Samuel*, 336.

116. Firth excuses "the unusual circumstance of sons being put to the death for their father's sin" on the account of covenant violation and generated bloodguilt (*1 & 2 Samuel*, 506). He, however, fails to reckon with the fact that the execution he calls unusual as well as the exposure of the corpses of the Saulide Seven (which he rightly notes as having prevented Yahweh from answering David's entreaty) were direct violation of the Torah, as we shall demonstrate subsequently.

117. Glück, "Merab or Michal," 73.

the events having their beginning during David's rule in Hebron is left to conjecture. Whatever that means, it is hard to conceive of any of these events happening during David's seven-and-a-half-year rule in Hebron, because prior to Abner's surrender, David would have had no way of ferrying away almost the entirety of Saul's male progeny for the hangman's noose without a robust and spirited resistance. The obvious conclusion is that these events relate to the period following David's ascendency over all Israel.

As the famine persisted for three consecutive years, David reportedly resorted to Yahweh. Herein lies one of the difficulties of this passage: all of the features usually associated with the discovery or disclosure of the will of the deity are absent. There is neither mention of a priestly official with an ephod or the Urim and Thummim (Exod 28:30; Num 27:21; Ezra 2:63; Neh 7:65) nor the mention of a prophetic figure or a seer. These two institutions (priest and prophet/seer) represent clearly defined means of obtaining the divine will in ancient Israel.[118] In the case of the priest with the ephod or the Urim and Thumim, the matter for which the divine will was being sought would be framed into a question that required a "Yes" or "No" answer so that either ends or sides of the instrument stood for an affirmation or a disaffirmation.[119] Indeed, in the Samuel narratives no mention of David inquiring of Yahweh is made until Abiathar joins the former's rebel band with an ephod in hand (1 Sam 23:1–12; 30:7–8).[120]

Campbell points out that the "phrase translated 'David inquired of the LORD' is unprecedented in Samuel for this meaning. It is used for Saul's seeking David (1 Sam 24:3 [Heb.; NRSV, 24:2]; 26:2; cf. 2 Sam

---

118. Occasionally the divine will was revealed through dreams as well, though this was much more common in the earliest and latest segments of Israel's tradition (see 1 Sam 28:6 where all the three means of revelation are mentioned). However, it is not even indicated that David received the revelation by dream or vision.

119. Friedman on the same note writes, "But the murder of Saul's remaining family members was not preceded by such a process. This time God was not consulted by the accepted binary process but was asked a general question about the cause of the famine and responded by blaming the house of Saul. The impression is that this was a cynical use of the deity in order to eliminate Saul's dynasty. An interesting aspect is the absence of any priests and prophets from the story. Either David claimed to have spoken directly to God and received an answer or he acted with the assistance of some priest or prophet but chose not to reveal any names" (Friedmann, *To Kill and Take Possession*, 161).

120. Even the other references to someone inquiring of the Lord for David prior to his wilderness wandering days has to do with a priestly figure (cf. 1 Sam 22:10, 15).

3:17; 5:17).ᵃ[121] The statement in 2 Sam 21:1 is ויבקש דוד את־פני יהוה ("And David sought the face of Yahweh"). The word בקש is rarely used of inquiring of the Lord. The most common word in that case is דרש (Gen 25:22; Exod 18:15; Deut 12:30; 17:9; 1 Sam 9:9; 1 Kgs 22:5–8; 2 Chr 34:21, 26). בקש is used with respect to looking or searching for someone or something that needs to be found in a literal sense. In other words, בקש is used with respect to searching for information within the human realm (Gen 24:57; Judg 4:20; 1 Sam 17:56). However, when reference is to inquiring to uncover the divine will (even through mediums) בקש is not used.[122] Rather, it is דרש and occasionally שאל that are used (1 Sam 28:7; 2 Kgs 1:2–6, 16; 1 Chr 10:13). Therefore, the use of בקש in this passage makes the reference to the divine will very suspect.[123] It is seems, therefore, that the narrator is using this linguistic dissonance to cast doubts on the supposed oracle that was used as the warrant for the execution of the Saulide Seven.

Another difficulty in this passage is that there is no antecedent reference to this act of Saul's aggression against the Gibeonites. Such an absence is baffling, to say the least, in consideration of the importance of the alleged offense, which was the ground for taking such an unusual step of not only annihilating almost all the male members of the premier Israelite family but doing so at the hands of people who were essentially aliens. Doing all that without previous reference to the offense makes the accusation against Saul suspect. The only other similar incident in the Hebrew Bible is that of Saul's murder of the priests from Nob by the hand of an Edomite (1 Sam 22:16–19). Yet, Saul did it more audaciously and with previous reference to the supposed offense. Viewing things in this way makes Saul even look better than David

---

121. Campbell, *2 Samuel*, 189.

122. In the few instances where בקש is used in the sense of seeking God, the reference is to seeking after God with the general meaning of returning in repentance and/or commitment to him, or seeking his favor in the face of imminent danger (Exod 33:7; 2 Sam 12:16; 2 Chr 11:16; Ezra 8:21; Ps 27:4, 7; 34:15; Hos 5:6; Zech 8:21–22). In these cases we may expect to find no direct divine response, a signal of divine disapproval, or an indication of a general favor of the deity. In a few cases where we find a direct divine response, the divine word is clearly indicated as coming through a prophet (2 Chr 20) or through an angelic being (Dan 9); such a clear manifestation of divine response is lacking in David's supposed oracle in this passage.

123. This suspicion is especially cogent in view of the dominant use of בקש in Samuel in the sense of looking for persons in order to end their lives (see 1 Sam 19:2, 10; 20:1; 22:23; 23:10, 15, 25; 24:3, 10; 25:29; 26:2, 26; 2 Sam 4:8; 2 Sam 16:11; 17:3; 20:19; 21:2).

because Saul would not hide under the name of the deity in pursuing personal vendetta. This understanding becomes more appealing in the face of the restrained defense of Saul, namely, that he committed the supposed injustice out of "his zeal for the Israelites and the Judahites." In general, patriotic and Yahwistic idealism rather than personal gain undergirded Saul's motivations throughout most of his reign (v. 2; cf. 1 Sam 11:1–13; 14:32–44; 28:9).[124] One wonders whether this defense of Saul was not the counter-testimony voice's spin on the Davidic apologia, offered for the murder of the Saulides, as a muffled comparison of David to Saul. This comparison with Saul is very telling, because in Saul's case all Israelites refused to put forth their hands against Saul's victims: did David anticipate such a refusal, hence the divinatory travesty that allowed the use of non-Israelites for this dirty job?[125] David

---

124. Commenting on this clause Glück similarly writes, "Such a remark must have placed Saul in a rather favorable light in the eyes of the Israelites (and the Judeans) and it is not likely that it was written by a Davidic court historian" (Glück, "Merab or Michal," 78). Reacting to the absence of evidence for Saul's murder of the Gibeonites, Brueggemann sees it all as a piece of Davidic fabrication that lacks historical support. He writes, "Saul is a scrupulously religious man who is unlikely to evoke such bloodguilt (cf. 1 Sam 14:45). We might expect Saul to have such restraining scruples. The narrative may suggest to us, in the guise of a simple report, that David has no such restraining scruple. Believing David's rationale and the accusation against Saul requires innocent credulity" (Brueggemann, *First and Second Samuel*, 338).

On the side of those who admit the possibility that Saul actually massacred the Gibeonites Robinson writes, "Saul may well have massacred them out of his zeal for the fulfillment of the *herem* institution, which the Gibeonites escaped earlier by playing a trick on the Israelites (cf. Josh 9). Saul is presented here as one to whom preservation of the purity of the people and their religion was of primary importance" (Robinson, *Let Us Be Like the Nations*, 265). Bergen, on the other hand, holds that Saul violated the centuries-old nonaggression compact with these Amorites and in effect prioritized nationalistic zeal over zeal for the Lord, the kingdom of Israel over the kingdom of God (Bergen, *1, 2 Samuel*, 444). Bergen's reference to the kingdom of God here is certainly anachronistic.

125. Friedman similarly writes, "It is significant that the justification for killing Saul's family is placed in the injustice that Saul did to the Gibeonites. They play a central role in the apologia designed to purge David of any responsibility for the extermination of the house of Saul. The members of Saul's family are not killed by Israelites, for had they done so at David's command, he would be held responsible, and the Bible seeks to keep him out of the murder" (Friedmann, *To Kill and Take Possession*, 161). I am of the opinion that if we understand the reported oracle in this episode as part of the retelling of the Davidic apologia in the context of counter-testimony, as we do here, then, it will be unnecessary to accuse the Bible of seeking to keep David out of a crime, especially as the Bible does not shirk from reporting anybody's offense—not even David (cf. 2 Samuel 11, 12). The question to ask is why did David have to use a pretext to kill the

had similarly employed the Ammonites, with no less subtlety, to snuff the life out of Uriah so he could take the latter's wife.

In normal circumstances, whenever an oracle was obtained, it was either applied to existing regulations or there was a clear direction from Yahweh on how to use the received revelation (Josh 7:10–15; 6:17–19; 2 Sam 5:23–24). But rather than check with Yahweh for clarification as to what to do in view of the received revelation, David turned from Yahweh to the Gibeonites to ask them what he needed to do to appease Yahweh. To borrow the analogy from Bergen, David was placing human vindictiveness in the place of divine justice, the Gibeonites in Yahweh's place. The Gibeonites, however, responded by saying that their case was not such that required monetary compensation, and that they had no right to put anyone to death in Israel. This reply is very poignant because it is in perfect agreement with Torah legislation. First of all, ransom was never to be taken in criminal murder cases (Num 35:30–33). Thus, they were right in denying that they had any money-matter with the house of Saul. Secondly, all the ordinances concerning murder unambiguously and emphatically state that it is the murderer who is the offender and he alone is condemned to capital punishment (Gen 9:5–6; Exod 21:12–14; Num 35:16–21; Deut 19:11–13). So again the Gibeonites were right to point out that there was no one in Israel for them to put to death ("And there is no one in Israel for us to kill," v. 4), since the alleged murderer, Saul, was already dead.

Commenting on the Gibeonite response Glück writes that such a response from a plaintiff usually was sufficient to terminate a criminal case and that David's rejoinder to their lackluster response clearly indicated his dissatisfaction with their reply.[126] Indeed, the Gibeonite response is redolent with a sense of finality since Saul, who would have been the candidate for such a judicial process, was no more. David then prods the Gibeonites further with a promise that he will do whatever

---

Saulides when latter kings did similar acts with no qualms (cf. 1 Kgs 14:10–11; 15:29; 16:3–4, 11–12; 2 Kgs 9:8–9; 10:11)? Some possible answer is that Yahwistic sensibilities were much stronger in these earlier times than they were in latter times. This is evident in the affair of Uriah's murder as well. Ishida also suggests that this may have been due to the popularity of Saul and his house long into David's reign (Ishida, *The Royal Dynasties in Ancient Israel*, 79). David, therefore, had to tread cautiously where Saul's house was concerned.

126. Glück, "Merab or Michal," 74.

they request. This implicitly places direct responsibility of the murders of the Saulide Seven on David.

It is in response to David's blank check, perhaps sensing the suggestiveness of the offer, that the Gibeonites then requested seven sons of Saul to sacrifice before Yahweh in Gibeon. Campbell notes that the Gibeonite request for seven sons of Saul employs the sacral number seven.[127] This concept of a sacral or mystical number (seven) indicates wholeness or completeness, thereby indicating the comprehensiveness of the ruin that was visited upon the house of Saul.[128]

What the Gibeonites proposed to do with the Saulides ("that we may execute them in Gibeon on the mountain of Yahweh," v. 6), to which David accedes, could be nothing other than human sacrifice, especially when considered in the context of the expiation that David was seeking.[129] This is further buttressed by the mention elsewhere in Israel's traditions of a prominent Yahwistic cultic center (high place) in Gibeon at least from the time of David (1 Chr 16:39; 21:29; cf. 2 Sam 20:8)—the place that would later play a very historic role at the inauguration of Solomon's reign (1 Kgs 3:3-14; 2 Chr 1:3-13). Most likely, it is on account of the location of this high place on a high hill that the place came to be called הר יהוה ("The mountain of Yahweh"). This sacral nature of the killings is troubling because there are strong sentiments in the Hebrew Bible to suggest that human sacrifice was alien to Yahwistic religion.

## *The Execution of the Saulide Seven*

After extracting the request for seven heads of Saulides, David proceeds to arrest them and hand them over to the Gibeonites for extermination. In this arrest, a statement is made about David sparing Mephibosheth, Jonathan's son, on the basis of a Yahwistic oath. This statement has become a source of intense debate in scholarly circles as to whether or not chapter 21 has chronological priority over chapter 9. Carlson, from the

---

127. Campbell, *2 Samuel*, 189. He observes that while the sacral number of seven may not have comprised all of Saul's descendents, it did eliminate all his sons (ibid., 190).

128. Robinson, on this account, writes, "'Seven sons' probably here refers to all the males born in the house of Saul. The evil that Saul intended on the Gibeonites is thus turned onto him—his house (or family) will have no portion in the territory of Israel" (Robinson, *Let Us Be Like the Nations*, 266).

129. Alter likewise comments, "'Before the LORD' is an explicit indication of the sacrificial nature of the killings" (Alter, *The David Story*, 331).

camp of those who grant priority to chapter 21, following Budde, holds that the evidence seems to show beyond question that 21:1–14 forms an original prelude to 2 Sam 9. To support this view he writes, "David's question in 9:1, 'Is there still any one left of the house of Saul that I may show him kindness for Jonathan's sake?' seems to presuppose that the description of the death of the seven descendants of Saul in 21:1–14 preceded chapter 9."[130] Those who give priority to chapter 9 object to the use of David's question in chapter 9 because, they insist, the question would still have been relevant even without the massacre of the Saulide Seven in view of the earlier deaths of Saul and his other sons. Segal, for example, writes, "The narrative of the Gibeonite blood revenge (xxi 1–14) is later than the coming of Mephibosheth to David (ix), as it [sic] clear from xxi 7. Here David has no need to enquire abous [sic] the identity and number of Saul's descendants (v. 8) or about their where-abouts as he had to do in ch. ix, because no doubt Ziba or Mephibosheth had already furnished him with all the information about the survivors of Saul's family."[131] If these chapters are taken on their own, the evidence will tilt one way or the other. However, when taken in the context of the entire book, especially considering our discussion on chapter 6, it becomes more convincing to accept that chapter 9 presupposes 21 in terms of story time, but chapter 21 has been placed where it is because of pragmatic reasons (some of which are highlighted above).

The Saulides delivered to the Gibeonites are listed as two sons of Saul by his concubine, Rizpah, and five sons of Michal (MT) or Merab (LXX and other translations). This is another point of disagreement among biblical scholars: the priority of either the MT or LXX is upheld by different scholars. From the latter group Friedmann writes, "The Bible speaks of five sons of Michal, Saul's daughter, by Adriel, but all the commentators agree that it was Merab who was Adriel's wife, while Michal was childless. The traditional explanation for the present text is that Michal raised her sister's children."[132] Friedmann's sweeping statement on the unanimity of all commentators in giving priority to Merab is more of his wishful thinking than a fact of life.

When one understands the enduring nature of blood feud (sometimes lasting for generations) in traditional societies, especially in the

---

130. Carlson, *David, The Chosen King*, 198–99.
131. Segal, "The Composition of the Books of Samuel," 36–37.
132. Friedmann, To Kill and Take Possession, 161.

Near East (to the present day[133]), it is hard to conceive that this would be a reference to Barzillai's five grandsons by Merab, considering his staunch support for David during the Absalom revolt. In recognition of this difficulty, Halpern rationalizes Barzillai's action by surmising that as the grandfather of these five Saulides that were killed, Barzillai only demonstrates that "his alliance with the House of Saul was a disposable product of dynastic politics. He was willing to throw over earlier partners in the process of advancing his own interests, presumably recognizing the uselessness of ties to a dethroned dynasty. Like the Gibeonites, Barzillai's non-Saulides descendents were rewarded with a berth in the temple hierarchy."[134] He adds that both Barzillai and Machir derived economic benefit from the Ammonite war, on which account they were willing to change sides. While such postulations are completely possible, their probability, which Halpern assumes, presumes too much on the greed and avarice of Barzillai, which is otherwise unattested in the biblical text.

On the contrary, our view of blood feud in the Near East is affirmed by Ahithophel's support of the Absalom revolt following David's murder of Uriah. This fact is underscored by Ahithophel's willingness to risk everything despite the fact that Uriah was not even a direct descendant, but the husband to his granddaughter, Bathsheba (cf. 2 Sam 11:3; 23:34; 15:12), and that he stood to gain more materially when his granddaughter became the king's wife. Joab's murder of Abner for the latter's killing of the former's brother is another case in point. Indeed, the Torah's promulgations on the blood avenger and cities of refuge are eloquent testimonies to this view.

Besides, arguments on the change of Michal's name to Merab derive partly from the fact that the LXX names the mother of the grandsons as such and that in 1 Sam 18:19 Merab is said to have been given to Adriel.[135] However, such arguments forget that the LXX does not even contain 1 Sam 18:19 at all, which fact further diminishes the role or place of Merab in the narrative, thereby making her less likely to be the one in view here. Glück points out that Michal (i.e., the mother) is the tragic

---

133. Robinson, "Breaking the cycle," 10–11.

134. Halpern, *David's Secret Demons*, 349. Firth, on the other hand, suggests that this Barzillai is different from the Gileadite, though he supplies no elaboration (*1 & 2 Samuel*, 505).

135. Campbell, *2 Samuel*, 349–50.

character in the episode; the mention of a husband is necessitated only because she had two. He further states, "The correct name of the children's father was so unimportant to the eyes of the scribe that he actually confused the name of Michal's husband with that of Merab's."[136] Glück further draws attention to the phenomenon of biblical inaccuracies with regard to patronymic references.[137] Indeed, he is of the opinion that

---

136. Glück, "Merab or Michal," 72–81.

137. Glück cites several examples of these that include some of the most prominent people or families in the histories of Israel and Judah. Some (not all) of the examples enumerated below are adapted from his "Merab or Michal," 76–77:

1. In 2 Samuel 23:8, for the MT's ישב בשבת תחכמני (Josheb-basshebeth a Tahchemonite), the LXX has Ιεβοσθε ὁ Χαναναῖος (Jebosthe the Chananite).

2. Compare 2 Sam 21:21 ([שמעה] (שמעי)־בן יהונתן, Jonathan the son of Shimei, using the Ketiv) with 1 Chr 20:6 (שמעא־בן יהונתן, Jonathan the son of Shimea), and 2 Sam 13:3 (יונדב בן־שמעה Jonadab the son of Shimeah). In all three instances the name of the father differs; similarly, the name of the son differs in the third instance; all three verses refer to the same person. Glück points out that Jonathan was a very common name in those days; indeed five men associated with David bore this name (1 Chr 27:25, 32; 2 Sam 16:27; 21:21; 23:32–33). The correct identification of this person (correct spelling of his name and his patronym) should have been important to the scribe, but the contrary is the case.

3. Compare the sons of Benjamin in Gen 46:21 (Bela and Becher and Ashbel, Gera and Naaman, Ehi and Rosh, Muppim and Huppim and Ard); with Num 26:38–41 (Bela, Ashbel, Ahiram, Shephupham, Hupham; and his grandsons through Bela were Ard and Naaman); with 1 Chr 7:6–10 (Bela, Becher, Jediael; the grandsons through Bela were Ezbon, Uzzi, Uzziel, Jerimoth and Iri; the grandsons through Becher were Zemirah, Joash, Eliezer, Elioenai, Omri, Jeremoth, Abijah, Anathoth and Alemeth; and the grandson through Jediael was Bilhan).

4. Compare Saul's genealogy in 1 Sam 9:1 (Saul is the son of Kish; Kish and Ner—Abner's father—are sons of Abiel, Abiel the son of Zeror, Zeror the son Becorath, Becorath the son of Aphia) and in 1 Chr 8:33; 9:39 (Ner rather than being the uncle of Saul is said to be the latter's father). So if the genealogy of even Israel's first king can be messed up, how much more should one expect that to happen to his daughter (a woman for that matter)?

5. Compare the list of the sons of Josiah in 1 Chr 3:15 (Jonathan, Jehoikim, Zedekiah, and Shallum) and in 2 Kgs 23–24 (Jehoahaz, Eliakim [Jehoikim], and Mattaniah [Zedekiah]).

6. Compare the two progenitors assigned to Athaliah: mentioned as the daughter of Ahab in 2 Kgs 8:18 and some mss of 2 Chr 22:2, but also referred to as the daughter of Omri in 2 Kgs 8:26 and most mss of 2 Chr 22:2.

this phenomenon is so prevalent that with regard to tribal genealogies "the inexactitudes are so frequent that they are more the rule than the exception."[138]

Consequently, arguing by merely citing ancient translation manuscript witnesses does not suffice in this situation. The hermeneutical key has to be found in the context of the narrative itself. In this case, between Merab and Michal the focus throughout the HDR was on Michal, with the paths of David and Merab not even crossing in the LXX. Even in the MT Merab receives no focus and is mentioned only as a foil to Michal. In the SN, we meet Michal again in 2 Sam 6. Indeed, in some regard, her story forms an inclusio around the SN, or what others prefer to call the Story of David's Middle Years (SDMY).

In addition, with the stature of David in biblical literature there would be a greater temptation for the redactors to mitigate the gravity of this incidence, to make the people killed more distant from David than to leave them as close relatives (stepsons). On the other hand, there is no sufficient motive for changing the name from Merab to Michal. Furthermore, the sons of Michal stood more proximate to the throne (having both a royal grandfather and a royal stepfather, coupled with a very strong-willed mother) and as such would constitute a greater threat to David's dynastic ambition than if they were Merab's sons. In like manner Ishida concludes that from the dynastic-political point of view, there were more "reasons for Michal's sons to be removed by David than Merab's. Hence, we prefer the emendation of 'Adriel' into 'Paltiel.'"[139]

The compositional use of the interconnection of David and Michal to bracket David's story in 2 Samuel is another reason to read this name as Michal not Merab. In the story of David and Michal we find an interconnection with Philistine wars (eight recorded wars in all). First, in a summary statement (quite unlike the elaboration in the case of Goliath) in 1 Sam 19:8 is a report of David's success against the Philistines. After this David exited Michal's life, we hear no more of his success against the Philistines, rather he even become a mercenary in their service. Right af-

---

7. The lists of Saul's sons given in 1 Sam 14:49 (the names of his sons are Jonathan, Ishvi, Malchi-shua; and the names of his two daughters are Merab and Michal) and in 1 Chr 8:33; 9:39 (the names of Saul's children listed are Jonathan, Malchi-shua, Abinadab and Eshbaal).

138. Glück, "Merab or Michal," 77.

139. Ishida, *The Royal Dynasties in Ancient Israel*, 79.

ter the return of Michal into David's life, he again experienced two great victories over the Philistines (2 Sam 5:17–25); the fourth war in this era is in 2 Sam 8:1. In all these wars, David was the center of attention: victory flowed from his actions. The theme of Yahweh's presence seems to underlie all these wars (cf. 2 Sam 5:17–25; 8:1, 6c).

This motif of Michal-David and Philistine wars resurfaces with the murder of Michal's children. There are four wars with the Philistines in the wake of these murders, in which Israel was successful, but in all of these David was not part of the success story. In the first battle, mentioned right after these brutal murders, David was almost killed by a Philistine warrior and was only saved by the timely intervention of Abishai, son of Zeruiah, Joab's brother. Then, in the three subsequent wars with the Philistines, Israel was successful but without David, who had been banished from warfare. In the previous wars (of the earlier times of David) the frequent commentary refrain was that Yahweh was with David. In these last wars Yahweh is not in the picture: in fact, one can insinuate that Yahweh was not with David at this point.

So there seems to be a direct correlation between Michal's presence in David's house and David's success against the Philistines. The success of David's rise and early reign years are characterized by the presence of both Yahweh and Michal with him. In David's middle years, however, Michal drops out of the picture, and we hear nothing of the Lord's presence with David. We note, however, that while the Lord does not overtly show solidarity with David as before, he nevertheless works against David's enemies (2 Sam 17:14). In David's twilight years, after he authorizes the murder of Michal's five sons, the Lord persistently fights against him in the characteristic Deuteronomistic retributive justice fashion with faintness in war (2 Sam 21:15–17), famine (2 Sam 21:1), and pestilence (2 Sam 24:1–15). Yahweh's anger against Israel in "the days of David" (21:1) seems to have persisted for some time after the murder of the Saulide Seven, as demonstrated both by David's near death encounter with the Philistines (21:18) and the census debacle (24:1), where it is stated that Yahweh's anger "continued"[140] to burn against Israel.[141]

---

140. I render the beginning of 24:1, ויסף אף־יהוה לחרות בישראל, as "Yahweh's anger continued to burn against Israel." The word (יסף) is traditionally translated as "again." However, its dominant or primary meaning is the idea of to "add," to "increase," or "do more," (BDB, 415). In other words, its basic meaning indicates a continuity of the same phenomenon even if manifested in different ways, rather than a discontinuous punctiliar iteration (though the latter may not be excluded, it is not primary), hence my idea of "to continue."

141. As has been argued above, while the stories in the so-called appendix occurred

Subsequently, the Gibeonites killed the Saulide Seven in Gibeon (see footnote 104 above). The sacral nature of the killings is recognized by many scholars.[142] Carlson, indeed, suggests that the phrase "before Yahweh" is a synonym for "before the Ark."[143] While such an equation of Yahweh's presence with the ark may be appropriated elsewhere in the Hebrew Bible, the appropriateness of such an understanding in this case is doubtful. A support for this is found in the account of Solomon's presentation of sacrifice and his reception of his inaugural vision at the Gibeonite high place long after David had brought the ark to Jerusalem (1 Kgs 3:4–14; cf. 2 Sam 6).

The end of this episode is as puzzling as the other elements contained therein. With the opening accusation of bloodguilt leveled against Saul and his house, one would expect that the sacrifice of the Saulide Seven would have brought closure to the issue at stake. Yet that was not the case. It is only after the granting of the "justice" that Rizpah's quiet protest demanded that true closure came.

## Rizpah's Search for Dignity for Her Dead

Having handed the Saulide Seven to the Gibeonites for massacre, David cared little about what became of their corpses. One can hardly miss the striking parallel here between David and Saul, the only monarchs in Israel who handed bona fide Israelites over to non-Israelites to kill (the Saulides to Gibeonites and the priests of Nob to an Edomite, respectively). The Gibeonites proceeded to massacre the Saulide Seven. The most appalling thing is that after their gruesome murder they were not even given the courtesy of a decent burial: their corpses were just exposed to the elements and scavenging birds and beasts. One supposes that it is this insensitivity to propriety on David's part, coupled with filial or kinship bond, honor of the dead, and purity of the land (*pace* Torah legislation; cf. Deut 21:22–23) that goaded Rizpah into action, though her motivation remains unstated.[144]

---

earlier in David's story, they have been pragmatically placed where they are to form a conclusion to the narrative.

142. Cf. Alter, *The David Story*, 331; Robinson, *Let Us Be Like the Nations*, 266–67; and Campbell, *2 Samuel*, 331.

143. Carlson, *David, The Chosen King*, 201, note 1.

144. Highlighting the absence of emotion and overt causal connection in the narrative that denies it of heroic defiance elements, Exum writes that the story "scandalizes us

In her bold and courageous action, Rizpah defies the king, elements of the weather, and wild beasts and camps out in the open, protecting the decomposing corpses of the scions of her late husband from being ravaged by either birds or beasts of prey. Her vigil is said to have begun in the early days of barley harvest (i.e., in the month of either Nisan or Iyyar—around March or April) and ended by the arrival of the first rain (i.e., in the month of either Tishri or Marheshvan—around October or November). It is the report of this protracted vigil that compels David to address this bestial desecration of the dead. David's response was to bury not just the bones of the most recent victims of Saul's house, but also those of Saul and Jonathan. The question to ask is, why go this extra mile? If it is part of David's loyalty to the house of Saul, then, why was it not done earlier? Could it be that David realized his violation of Torah prescription and was attempting an appeasement ahead of time? It is very instructive that we are told God responded to prayers for the land only after the burial of the Saulide Seven. This seems to be an indication of divine disapproval of what had transpired, for there was no divine order to kill the Saulides even in the purported oracle, and the manner of their disposal or the lack thereof was a flagrant violation of Torah legislation.

There are a number of parallels between this episode, coming as it does at the end of 2 Samuel, to what happened to Saul and his other sons at the end of 1 Samuel (ch. 31). In both cases they were killed by non-Israelites, they were dismembered, they were displayed in public, and some unusual means was used to extract their bones (burning the corpses in the first instance and exposure in the second). Most tellingly, we find in both cases the astonishing bravery of those who sought dignity for the dead: the people of Jabesh-gilead in the first instance and Rizpath in the second. In both cases these "redeemers" risked their lives for the dead; they underwent a period of self denial—a seven-day fast by the Jabesh-gileadites and about seven months of camping in the open (a kind of fasting, as it were) by Rizpah. The desired goals were achieved in both cases.[145] These "redeemers," in their own right, blazed the trail

---

without showing us directly the personal anguish of the characters. Neither Rizpah nor David—even less so the seven victims—seeks to avert the inevitable, though Rizpah's action serves as a powerful protest against the fate of Saul's sons" (Exum, *Tragedy and Biblical Narrative*, 110).

145. While we highlight the similarities between these two incidents, Exum draws attention to the dissimilarity. She writes, "When one considers David's praise for the

of how to fight for justice on the behalf of those who cannot speak for themselves.

## CONCLUSION

In this chapter we have studied the passages that deal with David's relationship to Michal, beginning from the earlier days of his rise, through the early period of his ascendency over both Judah and Israel, to later in his reign. David's relationship to Michal was as ambivalent and exploitative as his relationships with all other Saulides, and indeed, all his relationships with other people in the Samuel narratives.

Even in the earlier days of his rise, David manifested no affection or concern for Michal, who really loved him and risked everything to save his life. He was preoccupied with advancing his status and political career. He thus merely used Michal opportunistically to give himself a vantage point from which he would later contest for Saul's throne. It is with the same deviousness that, in his final thrust to grab Saul's throne, David sought to repossess Michal. She only served him the utilitarian value of granting him access to Saul's throne in her capacity as the late monarch's daughter. The claim he laid on her was no more than for a piece of estate that he acquired with a gross price. Her self-worth as a person, her dignity as God's image-bearer, and her emotional health mattered little to him. Later in his reign, David had passed beyond the point of only exploiting the Saulides, but now actively pursued their extermination through a supposed oracle that does not conform to the usual forms of Yahwistic oracles and effected the scheme via the agency of foreign elements within Israelite territory.

In the next chapter I shall conclude my investigation of the relationship between David and Saul's progeny by examining his interactions with Mephibosheth, the son of his supposed best friend.

---

men of Jabesh-gilead (2 Sam 2:5–7), his silence here becomes a telling commentary on his own ambivalent role in these events" (Exum, *Tragedy and Biblical Narrative*, 117).

# 6

# David and Mephibosheth

IN OUR CONTINUING STUDY of David's relationships with Saul's descendants, we have examined his relationship with Michal in the last chapter. We saw that Michal loved David from the start and sacrificed to secure his safety when his life was threatened. David, however, never showed affection for her. During the long years of their separation, he made no effort to retrieve her from Saul's sphere but found time to meet with Jonathan more than once. When it was convenient for David to reassert his status as son-in-law of the deceased monarch, in order to smoothen his path to Israel's throne, he once again remembered Michal—tearing her from the home of the husband who deeply loved her. Subsequent to her being plucked from the home in which she had found comfort, Michal was sequestered in David's palace. Even at the most momentous event of the ark's procession into Jerusalem, she was a mere onlooker, not a participant in the celebrations. She was only able to watch the events from the lattice behind which she remained picketed. Her venture to reprove David's intemperate gamboling only brought further humiliation and greater repercussions. We would hear no more of her till toward the end of the story of David, when we are told of the lamentable murder of her five sons and two half-brothers in a Gibeonite sacral event David sanctioned. In the present chapter, I will continue on the same trajectory by looking at the fate of Mephibosheth on David's watch.

The books of Samuel tell the stories of Israel's four leaders: two (Eli and Samuel) who reign as judges in the pre-monarchal era, and two (Saul and David) who were the founding monarchs of Israel. 2 Samuel chronicles the last lap of the story of David's ascendency to Israel's throne and his subsequent reign. Nevertheless, both the memory and the progeny of Saul refused to be eclipsed in this riveting story of David. Almost every time they surface, their appearance casts a dark shadow on David's career and character. The points at which Mephibosheth, in particular, is mentioned show an interesting pattern as shown below:

A      Mephibosheth mentioned in the story of the deaths of Abner and Ishbosheth at the hands of Davidic sympathizers (2 Sam 3 & 4)

    B    Saulide princess (Michal) confronts David (2 Sam 6:20–23)

        C    Mephibosheth invested with his grandfather's patrimony by David (2 Sam 9:7, 9)

            D    Mephibosheth divested of his grand father's patrimony by David (2 Sam 16:4)

    B'    Saulide sympathizer (Shimei) confronts David (2 Sam 16:5–8)

        C'    Mephibosheth partially re-invested with his grandfather's patrimony by David (2 Sam 19:30)

A'    Mephibosheth mentioned in the story of the death of the Saulide Seven at David's instance (2 Sam 21:1–14)

The story of David, as it is told in 2 Samuel, is bracketed by the accounts of the violent deaths of Saulides (both at the beginning and end; A and A' respectively), and in each case there is a cursory mention of Mephibosheth. Then, we have two accounts of Saulide confrontations with David: in the one case he is accused of impropriety (B) and in the other of shedding Saulide blood (B'). Similarly, there are two reports of David granting Mephibosheth the right to inherit his grandfather's estate: in the first instance (C), Saul's entire estate is bestowed on Mephibosheth with an elaborate Davidic speech; and in the second instance (C'), only half of the land is returned, with David speaking more or less tongue-in-cheek. At the core of the quasi-chiastic structure (D) is the report that David confiscates Saul's estate and bestows it on Ziba, Saul's steward.

In the above structure, David's portrait, especially with regard to his dealings with the house of Saul, is increasingly sullied. For an example let us consider the murders of Saulides reported in the outer rings of the quasi-chiasm (A) and (A') respectively. In the first case (A), there is a spirited effort to absolve David of blame, while in the second case (A′) he shares responsibility, if not guilt, for the murders. Regarding the confrontations, in the first instance (B), David turns Michal's accusation on its head by forcefully arguing that what Michal considers disgraceful is a manifestation of his piety, whereas in the second confrontation (B′), David shows piety by not answering the charge of being responsible for Saulide shed blood. The narrator affords the reader no luxury of explicit affirmation that silence here is to be taken as an acceptance of guilt. The double accounts of land grant, likewise, show a worsening portrayal of David. In the first report (C), he is portrayed as acting to fulfill covenant loyalty, while in the second account (C′), he seems to be bound to a man who had used graft to ingratiate himself with David. At the core is the account of David's hasty confiscation of Mephibosheth's land without affording him the opportunity to defend himself as required by the Torah, a matter we will return to in the next chapter. These accounts, together with the pattern in which they are reported, suggest the very manner of their telling to be a sad commentary on the way David administered (or failed to administer) justice.

The aforementioned point becomes poignant when we focus on 2 Sam 9, 16, and 19, in which the stories of Mephibosheth interlace with David's story. After the account of David's encounter with Mephibosheth in chapter 9, the next story involving an Israelite is that of David's adultery with, and expropriation of Bathsheba, after he ordered the murder of her husband (2 Sam 11). This dastardly act of injustice is roundly denounced by the prophet Nathan (2 Sam 12). On the heels of the Bathsheba fiasco follows the story of Amnon's skillfully orchestrated rape of his half-sister Tamar; David's failure to bring Amnon to justice would eventually result in the latter's murder by Tamar's brother Absalom (2 Sam 13). Indeed, for four years preparatory to his rebellion, Absalom demonstrated to all Israel that David's reign was a fraud as far as the dispensation of justice was concerned (2 Sam 15:1–7). Absalom's accusation is vindicated by the dramatized tale of the Tekoite woman (2 Sam 14).[1] Similarly, David's injustice to the Saulides, demonstrated in his (re)confiscation

---

1. It took the Tekoite's threefold appeals (2 Sam 14:7, 9, 11) to get David to make a categorical pronouncement on the fictional case she presented to him (cf. David's slow incremental responses in 2 Sam 14:8, 10, 11). This clearly brings to light the lack of adjudication of the cause of the oppressed during the reign of David, which Absalom would, in the following chapter, graphically demonstrate in the manifesto of his rebellion (2 Sam 15:1–4).

of Mephibosheth's assets (2 Sam 16:1-4), finds expression on the lips of Shimei, who minces no words in charging that David has Saulide blood on his hands (2 Sam 16:5-7).

There is a definite pattern that highlights David's unjust actions within these chapters. In the first two cases, the demonstration of the king's injustice is laid out first (the Bathsheba debacle and his failure to redress Tamar's humiliation, chs. 11, 13-14) before he is expressly called unjust (ch. 12:1-12; 15:1-4). In the case of Mephibosheth, the king's injustice is demonstrated twice (in the confiscation of the estate [16:1-4] and then in his half-hearted return of half of it [19:30, ET. 29]), while the verbalization comes in-between the two demonstrations (ch. 16:5-7). This pattern is illustrated in the schema below:

A        The murder of Uriah/the snatching of Bathsheba (2 Sam 11)
B        David declared unjust (2 Sam 12:1-12)

A'       The rape of Tamar/the inaction of David (2 Sam 13)
B'       David declare unjust (2 Sam 15:1-4)

A''      David confiscates Mephibosheth's Patrimony (2 Sam 16:1-4)
B''      David declared unjust (2 Sam 16:5-7)
A''      David fails to return Mephibosheth's Patrimony
         (2 Sam 19:30, ET 29)

The double demonstration of the king's injustice to Mephibosheth thus places greater emphasis on it than the first two cases. In short, the entire context in which David's encounters with Mephibosheth are recorded is so drenched in Davidic injustice that it forms the necessary background against which these events are to be read.

Of the three chapters dealing with the relations between David and Mephibosheth, 2 Sam 16 and 19 fall within the Absalom revolt narrative. Taking that revolt as the context of these two chapters, scholars have recognized their location in what Gordon calls "the mirror image" structure of the departure and return of David from and to Jerusalem (cf., 2 Sam 15:19—16:13; 19:17-41).[2] This structure, constituted with tales of rebellion at its outer margins (15:1-12; 19:42—20:22), is built around the two domains of conflict: the duel of the counselors (Ahitophel and

---

2. Gordon, *I & II Samuel: A Commentary*, 289.

Hushai) and the clash of the armies. Between the tales of rebellion and the domains of conflict are found the intermediate points of the "meeting scenes." An adaptation of Charles Conroy's chiastic structuring of these pattern is given below as follows:[3]

A    Rebellion breaks out (15:1–12)
    B    The King's flight: meeting scenes (15:13–16:14)
        C    Clash of counselors (16:15–17:23)
        C´    Clash of the armies (17–19:9)
    B´    The King's return: meeting scenes (19:9–41)
A´    The King returns to Jerusalem, and the final stirrings of rebellion are crushed (19:42–20:22)

Concentrating on the meeting scenes, which contain reports about Mephibosheth, Conroy points out the fascinating order and category of people who encountered David. During the king's flight, the meeting scenes begin with folks with the most congenial sentiments toward the king. The first sets of people to meet the king are the Davidic loyalists (Ittai and the Gittite mercenaries, the priests, Hushai); second is a man of doubtful loyalty (Ziba); and finally a man openly hostile to David (Shimei). On the homeward journey, the first person to encounter David is the repentant adversary (Shimei); second is a man of doubtful loyalty (Mephibosheth); lastly a loyal friend (Barzillai).[4] This symmetry can demonstrated in a chiastic structure as follows:

A    David and his loyalists—Ittai, the priests, Hushai (2 Sam 15:17–36)
    B    David and a man of doubtful loyalty—Ziba (2 Sam 16:1–4)
        C    David and an adversary—Shimei (2 Sam 16:6–12)
        C´    David and the repentant adversary—Shimei (2 Sam 19:18–19a)
    B´    David and a man of doubtful loyalty—Mephibosheth (2 Sam 19:25–31)
A´    David and a loyalist—Barzillai (2 Sam 19:32–40)

---

3. Conroy, *Absalom! Absalom*, 89. Cf. Anderson, *2 Samuel*, 202.
4. Conroy, *Absalom! Absalom!*, 89.

In this structure, the mention of Mephibosheth, both in the flight and the return meeting scenes, occurs within the sphere of the man of doubtful loyalty. In this way David's ambivalence toward him is implicitly suggested.[5]

For a clearer appreciation of this context (of Absalom's revolt), in which the Mephibosheth references are embedded, the "meeting scenes" during the flight from Jerusalem have to be examined carefully. In these meeting scenes, both the direction of movement and the landscape are employed for rhetorical effects (see the diagram below). As David departed the palace and proceeded to cross the Kidron Valley and to ascend the Mount of Olives, he was initially followed by members of his household, fighting squads, and the priests bearing the Ark of the Covenant (2 Sam 15:16–31). This group consisted of three categories of people: the large group of sympathizers composed of those who completely depended on David for their safety (household members); those upon whom David would rely for the defense of his kingdom (the fighting squads); and those upon whom David would lean for his intelligence gathering network in enemy territory (the priests).

**David's Meeting scenes on his Flight from Jerusalem through the Mount of Olives**

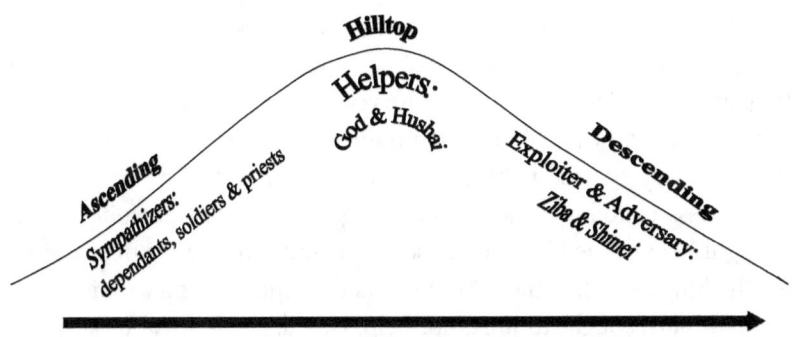

---

5. On the symmetry of the "meeting scenes," Alter writes, "There is an approximate symmetry between David's encounters in his exodus from Jerusalem and those that now occur in his return. Then he met a hostile Shimei, now he meets a contrite Shimei. Then he met Ziba, who denounced his master Mephibosheth; now he meets Mephibosheth himself, who defends his own loyalty. Then he spoke with Ittai, the loyalist who insisted on accompanying him; now he speaks with Barzillai, the proven loyalist who refuses to accompany him back to the capital. The encounter with Hushai, who becomes David's secret agent, has no counterpart here" (Alter, *The David Story*, 315).

At the top of the Mount of Olives, David encounters the second group, consisting of helpers (2 Sam 15:32–37). While one member of this group is implied (the deity), the other is explicitly mentioned (Hushai). During the ascent phase of the flight, David was informed of Ahitophel's defection to Absalom. In response to this cheerless news, the king whispers a prayer to the deity. Then, the narrator informs the reader of David's encounter with Hushai at the place of worship (most likely a high place). In his encounter with Hushai at this place of worship, David meets the answer to his prayer, and by implication the deity meets him here. On his descent from the Mount of Olives, David encounters Ziba, who exploits the present crisis vis-à-vis David's paranoia about Saulides to his advantage (2 Sam 16:1–4); and Shimei, an outright adversary (2 Sam 16:5–12).

There are a number of commonalities and divergences between these three categories of people, which help in our understanding of the narrator's characterization of Mephibosheth when David encounters him in the meeting scenes of the return from exile. A fuller consideration of these features will be taken up in our study of 2 Sam 19. The two most prominent features common to both sympathizers and helpers (of course, with the exception of the unnamed helper, the deity) were grieving with David—manifested by the signs of mourning that they bore—and their willingness to follow their king into exile (2 Sam 15:23–24, 30–37). Besides, they showed a willingness to help the king if they understood what they could do; yet it is the king who gives instructions to them on what to do. In contradistinction, both the exploiter and the adversary evinced neither a sign of mourning for the king nor the willingness to follow him into exile. Again, while the exploiter (Ziba) brought help to the king, he did so by his initiative rather than waiting for the king's word, as the other helpers did. The adversary (Shimei), on his own part, sought to hurt, not help, David. It is critical to keep this salient background in mind, therefore, as we explore David's interactions with Mephibosheth or with others concerning Mephibosheth.

# MEPHIBOSHETH AND THE TRIUMPHANT DAVID
## 2 Sam 9:1–13
## Chapter 9

1 Then David said,[6] "Is there indeed anyone still left of the house of Saul, that I may show him covenant faithfulness for Jonathan's sake?" 2 Now there was a steward of Saul's house; his name was Ziba. They[7] summoned him before David. And the king said to him, "Are you Ziba?" He said, "Your servant." 3 And the king said, "Is there no one anymore from Saul's house, that I may show him the covenant faithfulness of God?" Ziba said to the king, "There is a son left to Jonathan—Crippled Feet.[8]" 4 The king said to him, "Where is he?" Ziba said to the king, "Behold him[9] in the house of Makir son of Ammiel in Lo Debar.[10]"

---

6. Smith notes the abrupt opening of the present episode, and suggests that it should be taken from ch. 7:1 (Smith, *Samuel*, 310). Such observations, in some way, buttress our arguments above that the death of the Saulide Seven in 21:1–14 is prior to this story. Some commentators, like Smith, allow that this episode was preceded by the death of either Ishbosheth or the Saulide Seven (ibid., 310). McCarter, taking a stance akin to ours, writes, "The question of a survivor in the house of Saul is raised by the account of the execution of the Saulides in 21:1–14, which probably once stood before chap. 9" (McCarter, *II Samuel*, 260).

7. This is the use of the active theme in the impersonal third person plural to avoid the passive voice (cf. Williams, *Hebrew Syntax*, § 160).

8. The use of the adjective נכה here without an independent personal pronoun, coupled with the lack of a pronominal suffix on the noun "feet" (רגלים), makes it possible to take the adjective to be a substantive adjective—kind of a nickname that Ziba cynically gives to Mephibosheth. Knowing David's antipathy toward the lame and the blind, instead of Mephibosheth's name, Ziba volunteered a nickname "Crippled Feet"—a demonstration of Ziba's contempt for Saul's only surviving heir.

9. The two words (הנה־הוא) being bound together with a *maqqeph* become also closely bound up in meaning. They cannot, therefore, be translated separately as "Behold! He is . . ." Rather, the whole construction is a picturesque unveiling of Mephibosheth's hideout, "See him in the house of Makir" (cf. Gen 18:9). The combination of הנה and a proform (with a *maqqeph*) is usually done by affixing the proform (typically, a pronominal suffix) to the particle. In the majority of these occurrences this construction is in direct discourse and is followed by a participle (e.g., Gen 9:9; Exod 8:17; Num 24:14; 2 Sam 12:11; 1 Kgs 11:31; Jer 11:11; Ezek 4:16; Dan 8:19). Although translators usually render the participle with the future tense, the presentative function of the particle and its durative nature need to be taken into consideration. This combination conveys a strong emphasis on the here-and-now element of the fact being presented.

10. If my suggestion of cynicism on the part of Ziba in verse 3 above is correct, then, his use of the name of Makir's hometown may also contain a veiled pun—Mr. Crippled Feet lives in Nothing City.

5 Then David the king sent, and they[11] fetched him from the house of Makir son of Ammiel from Lo Debar. 6 So Mephibosheth son of Jonathan son of Saul came to David. He fell upon his face and he did obeisance. And David said, "Mephibosheth," and he replied, "I am your servant." 7 So David said to him, "Do not be afraid, for I will surely show you covenant faithfulness for the sake of Jonathan your father. I will return to you all the property of Saul your father; and you shall eat food at my table daily." 8 And he did obeisance, and said, "Who is your servant, that you should turn toward a dead dog such as I am?"

9 Then the king called Ziba, Saul's steward and said to him, "All of what belongs to Saul and all his house I bestow upon your master's son. 10 And you shall work the field for him: you and your sons and your servants. You shall bring in the produce that there may be food for your master's son[12] so that he may eat thereof;[13] for Mephibosheth, your master's son, shall eat food at my table daily." Now Ziba had fifteen sons and twenty servants. 11 And Ziba said to the king, "According to all that my lord the king commands his servant, thus will your servant do."

So Mephibosheth was eating at his table, like one of the sons of the king.[14] 12 Now Mephibosheth had a young son; his name

---

11. This is another instance of the use of the active theme in the impersonal third person plural to avoid the passive voice (cf. footnote 1 above).

12. The LXX[L] has εἰς τὸν οἶκον ("into the house"). Without the verb והיה, (as the LXX[L], Syriac, and Vulgate do not have it) this clause would mean something like "and you shall bring the food into the house." The "house" could very well be a reference to the palace. Some scholars like McCarter favor the Lucian rendition because of the special provision made for Mephibosheth's own upkeep (McCarter, *II Samuel*, 259). This would in itself raise further interesting questions, to which we will give more attention in our discussion of the text below.

13. Note the 3ms pronominal suffix attached to the 3ms *qal* verb (ואכלו). The obvious referent of the pronoun is the produce that is to be brought in that will constitute food for Mephibosheth.

14. This is a very difficult sentence. The way it is structured, it would have been more natural to read it as a continuation of Ziba's speech. However, the first-person pronominal suffix on the noun "table" (שלחני) disqualifies it from being Ziba's speech. I do not see why Keil calls it a circumstantial clause. I agree with him, however, that the participial form of the verb (אכל), in addition to the lack of explicit intimation that they were David's words, make it unlikely to be a direct quote from David (Keil, "Commentary on the Second Book of Samuel," 616). Alter, on the same note, argues that the Bible "never gives reported speech without an explicit introduction ('and David said')" (Alter, *The David Story*, 242). Smith likewise writes, "The second half of the verse cannot be correct as it stands"; but it is more likely that it originally existed in the form preserved by the LXX (Smith, *Samuel*, 311). I suggest an emendation of the MT's שלחני ("my table") to שלחנו ("his table"). In handwritten script with no vowel pointings, it is not hard to con-

was Micha. And all who dwelt in Ziba's house were servants to Mephibosheth. 13 But Mephibosheth was living in Jerusalem, because he had to eat[15] at the king's table daily, though he was lame in his two legs.

The understanding of 2 Sam 9 is enhanced when one keeps in mind its immediate literary context in 2 Samuel. Alter, in considering this passage, points to the return to dialogue after the long speeches of chapter 7 and the chronicles of chapter 8.[16] It is significant to also note that this chapter is sandwiched between two accounts of Davidic conquest wars waged against Philistia, Moab, and Aram (ch. 8) on the one hand, and Ammon and Aram (chs. 10–12) on the other. Placing the Mephibosheth episode in the midst of these wars against David's enemies, leaves one wondering if he is not another "Philistine" or "Ammonite" to be conquered, albeit with non-combative means.

Polzin extends the horizon of this contextual consideration beyond the immediate surroundings of the passage. He is of the opinion that a proper interpretation of David's belated move to protect the remnant of Saul's house demands we bear in mind David's singular inability to translate his covenantal loyalty to Jonathan's house into practical protection of its inhabitants. "We must look backwards and forwards in the story," he writes, "if we are to understand the form and function of David's *ḥesed*, his lovingkindness, to Mephibosheth here in chapter 9."[17] Besides the death of Saulides in the civil war years, where Mephibosheth is first mentioned (2 Sam 4:4), Polzin also points to 2 Sam 21, where David

---

fuse a *waw* for a *yod*. I believe this putative form may have been original to the Hebrew *Vorlage* that lies behind the LXX text. It is the ambiguity implicit in determining the antecedent of the pronominal suffix (Ziba or David) that the LXX clarifies by rightly replacing the pronominal suffix with David's name in its rendition Μεμφιβοσθε ἤσθιεν ἐπὶ τῆς τραπέζης Δαυιδ καθὼς εἷς τῶν υἱῶν τοῦ βασιλέως ("Mephibosheth was eating at David's table like one of the king's sons"). Indeed, the Syriac and Vulgate manuscripts also have "David's table" in the place of the MT's "my table." These ancient translations assume this sentence to be the beginning of the narrator's discursive comments.

15. Lit. "he was eating." His having to live in Jerusalem was required by his having to eat at the king's table daily. Driver similarly notes that Mephibosheth's eating at the king's table is the ground for his dwelling in Jerusalem (Driver, *The Books of Samuel*, 287). There is some hint of an imperative in the seeming generosity. The narrator's awkward repetition of this fact within the space of a couple sentences may be a subtle way of highlighting this implicit necessity placed upon Mephibosheth.

16. Alter, *The David Story*, 240.

17. Polzin, *David and the Deuteronomist*, 95.

hands over the descendents of Saul to the Gibeonites for execution.[18] On the same trajectory, McCarter goes all the way back to 1 Sam 20 to find an anchoring context for 2 Sam 9: "As an episode in the Deuteronomistic History, therefore, II Sam 9 joins with I Sam 20 to link separate components of the story of David into a narrative unit, while offering, like the episode of David and Michal in 6:20–23, a resolution to issues arising from earlier events in the larger story."[19] We will return to this linkage between the two passages later in our ensuing discussion.

Commenting on the content of 2 Sam 9, Eugene H. Peterson writes, "Some people when they become successful use all their energy and resources protecting and guarding their success. Others go out of their way looking for ways to share what they have, extending the realm of blessing. David went looking for ways to be generous."[20] One wishes things were as simplistic as Peterson construes them. Unfortunately, they are not. One should not be too piqued by such simplicity, bearing in mind the sermonic orientation of Peterson's book. That notwithstanding, when our goals becloud our methodology, the outcome becomes a far cry from the message the text presents—eisegesis not exegesis.

---

18. I have already suggested in chapter 5 that 2 Sam 21 precedes 2 Sam 9 in story time, a position that is not unique to me. McCarter, for instance, suggests that it was "Deuteronomistic editing that separated the story of the Gibeonites' revenge in 21:1–14 from its natural sequel here in chap. 9 and consigned it to an appendix at the end of the materials on the reign of David" (McCarter, *II Samuel*, 263). He further acknowledges, "it seems clear that David's question in 9:1 presupposes the events of 21:1–14 and is phrased with reference to them, and it is reasonable, therefore, to assume that 21:1–14 + 9:1–13 once stood in continuous narrative sequence. The separation, then must have been made by a Deuteronomistic editor, who saw David's treatment of Meribbaal in the context of his long-standing relationship to the house of Saul rather than of the suspicious circumstances of the Gibeonites' revenge" (ibid., 263).

Furthermore, the prepositional phrase "Afterwards" or "After this" (אחרי־כן) is used in Samuel, especially 2 Samuel, as a macrosyntactic marker—as a section initial phrase, not a section termination marker (1 Sam 24:6, 9; 2 Sam 2:1; 8:1; 10:1; 13:1; 21:18). However, the אחרי־כן ("after this") in 2 Sam 21:14 serves, in its present position, as section termination marker. Similarly, 2 Sam 9:1 begins rather abruptly. It makes perfect sense, therefore, to envision a smooth transition of 2 Sam 21:14 into 9:1 ("After this, therefore, David said, 'Is there . . .'"), when 2 Sam 9 was a direct sequel to 2 Sam 21:1–14. For similar views on this see Hertzberg, *I & II Samuel*, 299; Anderson, *2 Samuel*, 140; and Alexander Francis Kirkpatrick, *The Second Book of Samuel*, 315. For a contrary view, see Bergen, *1, 2 Samuel*, 354.

19. McCarter, *II Samuel*, 263.

20. Peterson, *First and Second Samuel*, 172.

David F. Payne, in characterizing this kind of overly sermonic approach to this passage, writes, "In Christian preaching, this story of David and Mephibosheth has often been used as an illustration of 'unmerited grace': the great king (Christ) goes out of his way to bring even a moral cripple to eat at his table."[21] While this may be one way of applying the text, it stands to reason that such an approach cannot be put up as authentic interpretation, as it fails to address the text on its own terms. In refuting such banality, Payne points out that the story is not so much about undeserved charity as about loyalty. He further cautions against taking the words of the characters at face value. He defends his position on the ground that Mephibosheth was not just anybody, but the son of David's best friend to whom he owed covenant obligation. Polzin, likewise, writes that the narrator characterizes David as someone given to expedient decisions that can conflict with his own prior commitments. He therefore questions "whether David is really the appropriate person to 'show the kindness of God' (2 Sam 9:3) to anyone, least of all to remnants of a rival house."[22]

2 Samuel 9 can be divided into four major segments, corresponding to three scenes and the narrator's discursive comments. These are (1) David's inquiry about Saul's surviving progeny (9:1–4), (2) David's interview with Mephibosheth (9:5–8), (3) David's instructions to Ziba (9:9–11b), and (4) the epilogue (9:11c–13).

## David's Inquiry into Saul's Surviving Progeny (2 Sam 9:1–4)

The first scene of the Davidic *ḥesed* episode is marked out by the preponderance of questions David asked. There are four questions in these four verses, a question per verse, and all aimed at discovering the whereabouts of Saul's surviving progeny, if there were any. The entire unit is a scenic composition, consisting almost exclusively of direct discourse with the singular exception of the *waw*-disjunctive sentence at the beginning of verse 2 that supplies the backgrounded information on Ziba. The first question (in verse 1) was, obviously, directed at David's courtiers, whose verbal response in not recorded. We are only told of their action in fishing out Saul's steward, Ziba. The rest of the scene then consists of David's conversation with Ziba.

---

21. Payne, *I & II Samuel*, 196–97.
22. Polzin, *David and the Deuteronomist*, 100.

David's third question (which is his second to Ziba,[23] in verse 3) is, more or less, a repetition of the one he had posed earlier to his courtiers in verse 1. This question has engendered different responses among interpreters. McCarter supposes that the triple repetition of *hesed*, twice in this scene (vv. 1, 3) and once in the next (v. 7), underlines it as David's singular motive for bringing Mephibosheth to his palace.[24] He explains it on the premise that David himself had once needed *hesed* from Mephibosheth's father to survive; and now, though David was in a position to kill Mephibosheth, he chose to show him *hesed*. In the same vein, Bergen sees this chapter as David's fulfillment of the pledge of familial support he made to Jonathan. Indeed, he understands that the narrator has portrayed David as the supreme Israelite example of covenant faithfulness—the highest virtue of the Hebrew society.[25] Furthermore, he considers the narrator's repetition of David's question as significant, though unnecessary, in establishing the theme of *hesed* in the chapter. To him, this underscores the fact that David was not an enemy of Saul's house.[26]

The conclusion that because David showed *hesed* to Mephibosheth he was not an enemy of Saul's house is quite a leap of faith. What Bergen fails to point out is that, while there is a threefold repetition of the *hesed* motif in the chapter, all the occurrences are found solely on the lips of David in his conversation with three different sets of individuals. There is a conspicuous absence of confirmation of this *hesed* toward the house of Saul either by the narrator or by any other character. That in itself serves to minify the potency of the theme in the narrative. Besides, while repetition serves to underscore emphasis, it can also be rhetorically pressed into service to yield a negative connotation (cf. Mark Antony's repetitious reference to Julius Caesar's ambition in William Shakespeare's *Julius Caesar*).

Kirkpatrick takes a more nuanced approach to the question. He allows that David's first motive in entertaining Mephibosheth was to fulfill his oath to Jonathan. Nevertheless, he also entertains the plausibility of political motivation lurking behind David's action in two ways. First,

---

23. David's first question to Ziba, the second in the scene, serves only to affirm his identity.
24. McCarter, *II Samuel*, 260.
25. Bergen, *1, 2 Samuel*, 354.
26. Bergen, *1, 2 Samuel*, 354.

David may have wanted to use this action as a way of conciliating the remnants of Saul's adherents. Second, David may have also thought it wise "to keep Mephibosheth in Jerusalem in order to prevent his becoming the tool of political intrigues."[27] With the complexity of David's character, it is probable that some permutation of those motives is operative in the narrative.

Therefore, it would not be out of sync with the tenor of the narrative to raise doubts on the integrity of David's declared motive. As if to dramatize the ambiguity raised by Kirkpatrick above, on the basis of all that has transpired heretofore, Polzin characterizes the question as "a compassionate query that could easily strike terror in the heart of anyone belonging to Saul's house who might hear of it."[28] Obviously, such terror is noticed in Mephibosheth's demeanor as he comes before David. It is warranted by how "David has been as singularly unsuccessful in his efforts on behalf of Jonathan as he has been eminently successful on his own behalf."[29]

The manner of the framing of the question in both verses 1 and 3 also reinforces these doubts. In verse 1, David asks, הכי יש־עוד אשר נותר לבית שאול ("Is there indeed anyone still left of the house of Saul . . . ?"). The double use of the emphatic particles כי (in this context, כי is not serving its customary conjunctive function but has the emphatic meaning of "indeed") and עוד ("still") intimates an expectation of a negative response (cf. Gen 3:1; 29:15; Job 6:22).[30] This expectation is less veiled in the reframing of the question in verse 3, האפס עוד איש לבית שאול ("Is there no one anymore from Saul's house . . . ?"). The verb אפס (meaning "to cease," or "to end") has been used in three principal ways in the Hebrew Bible, in most of which it yields negative connotations. First, it is used as a substantive verb in a propositional statement to indicate the end, nonexistence, denial, lack, or absence of something (cf. Gen 47:15, 16; Isa 5:8; 16:4; 29:20; 41:29; 45:6, 14; 54:15; Amos 6:10). Second, it is bound to the conjunctive particle כי in proclisis

---

27. Kirkpatrick, *The Second Book of Samuel*, 316.
28. Polzin, *David and the Deuteronomist*, 94.
29. Polzin, *David and the Deuteronomist*, 94. Polzin explains this by referring to the accounts in Samuel of how forces external to David conspired to eliminate Saulides while at the same time these same forces seemingly shield David from complicity in those deaths (ibid., 94–95).
30. Firth, likewise, hints at (albeit without demonstration) the doubts about the expectation of a Saulide survival that David's question engenders (*1 & 2 Samuel*, 403).

(though without a *maqqeph*, as would be expected in Hebrew) to form a contrastive conjunctive phrase (אפס כי, "however," "but," "nevertheless," etc.). The two conjoined words thus function as a contrastive conjunction whose sentential function is to oppose one element of the sentence to another (cf. Num 13:28; Deut 15:4; Judg 4:9; 2 Sam 12:14; Amos 9:8). On this note, there is an instance where אפס is used without the procliticizing כי but carries essentially the same effect (cf. Num 23:13). Third, it is used in interrogative sentences. In this last sense, it occurs only in two places in the Bible—in our passage of 2 Sam 9:3 and in Ps 77:9.

In both cases, consistent with the word's intrinsic function of negation, the answer to the question is expected to be negative, denying either the existence of a surviving Saulide or the perpetuity of divine wrath respectively. In our passage the combination of אפס and עוד is similar to the combination of כי and עוד in verse 1. In both cases, then, the expectation was for a disaffirmation of the stated fact of the question. Ziba's answer, therefore, must have been a perturbing surprise to David.

Ziba's attitudes toward and speeches to David tell a tall tale of his character, even though we find little about him by means of the narrator's direct characterization. First of all, in neither of his appearances before David does the narrator record that he did obeisance before the king. It could either be that he never did it out of self-conceit or that he did, but the narrator failed to report it so as to cast him in a hue more consistent with his character than if it were reported. Ziba's response to David's questions is equally interesting. To David's first question concerning his identity, he replies simply, "Your servant" (עבדך), without any of the niceties associated in the ancient world with speaking to royalty (or anyone of higher rank). To David's question about Saul's surviving progeny, Ziba answers with his characteristic economy of words, "There is a son left to Jonathan—Crippled Feet" (בן ליהונתן נכה רגלים).[31] He

---

31. The ambiguity that stalks Ziba's character is evident in his discourses; he is given to few words and taken to nominal rather than verbal sentences. In this first scene as whole, in response to three questions asked by David, Ziba uses fourteen words and no verb in the indicative form. All the speeches of Ziba in all of 2 Samuel put together consists of a paltry fifty-five words and only six of these are verbs in the indicative form (9:11; 16:3; and 16:4). Of the six verbs, four are presented as not really Ziba's words but words that merely reflect his response to David's command (9:11), or merely a report of Mephibosheth's supposed speech (16:3). Therefore, we truly have only two indicative verbs from Ziba's own thought (16:4), and those come out only after his goal of reclaiming Saul's estate for himself is achieved—his impugnable character finally coming to the surface.

not only readily volunteers the information the king desires, but also shows his disdain for Mephibosheth by calling him by a nickname that taunts him on his disability rather than giving his real name.[32] Evans correctly writes that Ziba was "well aware of Mephibosheth's existence and condition, but that he does not give a name perhaps indicates his attitude that Mephibosheth, as crippled, was a nobody."[33]

In verse 4, David inquires about Mephibosheth's whereabouts. Ziba's response is as terse as it is sentient (הנה־הוא בית מכיר בן עמיאל בלו דבר, "Behold him in the house of Makir son of Ammiel in Lo Debar"). Most of our English translation render it in the traditional way of translating nominal sentences, by understanding the pronoun הוא to be a nominative phrase (subjective, translated as "he") and inserting a copula verb ("is"). However, when we keep in mind the paucity of verbiage characteristic of Ziba's discourses vis-à-vis their ocular nature, then, it is reasonable to understand the pronominal phrase to be accusative in function—objective ("him"). This is what informs our rendition, in which הנה functions more like a locative deictic particle than a mere exclamatory particle and yields the sense of "There he is, in the house of Makir." Our position is all the more tenable because the exclamatory particle הנה ("Behold!") functions to stress the immediacy of the thing being talked about—its "here-and-nowness"—or the presentative function it performs in direct discourse in introducing a new fact.[34] Like the disappointment Ziba's answer might have given David, David's action in the follow scenes will blight Ziba's expectation.

---

32. See footnote 8 above for my explanation for this rendition.
33. Evans, *1 and 2 Samuel*, 174.
34. Waltke and O'Connor, *Biblical Hebrew Syntax*, 675–77. McCarthy commenting on the use of *hinneh* notes, "There is an emotional overtone when it is used. The user is moved about the connection, not neutral toward it, and the connective colors the thing connected ... In all this the expression remains exclamatory with an emotional note and we miss the language-user's full meaning if we simply *equate* the sentences with the suggested temporal or conditional or causal or purpose clauses. We get the meaning but not the feeling, and the two must be grasped to get the full force of the language" (McCarthy, "The Use of *wehinnēh* in Biblical Hebrew," 330–42). Considering Ziba's antics, as later events show, and in view of the systematic elimination of Saulides during David's reign, one can imagine the glee with which he was revealing the hideout of the sole surviving claimant to the Saul's estate, to which he (Ziba) might have had exclusive right since the demise of Saul and most of his progeny.

### David's Parley with Mephibosheth (2 Sam 9:5–8)

Upon learning about his whereabouts, David sent and Mephibosheth was fished out and brought to the palace. The next scene reports on this and the conversation between the two men. There are motific and thematic intertextual connections between this scene and other biblical narratives. Before taking a closer look at the dialogue itself, we will first explore the intertextuality between this scene and the earlier accounts of David's relations with the Saulides during his days at Saul's palace.

There are several (lexical and motific) correspondences between this passage and the events recorded in 1 Sam 20. These include first of all, the order to go and fetch someone—Saul orders Jonathan to go and fetch David in the first instance, and in the second, David directs his retainers to go and fetch Mephibosheth.[35] Second, there is the reference to Saul's estate (השדה, "the field")—first mentioned as a hiding place for the disclosure of Saul's intentions concerning David (1 Sam 20:5, 11, 24, 35), and in the second instance, with respect to the return of Saul's property to his grandson (2 Sam 9:7; cf. 9:9; 19:30). Third, there is the occurrence of the phenomenon of eating daily at the king's table (2 Sam 9:7, 9, 10, 11, 13; cf. 1 Sam 20:18–29). Fourth, both episodes contain reference to oneself as the servant of one's interlocutor (עבדך, "your servant")—first, David to Jonathan (1 Sam 20:7, 8), and, then, Jonathan's son to David (2 Sam 9:6, 8). Fifth, the reference to covenant loyalty—in the first instance, David and Jonathan make an agreement in order to safeguard the former's immediate safety, and in the latter passage David evokes this covenant loyalty as the guarantee of the safety of the latter's progeny.[36] Sixth, there are references to the deity in both passages.[37] Finally, the ac-

---

35. Saul had ordered Jonathan to send and fetch David for him to be killed (שלח וקח, "send and fetch," 1 Sam 20:31); which command Jonathan defied. David, however, sent and his retainers fetched Mephibosheth from his hiding place in Lo-Debar to the palace (וישלח דוד המלך ויקחהו, "David the king sent and they fetched him"). Indeed, the word "send" (שלח) appears eight times in Jonathan-David interlocution in 1 Sam 20 and all are with respect to giving David his freedom rather than binding him in the palace as King Saul wanted (cf. vv. 5, 12, 13, 20, 21, 22, 29).

36. There are three mentions of חסד ("covenant loyalty") in both 1 Sam 20 and 2 Sam 9.

37. God is the reference point of the covenant that Jonathan makes with David (1 Sam 20:3, 8, 14, 21–22), and he is called upon to be witness to the covenant obligations each owed to the other (1 Sam 20:12, 13, 15, 16, 23, 42). Later, after the demise of Jonathan, David anchors the covenant loyalty he is about to show to Mephibosheth in God (2 Sam 9:3) and his commitment to Jonathan (2 Sam 9:1, 7). This threefold

count of David falling on his face upon the ground and doing obeisance to Jonathan (ויפל לאפיו ארצה וישתחו, 1 Sam 20:41), finds its replica in Mephibosheth falling upon his face and doing obeisance to David (ויפל על פניו וישתחו, 2 Sam 9:6). With such striking common threads connecting these texts, it is imperative that the pathos of the former should guide our reading of the latter. To this very point we will return later. Presently, we will take a further look at the David-Mephibosheth parley itself.

Mephibosheth quaked with terror as he was ushered into the presence of King David. While there are numerous cases of people either falling upon their faces (ויפל על פני or its variants) or bowing in worship or to perform obeisance (וישתחו) before a deity or some dignified individual(s), the combination of the two verbs, rather as a hendiadys, is rarer than the occurrence of either of the verbs alone. It is often used in situations where the character so bowing is awe-stricken with either terror (Josh 5:14; 1 Sam 20:41), awe with a veiled hint of jubilancy (2 Sam 1:2; 14:22), or befuddlement (Job 1:20). The practice, as it occurs in 2 Sam 9:4, belongs more to the category of fear than either of the other two. On this Kirkpatrick comments, "Mephibosheth might be afraid that David had only hunted him out to treat him after the common fashion of oriental usurpers, who often put all their predecessor's kindred to death. He seems to have lived in concealment at Lo-debar."[38] Such fear, on Mephibosheth's part, would have been all the more warranted if, as we have suggested, this present episode was preceded by the gruesome murder of the Saulide Seven.[39]

After ascertaining his identity, David proceeded to pledge to render the covenant loyalty (ḥesed) he owed Jonathan. The ḥesed David

---

reference to חסד, "covenant faithfulness," corresponds to the threefold reference it has in the earlier events (1 Sam 20:8, 14, 15) thereby evoking the entire series of events. Yet Jonathan's strident evocation of Yahweh (eleven times in all, plus one appositional reference to Yahweh as the God of Israel) in 1 Sam 20 overwhelms David's meager twofold reference to the deity in 1 Sam 20. Indeed, in 2 Sam 9 David does not even take upon his lips the covenant name of Israel's God.

38. Kirkpatrick, *The Second Book of Samuel*, 316–17.

39. On the same note, Alter writes, "These gestures of abasement may have been standard etiquette in approaching a monarch, but Ziba is not reported making them. Mephibosheth is clearly terrified that the king may have summoned him in order to have him put to death—David's possible complicity in the deaths of other figures associated with the house of Saul might well have been a matter of continuing speculation in Benjaminite circles" (Alter, *The David Story*, 241).

promised Mephibosheth translates into three main offers: a reassurance that there is nothing to fear, the return of Mephibosheth's grandfather's patrimony, and a place at the royal dinner table. David's rhetoric here about covenant faithfulness seems convincing, and one may be easily taken in by it. Both Peterson[40] and Peter J. Leithart[41] consider David's act of offering *ḥesed* to Mephibosheth an extreme demonstration of love, since it is highly unusual for someone to seek out an enemy and a potential rival to show him love. Ackroyd, similarly, observes that in spite of Mephibosheth's initial apprehensions, he soon discovers the reality of David's loyalty to Jonathan.[42]

Such a rosy picture fails to do justice to the rich complexity of the text. Payne observes that though David's words seem admirable, there is the possibility that while outwardly honoring Mephibosheth by bringing him to the royal court, David was "in reality placing him where he could keep an eye on him and make sure that he was taking no action against David's interest. Perhaps, then, David, had ulterior motives, or any rate mixed motives."[43] Such a position is defensible on many counts, not the least of which is the manner of the offers that David placed before Mephibosheth. The return of the land itself was no more than a royal land grant, as it is both in the power and character of the king to give and take back (cf. 2 Sam 16:4). This is evident from David's instruction to Ziba in the next scene, in which he gave the management of the land to the latter. Mephibosheth was by now an adult (with a family of his own). If it was a full recovery of his inheritance, he would have been afforded free rein, to be able to do with it as he liked, and to hire and fire his workers.[44]

Furthermore, the motific intertextuality between 1 Sam 20 and 2 Sam 9 calls on us to look beyond mere verbal correspondences to the heart of the narrative: the correspondences are too deep and too many to be discounted as being purely fortuitous. Just like endangered

---

40. Peterson, *First and Second Samuel*, 173.

41. Leithart, *A Son to Me*, 209.

42. Ackroyd, The Second Book of Samuel, 93.

43. Payne, *I & II Samuel*, 197.

44. McCarter suggests that David had taken full control of Saul's property in Benjamin and elsewhere after the demise of Ishbosheth. He observes that the assignment of Saul's estate to Mephibosheth was only pro forma, as proven by David's future actions in 2 Sam 9:9–10; 16:4; 19:30 (McCarter, *II Samuel*, 261). On a similar note also see Anderson, *2 Samuel*, 141–42.

David fell upon his face before Jonathan when the latter spared his life by giving him free passage, a new endangered species, Mephibosheth, falls upon his face before the only person who could spare his life. Even though Jonathan was the man in whose hands the balance of power lay, he appears to have been more afraid of the future than David was of the present—a clear indication that he knew the ferociousness of his friend. His impassioned entreaty to David for his progeny, with a sworn covenant, is vindicated by the onerous violent elimination of Saulides. Only that covenant, which David now invokes three times, accounts for Mephibosheth's survival.

In addition, Saul's fields had served David for a hiding place at the time of his slough of despond; at the present moment the same fields would serve him for a different sort of hiding place—the apparent assignment of the property betokens his kindness to the Saulides. In addition, the narrator seems subtly to bespeak David's ambiguous perception of Mephibosheth through the double identification of Mephibosheth's pedigree in David's speech. In one breath, David referred to him as Jonathan's son (lit. "Jonathan your father"); in the next he refers to him as the son of Saul (lit. "your father Saul"). That Mephibosheth is identified with Saul just before David informs him that he will have to eat at the king's table daily calls to mind a similar requirement Saul made of David. In the former case a guaranteed seat at the king's table for David was Saul's way of keeping an eye on David. There is no sufficient ground for imagining that David's invitation to Mephibosheth to eat at his table does not have the same undertones as those of Saul.[45]

Finally, as David bowed before Jonathan and referred to himself as the latter's servant when the former's life was at risk, Mephibosheth likewise feels no less threatened and thus performs the same actions, falls upon his face before David and refers to himself as David's servant. It is as if David is now the new Saul, and the house of Saul (now represented in Mephibosheth) is the new David, except that the house of Saul lacks the element of divine favor that David enjoyed.

---

45. This perception of David is seemingly cynical, but if there is any cynicism it comes from David's own character. For example, while David seems to show much generosity and concern for Uriah and his family life, he turns around and hands the latter his death sentence to convey to his commanding officer (2 Sam 11). Similarly, while he could not offend Joab, nor order the murder of Shimei, David clandestinely orders their execution in his dying words (1 Kgs 2:5-6, 8-9).

In his reply to David, Mephibosheth displayed the kind of humility that is rarely found in persons of noble birth. He began by first of all prostrating before David again and then referring to himself a second time as David's servant.[46] As if those were not enough, in his obsequious deference to the king, Mephibosheth asks rhetorically, מה עבדך כי פנית אל הכלב המת אשר כמוני ("Who is your servant, that you should turn toward a dead dog such as I am?"). Mephibosheth's self-referential demeaning words have elicited divergent responses from Bible commentators. Jeremy Schipper charges Mephibosheth with animosity toward David, arguing that the use of noun phrase "dead dog" typifies relations of deep-seated antipathy (1 Sam 24:15 [ET v. 14]; 2 Sam 16:9–10; 2 Kgs 8:15). In particular, he connects 2 Sam 16:9–10 with our passage (2 Sam 9:8) and contends that notwithstanding the difference in the rhetorical import of these passages, the accusation of usurpation in the former passages applies to the latter as well, so that "Mephibosheth's seemingly obsequious response places him in the company of usurpers and political enemies."[47]

Schipper's comparison of Mephibosheth with Shimei is rather forced, as the conduct and speeches of both could not be more divergent. Mephibosheth's demeanor before and speech to David, in both his first and second meetings with David, are absolutely congruent: he was wholly submissive, self-debasing, and full of gratitude. Shimei's conduct and speech to David in their first and second encounters are poles apart. In the first, Shimei was violent in his conduct and verbally deleterious, while in the second he was very subdued in his conduct and conciliatory in his speech. With such divergences, one will be hard pressed to make their motivations coterminous. Payne takes a more or less agnostic approach to Mephibosheth's words. To him, they tell us nothing, especially bearing in mind the ancient Near Eastern royal court milieu where it was rather customary to speak in deferential terms.[48]

We need not despair of making sense of Mephibosheth's speech as Payne does: the pattern of usage of the humbling or humiliating phrase "dead dog," both in the Bible and extant ancient Near Eastern texts, af-

---

46. Mephibosheth evinces his humility both by his actions and his words. In just verses 6 and 8, where his actions are reported, the verbs that refer to prostrating before the king are used of him three times, and he calls himself David's servant twice.

47. Schipper, "'Why Do You Still Speak of Your Affairs?'" 344–51.

48. Payne, *I & II Samuel*, 199.

fords us clues on how to read it here.⁴⁹ In the DtrH, this phrase appears in four passages: three times in Samuel and once in Kings (1 Sam 24:15 [ET 24:14]; 2 Sam 9:8; 16:9–10; 2 Kgs 8:15). In all passages in Samuel where it occurs, the persons thus referred to (David, Mephibosheth, and Shimei) are respectively engaged in direct discourse or diatribe with the kings (Saul, David, and David). In the first and third instances the "dead dog" clearly views the sovereign as dangerous, if not vicious. In the first case, David had the chance and means by which he could have hurt the king but he would not, while in the third, Shimei would have hurt the king if he had the means and chance, but he could not. Mephibosheth is situated in between these two extreme: he had neither the means nor the chance to hurt the king; and we are not told whether he would have hurt the king if he could. We can only understand that he was a true son of his father, Jonathan, and so was truly grateful to David for sparing his life—his conduct and speech in 2 Sam 19 further depict this limpidly.

Therefore, Mephibosheth's self-referential denigration here certainly evinces his humility. For certain, in his case, as in the two instances of the use of the phrase in Samuel, there is a palpable dread of the sovereign— who at this time happens to be David. Mephibosheth's reply to David was couched in the form of a question. Though it is a rhetorical question, considering the dread with which Mephibosheth approached the king, it would have been so fitting for the king to offer him a reassuring response (as divine messengers normally give to the frightened recipients of their divine messages). That was never to happen.⁵⁰ King David rather turns

---

49. In the Amarna text, for instance, "dog" is used in reference to human persons in two senses. In the one, it is a self-deprecating term as a show of one's humility before his suzerain. The phrase "lone dog," used by Artamanja of Ziribašani, is the parallel to the "dead dog" of the Bible. Thus Artamanja's words, "Behold, to me thou hast written that (all) should be prepared for the archers. Verily, *who am I, a lone dog, that I should not go*" (*EA* I. 201.9–16, emphasis added; cf. *EA* I. 202.7–14), parallel those of Mephibosheth. Both Artamanja's words and those of Mephibosheth are to show their humility before their overlords. In the other sense, the phrase "dog" is used in the Armana letters to disparage an enemy. This is the sense that corresponds to Abishai's reference to Shimei as a "dead dog" (2 Sam 16:9). For instance, Rib-Adda of Byblos in complaining to the Pharaoh about Abdi-Aširta of Amurru, writes, "What is Abdi-Aširta, the servant, the dog, that he should take the land of the king to himself? What is his family?" (*EA* II. 71.16–20). For a further discussion of this see Galán, "What Is He, the Dog?," 173–80.

50. There are striking similarities and dissimilarities between the dialogues between David and Mephibosheth, on the one hand, and between Boaz and Ruth on the other. The similarities include, first, both dialogues were initiated by the authority figure; second, in either case both Ruth and Mephibosheth prostrated themselves; and third, both

his attention to Ziba. The interlocutory engagement of this duo constitutes the third and final scene of this episode.

### David's Instructions to Ziba (2 Sam 9:9–11a)

In his speech to Ziba, David repeats what he had told Mephibosheth, albeit with substantial differences. David had simply told Mephibosheth that he was bequeathing to him his father's estate and that Mephibosheth was to dine daily at David's table, whereas in his instructions to Ziba, David tells him that his is bestowing the estates of both Saul and all his house (a possible reference to Saul's grown sons who, as fighting men in the army, would have had properties of their own) to Saul's grandson Mephibosheth. He also now mentions that Ziba would be the manager of this whole holding. Besides, there is reason to believe that David indicates that Ziba is to make returns to the palace, which returns will be taken on the pretext of being provisions for Mephibosheth.

Scholars are not agreed as to the source of Mephibosheth's sustenance. Campbell prefers the Lucian LXX's "So that your master's house may have food to eat"[51] over the MT's והיה לבן אדניך לחם ואכלו ("that there may be food for your master's son so that he may eat thereof"). Kirkpatrick, similarly, favors following the Lucian LXX rendition. He argues that though Mephibosheth himself was to be a guest at David's royal table, "he would require the produce of this estate for the support of his household"; and he infers from the number of farmhands at Ziba's disposal that Saul's household must have been of considerable size.[52]

---

Ruth (Ruth 2:10, 13) and Mephibosheth (2 Sam 9:8) acknowledged their humble estates. The differences between the two dialogues include first, Ruth spoke to Boaz twice (2:10, 13), while Mephibosheth spoke to David only once, excluding the first time where he merely responds to the king's greetings (9:8). Second, Mephibosheth prostrated himself before David twice (9:6, 8), while Ruth did so before Boaz only once (2:10). Third, Boaz responded to Ruth's rhetorical question, and through this kind gesture, Ruth's hope of a possible "comforter" on the horizon is evident in her rejoinder to Boaz's response to the question (2:13). In contrast, David did not reply to Mephibosheth's response but rather turned his attention to a third party (Ziba, vv. 9–10), in which case Mephibosheth's apprehensions remained unaddressed. And finally, in the one dialogue Ruth had the final say (2:13), while in the other it is Ziba, not Mephibosheth, who had the final say (9:11). This presaged to whom the benefits were more likely to accrue the most in this new tripartite relationships of convenience between David, Mephibosheth, and Ziba.

51. Campbell, *2 Samuel*, 88.

52. Kirkpatrick, *The Second Book of Samuel*, 317. For a similar position also see McCarter, *II Samuel*, 262; and Mauchline, *1 and 2 Samuel*, 243.

Nothing could be further from the truth. Such a position fails to reckon with the fact that the biblical text nowhere attributes a large household to Saul (cf. 1 Sam 14:49–50; 1 Chr 8:33; 9:39). But then, his progeny were all but extirpated (cf. 1 Sam 31:2; 2 Sam 4:5-7; 21:8-9). Even Saul's harem, which he may have acquired later in his reign—though not mentioned in the narrative—was taken over by David (2 Sam 12:8). Thus, to speak of a large Saulide household is illusory and a *non sequitur*. The large number of servants at Ziba's disposal, along with his many sons in the same service, may be indicative of his high rank in Saul's palace—comparable to a contemporary chief of staff of a president or a governor—wherein a large retinue of servants would have been imperative for the maintenance of palace services.

Such stances as those of Campbell, Kirkpatrick, and McCarter are in one sense attributable to the insufficient attention given to the MT on the a priori assumption of the superiority of the LXX (even when it is a recessive text like that of Lucian). We note that most modern English versions take into account the 3ms pronominal suffix attached to the purpose clause ואכלו (lit. "that he may eat of it"), even though they do not render it as literally as we have done here (cf. KJV, ESV, NASB, and NIV).[53] That being the case, then, the antecedent of the affixed pronoun is the crop that Ziba is to bring from Saul's fields. Yet in the next sentence, David insists that Mephibosheth must eat at the former's table. The logical deduction to be made from all this is that Ziba was to furnish David's kitchen with the produce from Saul's fields so Mephibosheth, who will now partake of David's table, will have food to eat. This is why we agree with Gunn that David's supposed generosity is programmed to result in a "healthy subsidy" for the king's court.[54]

---

53. For the nature of purpose clauses following imperatives see Williams §187, 189; Waltke and O'Connor, *Biblical Hebrew Syntax* § 34.6, 39.2.2.

54. Gunn writes, "The gift of Saul's kingdom to David is followed by David's gift of Saul's land and servants to Mephibosheth, Saul's grandson, as a token of his loyalty (*ḥsd*) to Jonathan. At least that is ostensibly what it is about. Yet again there are indications in the text that suggest another possible perspective. The gesture is perhaps less magnanimous than David suggests: it is not merely without cost to himself (since he is giving away someone else's land and labor), but it is also likely to result in a healthy subsidy for the court (cf. 9:9–10), and (as often noted by commentators) it will enable him to keep this last scion of the house of Saul under perpetual surveillance. There is a delicate irony in the possibility that in 16:1–4 Ziba's gesture of generosity to the dispossessed David may be no less devious than David's to the dispossessed Mephibosheth" (Gunn, *The Story of David*, 96–97). For a similar view, see Halpern, *David's Secret Demons*, 343.

Ziba accepted the king's directives readily, yet not without leaving hints of what is to come. Very uncharacteristically, Ziba used two verbs in the indicative form. Both of these verbs are imperfective in form (ככל אשר יצוה אדני המלך את עבדו כן יעשה עבדך, "According to all that my lord the king commands his servant, thus will your servant do"). Particularly, with respect to the king's directive, Ziba did not construe it as the final word, hence his reluctance to say something like, "According to all that my lord the king has *commanded*." His usage of the non-perfective tense leaves room for yet other commands of the king, thereby adumbrating David's further new commands in 2 Sam 16:4 and 19:30. Besides that, the repetition of and the manner of use of the noun "servant" and its verbal form "serve" (√עבד) in itself leaves doubts as to whether Ziba will truly serve Mephibosheth.

The word root עבד appears nine times in this chapter. In its occurrence, Ziba is called Saul's servant twice by the narrator (v. 2, 9)—David referred to Ziba as Saul's servant twice without using the עבד root (בן אדניך, "the son of your master" vv. 9–10); Ziba referred to himself twice as David's servant (vv. 2, 11); Ziba himself is said to have had twenty servants (v. 10); and Mephibosheth called himself David's servant twice (vv. 6, 8). However, only the narrator, drawing inferences from David's pronouncement, referred to Ziba and his household as Mephibosheth's servants (v. 12). There is a perspectival dissonance here: neither David nor Ziba see anyone as Mephibosheth's servant. Mephibosheth may have misinterpreted David in assuming that Ziba and his household were his servants (cf. 2 Sam 19:27, ET 19:26). From David's perspective, Ziba and those in his employment were only to till the ground for Mephibosheth (v. 10). Seen in this way, then, they owed their allegiance not to Mephibosheth, but to the king; hence Ziba's expectation to receive further instructions from David.[55]

---

55. Regarding the delicate balance in this interlaced reference to the word root עבד, Fokkelman comments, "The multiple occurrences of 'servant' and 'serve' in II Sam 9 raise the question as to whether Ziba is indeed going to be a loyal servant to Mephibosheth. In verse 11bc, Ziba bows so deeply before David, and his court manner is so perfect that I have my doubts about his intentions" (Fokkelman, *Narrative Art and Poetry in the Books of Samuel*, 28).

## The Epilogue (2 Sam 9:11b–13)

The literary arrangement of the epilogue is very telling in the subtlety of its depiction of Mephibosheth's predicament in the offer or, rather, the requirement placed upon him to dine at the king's table daily. There are four sentences in the epilogue, each of which contains Mephibosheth's name. It is constructed as an inclusio; see the illustration below:

A  ומפיבשת אכל על שלחני כאחד מבני המלך

So Mephibosheth was eating at his table, like one of the sons of the king—

B. ולמפיבשת בן קטן ושמו מיכא

Now Mephibosheth had a young son; his name was Micha.

B′ וכל מושב בית ציבא עבדים למפיבשת

And all the dwellers in Ziba's house were Mephibosheth's servants.

A′

ומפיבשת ישב בירושלם כי על שלחן המלך תמיד הוא אכל והוא פסח שתי רגליו

But Mephibosheth was dwelling in Jerusalem, because he had to eat at the king's table daily, though he was lame in his two legs.

Both the first (A) and fourth (A′) sentences deal with Mephibosheth's eating at the king's table (two key lexemes אכל, "to eat," and שלחן, "table," are found in both sentences). In addition, both sentences begin with a *waw*-disjunction clause, with the *waw* prefixed to Mephibosheth's name. Both sentences consist of the main clause being followed by subordinate prepositional clauses, prefixed with a כי ("like," and "for," or "because,"). The two sentences in between (the second [B] and the third [B′]) deal with people who belong to Mephibosheth, a son and servants respectively, and their relationship to him are indicated with the preposition ל (meaning "for" or "to") prefixed to Mephibosheth's name.

The four sentences are paired in yet another way—with key lexemes. The first two are linked by the lexical form בן; one in the plural ("sons"), the other in the singular form ("son"). While Mephibosheth is a father, having his own son, he is reduced to a dependent status like that of a child, one among many of another man's sons. We are not told the whereabouts of his son. But the linkage observed above between the second and third sentences may be a hint that Micha may have been left behind in the house of Ziba.[56] The third and fourth sentences are paired by the lexeme יָשַׁב ("to dwell"): one in the noun form ("dwellers" or "inhabitants") and the second in the participial form ("to be dwelling"). While those who are to serve Mephibosheth dwelt under the authority of another man, Ziba, Mephibosheth himself is severed from them—dwelling under the authority of another man, David. Thus, eating at the king's table (pragmatically placed at the margins of this inclusio) separates Mephibosheth from those to whom any household head would love to be close, both progeny and servants (placed at the core of the inclusio). This makes him out to be no more than a privileged hostage or prisoner.[57]

Understood in this fashion, the treatment of Mephibosheth is very akin to the treatment accorded Jehoiachin, the last monarch of the Davidic dynasty, who was held captive in Babylon. Just as the Deuteronomist speaks of Jehoiachin's throne being exalted above the thrones of all the other captive kings (2 Kgs 25:28), Mephibosheth is also raised from obscurity to a status comparable to that of princes of the reigning dynasty. Yet, just as there was no hope of Jehoiachin being restored to his throne

---

56. Sounding a different note, Anderson writes, "It seems that this reference to Mephibosheth's son may have been intended to emphasize the unending loyalty of David to Jonathan" (Anderson, *2 Samuel*, 142). To him, the essence of the chapter as a whole is to showcase David's loyalty to Jonathan, as is indicated by the threefold repetition of David's intention to show his covenant faithfulness to any surviving Saulide (ibid., 143). In an opposing view, Hertzberg notes the lack of emphasis on Mephibosheth's little son. He, however, believes David was playing safe by keeping a watchful eye on a potential claimant to the throne to avoid any surprises as the kind found in 2 Kgs 11), where a royal kid raised in secret supplanted the queen (Hertzberg, *I & II Samuel*, 301). Sternberg likewise distrusts David's intentions. In view of David's distaste of the disabled (2 Sam 5:6–8), he suspects David's decision to give the lame Mephibosheth a permanent seat at the royal dinner table (9:3, 13). Sternberg concludes, "Is David willing to undergo such a daily ordeal just in memory of his friendship with Jonathan, as he himself declares, or as the price for keeping an eye on the last of Saul's line? Considering David's genius for aligning the proper with the expedient, he may even be acting from both motives" (Sternberg, *The Poetics of Biblical Narrative*, 255).

57. Fokkelman points out that the exact meaning of the phrase "to eat bread at the king's table"—as a manifestation of *ḥesed*—can be correctly determined only against the background provided by the threefold use of the same term in 1 Sam 20: "Even more striking is the fact that the word 'table' does not occur elsewhere in the books of Samuel, except twice in 1 Sam 20, and there again it concerns 'eating at the king's table'! Hence we ought to ponder the connection between 1 Sam 20 and II Sam 9" (Fokkelman, *Narrative Art*, 29). As discussed above, the requirement that David eat daily at Saul's table was overtly an honor to him, while it covertly served Saul as a way to keep close watch on him. The same surreptitious and hideous motivation seems to be at work here again.

in Jerusalem, there is no hope of Mephibosheth regaining Saul's throne in Gibeah. We will give more attention to the similarities and differences between the last scions of the Saulide and Davidic dynasties in the next chapter. Suffice it to point out that as the ensuing events that we will be discussing in the following sections of this chapter reveal (16:1–4; 19:25–31), David, at best, was combining loyalty to a dead friend with *Realpolitik* by sequestering Mephibosheth under his watchful eyes in order to forestall any irritations to the stability of his kingdom.[58]

Before concluding this section, we note that the epilogue ends with a clause that highlights Mephibosheth's disability, והוא פסח שתי רגליו ("though he was lame in his two legs," v. 13c). The placement of this piece of information at this point is very important for both its backward and forward looks. The backward glance looks, first of all, to the initial intimation of Mephibosheth's disability in the account of Ishbosheth's death. In the tragic narrative of the fate of Saul's progeny, the only person left standing before king David is the crippled Mephibosheth. McCarter suggests that more than fortuity accounts for this phenomenon. He writes, "It may be more than accidental, moreover, that the one male Saulid who survived the purge was lame."[59] While disabled persons of the priestly line could not officiate in the cult, there is nothing that bars any disabled person from the kingly role in Israel. However, the interconnectedness of the sacred and the secular in ancient Israel, with the monarchs often officiating or presiding over the cult (1 Sam 13:9–12; 2 Sam 6:17–18; 2 Kgs 16:12–13; 1 Chr 21:26; 2 Chr 29), makes it imperative that the one who ascends the throne be without any physical blemish.

The first mention of Mephibosheth's lameness, in the account of Ishbosheth's death, is preceded by the notice of the enfeeblement of Saul's house vis-à-vis David's virility (2 Sam 3:1). The persistence of the lameness motif serves to buttress another motif, that of weakness and its impact on holding onto the throne. The motif of weakness and dynastic rule stretches from Samuel to Kings. Any time a king is mentioned as being weak, his rule is at its twilight. The difference between the house of Saul and the house of David hinges on whether or not a king's weakness accompanies his progeny. Saul is eliminated after his weakness is noted (1 Sam 28:20); weakness continues to plague his house (2 Sam 3:1; 4:1;

---

58. For a similar conclusion see Hertzberg, *I & II Samuel*, 300–1. For a glowing tribute to David's loyalty to his dead friend, see Bergen, *1, 2 Samuel*, 355–56.

59. McCarter, *II Samuel*, 265.

9:3, 13; 19:27, ET 19:26) and is epitomized by Mephibosheth's lameness. Similarly, David's hold on power becomes elusive once weakness is noted in him (2 Sam 16:14; 17:2; 21:15; 1 Kgs 1:1–4). However, such a weakness is not attributed to his progeny, hence the longevity of his dynasty.[60]

In the backward look, we are also reminded of how the Jebusites had declared that David could not take the fortress of Zion—that the blind and the lame would keep him at bay (2 Sam 5:6). Upon seizing the fortress, David barred the blind and the lame from his palace because they were loathsome to him (2 Sam 5:8).[61] There is an ironic turn of events in this respect: David, whom the blind and the lame were supposed to keep away from Jerusalem, takes residence in Jerusalem. Similarly, David, who had barred the blind and the lame from his citadel, compelled the lame Mephibosheth, who might have preferred to reside elsewhere, to not only dwell in Jerusalem but dine at the king's table daily.

In the forward look, the restatement of Mephibosheth's lameness anticipates the extrication of Mephibosheth from the death faced by the Saulide Seven (2 Sam 21:1–14). As stated in the previous chapter, while we understand that incident to precede this present episode in story time, it has been placed at the end of David's story, in narrative time, to give finality to the fate of Saul's house. In that incident, it is only the lame Mephibosheth (from among Saul's surviving male progeny) that is spared certain death at the hands of the Gibeonites. Given the sacral nature of the killings, his lameness certainly may have been a pleasing disqualifier for him.[62] The forward look is also anticipatory

---

60. In recognition of the potency of the motif in the rhetorical portrayal of the antithesis between the fates of the two houses, Alter comments, "This notice at the end about Mephibosheth's lameness also underscores the continuing antithesis between the fates of the house of Saul and the house of David: King David came into Jerusalem whirling and dancing before the LORD; the surviving Saulide limps into Jerusalem, crippled in both legs" (Alter, *The David Story*, 243).

61. For a fuller discussion of what הבית ("the house") in 2 Sam 5:8 means, see Vargon, "The Blind and the Lame," 496–514.

62. While acknowledging the improbability of offering a blemished sacrifice, Glück gives David some credit for sparing Mephibosheth: "It can be surmised that on account of his lameness he would not be considered a suitable 'offering,' but the king, as the supreme judge, had the right, in any case, to commute a death sentence and thus save Mephibosheth even if he was suitable" (Glück, "Merab or Michal," 75, note 17). We could sharpen the credit to David by reversing Glück's statement: even though Mephibosheth's lameness disqualified him from being a suitable "offering," the king as the supreme judge had the right to have had him killed anyway.

## David and Mephibosheth

of Mephibosheth's failure to accompany the king when the latter fled Jerusalem during the Absalom uprising, whereupon Mephibosheth was taken undue advantage of by Ziba through calumny (2 Sam 16:1–4). Mephibosheth would finally proffer his lameness for his vindication in his interview with David, upon the latter's return from exile (2 Sam 19:27–29). To these last two issues we presently turn.

## MEPHIBOSHETH AND A DISGRACED DAVID (2 SAM 16:1–4)

### CHAPTER 16:1–4

> 1 Now David had barely crossed over the summit *of the hill*, and behold![63] Ziba, Mephibosheth's steward, *on hand* to meet him with a pair of saddled donkeys, and upon them two hundred *loaves of* bread, a hundred cakes of raisin, a hundred summer fruits, and a pitcher of wine. 2 Then the king said to Ziba, "What do you mean by *bringing* these?"[64] Ziba replied, "The donkeys are for the king's household to ride, the bread,[65] and the summer fruits are for the troops to eat, and the wine is for the weary to drink in the wilder-

---

63. Distinctions are drawn between הנה and והנה on the basis of the contexts in which they are usually used. Zewi lists the most prominent contexts of their occurrence as follows: (1) הנה normally follows an inflected form of the biblical Hebrew verb of speech אמר, and introduces direct speech; and (2) והנה usually follows verbs of sight or descriptions of dreams, visions, or revelations, and customarily introduces content clauses related to verbs of sight or to some other previous context. She further adds, "Although these occurrences are very common, a large number of instances do not share any of these characteristics. A thorough examination suggests that the contexts are very close to those involving verbs of sight and that they always entail some kind of watching activity. The verbs preceding והנה in these cases are frequently verbs of motion and are followed by an act of watching or listening (e.g., to come, to send, to rise early, to go, to descend, to ask)" (Zewi, "The Particles הִנֵּה and וְהִנֵּה in Biblical Hebrew," 21–37). While the particle והנה in our passage does not follow a verb of sight it perfectly fits into the ways in which it is characterized: our context also requires some kind of watching activity, and the verb preceding it is a verb of motion עבר ("cross over").

64. Lit. "What are these to you?" For similar questions see Gen 33:5, 8; Exod 12:26; Josh 4:6; and Ezek 37:18 (cf. Driver, *The Books of Samuel*, 318). David began asking the right question about Ziba's motive for bringing these gifts, which question the latter skillfully evaded. Sadly enough, David did not follow through on his initial question and thereby provided Ziba with the needed opportunity to malign his supposed master.

65. I follow the *Qere* reading (והלחם, "and the bread") rather than the *Ketiv* (ולהלחם, "and as for the bread") as do most of the ancient versions. On the ל prefixing the *Ketiv*, Driver comments, "The ל affords an example of the accidental repetition of a letter from a preceding word, such as has taken place—though it is not there corrected by the Masorah." (Driver, *The Books of Samuel*, 318).

ness." 3 And the king asked, "But where is your master's son?" And Ziba replied the king, "Behold! He is staying in Jerusalem. For he said, 'This day the house of Israel shall return to me my father's kingdom.'" 4 Then the king said to Ziba, "Behold! To you *belongs* everything that is Mephibosheth's." And Ziba replied, "I prostrate myself. May I find favor in your eyes, my lord the king."

This scene is part of the subplot of the Absalom narrative that deals with David's flight from Jerusalem, which begins in 2 Sam 15:14 and goes through 17:22. In David's flight, his relationship with the subjects who interacted with him are characterized by three key terms, namely, עבר, "to cross over," which appears twenty times in the unit (2 Sam 15:18, 22, 23, 24, 28, 33; 16:1, 9; 17:20, 21, 22); שוב, "to turn, or return," which appears six times (2 Sam 15:19, 20, 25, 27, 29, 34; 17:3); and ישׁ, "to remain, stay, or dwell," which is found four times (2 Sam 15:19, 29; 16:3, 18). The first word relates to those whom David allowed to follow him in his flight; they "crossed" with him. The second and third words relate to those whom David had asked to "return" to Jerusalem, and "remain" with the usurper. Both groups were working for David; a part of the first group would constitute the force that later battled the rebels, while the second would return, remain and engage in counterinsurgency behind enemy lines—working toward the return of the king.

The use of literary artistry for rhetorical effect in our scene (16:1–4) is noteworthy. The scene opens with David crossing over (עבר) the summit of the Mount of Olives (where he had just met God, through answered prayer, and Hushai, the answer to his prayer); and strategically stationed to meet him is Ziba. The people who had come out to David since the beginning of the flight had offered themselves to the king—to follow him whither he went. It is in response to such self-presentation that David determined who should cross over and who should return and remain behind. Ziba presented not himself but material things to David: there is no overt statement as to whether he was for or against the king—he remains opaque. Hence, the king uses neither "crossover" nor "return and remain" to address him. Rather, since he had come to the king with "things," he went away with a "thing"—property. Ziba, however, accused Mephibosheth of remaining (ישׁב) behind on the latter's initiative (a decision that was the king's to make for loyal subjects) and of staying behind to work for himself against the king's interest. The implication of this is that Ziba presented Mephibosheth's alleged usurpation of the king's prerogative of determining who remains behind as proof of Mephibosheth's high treason. This accusation incited the disgraced and vulnerable David enough that he decreed the confiscation of Mephibosheth's inherited property and the transference of the same to Ziba.

In this scene, the narrator calls Ziba the *na'ar* (נער)[66] of Mephibosheth. In our first encounter with Ziba, in chapter 9, he was first called the servant of Saul (9:1) and then the *na'ar* of Saul (9:9). In that capacity, whether as Saul's or Mephibosheth's steward, Ziba is expected to protect Mephibosheth's interest. Contrary to that expectation he is found here not only sabotaging but actively subverting Mephibosheth's interest, and perhaps his very existence, for personal gain. To realize this gain, Ziba strategically stationed himself on David's anticipated escape route out of the city so as to avoid being interrupted by the many loyalists engaging the king's attention on his flight from the city, but also to be close enough to the outskirts of the city so as to meet the king in his traumatic moment of mystification and stupor.[67]

---

66. The way this term is employed in the Hebrew Bible shows it has four or, perhaps, five distinct uses. First, it is used in reference to one who is young in age, either a child or a young adult (Gen 37:2; Exod 2:6; Deut 22:23; 1 Sam 17:33, 42). Second, it is used in referring to someone who is a lieutenant, an associate, or even someone who is second in command to a high ranking official (Exod 33:11; 2 Kgs 8: 4). Third, it refers to a servant who waits upon a master (1 Sam 2:13, 15, 18; 20:38; 1 Kgs 3:7). Fourth, *na'ar* refers to footmen among fighting troops (1 Sam 16:18; 30:17; 2 Sam 2:21). A common thread in all these uses of the term is that the *na'ar* is expected to be loyal to his superior. Ziba does not fit strictly in any of these categories. Ziba may have been a high-ranking official in Saul's court who had managerial duties (which places him more in the second category above than any of the others). He is now charged with the responsibility of managing the late king's estate, hence I have called him "steward."

67. Hertzberg's supposition that Ziba acted on the spur of the moment and took with him what he had at hand cannot be substantiated (Hertzberg, *I & II Samuel*, 345). The list of things that Ziba brought along for the king and his entourage consists of the kinds of things that one could not just go into the barn and pull out, bearing in mind that this was three thousand years ago, when one could not just walk into a grocery store to pick off the shelf two hundred loaves of bread.

Gordon rightly sees through Ziba's dissimulation as he writes that Ziba, as an opportunist, sought to take advantage of David's vulnerability and profit at the expense of Mephibosheth (Gordon, *I & II Samuel*, 277). Unlike Gordon, Anderson believes Ziba had real sympathy for David because he could not have predicted the way the war would (Anderson, *2 Samuel*, 205). What Anderson fails to take into account is that David had on his side his striker brigade that had been with him from his wilderness wandering days: all his commanding officers and all the well-motivated and experienced mercenaries were still with David. When you juxtapose this vis-à-vis Absalom's

Along with him, Ziba brought a pair of donkeys, two hundred loaves of bread, a hundred raisin cakes, a hundred cakes of summer fruits (probably figs), and a keg of wine.[68] When David, perhaps suspicious of Ziba's motive, questioned Ziba why he had brought all this items, he responds with a diversionary tactic. Rather than put forth the ethical motivation for his action, which was most probably what David's query sought from him, Ziba went on describing what is to be done with the things he brought: Even a child would know that asses are for riding and food is for eating. Yet, David was taken in by Ziba's dissembling.

Persuaded by Ziba's lackluster response, David proceeded to inquire about Mephibosheth's whereabouts. All of the discourses in Samuel that involve David directly talking to or about Mephibosheth are initiated with a question that David asked about or to Mephibosheth, indicative of the former's doubts about the latter. In the first two of these (2 Sam 9 and 16:1–4), the inquiry concerns Mephibosheth's whereabouts. In 2 Sam 19, David queried Mephibosheth for desertion. In the present passage (2 Sam 16:1–4), David's question (ואיה בן אדניך, "Where is your master's son?") betrays the discrepancy in the perspectives of the narrator and David. The narrator views Ziba as Mephibosheth's servant, while David considered him Saul's servant. On this note, Alter is mistaken in thinking that David calls Ziba Jonathan's servant.[69] Jonathan never was Ziba's master anywhere in the entire text of Samuel, nor is Ziba anywhere referred to as Jonathan's servant. David directly linked Mephibosheth with his enemy Saul; and by that association, at this critical juncture of

---

untested and inexperienced rabble, it becomes apparent that the scales tilted, however delicately, more in David's favor than in Absalom's.

68. Gunn has compared this list to that found in 1 Sam 25:18, and the similarities are striking. Besides the similarities of the items and their quantities that were brought to David, Gunn writes, "Both verses belong to a context where someone, attached to a potential enemy of David but acting independently of him, brings provisions to David as a conciliatory gesture. The people concerned are, respectively, Abigail the wife of Nabal, and Ziba the servant of Mephibosheth" (Gunn, *The Story of King David*, 50). We also note that both Abigail and Ziba state that the food items they brought were for David's troops (נערים, cf. 1 Sam 25:27; 2 Sam 16:2). Furthermore, just as Abigail had expected to be rewarded by David for her act (cf. 1 Sam 25:31), which he did by taking her into his harem upon her husband's death, Ziba's help was also not altruistic—he apparently had his eyes on Saul's estate.

69. "It is noteworthy that, at this late date, David still refers to Mephibosheth as 'your master's son,' still thinks of the long-dead Jonathan as Ziba's real master" (Alter, *The David Story*, 291).

defining where people stand, he now overtly lists Mephibosheth among his enemies.

Seizing on this question that scarcely masks David's suspicion of Mephibosheth, Ziba opened his response with the exclamatory particle הנה ("behold"), which accentuates the presentative effect and, hence, the immediacy of the fact being introduced. Ziba's response to the king in 16:3 can equally be translated "Behold, the inhabitant of Jerusalem." The phrase יושב בירושלם in the present text parallels a similar phrase in 2 Sam 5:6 יושב הארץ (which most translations render as "the inhabitants of the land,"). This latter phrase is appositional to the gentilic noun phrase (more properly a substantive adjectival phrase) היבסי ("the Jebusite"), which has no gender or number in and of itself—these properties can be determined only by the context. I submit, then, that the plural rendition of this phrase as "inhabitants of the land" needs to be revised: the participle יושב is masculine singular. Therefore, the focus is on one person, namely, the king of the land—the Jebusite king of Jerusalem. When the Bible intends the plural (which is the most common form), it states it categorically (cf. Num 33:55; Jos 2:9; 9:3; Judg 10:18; 1 Chr 22:18). Thus, in 2 Sam 5 David had defeated the Jebusite king of Jerusalem, but he let the lame Mephibosheth live there. Just as the narrator in 1 Samuel portrayed Saul as the new Philistine whose fight against David would amount to naught, Ziba now casts Mephibosheth as the new "inhabitant of Jerusalem"—the new Jebusite that David needs to dispossess.

The veracity of Ziba's inculpation of Mephibosheth remains a bone of contention among biblical commentators. There are those, like Peterson, who would rather gloss over it without dealing with it.[70] Such a stance is obscurantist, to say the least. Gordon, on the other hand, places serious doubts on Ziba's verity on the basis of circumstantial evidence.[71]

---

70. Peterson argues, "The storyteller doesn't make it clear to us whether Ziba is telling the truth or making it up. Later, Mephibosheth will present a different version of what happened (2 Sam 19:24–30). But for now David believes Ziba, accepts his help and turns over all of Mephibosheth's possessions to him. We do not have to decide whether Ziba is telling the truth or not to see that he is bent on using the David-Absalom crisis to his own advantage" (Peterson, *First and Second Samuel*, 211).

71. Gordon observes that only a monumental miscalculation could have deluded Mephibosheth into imagining that the events of Absalom's revolt would result in him, Mephibosheth, being crowned when indeed it was Absalom's rebellion and for whose sake all Israel was amassing (Gordon, *I & II Samuel*, 277).

Kirkpatrick outrightly calls it an audacious fiction of Ziba's invention.[72] Indeed, it is nothing other than pure chicanery, which Ziba had contrived for expropriating Mephibosheth's inheritance.

In his attempt to determine the candor of Ziba's statement, Sternberg begins by outlining the compositional technique of repetition. He observes that there are three categories of members that constitute the fabric of repetition in the dynamic of the biblical plot. These three categories are forecast (prophecy, command, or scenario), enactment (performance, realization, or, rarely, state of affairs), and report (of the fulfillment of the "forecast" or "enactment").[73] He notes, however, that the order of this structure, which was the habitual format in ancient literature, is not always conformed to by biblical literature—modern literature does not conform to it either. Nevertheless, the structure of repetition, he writes, receives immunity from temporal displacement: excepting prophetic messages it seldom happens "that the utterance of a forecast or the occurrence of an event emerges only from a later scene of report. So much so that when the reader finds the natural order subverted, he is entitled to take it as a question mark about the reliability of the report or the reporting character. Given the unique norm, temporal comes to imply perspectival divergence."[74] When we apply this principle to Mephibosheth's speech reported here by Ziba without its antecedent occurrence, we are bound to read it as the narrator's compositional question mark on Ziba's reliability.

Ziba's reply excited and incited David enough that at the spur of the moment he spewed such a far-reaching verdict that instantly disinherited Mephibosheth.[75] David's passionate emotion is conveyed in his

---

72. Kirkpatrick, The Second Book of Samuel, 368.

73. Sternberg, *The Poetics of Biblical Narrative*, 376. Explaining further, he writes, "The order in which the members appear usually reflects their chronological sequence: planning before performance, decree before fulfillment, action before its reporting as a thing of the past" (ibid., 378).

74. Sternberg, *The Poetics of Biblical Narrative*, 379. One example that Sternberg gives of this phenomenon is Gen 50:15–17, where Jacob's sons quote their father's speech without its prior occurrence in the narrative. Every reader of that text is inclined to understand it as the invention of Joseph's brothers, out of fear of possible retribution from their brother.

75. Hertzberg interprets Ziba's easy influence on David as a demonstration of how the latter's mistrust of the house of Saul had not really been banished from his innermost thoughts (Hertzberg, *I & II Samuel*, 345). Kirkpatrick considers David's action in passing a verdict on Mephibosheth without an inquiry as both rash and hasty, and reflective of David's unreflecting impetuous character (Kirkpatrick, *The Second Book of*

employment of the emotive exclamatory particle הנה accompanied by a nominal sentence, very unlike David (compare this with 9:9, where David returned Saul's estate to Mephibosheth).[76] In that flurry of furious words, David consigned Saul's estate to Ziba. Ziba's reaction is as intriguing as the Davidic donation.[77] We have to remember that since we have met Ziba, he has never bowed to David. Now, in gratitude to David, the first word that came out of his mouth is השתחויתי ("I prostrate myself," v. 4). However, if one is prostrating one would scarcely need to mention that fact: it is more likely that Ziba bowed with his mouth than with his body.[78] Furthermore, Ziba's hauteur comes through, in spite of his smokescreen of phoniness, in his use of the first person pronominal suffix rather than the deferential third person pronoun that is the customary form of address to royalty. Then he continues with the usual courtly courtesies. The text displays a reversal of rhetorical preferences here: David, normally verbose, has now taken to terseness and the use of a nominal sentence, while Ziba, usually laconic and given to nominal sentences, has now employed two indicative verbs in this short discourse of six words.

The reversal of rhetorical preference between David and Ziba is symptomatic of the reversal of fates between David and Mephibosheth. David, who had previously danced and skipped into Jerusalem, now scurried out of town, while Mephibosheth, who had limped into the city previously, now remained in it. Similarly, David who would have loved to remain in the city is forced out of it, whereas Mephibosheth, who was prepared to leave the city with David, is compelled to remain therein. We also note that David, who had undertaken to take care of Mephibosheth, now needed the care of the former caretakers

---

*Samuel*, 368).

76. Fokkelman notes that both Ziba and Mephibosheth are introduced by *hinneh* (16:1b, 3d), and what connected them both (the land) is also now introduced with a *hinneh* (16:3d) (Fokkelman, *Narrative Art*, 31).

77. Anderson observes that David's action in this passage "illustrates the use of the royal prerogative to confiscate land or property from an enemy or opponent, and to give it to another person as a land-grant (cf. 9:7)" (Anderson, *2 Samuel*, 205).

78. Fokkelman misses this point in his assumption that Ziba actually bows to David, when there are no hints for such a supposition in the text. He writes, "This meeting concludes with Ziba's thanks. The man whom we did not see bow in A now bows indeed! His prostration occurs just when he is promoted to being a big landowner, and not before" (Fokkelman, *Narrative Art*, 31).

of Mephibosheth (Ziba and Makir, cf. 2 Sam 16:1–2; 17:27–29). All this presages the ultimate similarity of the fate of the house of David to that of the house of Saul, even though David's house received by far a better deal from Yahweh than the house of Saul. To this theme we will return in the next chapter, where we will be situating our study in Samuel within the larger biblical context.

## MEPHIBOSHETH AND A COMPROMISED DAVID
## (2 SAM 19:25–31; ET 19:24–30)

### Chapter 19:25–31 [ET 19:24–30]

25 Then Mephibosheth son of Saul came down to meet the king. Now he had not cared for his legs, neither did he trim his moustache; even his garments he did not wash from the day the king went out to the day on which he returned in peace.

26 When he came from[79] Jerusalem to meet the king, the king said to him, "Why did you not go with me, Mephibosheth?"

---

79. There is no prepositional prefix in the MT. The usual way of translating such a construction would have been to insert "to" rather than "from." There are several places in the Hebrew Bible where the verb בא is used in conjunction with the preposition כי, either in a circumstantial or subordinate clause. I have identified three distinctive uses. The first is where they are used with a preposition that indicates direction, which always tends to be motion toward, rather than motion from, an object (cf. Exod 15:19; 1 Sam 26:3; Jer 37:16). The second is where the two-word combination is used with a preposition prefixed to an infinitive construct to indicate purpose, which also at the same time has an implicit directional element that implies motion toward an object (1 Sam 26:15; 1 Chr 16:33; Ps 96:13). Lastly, as in the case at hand, there are situations in which the word combination is used without an accompanying prepositional phrase, but a spatial directional motion toward an object is implied (Num 21:1; 1 Sam 23:7; 2 Sam 19:26; 2 Chr 32:2). McCarter observes that only a few LXX minuscules support the reading "*from* Jerusalem to meet the king;" which rendition he notes was nevertheless favored by both O. Thenius and J. Wellhausen (*II Samuel*, 417).

On the basis of the foregoing, then, we ought to insert the preposition "to" before Jerusalem. However, the context of this circumstantial clause demands a different approach. The context of 2 Sam 19:16–40 [ET 19:15–39] is at the Jordan River. After the men of Judah had given the king the green light to return, he came as far as the Jordan, where he was met by the men of Judah (v. 16), Shimei and the Benjiminites (vv. 16–17a), and Ziba and his entourage (vv. 17b–19). Then, at the end of the Jordan encounter episode, David converses with Barzillai, still at the Jordan, in verses 32–39. It is only after this latter conversation that we are told that the king crossed over to proceed to Jerusalem via Gilgal (vv. 40–41). In between the first set of encounters and the last dialogue the king had with Barzillai is located his interview with Mephibosheth (vv. 25–31). Indeed, both the narrator's and Mephibosheth's use of the prepositional adverbial phrase "in peace" (בשלום) would be more appropriate if this encounter took

27 He replied, "O my lord the king, my steward betrayed me; for your servant had said to him, 'Saddle for me an ass[80] that I will ride upon it and go with the king'—for your servant is lame. 28 However, he slandered your servant to my lord the king; but my lord the king is like the angel of God. Let him do what is good in his eyes. 29 For my father's entire house was nothing but dead men before my lord the king, yet you have placed your servant among those who eat at your table. What right do I have anymore to still cry out to the king?"

30 Then the king said to him, "Why do you argue your case further? I have decided: you and Ziba will divide the estate." 31 But Mephibosheth said to the king, "Let him even take everything, now that my lord the king has come be in peace to his throne."[81]

This narration of Mephibosheth's interview with David is part of the story of the return of the king from the latter's self-imposed exile consequent to Absalom's revolt. In this episode of the king's return, the scene reporting Mephibosheth's interview with the king contains twice the number of words in direct discourse as in narration.[82] This contrasts sharply with the previous passages we have dwelt with (2 Sam 9 and 16:1–4), where there is an almost one-to-one correspondence between direct discourse and narration. Fokkelman sees this as the narrator's way of tipping the scales in favor of Mephibosheth.[83] Mephibosheth not only speaks more than David, he also has the final word, both of which contrast sharply with what happened in 2 Sam 9. This, when taken in concert

---

place at the Jordan, prior to the new insurrection that arose when the king's procession reached Gilgal. Clearly the pragmatic implication of this context is that Mephibosheth's encounter with the king also took place at the Jordan River, hence we have inserted the preposition "from" before Jerusalem.

80. The ancient translations (the LXX, the Syriac and the Vulgate) have this clause in the 2ms imperative. It would make better sense if Mephibosheth had given orders for his ass to be saddled than for him to attempt to saddle it for himself, since he was crippled. Perhaps it is therefore possible that while he was dressing or waiting for Ziba to get his ass ready, the latter stole way to meet David in his own right.

81. Lit., "House." However, if our suggestion above that Mephibosheth met David at the Jordan River is correct, then the king had not yet reached his "house" (palace or even capital city) in the literal sense. However, his restoration to his throne was not in doubt. This interpretation is in consonance with the use of house, in word-play, in 2 Sam 7 in reference to kingship (dynasty).

82. Fokkleman gives the ratio or words in direct discourse and narration in this episode as 83:42, approximately 2:1 (*Narrative Art*, 23).

83. Fokkelman, *Narrative Art*, 23.

with the content of Mephibosheth's locution, is a possible signification of the higher moral ground (vis-à-vis David) from which he speaks.

As the people of Judah proceed to the Jordan River to welcome David, Shimei leads an entourage of a thousand warriors (lit. chosen men) from Benjamin to tender his apology to the king. Ziba comes along with his household to bring the king across the river. At the Jordan River crossing, Barzillai and his associates stand to bid the king farewell. It is in midst of the enumeration of these welcoming and farewell parties that Mephibosheth is also listed.

In giving the account of Mephibosheth's encounter with David, the narrator first gives a backgrounded account of how Mephibosheth conducted himself in the absence of the monarch (with a *waw*-disjunctive construction). From the day David fled Jerusalem until the day of his return, Mephibosheth completely neglected all the rules of personal hygiene: he never had a bath, neither did he trim his moustache nor wash his garments. Mephibosheth compensated for his inability to share in the king's risk from enemies by placing his health at risk by adopting the customary forms of mourning of the time for a rather extended period of time.[84]

There are different scholarly stances on the narrator's account of Mephibosheth's conduct in David's absence. While an overwhelming majority of scholars see it as proof of his loyalty to David, a few read it as being phony. J. Kirsch, for example, compares Mephibosheth's conduct to that of David before Achish the Philistine king of Gath (1 Sam 21:14).[85] Halpern makes a case for Mephibosheth's loyalty to David; however, he argues on for the possibility that Mephibosheth's disheveled veneer, which he presents as proof of his mourning for the king, could as well have been presented as his self-effacement before Absalom in the desire

---

84. Bergen, commenting on 2 Sam 19:24, is of the opinion that the unflattering appearance of Mephibosheth was proof enough that he was in deep mourning in the king's absence and that he did not look a pretender to the throne as charged by Ziba (Bergen, *1, 2 Samuel*, 430). Expatiating on the modes of mourning in ancient Israel, Mauchline writes, "This neglect of personal care was practiced in various ways during occasions of mourning (cf. 2 Sam 12:20; 14:2); other practices were to shave the hair and beard (cf. Job 1:20; Jer 16:6; 41:5; 47:5; etc.), to wear sackcloth and cast earth on the head (1 Sam 4:12; Job 2:12; Neh 9:1); etc.) and to sit or lie on an ash-heap (Isa 58:5; Jer 6:26; Ezek 27:30)" (Mauchline, *1 and 2 Samuel*, 292).

85. Kirsch, *King David*, 254; as quoted in Schipper, "'Why Do You Still Speak of Your Affairs?" 345, footnote 5.

that vengeance be visited on David for decimating his family.[86] Ackroyd, similarly, likening Mephibosheth's conduct to the dissimulations of the Gibeonites in the conquest era of Joshua, asks quizzically, "Can we be sure that Mephibosheth was not being similarly astute?"[87] Views such as these fail to reckon with the diversity of rhetorical strands that a narrator weaves into the fabric of a narrative. Mephibosheth, in his speech before David, made no reference to his appearance. Rather, it is the narrator who, in his discursive comment, draws the reader's attention to Mephibosheth's act of mourning. It is, therefore, unfair to ascribe such sinister motives to Mephibosheth's well-intentioned devotion.

Contrary to the preceding views on Mephibosheth's appearance, Fokkelman sees it as proof of his integrity and shows how Mephibosheth's immaterial *ḥesed* sincerely responds to David's *ḥesed* toward him and stands in contrast to Ziba's material *ḥesed*. This, he believes, completely belies the charge of treason that Ziba had leveled against Mephibosheth.[88] Sternberg likewise highlights the significance of Mephibosheth's conduct coming from the narrator. He thus sees it as a vindication of the reader's distrust of Ziba and proof of Mephibosheth's loyalty to David.[89] Vargon even goes a little further in reading the narrator's comments here as a subtle critique of David.[90]

In between these two extremes are those who either seek to avoid a commitment on the matter either way and those who strive for a nuanced position. C. Conroy understands the narrator's failure to make a categorical judgment on either Ziba or Mephibosheth as a subdued way of showing that both of them are worthy of the reader's disdain.[91] Schipper similarly sees more complexity than clarity in the whole episode. He insists that textual evidence does not reveal any clues to assist a reader in ascertaining Mephibosheth's truthfulness.[92] While Peterson acknowl-

---

86. Halpern, David's Secret Demons, 50.
87. Ackroyd, The Second Book of Samuel, 181.
88. Fokkelman, *Narrative Art*, 32.
89. Sternberg, *The Poetics of Biblical Narrative*, 380.
90. "At first sight, the narrator does not criticize David directly, but there is implied criticism of his deeds" (Vargon, "The Blind and the Lame," 507).
91. Conroy, *Absalom Absalom!*, 106.
92. Schipper, "Why Do You Still Speak of Your Affairs?" 346. Along the same lines, Anderson concludes that considering all the available data, "in the end we are unable to decide with any certainty as to who told the truth" (Anderson, *2 Samuel*, 238).

edges that Mephibosheth's looks belie Ziba's claim that Mephibosheth is a dynastic pretender anticipating a personal coronation, he suggests that there is a deliberate withholding of a verdict so as to set David's response in bold relief. His view is that as David listens, "he knows that both stories cannot be true. Here the narrative takes us into new territory: David doesn't *care* who is telling the truth. There is no cross-examination, no calling in of witnesses. David accepts both men, Ziba and Mephibosheth, back into his city. His love is large enough, expansive enough, to handle faithlessness, fecklessness, lies, and hypocrisy. David does not insist on having a 'pure church.'"[93] Peterson's pastoral concerns trump his better exegetical judgment. He leaps to appropriation, completely bypassing the prior step of explication wherein one necessarily explores the world of the text. The foregoing skepticism notwithstanding, a close reading of the text does find clear clues that would inform the reader's exegetical endeavor.

As we take a closer look at Mephibosheth's speech, we ask how Sternberg's theory of repetition in the structure of plot dynamic applies here. There is no antecedent enactment of Mephibosheth's speech to Ziba, which he now reports to David (19:27–29, ET 19:26–28). If we follow Sternberg's pattern of argumentation superficially, then, Mephibosheth shall be construed as being downright mendacious. However, this situation is ameliorated by the narrator's prior positive report on Mephibosheth (19:25, ET 19:24). It is against the template of the narrator's positive perspective on Mephibosheth that the latter's speech ought to be read, in which case he is to be understood as being veridical.

Probing further into his speech, we note the use Mephibosheth makes of a key Hebrew word, רמה (to "deceive," "deal treacherously with," or to "betray;"[94] 19:27, ET 19:26) vis-à-vis its use in other places in Samuel and indeed elsewhere in the biblical text. In both of the other instances where the same word is used in Samuel, actual deceit is involved. The first instance involves Michal's deceit of her father, which allowed David to escape (1 Sam 19:17), and the second involved Saul's deceit of the witch of Endor so she could vaticinate for him by her necromancy (1 Sam 28:12).[95] It is, therefore, natural to expect that the third use of the

---

93. Peterson, *First and Second Samuel,* 232.
94. BDB, 941
95. For further use of רמה in the Hebrew Bible see Gen 3:13; 29:25; Josh 9:22; Lam 1:19; Obad 1:7; Job 13:7; 27:4; Pss 78:57; 101:7; and Hos 7:16.

word in Samuel would also involve actual deceit. Besides, we observe that in all these three instances, the deceit involves Saulides, and the outcome of the deceit is also detrimental to them. Additionally, in all these instances the deceiver stands in a relationship of trust to the deceived. Thus, there is no sufficient ground to doubt that Ziba had acted perfidiously toward Mephibosheth.

In his refutation of Ziba, Mephibosheth employed an epithet in reference to David that is used elsewhere in the books of Samuel as well, namely, the king is like *an angel of God* (ואדני המלך כמלאך האלהים, v. 28, ET v. 27). The same phrase was used by the wise woman of Tekoa, who stood proxy for Joab (1 Sam 14:17, 20). In addition, the Philistine king Achish of Gath had also used the same expression in reference to David (1 Sam 29:9). In noting the occurrence of this phrase in 2 Sam 14 Schipper proceeds to also compare Mephibosheth with the Tekoite and concludes,

> In v. 28b, he says to David, "my lord the king is like the angel of God (*kml'k h'lhym*)." Again, one again hears traces of texts involving deception and disloyalty. In 2 Sam. xiv 20, the wise woman of Tekoa compares David's wisdom to the wisdom of "the angel of God" (*ml'k h'lhym*) when she asks David to judge her fictitious dispute with her family. This intersection with a text in which David is deceived when called upon to make a judgment subtly introduces the possibility that Mephibosheth is being less than sincere. His constant use of self-abasing speech actually reveals very little to the reader about his motives or his truthfulness.[96]

96. Schipper, "Why Do You Still Speak of Your Affairs?" 350. In a similarly flawed analysis, Schipper wrongly compares 2 Sam 19:26 (ET 19:25) with 16:17—the passages deal with the questions asked respectively to Mephibosheth and Hushai by David and Absalom. He then equates Mephibosheth's answer with Hushai's deception (ibid., 349–50). However, that kind of approach takes literary artistry to absurdity. Such a comparison has to be anchored in more than just one apparent similarity. The disparities between these two passages are too grave to be overlooked. First of all, in the case of Hushai, it is the narrator who clearly states that David had planted the former in Absalom's camp to undermine the rebellion. No such categorical statement anywhere in the literature imputes ulterior motives to Mephibosheth. Secondly, in the case of Hushai, the structure of the communication is quite different. There the question is being asked of an interlocutor about his loyalty to a third party, while here in the case of Mephibosheth, the question is set in a I-thou context; we note also that in this case, unlike in the former, the integrity of the second party has been asseverated by the narrator's favorable comments on him. Finally, in the case of Hushai, there already exists an antecedent case of a loyalist deserter in David's cabinet (Ahithophel) to make Absalom trust Hushai; in the case of Mephibosheth there is no agreement between his conduct

Schipper's comparison of Mephibosheth to the Tekoite woman is flawed: that the Tekoite presented her case in a concealed form cannot be called deception as it is a common rhetorical tool also used by the prophets to bring about a rude awakening in their audience at the punch line for maximum rhetorical effect (cf. 2 Sam 12:1–7; 1 Kgs 20:35–42). Additionally, the use of the figure of speech ("the angel of the God") in ch. 14 was devised by a loyalist, Joab, working for the good of the king—that he may bring back the son the king loved and missed badly (cf. 2 Sam 13:39—14:3). On a similar note, the intentions toward the king, which the narrator apparently ascribes to Mephibosheth right from the beginning of the scene, are good ones.

Contrary to Schipper's suggestion, I envisage that both passages highlight David's weakness in failing in each case to reach the crux of the matter at stake. David, as Yahweh's anointed, was certainly the messenger of God (recall the endowment of the Spirit that he received in 1 Sam 16), and as such was expected to be capable of deciphering truth from falsehood. In both cases he showed a colossal want of sagacity and the attendant ability to fathom the matter at hand. In the case of the Tekoite, the concern was with the restoration of the king's estranged son and his installation as the heir, in order to avert imminent danger to Yahweh's heritage (14:4–13). David went only halfway in bringing Absalom back, without installing him as the heir to the throne, which was the crux of the Tekoite (Joab's) petition (14:7, 16). In like manner, with respect to Mephibosheth, where the same figure of speech is used, David fails to grasp the heart of matter, now that he has both Ziba and Mephibosheth at hand. Furthermore, in 2 Sam 14:1–3, the prelude to the usage of this sobriquet is a pretended mourning that is meant to work for David's good (since his heart was yearning for Absalom). Similarly, in 2 Sam 19:25, prior to the usage of this epithet, there is an actual mourning concerning the well-being of David.

Additionally, Mephibosheth, in his speech, deftly paints a telling picture of the precarious position in which Ziba had placed him now. He states that all the members of his father's house were condemned men before David when the latter chose to spare his life (v. 29, ET v. 28).[97]

---

(and speech) and the behavior of his counterpart (Ziba), neither does his conduct square up with his alleged crime. This makes the need to determine the truth even more urgent than ever, which need David completely overlooks.

97. The Hebrew phrase Mephibosheth employs, אנשי מות, literally translates as "men of death," that is, condemned men. This presupposes some kind of sentence to that

This simple statement serves both to allude to David's complicity in the murder of the Saulide Seven (ch. 21)[98] and to explain Mephibosheth's own terror when he first appeared before David (ch. 9). Having been implicated by Ziba, and in view of his pedigree in the fated house of Saul (and the death sentence passed on them, as he perceives things), coupled with the ancient Near Eastern custom of decimating the male members of a deposed dynasty, Mephibosheth acknowledges that he has no legal right to claim before David.[99] He then leaves the matter with David, allowing him to decide as he wills.

David's response to Mephibosheth is as puzzling as his initial response to Ziba. Certainly, David's actions both in chapter 16 and chapter 19 do not present him as one who dispensed justice to the nation, as the Torah requires; but we will reserve that discussion for the next chapter. His hasty dispensing with Mephibosheth's case smacks of an uneasy conscience recoiling from confrontation with the naked truth.

---

effect issued by some authority figure. The authority figure may be one invested with legal authority (cf. 1 Sam 20:31; 2 Sam 12:5; 1 Kgs 2:26). The sentence may also be issued by someone without stately authority but possessing violent power, such as when a rebel leader pronounces a death sentence on rival elements or defectors, or the sort of *fatwa* that fundamentalist terrorists issue for the death of their enemies (cf. 1 Sam 26:16). In either case the person making the pronouncement has either the authority or the capability to execute it. When all the biblical passages cited here are taken into consideration, one is left in no doubt that Mephibosheth alludes to a scheme orchestrated, on David's watch, to eliminate Saulide contenders to the throne of Israel.

98. Kirkpatrick understands Mephibosheth to be suggesting that David might have put all the members of Saul's house to death. He also connects this statement with the incident in 2 Sam 21:6-9 (Kirkpatrick, *The Second Book of Samuel*, 395).

99. The term used here is צדקה, which is usually rendered as "righteousness." Underlining the term, however, is the concept of an established norm of just order for regulating conduct, both in the larger society and for individuals, whether in the sacred realm (with emphasis on morality and conduct) or in secular affairs (stressing integrity and justice in the marketplace, in the polity, or in the court). When used, especially but not exclusively, in combination with משפט as a hendiadys (or word pair), צדקה signifies an inherent requirement for conformity to an established norm (cf. Lev 19:36; Deut 1:16-17; 25:13-16; Job 8:3; Ps 94:15; Jer 22:12). To the person who stands to benefit from this norm, it is a right to be claimed. Conversely, there is an implicit duty placed upon the person who is in the position to make the conformity to such an established norm possible (for instance, it is incumbent upon a judge to ensure that justice is dispensed without fear or favor, cf. Lev 19:15; Deut 16:18-20; Prov 31:9). This is what, in today's parlance, is termed human rights. It is this that Mephibosheth, in his predicament, disclaims before the monarch. For similar positions see Kirkpatrick, *The Second Book of Samuel*, 396; Gordon, *I & II Samuel*, 291; and Ackroyd, *The Second Book of Samuel*, 181-82.

Biblical commentators have struggled over time to find some explanation for David's untoward action in this case. K. Budde supposes that regal dignity would not allow David to eat up his words, so he made only a partial retreat.[100] Kirkpatrick suggests three possible reasons why David was content with a compromise verdict: he was either suspicious of the truthfulness of Mephibosheth's story, or he was unwilling to alienate Ziba (and possibly a large contingent of Benjaminites) by revoking the grant he had given to Ziba, or it could just have been a confirmation of the initial lease arrangement.[101] I find all the reasons unsatisfactory. First of all, if he was not sure of the truth of the matter, it was incumbent on him as the ultimate judge of the land to search this matter out and arrive at the truth (Deut 13:13–16, ET 13:12–15; 17:2–5; cf. 1 Kgs 3:16–28; Prov 25:2; Ezra 4:19; 5:17; 6:1; Job 29:16). Second, there is no evidence to suggest that Ziba had such a following in Benjamin that pitching him against the grandson of Saul (Israel's popular king), the Benjaminites would have preferred Ziba over Saul's heir. Third, lease arrangements are not coterminous with inheritance rights. This is even more so in Israel's covenant context, where land holdings, as a fief from Yahweh, were never to be permanently alienated from the family. The issue, therefore, is not that David *could* not get to the truth but that he *would* not. All that notwithstanding, Mephibosheth still comes through with integrity and dignity, showing himself standing tall on a higher moral plane than either Ziba or David: he shows that he valued his relationship to his sovereign over and above property.

There are clues in the text on how to assess the ethics of David's actions in this matter. There is a striking similarity to the narrator's stance

---

100. Budde, *Die Bûcher Samuel*, 292; as quoted in Vargon, "The Blind and the Lame," 508 n. 29.

101 . Kirkpatrick, *The Second Book of Samuel*, 299. For others who similarly account for David's action on the basis of either his distrust of Mephibosheth or his inability to decipher the truth see Gordon, *I & II Samuel*, 291; and Anderson, *2 Samuel*, 238.

Payne makes the distinction between the perspectives of the narrator and that of David: "It is clear that the biblical writer believed his story, but it is not so clear that David did" (Payne, *I & II Samuel*, 251). He nevertheless excuses David, unconvincingly, on the account of the loyalty of Ziba, adding that David may have had the desire of not visiting reprisal on anyone. I find McCarter's comments on the matter puzzling. He writes, "David settles this contest of obsequiousness by declaring it a draw" (McCarter, *II Samuel*, 424). The affairs of the state, and especially the administration of justice, are of such a serious nature that it is reprehensible if they are attended to as if one were a judge in some comic TV reality show.

on David in this passage and that of 2 Sam 3. In the events of chapter 3, David's motives are not clearly stated. However, the narrator's intimation that people were doing things that were "good in the eyes" of others or one another hints at the ethical perspective in which they were to be viewed: there was a movement toward expediency instead of a drive to the divine will. The same pattern resurfaces here with the use of the concern with people doing things that were "good in the eyes of David," and David doing things that were either good in his own eyes or in the eyes of others (2 Sam 19:19, 28, 38, 39; ET 19:18, 27, 37, 38). In this passage, as in the other, expediency tramples propriety. It is fascinating that David, in despair and at the nadir of his reign, during Absalom's rebellion, sought what is good in Yahweh's eyes (15:26). Yet, in his moment of triumph, others seek what is good in his eyes and he himself seeks what is good in the eyes of others: he cares less about what is good in the eyes of Yahweh now.[102]

David's "resolution" of the seeming stalemate in the conflict between the testimonies of Mephibosheth and Ziba without attempting to get to the bottom of the matter (2 Sam 19:30) contrasts sharply with the approach taken by Solomon to fathom the stalemate of a similarly, if not even more, complex nature (1 Kgs 3:16–27). David's solution only approximates Solomon's heuristic device for discovering the truth of the situation. While Solomon pursued the truth when faced with similar circumstances, David only employs volte-face diplomacy to speedily dispense with the situation at hand. The similarity between Mephibosheth's concluding remarks and that of the true mother of the living son in 1 Kgs 3 sets in bold relief the difference in the judgments of the two kings.

## Conclusion

Reflecting over the three accounts that relate David's dealings with the sole surviving male Saulide (2 Sam 9; 16:1–4; 19:25–31), we observe how the three crucial founding motifs of the Israelites as a people (blessing, progeny, and land) play out in Saul's family. The decimation of Saul's progeny indicates that it is the curse, rather than the blessing, that is operative in Saul's house. It leaves one wondering if the memory of Saul's

---

102. This pattern identified here compares well with David's conduct in the HDR. Throughout the early stages of the HDR David constantly sought after the divine will, but toward the end of the HDR (at his ascendency to Israel's throne) the preoccupation was with what was pleasing to human beings (either David or other Israelites).

name will survive in Israel. The mention of Mephibosheth's son, Micha (2 Sam 9:12), as a kind of remnant, is an intimation that Saul's name will not be completely cut off from among his people. The restoration of his estate to his grandson (2 Sam 9:7, 9) provides footing for Saul's progeny to be planted amongst his own people in the tribe of Benjamin. The king's (re)confiscation of Saul's estate (2 Sam 16:4) shows the precarious existence of Saul's progeny vis-à-vis the ironic fugacity of Davidic *ḥesed*.

The decimation of Saul's family and the confiscation of his family land holdings evince the dominant operative force of retribution. Whether it accrues from Yahweh's curse or Davidic vendetta is another question entirely. At the same time, the presence of a remnant (however insignificant) in Saul's house, coupled with the grudging return of half the estate to Mephibosheth (2 Sam 19:30), indicates that Yahweh would not completely wipe out Saul's family. Indeed, even in Samuel's prophetic diatribes against Saul, only the kingship was to be taken away from him: he said nothing of Saul's loss of progeny (1 Sam 13:13–14; 15:26–28). Even at the shrine of the Endorite witch, though Samuel said Saul would die with his sons (1 Sam 28:15–19), there was no indication that it was to be a perpetual annihilation of his house as the case was with the house of Eli (cf. 2 Sam 2:31–35; 3:11–14). This is why it becomes questionable whether or not divine retribution against Saul extended beyond those who died with him in the Philistine war. In view of all this, we are inclined to agree with Polzin that Mephibosheth, "the one still left in Jonathan's house, is a living reminder of David's complicity—whether justified or not—in transforming Saul's house into a barren establishment, and his own pact with Jonathan into a broken covenant."[103]

In the next chapter, I will assess our research findings in the light of Deuteronomic legislation. I will also attempt to situate our research findings in the larger biblical context. The purpose of this will be to determine how our findings relate to the biblical data elsewhere in Scripture, especially with regard to David in view of his larger than life stature in Scripture and the traditions of the church and synagogue.

---

103. Polzin, *David and the Deuteronomist*, 100.

# 7

# An Integrative Reading of Research Findings

I HAVE EXPLORED THE relationships between David and Saulides, with a narrative critical approach, in the last three chapters. In chapter four, which deals with the civil war years, two prominent Saulides, Abner and Ishbosheth were brutally murdered in cold blood. While there were no sufficient grounds for directly linking David with Ishbosheth's murder, there was significant circumstantial evidence implicating him in Abner's murder. David's dealing with Michal and her kin was the subject of study in chapter 5. David not only abandoned Michal when he fled Saul's palace, but upon his return to Israel had her removed, without concern for her feelings, from the home of a husband who deeply loved her. David eventually publicly humiliated her, and ultimately ordered the ritual killing of her five sons and two half-brothers. In chapter 6, I laid out how David first returned Saul's patrimony to Mephibosheth, without the latter requesting it, only to retake it later (when Ziba denounced Mephibosheth before David) without giving him the opportunity to defend himself. Even when Mephibosheth eventually defended himself satisfactorily, as I argued, David returned only half the estate he had seized. These acts of David violate Yahweh's law as laid out in Deuteronomy.

In the current chapter, I will be focusing on two main things. First, I will evaluate the major findings of this study on the basis of the Deuteronomic Code. Since this code is presupposed in these narratives, how do these findings fare in the light of Deuteronomy's requirements for justice in the covenant community? Second, I will analyze the findings from a biblical-theological perspective, especially in view of the prominence David has in biblical literature.

## A DEUTERONOMIC EVALUATION OF THE RESEARCH FINDINGS

It is commonly agreed in contemporary biblical scholarship that the book of Deuteronomy prefaces the final redaction of the Former Prophets, and the implied author expects the implied reader to presuppose Deuteronomy in his reading of the Former Prophets. Arnold, in this regard, writes, "These books present a theological history of Israel, evaluating Israel's past in light of the covenant relationship established in Deuteronomy and relying on the so-called 'retribution theology' established there."[1] This evaluation becomes even more poignant when we remember that history writing is always driven by a purpose, according to which authors make selective use of the raw data at their disposal. Ultimately, every history expects its readers to draw conclusions on the basis of its presuppositions. For the Deuteronomistic History, those fundamental presuppositions are articulated in Deuteronomy.

As noted earlier, the theme of justice is central to Deuteronomy. In the series of homilies that make up the book, Moses repeatedly summons the people to just living because they are family, on account of the covenant. Speaking to this matter Goldingay writes, "When Deuteronomy sets up the standards for life in the promised land, one aspect of its vision is that the people of God is a family in which people are each other's brothers and sisters. This is Deuteronomy's distinctive basis for an appeal for what we might call civilized or generous life in the people of God. Surely you will want to be considerate rather than oppressive, liberating rather than enslaving, it says, because the people you are relating to are family."[2]

The same requirement for justice applies to the anticipated institution of kingship. The Law of the king (Deut 17:14–20) epitomizes this. Israel's rejection of judgeship, as it opted for the introduction of kingship, was occasioned by the perversion of justice by Samuel's sons (1 Sam 8:1–5). At the inauguration of Saul's reign, Samuel set forth his own impeccable life of conformity to the covenant in public service as a model of just leadership (1 Sam 12:1–5). This *inclusio* that frames the narration of the introduction of kingship in Israel (1 Sam 8–12) by the justice motif (1 Sam 8:1–5 and 1 Sam 12:1–5), therefore, establishes one of the criteria

---

1. Arnold, *1 & 2 Samuel*, 26.
2. Goldingay, *Men Behaving Badly*, 201.

for evaluating kingship.³ The question, therefore, that hung over this new institution was whether Israel's kings would live up to these criteria. It is particularly on the basis of the justice criterion that I proceed to evaluate David's relationships with Saul's progeny.

## Deuteronomy and David in the Civil War Years

In the fourth chapter, I argued for David's complicity in the death of Abner on the basis of strong circumstantial evidence (2 Sam 3). I contrasted David's alacritous execution of Saulide murderers (presumed or real) with his lethargic approach to Abner's murderer, Joab. There is, then, the need to reconsider David's action against Joab vis-à-vis the stipulations of the Law.

The only actions that David took against Joab was to pronounce curses on him and to compel him and his accomplices to engage in traditional mourning rites (2 Sam 3:29-31). The Deuteronomic Code, however, does not list cursing and mourning rites as sanctions against murderers. Rather, in unequivocal terms, it demands that murderers are to face capital punishment for their crimes (Deut 19:1-19). The main focus of this passage is the provision of cities of refuge to ensure "that innocent blood should not be spilt as a result of a false conviction"⁴ of persons involved in involuntary manslaughter (Deut 19:1-10). The implication of shedding innocent blood (whether through murder or miscarriage of justice) is the pollution of the land (Yahweh's inheritance given to Israel), which would then bring guilt and the concomitant curses upon the whole land (Deut 19:10, 13; 21:1-8; cf. 2 Kgs 21:16; 24:1-4). However, it is evident that the penalty for murder is capital punishment (cf. Exod 21:23-25; Lev 24:17-21; Num 35:16-25). David's action, therefore, must be seen as either a subterfuge (if he were personally implicated in the murder) or a miscarriage of justice (if he were innocent but just failed to implement the requisite sanctions against the offender). In either case, his action was unjust in light of the Law.

---

3. For a similar position see McConville, "King and Messiah," 271-95. For the other criteria see chapter one of this present book, especially pp. 24-25.
Furthermore, it is to be noted that the first leadership change recorded in Samuel (from Eli to Samuel) was similarly occasioned by the Elides's perversion of the cult and oppression of the worshipers and cult attendants (cf. 1 Sam 2:12-17, 22).

4. McConville, *Deuteronomy*, 310.

## *Deuteronomy and David and Michal*
## *(with Her Sons and Half-Brothers)*

The relationships between David on the one hand and Michal and her kin on the other were the focus of chapter 5. I have already shown that while Michal helped David to escape certain death from her father's henchmen, he made no effort to retrieve his wife from Saul's sphere. That David met with Jonathan a couple of times after his flight from Saul's palace suggests that he *could* have retrieved Michal from Saul's grip but he *would* not. Contrary to the Deuteronomic Code's demand that the husband issue divorce papers to a wife in whom he finds something offensive (Deut 24:1), David just left Michal in the limbo. The narrator is deafeningly silent on David's communication with Michal, or the lack thereof, after David escaped from the palace. The narrator is equally ambiguous as to the chronology of the events around the (re)marriages of David and Michal. Nevertheless, it is seems that David's new marriage(s) confirmed his lack of interest in Michal. If my supposition that David had entered into at least one marriage prior to Michal's remarriage to Paltiel is correct, then that event may have further furnished Saul with sufficient grounds to Saul to give Michal in marriage to Paltiel (1 Sam 25:42–44). Michal's contrived conversation with David, in which he allegedly threaten to kill her, would have already enraged Saul (indeed, any father) enough to see that as severance of relations. Overall, I have argued that David dealt with Michal rather underhandedly.

While the Bible does not say how long David was separated from Michal, gleanings from the narrative intimate that it was for a long time; certainly it was not less than nine years. David, after his flight from Saul's service, ranged the southern tribal areas as a renegade for an unspecified period of time. Nonetheless, it was long enough to allow him the time to marry two wives (1 Sam 25:42–43). After these incidents, David entered the service of Achish, the Philistine king of Gath, for sixteen months before Saul's demise (1 Sam 27:7). Following Saul's decease, David relocated to Hebron, where he reigned as king for seven-and-a-half years before the opportunity came for him to seize Saul's throne (2 Sam 5:5), at which time he also retrieved Michal from Paltiel's home. Thus, even beginning from when David entered the service of the Philistines alone, he and Michal were separated for about nine years. It is within this time period that Michal had her five sons with Paltiel.

# An Integrative Reading of Research Findings

In chapter 5, I argued that David lacked moral warrant for reclaiming Michal after the latter's marriage to Paltiel, contra Ben-Barak.[5] The whole point of the DtrH, especially in the exilic milieu of its final redaction, is that Israel was meant to be different from the nations (Deut 7:6; 14:2; 26:18–19; 32:8–9; cf. Exod 19:5–6; Isa 43:21; Ps 135:4). Thus, the DtrH perspective is better served by the distinction it makes between Israel and the nations, not by the congruence we see between them. This distinction is what should inform our understanding of Deut 24:1–4, which will become a legitimate basis for evaluating David's retrieval of Michal from Paltiel.

Deuteronomy 24:1–4 prohibits a husband from taking his divorced wife back if she has married another person and subsequently becomes divorced or widowed. This passage's prohibition hinges on moral (perhaps, cultic), but not particularly on legal grounds, because the wife has become defiled (הטמאה) to her first husband (cf. Jer 3:1). Because of this defilement, taking her back is an abomination in the sight of Yahweh (כי תועבה הוא לפני יהוה) and would bring sin upon the land that Israel received as an appanage from him (ולא תחטיא את־הארץ אשר יהוה אלהיך נתן לך נחלה) (Deut 24:4).

From the above, it is to be observed, first of all, that the yardstick for human conduct is not human standards but the divine norm. Secondly, the moral basis of the prohibition draws upon the age-old biblical tradition that marriage is a lifelong commitment between a man and a woman. This commitment restricts the involvement of a third party; hence the stringent legislation regarding adultery, which one transgresses on the pain of death (Deut 22:22–24; cf. Gen 2:24; 1 Cor 6:16–17). Thus, even in a non-adulterous relationship (as Deut 24:1–4 envisages), the defilement of the wife remains for the first husband, once she has been with another man. This, possibly, is the reason why Jesus gave adultery as the exceptional ground on which divorce is allowable (Matt 5:32; 19:3–9).

J. A. Thompson observes that the notion that unchastity defiles is found elsewhere in Scripture as well (cf. Lev 18:25, 28; 19:29; Num 5:3; Jer 3:2, 9; Hos 4:3). With regard to the purpose of the prohibition, he writes, "[T]here is value in the proposal that these laws were intended to preserve the second marriage. Once the divorcee has entered a second marriage there is no possibility of the husband reclaiming her. Reunion

---

5. Ben-Barak, "The Legal Background," 74–90.

is forbidden and the second marriage is guaranteed."⁶ Christopher Wright similarly writes, "The practical effect of this rule is to protect the unfortunate woman from becoming a kind of marital football, passed back and forth between irresponsible men. It is likewise for the woman's protection that a certificate of divorce is to be given to the woman (lit. 'into her hand'), since it proves her status as free to marry the second man."⁷ David deprived Michal of both rights guaranteed her under the Deuteronomic Code: the right to a divorce certificate (since he showed no interest in her anymore) and the right to be secure in the home of her new husband. If even a divorced woman was prohibited from the former husband, how much more she who was still actively married to her second husband ought to have been let alone. Remarriage to her, therefore, is an abomination before the Lord and thereby brings guilt upon the heritage of the Lord.⁸

The moral offense of Michal's retrieval from her husband's home extends beyond the cultic element to the social realm as well. This offense becomes very apparent, when we recall its context in 2 Sam 3. There, the narrator fills in the reader with information on David's growing harem—he now has six wives (vv. 2–5). Kessler comments tellingly on these verses, "It is noteworthy that this mention of David's four additional wives *precedes* his demand for the restoration of Michal (cf. 1 Sam 25:43–44, where such a notice *follows* his marriage to Abigail). Thus, the audience approaches David's demand for Michal in 2 Sam 3:12–13 with the freshly acquired knowledge that the man who will deprive Paltiel of his one cherished wife already has six other women. This motif reappears in 2 Sam 11–12 with infinitely greater intensity."⁹ By naming David's six wives just before he describes David's

---

6. Thompson, *Deuteronomy*, 244.

7. Wright, *Deuteronomy*, 255.

8. Brueggemann holds that the primary concern of this casuistic law was neither the marriage nor the status of the woman but the purity of the land. "The issue turns on the characteristic terms 'defile' and 'abhorrent.' The second marriage has made the woman a 'used' woman as far as the first husband is concerned. For the first husband to reengage with her sexually would be to relate to a 'used' woman, which could only bring *contamination* to the community and to the land ... The law operates on the assumption that anything 'out of order' will threaten the order of everything else; a sequel of sexual interactions that is not 'normal' is a disruption and a threat" (Brueggemann, *Deuteronomy*, 236).

9. Kessler, "Sexuality and Politics," 416.

demand for the return of Michal—that is by his "showing" not necessarily "telling"—the narrator casts David in lights that make him out to be not only a violator of cultic purity but also a greedy oppressor of the people. In this regard, David compares unfavorably with Samuel, who at the end of his tenure disavowed having either coveted anyone's possession or oppressed the people.

Both the account of David's handling of Abner's murder and his actions (and inactions) towards Michal defile the land to the extent that we would expect repercussions to be visited on the land at the commencement of David's reign. Notwithstanding, when there was famine at the beginning of David's reign, the blame for it was foisted upon the long-dead Saul through an oracle that does not fit the profile of such Yahwistic oracles (see my detailed discussion in chapter 5). To atone for Saul's alleged treachery against the Gibeonites, David authorized the ritual killing of Michal's five sons and two half-brothers (2 Sam 21:1–14).

Two aspects of this event directly contravene the Deuteronomic Code. In the first place, Deut 24:16 states: לא יומתו אבות על בנים ובנים לא יומתו על אבות איש בחטאו יומתו ("Fathers shall not be executed on account of their children; and children shall not to be executed on account of their fathers. Each person shall be executed for his own sin"—author's translation; cf. 2 Kgs 14:5–6; Jer 31:29–30; Ezek 18:2–4). Recognizable in this verse is the inestimable value God places on human life, such that he would not want the life of any person to be wasted for a cause that person knows nothing about.

On a similar note Eugene H. Merrill observes that the individual's supreme worth and responsibility before God is here attested to in the individual's personal accountability as a sinner (v. 16). He also notes that while the notion of corporate identity was pervasive throughout the OT, it was never to be employed at the expense of the solitary person. Merrill further comments, "Moreover, this very precept was appealed to in later times to justify the sparing of the innocent when judgment was being meted out to their relatives (2 Kgs 14:5–6; 2 Chr 25:3–4)."[10] That the DtrH appeals to Deut 24:16 to explain why Amaziah did not execute the children of his own father's murderers, therefore, is a clear indication of the intra-textual consciousness that undergird the corpus. In this light, then, one can say with confidence that David's authorization of the

---

10. Merrill, *Deuteronomy*, 322–23.

murders of Saul's surviving male progeny in 2 Sam 21 was viewed by the Deuteronomist as a contravention of Yahweh's law.

In the second place, the desecration of the Saulide corpses also ran afoul of Yahweh's law and Israel's practice. Deut 21:22–23 required that if any capital offender was hung on display, he must be brought down and buried at the end of the day: he must not be left hanging without burial even for one night. Such an act would defile the land that Yahweh gave Israel as a fief: It had the same implication as that of spilling innocent blood or remarrying a wife who had become defiled to her first husband through union with another man. As in these other matters, David offended in exposing Saulide corpses.

Indeed, this appears not to be first time the corpses of people, whose executions David authorized, were hung up (and left hanging for an extended period of time). In the case at hand, the text unambiguously states in 2 Sam 21 that the Saulide corpses were exposed for at least six months, from the beginning of the barley harvest to the beginning of the rainy season (i.e., from March/April to October/November). In the other case, where David authorized the execution of the Rimmon brothers, their bodies were mutilated and hung by the pool of Hebron (2 Sam 4:12). While this passage does not state categorically that the bodies of the Rimmon brothers were left there longer than expected, that implication is not lost on a keen reader. This is even more evident when one considers the contrast between what was done with their bodies and what was done with the head of Ishbosheth.[11] This behavior deviates not only from the stated legislation but from prior praxis as is evident from Joshua's treatment of the corpses of executed Canaanite kings in strict compliance with the Deuteronomic Code (cf. Josh 8:29; 10:26–27).

---

11. In the MT, the clause dealing with the burial of Ishbosheth's head begins with a *waw*-disjunctive followed by perfective verbs (ואת ראש איש בשת לקחו ויקברו בקבר אבנר בחברון), "But the head of Ishbosheth they took, and buried it in Abner's grave in Hebron."). This contrasts sharply from the *waw*-consecutive verbs used with respect to the bodies of the Rimmon brother (ויצו דוד את־הנערים ויהרגום ויקצצו את־ידיהם ואת־רגליהם ויתלו על־הברכה בחברון) "So David commanded his militia, and they slaughtered them. Then they cut off their hands and feet, and hung them by the pool of Hebron."). In this way, the very grammatical construction of the report indicates the contrast that is being made between the actions taken regarding the two sets of dead people: the head of the one was buried, while the bodies of the other two were hung by the pool of Hebron.

## Deuteronomy and David and Mephibosheth

The treatment David accorded Mephibosheth—both during the former's flight from Jerusalem, when Ziba accused the latter of royal pretensions, and during his return from exile, when Mephibosheth defended himself against the false accusation—has a feel of injustice. I will address two aspects of David's treatment of Mephibosheth: David's condemnation of Mephibosheth in absentia, and his partial nullification of his earlier verdict.

Deut 19:15 directs that in all judicial matters, no one is to be convicted on the testimony of only one witness. The crime that Ziba accused Mephibosheth of (i.e., treason) was one for which the offender could easily receive capital punishment (cf. 1 Sam 11:12; Luke 19:27). The crime of treason was of the same magnitude as the crime of idolatry, since both crimes were capital offenses. Therefore, the judicial procedure prescribed for the one would apply to the other as well. In the case of someone standing trial for idolatry, the Deuteronomic Code required that a thorough investigation be instituted to verify the accusation and that there should be at least two or three witness (Deut 17:4–6) before a verdict was to be pronounced. This requirement is an illustration of the law of witnesses touching any criminal matter articulated in Deut 19:15. In addition to the above, another rule regarding criminal proceedings outlined in the Deuteronomic Code required that the accused appear before the judges in person to make his defense (Deut 1:17; 19:16–17; cf. John 7:51). Moreover, the Law prohibited the judges from taking bribes, so that they would not be swayed one way or another and thereby pervert justice (Deut 16:19; 27:25; cf. Exod 23:8; Isa 1:23).

Thus, the Deuteronomic legislation had outlined at least four clear rules of proceedings for criminal cases that were meant to guarantee justice for all members of the covenant community, especially for its disadvantaged members like Mephibosheth.[12] First of all, an accusation against an alleged offender was to be thoroughly investigated before prosecution. Second, the accused was to be guaranteed fair hearing and the right to due process whereby he would be able to defend himself. Third, there were to be credible testimonies confirming the accusation: This is the equivalent of the requirement that the prosecutor/plaintiff prove his

---

12. Indeed, Ziba's action in beguiling a disabled person was a flagrant violation of Yahweh's stringent requirement for the protection of the dignity and well-being of the disabled in the covenant community (Deut 27:18–19; Lev 19:14–16; cf. Job 29:11–16).

case beyond reasonable doubt in today's criminal justice system. Finally, the judges were barred from accepting gifts from any party in a case before them. In judging Ziba's case against Mephibosheth, David essentially broke all these rules. There was no investigation of the accusation, Mephibosheth's right to fair hearing was not honored, the case was not proven beyond reasonable doubt (only one witness—the plaintiff); and the judge (David) also took bribes from the plaintiff (2 Sam 16:1–4). In every respect, therefore, justice was not served by David's verdict.

In due course, Absalom's revolt, from which David had fled into exile, was quelled. Upon his return, David was met at the Jordan River by Mephibosheth, Ziba also being present. Mephibosheth, on this occasion, defended himself very satisfactorily (see the discussion of 2 Sam 19 in chapter 6). Yet, even at this time, David's response fell short of the provisions of the Deuteronomic Code. The Code provides that when an accusation is brought against any person, and if it is discovered that the witness had lied against the accused, such a witness should be made to bear the sanction for the offense that was leveled against the accused (Deut 19:16–21). The punishment for treason was death, so ideally Ziba should have been made to face that consequence. Even if it is argued that David did not order Mephibosheth executed, the least that ought to have been required of Ziba was not only the forfeiture of Saul's estate, which David granted to him, but he should have, in addition, forfeited his own patrimony to Mephibosheth. Nevertheless, it is Mephibosheth who still ends up losing half of his inheritance to Ziba. It is safe to conclude that as far as the Saulides were concerned, David never acted in ways consistent with the just living that the covenant document required of the members of the covenant community, especially of its leaders.

## READING THESE STORIES OF DAVID FROM A BIBLICAL THEOLOGICAL PERSPECTIVE

My evaluation of David on the basis of the Deuteronomic Code turns up a darker portrait of the man who is highly venerated in other parts of the biblical canon and in the traditions of both the church and the synagogue. Even within the books of Samuel, he is called by such honorific epithets as "a man of Yahweh's own choosing" (1 Sam 13:14),[13] "the

---

13. The more traditional rendition is, "a man after Yahweh's own heart." I am here following Kessler's rendition of this passage (Kessler, "Sexuality and Politics," 409).

## An Integrative Reading of Research Findings 281

servant of Yahweh" (2 Sam 3:18; 7:5, 8, 26), and "Yahweh's anointed" (2 Sam 19:22; 22:51 [cf. Ps 18:50; 89:20]). The NT is no less reverential and eulogistic of David than the OT (Luke 20:41; Acts 13:22–36). In spite of all these, as Kessler observes, "[T]he narratives in 1 and 2 Samuel paint a very different portrait of him."[14]

In this section, I will attempt to locate the story of David in the larger context of Scripture, attending to the themes and motifs of this story that resonate with similar themes or motifs in the different corpuses of biblical literature.

### The Torah and David's Story

Several themes or motifs interconnect the story of David with the Torah. The few I will be considering here include the impact of human conduct on nature; the relationship between election and character; sacred spaces and sacred toponyms; and Jacob's blessing on Judah and the rise of the Judahite dynasty.

In the interlaced narratives of David and the Saulides, one place where the theme of the impact of human conduct on nature features prominently is in 2 Sam 21:1–14. This comes up, first of all, in the allegation that the famine that persisted in the early years of David's reign resulted from Saul's covenant unfaithfulness to the Gibeonites. This allegation flies in the face of the above reading of 2 Sam 21. Besides, we have also seen that several of David's violations of the Yahweh's covenant stipulations (at least three of these) are directly listed in the Torah as offenses that would defile and bring guilt upon the land. Additionally, the drought that brought the famine, in the first instance, never really abated until the desecrated corpses of the Saulides were given proper burial.

This phenomenon of connecting the fate of the environment to human behavior finds its roots and antecedents in the Torah. In the fall narrative, the curse that Adam (as a lawbreaker) received was the curse that was placed upon nature for his sake, as Yahweh pronounced, ארורה האדמה בעבורך ("Cursed is the ground because of you," Gen 3:17).[15] The account of the deluge in Noah's time records the devastation

---

14. Kessler, "Sexuality and Politics," 409.

15. Commenting on this passage, Robinson writes, "That human sin affects the harmony of nature is a fact underlined by biblical teaching on sin (Gen 3:17). Religious traditions sought to restore the harmony of nature by rectifying the disorder in human relations. This teaching, that human sin affects the order of nature, gains relevance

of the entire created realm on account of human sin (Gen 6–8; esp. 6:13; 7:20–23). Similarly, the region of Sodom and Gomorrah, which was compared to the Garden of Eden for its luxuriant vegetation (Gen 13:10), was scorched to salinized barrenness on account of human wickedness (Gen 19:24–25). Likewise, the hard-heartedness of the Pharaoh had brought great ruin on humanity, beasts, and vegetation alike in Egypt. Beyond the Torah, the implications of human recklessness on the environment were not lost on the prophets either (cf. Isa 24:1–8; Jer 12:4, 11–13; Jer 14:1–7; Hos 4:1–3).

When considering the relationship between election and character, it would be desirable for the one to lead naturally to the other, but that is not the case. In other words, election is not coterminous with one's progressive perfection in character (sanctification). Alter perceptively highlights this as he observes, "one of the most probing general perceptions of the biblical writers is that there is often a tension, sometimes perhaps even an absolute contradiction, between election and moral character."[16] Election is a gracious act of God (not based on merit), while character is developed over time through conscious compliance with the divine will. Thus, God's elect are still very much human and are as such implicated in the sinfulness that has pervaded human nature since the fall. The flawed humanness of God's elect, which is very obvious in David's life, is seen in the life of the patriarchs as well. Abraham, for instance, though assured of Yahweh's protecting presence, made it his cardinal survival strategy to lie about his relationship to his wife Sarah (Gen 20:13) and ended up forfeiting her twice to other men to save his skin (Gen 12:10–20; 20:1–16). In the same vein, Jacob was a fraudster, even though he was chosen to preeminence over his brother right from the womb—cheating his brother twice (Gen 25:23–34; 27:1–23) and even cozening his father-in-law (Gen 30:37–43).

The abiding significance of sacred spaces and the perpetuity of sacred toponyms, sometimes involving the transfer of a sacred toponym from one sacred space to another, is another motif that connects David's story with the Torah. Keen readers would recognize that it was a deft political move on David's part to capture the Jebusite city of Jerusalem and

---

today as well. Ecological scientists confirm the fact that human greed and avarice and the consequent plunder and destruction of nature are the root cause for drought and famine in many parts of the world" (Robinson, *Let Us Be Like the Nations*, 267–68).

16. Alter, *The Art of Biblical Narrative*, 117.

name it his capital city. David used the strategic location of Jerusalem as the mortar with which to cement the union of northern Israel and southern Judah. His transfer of the Ark of the Covenant to Jerusalem is a further display of his astuteness in *Realpolitik*: That act would later become the basis for forging a Davidic dynastic ideology of Zion.

In his choice of Jerusalem as the cult center (in addition its status as his political capital), David was treading the well-beaten ancient Near Eastern path, wherein the choice of holy places was not left to human arbitrariness "but was determined by a manifestation of the god's presence, generally at a certain site with special natural conditions, such as springs, sacred trees, mountains, and so forth. It is thus legitimate to suppose that David intended to utilize the ancient religious traditions of Jerusalem for the creation of the new Yahwistic tradition in the city."[17] David's choice of Jerusalem derives from its cultic importance as far back as Abraham's days. After he had defeated the Mesopotamian coalition that had taken his nephew Lot captive, Abraham was entertained and blessed by Melchizedek the king of Salem (most likely, Jerusalem[18]), while he himself paid tithes to the latter. Melchizedek is also called the priest of God Most High (Gen 14:18–20), signifying the existence of a major cult center in his city, hence Jerusalem's status as a sacred space.

Additionally, in the time of the Jebusite, the citadel of Zion was renowned for its invincibility, which is witnessed to in the way its inhabitants taunted David before he captured it (2 Sam 5:6–7). David wove into this preexistent tradition of invincibility new layers of tradition: both of his own election and Yahweh's choice of his new capital city as a fulfillment of the Deuteronomic expectation (2 Sam 7; Deut 12:5–14; 14:23–25; 15:20; 16:2–16; 31:10–11). Eventually, when Solomon built the temple on the threshing floor of Araunah, which David had purchased, the sacred toponym, Zion, was now transferred from the old citadel to the Temple Mount (Ps 74:2; 78:68). The Chronicler even recognizes the Temple Mount as an ancient sacred space, the site of the *Akedah* (2 Chr 3:1; cf. 1 Chr 21:18; 22:1; Gen 22:1–18). Therefore, all these elements—the preexisting traditions of Zion's invincibility; the enduring status of Zion, either as the old citadel or the Temple Mount, as sacred space; David's election and Yahweh's eternal commitment to his dynasty; and Yahweh's abiding presence through the Ark of the Covenant—were the building

---

17. Ishida, *The Royal Dynasties in Ancient Israel*, 121–22.
18. So Archer, *Encyclopedia of Bible Difficulties*, 91; and K & D I, 132.

blocks for developing the Judahite dynastic religio-political ideology of the inviolability of Zion (Pss 48; 125:1; 132:13–14; Jer 7:4–14). It is interesting to note that the NT writers continued the tradition of transferring a sacred toponym to new sacred space as they transferred the names (Jerusalem and Zion) to both the church and the celestial city (Gal 4:26; Heb 12:22–23; 13:14; Rev 3:12; 21:2, 10).

Finally, we consider Jacob's deathbed blessing of his children and the rise of the Judahite dynasty. Gen 49 records Jacob's dying words to his sons. Verses 8–12 describe his blessings on Judah, in which Jacob predicts Judah's leadership over his brothers. The issues this passage addresses regarding Judah, no doubt, are customarily the prerogatives of royalty: Judah's brothers will bow to him; he triumphs over his enemies; he possesses the scepter and the ruler's staff; and his supplies overflow abundantly. Derek Kidner characterizes the theme of verses 8–10a as "the fierce dominance of the tribe among its fellows."[19] Similarly, after making references to both 1 Chr 5:1–2 and Ps 78, John Sailhammer observes that in these biblical texts, "the words of Jacob regarding Judah in Genesis 49 anticipated in many details the future rise of David to Israel's throne."[20] The royal implications of this passage are also not lost on the Targumim. The Targumim render the MT's לא יסור שבט מיהודה ("The scepter will not depart from Judah") as "The ruler shall never depart from the House of Judah."[21] They transform the more suggestive symbol of a scepter to the explicit statement of "ruler." Similarly, the mere mention of Judah assumes for them the form of the Judahite dynasty (the "House of Judah"). This prophecy concerning Judahite kingship now finds fulfillment in the story of David's displacement of the house of Saul. Indeed, the messianic expectation associated with the Davidic line also finds its moorings in this passage, especially the rather difficult second part of verse 10 (cf. Ezek 21:31–32 [ET. 21:26–27]). Christian interpreters readily see the connection between Judah's tethered donkey (v. 11) and Jesus riding a donkey into Jerusalem (Matt 21:1–9; cf. Zech 9:9).

---

19. Kidner, *Genesis*, 217.
20. Sailhammer, "Genesis," 1–284 (276).
21. Aberbach and Grossfeld, *Targum Onkelos to Genesis*, 158, 163.

## The Deuteronomistic History and David's Story

The monarchy will be the main theme under consideration as we look at the story of David in the context of the DtrH. I will explore the nature of the monarchy as an institution in terms of what it was initially expected to be and what it turned out to be. Other facets of kingship that I will survey include the phenomenon of the kingdom being taken away from one person (or dynasty) and given to another; the attitude(s) in DtrH toward kingship; and the ends of the first two dynasties.

### THE NATURE OF THE MONARCHY

Leadership in Israel from the time of Moses through the era of the judges was charismatic in nature.[22] In the first attempt to institute monarchy, the call for Gideon to cross over from judgeship to kingship arose after his spectacular display of charismata in his brilliant victory over the Midianites (Judg 7–8). The History of Saul's Rise (HSR) records two accounts concerning the choice of Saul as Israel's king: The first relates to divine election (1 Sam 9:1—10:16), and the second involves the entire congregation of Israel (1 Sam 10:17-27). In addition, the people's support of Saul's ascendency was underscored after he displayed his charismatic leadership in the rescue of the Jabesh-gileadites from the Ammonites (1 Sam 11).

The traditional historical-critical reading of these narratives is to see them as two, possibly three, competing accounts of the rise of the monarchy.[23] Such an approach fails to read the DtrH on its own terms and therefore fails to see that from the beginning it stood for charismatic monarchy that involved both divine election and the people's acclaim. This stance is evident in the kingship law in Deut 17:14-20. Foreseeing that at some point the Israelites would want a king so that they could be like the nations around them, Yahweh permitted them to choose a king from among their own kith and kin. Yet the king they were to set over themselves had to be a person of Yahweh's choosing (vv. 14-15).

---

22. The adjective *charismatic* as used here refers to the combined factors of a person being elected by the deity for some special task and therefore uniquely endowed with the enabling presence of the deity, as manifested by the descent of the deity's spirit upon the person or some other palpable evidence of divine presence upon the person coupled with the individual's manifestation of exceptional abilities, especially with respect to securing deliverance for his or her people.

23. Bright, *A History of Israel*, 187-88; and Rad, *Old Testament Theology*, 325-26.

Israel's coronation of the person Yahweh chooses is congruent with the usual ancient Near Eastern covenant practice, where the suzerain exercised oversight over any vassal state's choice of her king.[24] In this legislation, Brueggemann observes the hesitancy about the monarchy that becomes more explicit in 1 Sam 8.[25] What is problematic in the desire for a king is the lingering possibility of the obliteration of Israel's distinctiveness among the nations—the very heart of her calling—which is a theme very dear to the Deuteronomist's heart (Deut 4:5–8, 19–20; 7:6; 14:2, 21; 1 Kgs 8:53; cf. Exod 19:5–6; Ps 135:4; Jer 10:14–16). To guard against this envisaged threat, Yahweh, through his servant Moses, provides for Israel "a monarchy that will maintain the distinctiveness of Israel as YHWH's chosen people, that is, a monarchy 'like all the nations' for a people that is to be *unlike* all the nations."[26] Hence, while the other nations had either divinely elected or hereditary monarchies (with an occasional possibility of authorization by the overlords), or a combination of both,[27] Israel was to have a charismatic monarchy.

The central elements in charismatic monarchy are the elective principle, the endowment of divine charismata, and the people's acclaim. All these elements were part of the process involved in the choice of the first two kings of Israel as recorded in 1 Samuel (10–11; 16–17). The divine choice of Josiah, the most acclaimed king in Judah in the DtrH,[28] was announced several centuries before he was even born (1 Kgs 13:2). Yet even with regard to Josiah, divine election had to be confirmed by popular acclaim, as was the case at the beginning of the monarchy (2 Kgs 21:24; cf. 1 Sam 11:12–14; 2 Sam 2:4; 5:1–3). After the division of Israel, the northern kingdom generally maintained a loosely charismatic monarchy, more as a result of a corruption of the Deuteronomic Law of the king than a strict compliance to it. There are clear examples of kings going through the two-step process of divine election and popular acclaim in apostate northern Israel as well: Jeroboam (1 Kgs 11:29–39; 12:15–20)

---

24. Thompson, *Deuteronomy*, 205.
25. Brueggemann, *Deuteronomy*, 184.
26. Brueggemann, *Deuteronomy*, 184.
27. Ishida, *The Royal Dynasties in Ancient Israel*, 6–25.
28. On Josiah's renown among Judah's kings, McConville writes, "Among the kings the greatest accolades are heaped upon Josiah of Judah, peerless before and since (2 Kgs 23:25), and evoking both Davidic and Mosiac echoes. He is so eulogized that he has seemed to many to be the real climax of a story that saw in him the fulfillment of Davidic promise" (McConville, "King and Messiah," 272).

and Jehu (2 Kgs 9:1–13; 10:5). This DtrH model of kingship, however, was not the dominant form in Israel and Judah. Most of their kings were not first so designated by Yahweh, which the prophets showed to be a covenant violation equal to idolatry (Hos 8:1–4).

Even the dynastic promise to David (2 Sam 7:11–16) did not replace the original two-step operational principle of the monarchy. 2 Sam 7:12 confirms the law of the king (Deut 17:14–20): Yahweh himself was to raise up a descendant of David to the throne.[29] Indeed, the Deuteronomic Code's subordination of the king to the Torah (and by implication the holders of the sacral offices, who were the interpreters of the sacred word—priest and prophet) is even confirmed in David's dying words to his successor (1 Kgs 2:1–4). Therefore, David's authorization of the anointing of Solomon as his successor was a direct violation of the founding principle of Israel's monarchy. This then paved the way for the failures that followed.

## Similarities between the Ends of the Saulide and Davidic Dynasties

In the last recorded encounter between David and his wife Michal, in which the latter had rebuked the former for inappropriate exposure in a religious ceremony, David justified his action by touting Yahweh's choice of himself and rejection of Saul (2 Sam 6:21). The distinction that David made here between the two dynasties will eventually prove, in some regards, to be more quantitative than qualitative in nature. David's house will in due course suffer the same fate as Saul's house, which the DtrH shows through the use of both linguistic and motific parallels.

There are numerous linguistic clues pointing to the similarities between the ends of the Davidic and Saulide dynasties. The first such linguistic clue appears early in Saul's reign and again toward the end of Solomon's reign: The use of the Hebrew verb form קרע ("to tear" or "to rend"), which appears in DtrH about twenty-nine times. Of these twenty-nine occurrences, nineteen relate to the tearing of clothes, two

---

29. I disagree with McConville, who conceives of these two passages as polar opposites of the dialogue between law and narrative about the nature of Israel's kingship. He sees the contrast between law and narrative to be most marked in the portrayal of Solomon (McConville, "King and Messiah," 271–73). The disparity arises on account of the Davidic dynasty's departure from the Deuteronomic norm. My stance is more akin to Halpern's idea of the monarchy under the Torah (Halpern, *The Constitution of the Monarchy in Israel*, 230–32).

concern Yahweh's rending the kingdom from Saul (1 Sam 15:28; 28:17), and six deal with the ripping of the kingdom from a Davidide (1 Kgs 11:11-13, 31; 14:8; 2 Kgs 17:21). Just as the announcement of Yahweh's judgment against Saul did not lead to the immediate end of Saul's reign but was fulfilled in his son's reign, the pronouncement of the verdict against Solomon's reign was fulfilled in the reign of Solomon's successor. Similarly, as Saul's kingdom was bequeathed to his subordinate, David, the greater part of David's realm went to Solomon's lieutenant, Jeroboam. By these linguistic and thematic means, the two houses are shown to share an astonishingly similar fate.

There are a series of subtle linguistic and thematic intimations of the connection between the fates of Saul and David's scions, which points to the similarity between the ends of the two dynasties. In his understanding of David's rehabilitation of Mephibosheth in 2 Sam 9, Polzin observes, "A hint that what happens to Mephibosheth, the remnant of the house of Saul in 2 Samuel 9, is compositionally connected to what happens to Jehoiachin, the remnant of the house of David in 2 Kings 25, lies in the immediate linguistic and thematic similarities between the two passages, as intermediate and final fulfillments respectively, of God's prophetic—and the Deuteronomist's programmatic—oracle in 1 Samuel 2."[30] In 1 Sam 2:27–36, a man of God reproved the priest Eli for taking his election to perpetual priesthood lightly and warned him that he was going to lose that privilege. The unnamed prophet also told Eli that his remnant would crouch before Yahweh's newly chosen priest in order to eat. This, Polzin points out, adumbrates the fate of Saul and his dynasty but ultimately that of David as well. Both were chosen by God, and both abused their positions; moreover, the last scions of both dynasties ended up as dependents at the tables of their conquerors.[31]

The fates of Mephibosheth (2 Sam 9) and Jehoiachin (2 Kgs 25:27–30) are also linked by the striking similarity in their ambivalent rhetoric. Both passages describe the captivity of a descendant of an Israelite dynasty and the survival of a remnant of that crushed dynasty, thereby raising a subdued hope. Just as David had brought Mephibosheth out

---

30. Polzin, *David and the Deuteronomist*, 103.

31. Note the use of common terms in both the case of Mephibosheth (כי על־שלחן המלך תמיד הוא אכל), "for at the king's table *he was eating continually*"; 2 Sam 9:13) and Jehoiachin (ואכל לחם תמיד לפניו, "and *he ate* food *continually* before him [Evil Merodach]"; 2 Kgs 25:29).

of hiding, given him a seat at his table (a position no Saulide would have dreamed of), and spoken words of encouragement to him (2 Sam 9:5–7), Evil-Merodach also lifted Jehoiachin out of prison, gave him a more privileged seat than other captive kings, and spoke kindly to him (2 Kgs 25:27–28).[32] However, in neither case does the hope culminate in the restoration of the vanquished dynasty.[33] Indeed, Jeremiah does indicate in his prophecy the finality of the end of Jehoiachin's rule, and by implication the end of the Davidic dynasty (Jer 22:24–30). Nevertheless, the kindness to a scion of a vanquished dynasty does raise the prospects of an heir. In the case of Saul, the patrimony at stake was his estate, while in David's situation, as the Second Temple period would prove, the patrimony would ever so slowly crystallize in the messianic hope.

32. Polzin writes that while the king of Babylon and Jehoiachin may have respectively replaced David and Mephibosheth, in the final analysis, God and Judah are the new David and Mephibosheth respectively. "At the end, Judah in Babylon embodies the 'lovingkindness of the LORD' and his long awaited justice at one and the same time; this exiled nation is *hannôtar*, the living remnant that now suffers 'the pangs of dispriz'd love' as it once enjoyed 'the law's delay.'" Polzin, *David and the Deuteronomist*, 106.

33. While the release of Jehoiachin from prison and the preferential treatment he received does not intimate a prospect for the restoration of the Davidic kingdom, it raises a ray of hope for an improved or at least a more tolerable quality of life for the Judean exilic community. Cogan and Tadmor comment, "Exilic readers might have found some measure of consolation in the preferred treatment of their aged king; from this point of view the book of Kings does end on a positive note ... The motif of the elevation of a Judean to a position of influence at a foreign court was a popular one in exilic literature, e.g., the story of Daniel at the court of Nebuchadnezzar, and that of Mordecai at the court of Ahasuerus" (Cogan and Tadmor, *II Kings*, 330 n. 5; as quoted in Jeremy Schipper, "'Significant Resonances' with Mephibosheth," 344–51). For a similar position see Murray, "Of All the Years the Hopes—or Fears? 245–65.

Begg, however, does not see any huge significance in Jehoiachin's treatment under Evil-Merodach. His point is that the passage lacks the Deuteronomistic trademark of pointing to Yahweh's initiative in events of true significance. Not only that, he also points out that the account is bereft of any reference to Jehoiachin's repentance, a common Deuteronomistic way of initiating Yahweh's intervention in the behalf of a bad king (and Jehoiachin was one such bad king, per the Deuteronomist). Indeed, even the Solomonic prayer for help for God's exiled people was hinged on their repentance (1 Kgs 8:33–34, 46–53; cf. Deut 4:29–31; 30:1–10). Thus, this event, arising purely from the initiative of a pagan king, held no promise for the future. Therefore, Begg concludes, "Even more significantly, 2 Kgs 25.27–30 makes no reference to the personal privileges accorded Jehoiachin being extended, whether in the present or for the future, either to his sons or to his people as a whole. Such observations suggest that Evil-Merodach's initiative has to be seen as a matter of limited import even for Jehoiachin himself and quite without significance for anyone else" (Begg, "The Significance of Jehoiachin's Release," 49–56).

Finally, another thread correlating the collapse of these two houses is the motif of weakness or disability. In the last chapter, I discussed how the motif of weakness trailed the Saulides to their extinction, beginning with Saul himself (1 Sam 28:5, 20), through Ishbosheth (2 Sam 4:1), and ultimately to Mephibosheth's disability (2 Sam 4:4; 9:3, 13; 19:26). I also showed that once weakness had crept into David's life, the end of his reign was in sight (2 Sam 16:14; 17:2; 21:15). I also discussed the use of disability with respect to Jerusalem, to indicate who had the upper hand in the city. The Jebusites had taunted David with the avowal that even the lame and the blind would stop him from taking their invincible royal city (2 Sam 5:6). When David captured the Jebusite citadel of Zion and made it his capital city, he decreed that the lame and blind (פסח ועור) would not enter his palace.

Evidently, there is a dynamic correlation between the surfacing of a disabled (lame or blind) person in a dynasty and its imminent end. The appearance of a disabled member of either of these dynasties sealed the fate of the dynasty he represented: Mephibosheth appeared with lameness (2 Sam 9), and no Saulide ascended to the throne of Israel. Similarly, when Zedekiah was gruesomely blinded by the Babylonians, no Davidide succeeded him on the throne of Judah. As the end of the Saulide dynasty was betokened by the presence of the first aspect of the word pair ועור פסח ("lame and blind")—the lame Mephibosheth—the end of the Davidic dynasty was signified by the specter of the second—the blind Zedekiah (2 Kgs 25:7; cf. Jer 39:6–7).[34] It is equally salient that both of

---

34. This observation is significant because of the uniqueness of these adjectives (עור ופסח) in the DtrH. Outside of Deuteronomy these adjectives are found in the entire DtrH only with respect to Mephibosheth and Zedekiah. Commenting on this, with regard to how the end of the Davidic dynasty mirrors that of the Saulide dynasty, Schipper writes, "This linguistic connection does not simply foreshadow the Davidic dynasty's fate, but, together with the motif of entering Jerusalem, continues the use of imagery of disability to highlight its collapse through a devastating reversal of insiders and outsiders. The story of Jerusalem's destruction in 2 Kings 25 echoes the story of its establishment as David's capital in 2 Samuel 5 with a tragic reversal of fortune. In 2 Kgs 25:7–8, Nebuchadnezzar's captain, Nebuzaradan, and his troops become the last characters in the Deuteronomistic History to come into Jerusalem (esp. v. 8, סלשורי . . . דאראזובנ אב). The Davidic king Zedekiah, however, ends up disabled and outside Jerusalem (v. 7). In fact, at the conclusion of the Deuteronomistic History, both Zedekiah and Jehoiachin end up outside Jerusalem. The story concludes in Babylon, where Zedekiah is now blind and Jehoiachin occupies a position similar to that of Mephibosheth, who is 'lame'" (Schipper, "Reconsidering the Imagery of Disability," 432–33).

these men suffered their disability in the throes of the excruciatingly violent events that swept away the dynasties to which they belonged; and both had to live in the royal cities of their captors (Jerusalem and Babylon respectively) away from their own cities (Gibeah and Jerusalem respectively).

Though the books of Samuel censure David as much as, if not more than, they venerate him, there seems to be a strongly positive view of him in the books of Kings, as he becomes the yardstick for measuring the performance of other kings. One way of looking at the positive view of David in Kings is to understand that he, as the model king, functions in the DtrH as a limiting concept not necessarily the ultimate example. On the human level, he is the anticipation of the king par excellence, Josiah, who typifies the ideal king as set out in the Deuteronomic Code.

Besides, David is reputed for possessing many gifts and talents that revolve around piety and worship. These include his possession of the Divine Spirit for which he was renowned (1 Sam 16:13, 18; 18:12–14),[35] his musical acumen with its accompanying powers of exorcism (1 Sam 16:16, 23), his role as a composer and/or singer of psalms, and his organization of the Yahwistic cult in Israel with its center in Jerusalem (2 Sam 23:1; 6: cf. 1 Chr 15:16—16:43; 21:25—22:19; 28–29). In addition, David was known to repent readily whenever confronted with his transgression of Yahweh's ordinances (2 Sam 12:13; 24:9; cf. Ps 32:3–5; 51:4). And since repentance is such a major theme in the DtrH—on the basis of which Yahweh abates his judgment on his people (cf. Deut 4:29–31; 30:1–5; 1 Sam 7:3–10; 1Kgs 8:47–50, 21:20–29)—it is all the more understandable that David, the paragon of repentance, would become the iconic model king in the DtrH.[36]

Further, although his praxis was varied greatly from his theory, David was someone who had an acute sense of what is right and just (2 Sam 12:5–6). It is not hard therefore to see how such Davidic oracular traditions, such as the one on the just ruler (2 Sam 23:3–4) to which he

---

35. We should remember that possession of God's Spirit is not coterminous with living a virtuous life. This is evident both from the books of Judges and the Pauline epistles of Corinthians.

36. Borgman has given an in-depth study of this feature of David's life using the pattern of sin-confrontation-consequence-response (Borgman, *David, Saul, and God*, 204–15). I would suggest a re-ordering of the pattern. From such passages as 2 Samuel 12, 24, the pattern tended to be rather sin-confrontation-response-consequence: consequences always followed, even though they were mitigated after repentance.

appends Yahweh's commitment to his dynasty (v. 5) first mentioned in 2 Sam 7, could be mistaken in latter generations for his own character. This is very true for traditional societies, whose natural tendency is to locate their golden age in the past. What is more, a people whose existence and identity are threatened by exile have a proclivity for embracing their glorious past as a confidence building measure and as a means for re-imagining or recreating home away from home. David, with his unsurpassed record of military successes over Israel's enemies, therefore, would certainly become iconic in an age when Judah was bedeviled with inept kings and at the same time was being buffeted on every side by more powerful enemy forces, ending up in exile in Babylon.

## *The Latter Prophets and David's Story*

Of the themes that arise from the story of David (especially as it interconnects with the Saulides), I shall survey the resonances of just three in the Latter Prophets: marriage, Judahite Zion ideology, and the future of the Davidic dynasty.

### Marriage

Two aspects of David's marriage relationships are of interest here: his polygamous marriages, and his relationship to Michal. The Deuteronomic circles, as Kessler observes, viewed polygamy and the use of political marriage as both dangerous and suspect. "While such circles were prepared to tolerate polygamy and concubinage as a concomitant of the royal lifestyle, they viewed them as practices inherently inimical to Yahweh's ultimate will for life and detrimental to those involved."[37] The story of David (as far as his marriages are concerned) squares with this suspicion. In the Latter Prophets, there is a remarkable absence of reference to polygamy. The prophets who are mentioned as having been married were in monogamous marriages (Isa 8:3; Ezek 18:16–18). Even Hosea was asked to go and redeem his unfaithful, adulterous wife, who by the standard of the Torah was defiled to him (Hos 1–3). In this way, the Latter Prophets had come full circle, returning to the beginning wherein monogamy was the standard. Almost all the standard bearers in the Torah were in monogamous marriages: Adam, Noah, Isaac, the priests, and most of Israel's

---

37. Kessler, "Sexuality and Politics," 421.

earlier leaders. Even those who did not strictly have one wife are shown to have been unwilling polygamists.[38]

There are other ways in which the Latter Prophets paint pictures of marriage that contrast sharply with the images seen in David's marital affairs. Isaiah characterized Yahweh's redemption of Israel from exile as a passionate marriage (Isa 54:1–10). The imagery he set out here depicts a marital relationship that is the very opposite of what David had with Michal. Whereas Yahweh promised to make his barren bride a mother of many children, David had made Michal, the mother of five sons, childless. While Israel's marriage had a sad beginning but was to be turned into a happy ending, Michal's began happily (as it seems—otherwise she would not have risked her life to save David's) but ended sadly. In the place of Yahweh's promise to never be angry with Israel, David angrily shamed Michal. Whereas Yahweh pledged his unfailing love to Israel as an unshakable covenant commitment, David never showed love to Michal; neither did David rejoice over Michal as Yahweh rejoices over Israel his bride (Isa 62:5). In the descriptions of Yahweh's relationship with Israel, the prophet shows a beautiful picture of what marriage should be.[39] Similarly, Malachi speaks specifically to the issue of unfaithfulness to the wife of one's youth (Mal 2:13–16). In his statement (through a rhetorical question) about God making them one in flesh and in spirit (v. 15), the prophet calls to mind the creation order set forth

---

38. Sarah thrust Hagar upon Abraham (and as suddenly as her initial action, Sarah took Hagar away when Abraham was beginning to love the whole affair), while Jacob was basically tricked into marrying the Laban sisters, and the sisters in their rivalry turned their maidservants over to him. This picture contrasts sharply with either David who gained notoriety as a wife snatcher or Solomon who had the unbeatable record of marrying a thousand wives and concubines.

39. Two visions of marriage are found in the DtrH: the one projected by the royalty and those associated with it, as seen in the likes of David and Solomon, which is a perverse version of marriage; and the other displayed by ordinary folks, which represented the veritable version of marriage. On this latter, Kessler writes, "The second and alternative vision of marriage and sexuality is reflected in the *dramatis personae* of Paltiel and Uriah and in the parable of Nathan. Here, marriage is monogamous rather than polygamous. It is not a political tool but a locus of tenderness and attachment (of Paltiel to Michal, and of the poor man to his lamb). It provides nurture and comfort. Its dissolution brings severe emotional grief. This general perspective is echoed in other narrative passages (e.g., in Ruth 1:9; 1 Sam 1:8), in wisdom traditions (e.g., in Prov 5:15–20; Eccl 9:9), and in prophetic traditions (e.g., Ezek 24:15)" (Kessler, "Sexuality and Politics," 422).

for marriage (Gen 2:23–24). David certainly did not keep faith with the wife of his youth, Michal.

The prophets also bristle with rage against the people for their pursuit of their neighbor's wives (Jer 5:8–9; Ezek 18:5–17 [esp. vv. 6, 11, and 15]; 22:11; 33:23–29). This is given as one of the reasons for which Judah was now being sent into captivity. It is in some way a legacy that comes from David's time: both he and his son Absalom had neighed like stallions after their neighbors' wives.

The above comparisons clearly set out the narratives of the monarchy in the DtrH as deviations from the divine norm. What is perplexing is that the narratives seem to suggest God's approval of both polygamy and political marriages (2 Sam 12:8). This raises a very important hermeneutical question of how to treat these visions of marriage, since Yahweh is implicated in both. Kessler, in my view, correctly argues that even though both visions of marriage are connected with Israel's God, the manner of presentation of the events in 2 Sam 3, 11–12 seem to suggest that the second vision is the one that truly reflect Yahweh's purposes for marriage. On this trajectory he concludes, "Hermeneutically speaking, it may be appropriate to say that while Yahweh may be associated with a variety of motifs in a text, some of these may be more profoundly affirmed than others."[40] In other words, these two versions of marriage reflect, in the first instance, divine toleration or accommodation of human weakness (as in the case of divorce, Deut 24:1–3; Matt 19:1–9; Mal 2:16), and in the second, the divine design for marriage (Gen 2:22–24; Matt 19:3–9).

## Jerusalem

The Latter Prophets are very conflicted about Jerusalem. On the one hand, they show a very loathsome image of the city that is called a harlot, deserving nothing but God's judgment (cf. Isa 1:21–31; Lam 1:8–9; Ezek 22:1–7; 24:6–9); and the history of most of the things that are leveled against her go back to the early days of the monarchy. On the other hand, there are passages that speak glowingly about Yahweh's eternal commitment to Jerusalem and how he will work for her redemption and restoration (cf. Isa 52:7–9; 62:1–12; Jer 31:6; 50:4–5). In the late pre-exilic period, the traditions of Davidic Zion ideology had been

---

40. Kessler, "Sexuality and Politics," 422. Kessler compares his views here to Goldingay's categories of central and peripheral issues in the ethical evaluation of Old Testament texts (Goldingay, *Theological Diversity*, 97–133).

fully etched in the psyche of the Judeans. Brief moments of triumph or, more correctly, reprieve—such as when Jerusalem was spared from the ravages of Sennacherib during Hezekiah's time (Isa 37:33–38; cf. 2 Kgs 19:32–35)—were critical junctures for recalling the traditions of Zion's inviolability and imaginatively recreating and reinforcing them with these new experiences.

With the passage of time, about a hundred years after Hezekiah, this Judahite ideology of Zion's inviolability had so filled the consciousness of the society that it became calcified to the point that its people expected God to do right by them. Consequently, they became indurated in their flagrant violations of Yahweh's covenant requirements and cared not a whit about fulfilling their covenant obligations. Yet, they superstitiously believed that, because of Yahweh's presence in his temple and his eternal commitment to the Davidic dynasty, no harm could come to Jerusalem,[41] irrespective of how they lived. It is this credulity that Jeremiah frequently addresses in his sermons (Jer 5:1–5; 6:1–15; 7:1–14; 26:1–15).[42] The Judeans' presumptuous obstinacy prevented them from harkening and repenting that they might be saved. Consequently, certain destruction was decreed against Jerusalem that would end both the temple and the Davidic dynasty (Jer 5:6; 6:16–30; 22:24–30; Ezek 24:21).

Jerusalem eventually fell, in accordance with the word of Yahweh by the mouth of his servants the prophets. That notwithstanding, the writings of the exilic and post-exilic prophets demonstrate that traditions die hard. The sanctity of Jerusalem was preserved both in the people's memories of its violent destruction (see the book of Lamentations[43]) and

---

41. There were precedents of either Yahweh's actions on their behalf or his statements that may have led them to believe that he would always do right by them (Isa 37:35; cf. 1 Kgs 11:12–13, 36; 15:4; 2 Chr 21:7).

42. On Jeremiah's preaching and what he faced, MacKenzie writes, "Against this magical notion Jeremiah protested with such forceful eloquence that he had a narrow escape from being lynched for blasphemy. His hearers were not willing to amend their ways, but they were willing to defend God's honor against a man who maintained that God was not strictly bound to a particular earthly locale. So much, at that time, had the mystique of the city invaded and degraded the religion of Israel" (MacKenzie, "The City and Israelite Religion," 60–70).

43. MacKenzie compares the more sober reflections in Lamentation to the vehement revulsion of the Judeans to Jeremiah's prophecies of doom. He writes, "The same feeling, the same conviction that it was blasphemy to say anything against Jerusalem, lies behind the book of Lamentations and its vivid psychological picture of the state of mind of the survivors, after temple and city had been destroyed. Not only desperate grief and

in their aspirations for the future (Zech 12:1–9). Ezekiel, who had prophesied on either side of the catastrophic events of 587/6 BC, had a more or less bifurcated message: destruction and restoration. Even though he was one of those who had decried the perversion of the temple *cultus* in the buildup to the Babylonian captivity (cf. Ezek 8:16—9:11), he could not envisage a restoration without a renewed temple *cultus* that would confer special status on Jerusalem (Ezek 40–48). The tradition was too deeply engrained in their perception of Yahwistic religion to be given up readily.[44] Indeed, the exiles' re-imagined perspective on Jerusalem was that of a chastised, cleansed, and restored Zion, which would become the center of Yahweh's global kingdom (Jer 50:1–5; Ezek 20:27–40; Zech 8:20–23; 13:1–9; Mal 1:11). This re-imagined glory of Zion generated a renewed impetus for rebuilding the temple and the walls of Jerusalem in the post-exilic period (Hag 2:1–9), as is chronicled in the memoires of Ezra and Nehemiah.

## The Davidic Monarchy

David had taunted Saul's daughter Michal about God's rejection of the latter's father and his entire dynasty vis-à-vis God's election of the former. David's dynastic ambitions are reflected both in his prior protestations of innocence in the murder of Abner (2 Sam 3:28) and in his prayer in response to Nathan's oracle revealing Yahweh's eternal commitment to build him a dynasty (2 Sam 7). This Davidic dynastic concern occupies the rest of the DtrH. However, the Law of the King in the Deuteronomic Code makes no reference to the Judahite origins of the king to be chosen, even though Genesis (49:8–12) hints of this. Yet subsequent to the removal of the Ark to Jerusalem, Davidic traditions developed the

---

misery are expressed: there are also amazement and incredulous horror that Yahweh could bring himself to do such a deed. (It is pictured as his work, the Babylonians being merely his instruments.) Yet the truth is faced up to honestly. The writers realize that their God has vindicated his prophets, and in so doing has contradicted one of his people's dearest beliefs. The catastrophe has not in the least shaken the faith of the authors of Lamentations in Yahweh's power, or even his will, to save. But obviously the necessity of abandoning their superstitious trust in his obligation to defend Jerusalem was a severe psychological shock" (MacKenzie, "The City and Israelite Religion," 67).

44. MacKenzie explains, "This is quite understandable, when we remember that the great majority of these sixth century exiles came from Jerusalem itself or its near environs. Hence the city, rather than the people of Israel as such, held the central position in the development of 'exilic' piety and theology" (MacKenzie, "The City and Israelite Religion," 68).

Zionist royal ideology that became much more influential in the late pre-exilic period. The Davidic royal ideology traditions of Zion can be summarized in the following three points: first, Yahweh reigns as king over Israel and the nations and their gods; second, Yahweh has affirmed, with an eternal covenant, his election of David (and his house) as his earthly vicegerent; and thirdly, Yahweh chose Jerusalem as the earthly seat of his rule, with his throne being over the Ark of the Covenant.

Credulity to this Zionist royal ideology became the bane of the Judahites and their leaders in the late pre-exilic era. Deceived by their equation of the eternal Davidic covenant to the inviolability of Zion, they became brazen in their rejection of Yahweh as king (in their defection to idolatry and violation of their covenant obligations in the treatment of their fellows). Consequently, both the people and their kings would be visited by Yahweh's devastating judgment, culminating in the exile and the destruction of the temple. The writings of the Latter Prophets span both the pre-exilic monarchical period of Israel and Judah's history and the post-exilic period when both kingdoms ceased to exist.

Yet, even during the pre-exilic era, when they acerbically denounced the people and their kings, the prophets still indicated hope for the rebirth of the house of Jacob as a nation with a righteous and just king over them. There is an element of complexity in the nature of the new king in the prophetic expectation. In Amos, probably the earliest of the Writing Prophets, there is a promise for the rebuilding of the fallen booth of David (Amos 9:11–12). It is hard to say with certainty what the fallen booth of David is: the Davidic dynasty (from the "sure house" of 2 Sam 7:11) or the Judahite kingdom. C. F. Keil understands that it refers to the restoration of the Davidic dynasty, albeit one that is in a degenerate state, as one considers the physical difference between a house (בית) and a booth or a hut (סכה). Keil, however, notes that both the dynasty and the kingdom are inseparable. He observes that the stately image of a house (palace) figuratively represents the greatness and might of the kingdom, while the imagery of the fallen hut symbolizes the utter ruin of the kingdom.[45]

Thomas Edward McComiskey, like Keil, recognizes the implication of this passage for both the dynasty and the kingdom. As far back as Amos' time, the dynasty was already only a shred of its original glory as a result of the division of the kingdom. McComiskey, therefore, lays

---

45. K & D, X, 220.

emphasis on the active voice of the participle הנפלת (which he renders as "the falling"), indicating the continuing deteriorating state of the dynasty.[46] Yet, the devastating catastrophes that eventuated in the exile would not seal the fate of the dynasty, because of Yahweh's eternal commitment (2 Sam 7:12–13). It will be restored, and its restored kingdom will possess the nations. In this, both McComiskey and Keil see the messianic expectation that James picks up at the Jerusalem council in Acts 15:12–21.

Hosea, probably a younger contemporary of Amos, similarly spoke of a time of judgment wherein the Israelites would be without king or temple, but in their repentance they would return and seek after Yahweh their God and David their king (Hos 3:4–5). This statement is rather curious because it does not include any mention of a reestablishment of the Davidic dynasty over the people. In fact, earlier Hosea had spoken of the Israelites (both the northerners and southerners now reunited) appointing a single leader (ראש אחד, lit. "one head;" Hos 2:2 [ET, 1:11]) over them, as they return from the land of their captivity. However, the passage does not suggest that the one so appointed would assume any royal status; neither does it indicate that he would need any royal pedigree.

Overall, in Hosea's prophecies there is a much diminished perception of the monarchy. In their hour of trouble the king was completely impotent. Indeed, in Hosea, the rise of kingship in the covenant community was understood to be an error—in agreement with Samuel's thinking (1 Sam 8:4–20; 12:7–19); it is something that Yahweh approved in anger and has taken away in rage (Hos 13:10–11; cf. 8:4).[47] The prophet foresaw

---

46. McComiskey, "Amos," 269–334 (esp. 329–30).

47. Many tend to see these oracles solely as referring to the northern kingdom of Israel, perhaps with good justification based on the context especially of 8:4, cf. Smith, *Hosea, Amos, Micah*; and Garrett, *Hosea, Joel*. However, it should be observed that while Hosea ministered primarily to the northern kingdom of Israel, he constantly had Judah in his purview as well (Hos 1:7, 11; 6:4, 10–11). Indeed, his use of the term Israel is often suggestive of the inclusion of Judah. In such cases, he employs *Ephraim* and *Judah* to differentiate the northern and southern kingdoms (Hos 5:5–14; 10:11; 12:1–6 [ET 11:12—12:5]). The retelling of the exodus in the earlier verses of Hosea 13 places vv. 10–11 in the context of all Israel, as there is no record of either of the kingdoms separately asking for a king. James Luther Mays is, therefore, correct in linking verse 10 here with the tradition in Samuel. He writes, "The tradition about the history of Israel's kingship in which Hosea stands attributes their existence to the petition of the people. Having a royal court was their idea and the quotation sounds like an echo of the old antimonarchical source in the early chapters of Samuel (1 Sam 8:6)" (Mays, *Hosea*, 178).

that in exile the people's attitude toward the monarchy as an institution would wax indifferent (Hos 10:3). As far as one can see, Hosea's prophecies do not speak of a role for the Davidic dynasty. They only conceive of it as a haunting memory of its irrelevance and its ineffectiveness in defending the Israelites against their enemies—the very raison d'être for which they had asked for a king in the first place.

There is a greater place assigned to kingship in general and the Davidic dynasty in particular in the succeeding prophets, such as Isaiah, Micah, Jeremiah, Ezekiel, and Zechariah, than in either Amos or Hosea. The latter prophets' hope for the restoration of Israel after her chastisement also contains the expectation of a restored kingship, perhaps even a Davidic kingship. However, the nature or the pedigree of the king varies with the prophets. The prophets who ministered prior to the Babylonian exile tended to predict a return *ad fonte*. Isaiah (11:1), for instance, speaks of a branch pullulating from the stump of Jesse (חטרמגזע ישי), and a shoot sprouting from Jesse's root (ונצר משרשיו). By this means the prophet bypassed the Davidic line of his time to the source from where it arose, and proclaimed Yahweh's new initiative that would produce the right king for the restored nation.[48]

In Micah's prophecy, there is a similar preference for bypassing the current Davidic kings of his time and returning to the humble origins of

---

48. The difference Isaiah highlights here need not be necessarily genealogical, as if the branch or shoot would not descend from David. In the context of the chapter, the distinction is found in the character and ethical quality of the branch, which would not follow the perversion of latter Davidides but retain the purity of the earlier generation. Oswalt underscores this as he comments, "The Messiah is not merely promised or announced but is depicted as ruling. In place of the craven and petty house of David, or the arrogant and oppressive empire of Assyria, here is a king in whose hands the concerns of the weakest will be safe. He will usher in a reign of safety and security to which the weary exiles may come streaming in return" (Oswalt, *The Book of Isaiah*, 277).

Webb similarly writes, "Moreover, in view of the promises made to David it was natural that the Davidic house should have held a central place in the hopes of those who looked for God's will to be done in their midst. But it is also natural that, as the Davidic dynasty proved to be more and more of a disappointment, their expectations should have moved away from the current kings in Jerusalem toward a future ideal ruler, *the* Messiah, whom God would send to lead them. This process is clearly at work in chapter 8–11 of Isaiah, against the background of the faithlessness of Ahaz in chapter 7. We first met this ideal figure in 9:6–7; now we are given a fuller account of his character and reign ... The expression *the stump of Jesse* (1, cf. 10) indicate his humble origins, bypassing all the ostentation of the Davidic house as it subsequently developed. His fitness to rule will consist essentially in his endowment with *the Spirit*, giving him *true wisdom*, grounded in *the fear of the LORD* (2–3)" (*The Message of Isaiah*, 75).

the Davidic dynasty. Micah announced that Israel would be abandoned until the time of the deliverer king, who was to be born in Bethlehem in Ephrathah, the smallest of the clans of Judah. Kenneth E. Pomykala understands the characterization of this future ruler to be mysterious and as making his relationship to the tradition of Davidic dynasty ambiguous. To him, this new ruler "will not emanate from the Davidic line currently in power in Jerusalem. Consequently, some kind of genealogical break with the currently ruling royal line is envisioned, thus indicating a tradition here that is in opposition to the dynastic promise found in 2 Sam 7:11-16 and Psalm 89."[49] The passage in Micah is of the same nature as that of the passage in Isaiah discussed above. Thus, it is preferable to understand the distinction the prophet was making here between the future ruler and the corrupt Davidic line in the terms that are outlined in his work—in terms of its humble origins in Ephrathah and in terms of the future ruler working in the strength and majesty of Yahweh's name for the security and peace of the people. This perception of the future ruler contrasts sharply with the arrogance and self-serving demeanor of the Davidides who were contemporaries of the prophet.[50]

49. Pomykala, *The Davidic Dynasty Tradition*, 18. Mays, with a similar interpretation of this oracle, comments, "The time of David is viewed as an era of the distant past belonging to 'ancient days.' That the new ruler comes from the people of David's origins, and not his line, may suggest that no Davidide is living or available. If that is the case, exilic times seem the most likely setting. On the uncertain assumption that Isa 9:1-6 and 11:1-9 were spoken by Isaiah, it is conceivable that vv. 2 and 4 could come from a time as early as the end of the eighth century. But they belong to a literary context whose organizing material seems to come from the late seventh and sixth century, and that suggests a later date" (Mays, *Micah*, 113). It appears, however, that concern for the dating of the oracle seems to be the driving motivation for his interpretation.

50. In spite of Mays' mischaracterization of the passage as the revision of the founding oracle of 2 Sam 7, he correctly captures one of the true essences of the passage when he observes, "The characterization of Bethlehem as 'small(est) (*sāʿîr*) among Judah's clans (*elep*)' recalls the procedure by which YHWH selected directly an individual to lead Israel, a procedure that had been replaced by the election of the Davidic successor as bearer of kingship. Gideon protested that he could not save Israel because 'My *'elep* is the weakest in Manasseh and I am *hassāʿîr* in my father's house' (Judg 6:15); and Saul said that he was a Benjamite from the least (*qtn*) of the tribes of Israel and his clan (*mišpāḥāh*) was the smallest *hassāʿîrah*) of all the clans of the tribe (1 Sam 9:21). The motif is also present in the narrative of David's selection; he was the youngest of Jesse's sons and the last to be considered (1 Sam 16:11). The motif emphasizes the marvel of God's intervention, who brings forth a man to save his people from the most unlikely and unexpected quarter. From such an unlikely source shall emerge one who will specifically belong to YHWH ('to me/YHWH') is emphatic in its sentence). He will serve as (*mōšēl*) over Israel. Perhaps the title 'king' (*melek*) is avoided to reserve the language

The prophets who experienced the crises brought by the Babylonian invasion and preached in the early exilic era had a predilection for embracing the Davidic tradition, though not without some reticence. Rather than returning to the source, as did both Isaiah and Micah, both Jeremiah and Ezekiel are content to go back as far as David. The branch of Jesse in Isaiah becomes the branch of David in Jeremiah (23:5). Indeed, Jeremiah appeals directly to the Zion tradition of Yahweh's eternal and inviolable covenant with David as the basis for indicating the terminal point of the refining period, when Yahweh will raise up for his people a Davidic redeemer king (33:14–26).[51] Ezekiel, likewise, promised that Yahweh will return to save his people, be their God, and appoint "David my servant" as king over them (34:23–24; 37:24–25).

Zechariah, who prophesied to the first set of returnees in the postexilic era, seems to have been more enthusiastic about the Davidic dynasty than his predecessors. He apparently invoked all the themes of the dynastic traditions of Zion: the renewal of the doctrine of the inviolability of Zion (Zech 2:4–5; 12:1–6); Yahweh's presence with his people both through a reestablished temple *cultus* (Zech 4:9; 6:15; 8:8–9; 9:8) and the divine Spirit (Zech 4:6; 12:10); and the forgiveness and rehabilitation of the Davidic dynasty (Zech 12:8; 13:1). It is understandable that Zechariah's expectation of a renewed Davidic kingdom brimmed over with exuberance in view of the rise of Zerubbabel, a Davidide in all probability, as the governor of the Persian province of Judah. Looking toward

---

of kingship for YHWH alone and to subordinate the *mōšēl* to YHWH. His dependence on YHWH is specifically elaborated in v. 4" (Mays, *Micah*, 116).

51. Brueggemann thinks the inclusion of the Zion ideology of the promise to the Davidic house surprising and unexpected because "the larger casting of the Jeremiah tradition regards the dynasty as a main problem for Israel (cf. 22:13–18, 24–30), and does not characteristically envision a David-shaped future. Nonetheless, God's good inclination toward the dynasty and family of David belongs to Israel's central stock of promises. It is therefore included here among the many ways in which Israel voices its hope. Indeed, this chapter seems to want to collect all Israel's possible ways of speaking of God's good future" (Brueggemann, *A Commentary on Jeremiah*, 318). This turn of events is not too surprising when we remember that the messages of all of Israel's prophets were not unidirectional, containing only messages of doom. They all always threw out a lifeline of hope that looked forward to a time of Yahweh's favor wherein redemption might be found. If this hope was held out for the nation as whole, there would be no justifiable reason to think that it would not be extended to the central institutions, which, indeed, described the boundaries of existence (i.e., identity markers) for the people. It is little wonder that the Davidic tradition would receive greater attention at the point when the people's existence and identity were most threatened.

the renewal of temple worship, Zechariah conceived of Zerubbabel as the temple builder (Zech 4:6–10).

Zechariah also now applied the title of the Branch, spoken of by the earlier prophets, to Zerubbabel (Zech 6:12–13). He, however, portrayed a Davidic kingship that is much diminished in power or importance. Even though both a priest and a royal figure are put forth as Yahweh's anointed ones (Zech 4:14), the priest apparently has more clout than the royal figure: The priest is mentioned first, for instance. It is the priest Joshua who is given the promise of ruling over Yahweh's people, a duty previously an exclusive preserve of the Davidic dynasty (Zech 3:7; cf. 2 Sam 7:11–16; 1 Kgs 2:1–4; 11:38), while the only significant role Zechariah assigned the royal figure, Zerubbabel, is that of a mere temple builder (4:6–9)—still a royal prerogative in the ancient Near East. Most significantly, in Zechariah, Israel comes full circle to the pre-monarchical state where Yahweh was the sole king over his people and, indeed, over the whole universe. Once again, Yahweh is acknowledged as the sole Lord in Jerusalem (14:9–11). This, then, explains the diminished status of the Davidide in Zechariah, even though his presence is hailed and enthusiastically celebrated.

The common thread in all these prophets is that the new David they expected would be quite different from the Davidic dynasty they had known. He would be specially endowed with God's Spirit or strength for the task (Isa 11:2; Mic 5:3 ET, 5:4; Zech 4:6); he and his people would be purged from their impurities and become submissive and obedient to the divine will (Isa 4:4–5; Jer 30:9; Hos 3:5; Ezek 37:23–24; Zech 13:1–2); and, unlike the previous Davidides, his throne will be established by (and will usher in) truth, justice, and righteousness for all the people (Isa 11:3–5; Jer 23:5; 33:15). Besides, this king is rather of a supra-human character, based on the epithets by which he is called, such as "Mighty God," "Everlasting Father," "Immanuel," and "The Lord our Righteousness" (Isa 7:14; 9:6; Jer 23:6). The peace and prosperity of his reign surpasses all human capabilities (Isa 11:6–9; Ezek 34:25–31; Hos 2:18; Mic 4:3–4). Similarly, the boundaries of his realm extend beyond Judah, and have a global reach (Isa 9:7; 11:10; Mic 4:2; Zech 8:20–23).

Such optimism was short lived. The stark realities of unfulfilled expectation eventually led to disillusionment. The prophets and writers of the late post-exilic era despaired of any this-worldly resurgence of the Davidic kingdom. The *Golah* community had experienced such cognitive dissonance that it even doubted God's love for them (Mal 1:2). The temple *cultus* itself had become so degenerate that the prophet Malachi desired that even the very doors of the temple would be shut (Mal 1:6–10). It is this turn of events that will gradually chart the path from OT prophetic eschatology to Second Temple apocalyptic eschatology[52]—from the hope of the renewed this-worldly Davidic kingdom to a supra-natural Messianic hope of a heavenly Son of Man.

## *The Writings and David's Story*

The Writings, as a corpus, is the most diverse corpus of all, especially as it relates to David. It ranges from books that have nothing about Davidic kingship (for example, Job, Ecclesiastes, Proverbs, Song of Songs, and Esther) to those with a mere fleeting mention of David (such as Ezra-Nehemiah or the Davidic genealogy in Ruth) and to those that contain voluminous material on David (the Chronicler and the Psalter).

Of these last two, Chronicles reels out the glorification of the past era of the Davidic dynasty but has little expectation of a future for a Davidic kingship in the *Golah* community. Two main views are espoused by biblical scholars respecting the place of the Davidic dynasty in Chronicles. The one position sees the Chronicler as making a strong case for the continuation of the Davidic dynasty. A.-M. Brunet, for instance, sees greater eloquence in the Chronicler's silence than in even what he positively affirms. There is a palpable absence, or at best a very fleeting mention, of Israel's earlier traditions regarding the patriarchs and the Sinaitic Covenant in the Chronicler. For Brunet, the Chronicler envis-

---

52. Hanson defines prophetic eschatology "as a religious perspective which focuses on the prophetic announcement to the nation of the divine plans for Israel and the world which the prophet has witnessed unfolding in the divine council and which he translates into the terms of plain history, real politics, and human instrumentality; that is, the prophet interprets for the king and the people how the plans of the divine council will be effected within the context of their nation's history and the history of the world." And, he defines Apocalyptic eschatology as "a religious perspective which focuses on the disclosure (usually esoteric in nature) to the elect of the cosmic vision of Yahweh's sovereignty—especially as it relates to his acting to deliver his faithful—which disclosure the visionaries have largely ceased to translate into the terms of plain history, real politics, and human instrumentality due to a pessimistic view of reality growing out of the bleak post-exilic conditions within which those associated with the visionaries found themselves. Those conditions seemed unsuitable to them as a context for the envisioned restoration of Yahweh's people'" (Hanson, *The Dawn of Apocalyptic*, 11–12; as cited in Carroll, "Twilight of Prophecy or Dawn of Apocalyptic?" 3–35).

ages that Sinai and the exodus were no more than mere stepping stones toward the Davidic covenant, and, as such, there was no need even to allude to the scaffolding once the edifice itself was completed.[53]

The other position understands the Chronicler as asserting that the ancient promise Yahweh made to David of an eternal dynasty was brought to fruition in the succession of Solomon to the Davidic throne and in the founding of the Jerusalem temple and its cult by the first two forebears of this dynasty. The implication is that because the second temple—constructed after the exile—and its cult are legitimate heirs to the Davidic-Solomonic establishment, the initial Yahwistic eternal promise to David remains operative through the temple *cultus* during the Chronicler's time.[54] Murray points out that the Chronicler displays an arresting lack of interest in the fate of the last few Davidides in the run-up to the Babylonian exile.[55] The usual notices of the king's accession and his activities, death, and succession are completely skirted over. Rather, the end of Chronicles focuses on the actions of, and the conse-

---

53. Brunet, "La théologie du Chroniste," 391; as referenced in North, "Theology of the Chronicler," 369–81). North, affirming his own conviction on the matters writes, "My own conviction is that the Chronicler aimed at nothing less than to rectify an existing popular misconception. The primary vehicle of Israel's 'chosenness,' he shows, was not Moses on Sinai at all. No, it was David on Zion! Only some such firm and avowed intention accounts for the ruthlessness with which he suppresses any allusion to the whole exodus event" (North, "Theology of the Chronicler," 378). I am not, however, persuaded by North's explanation of the absence of an affirmed future for the Davidic dynasty on account of the Chronicler's desire not to become fixated on the imperfections of the dynasty, which was wont to engender rebellion (ibid., 380–81). If the dynasty had to be protected through quiescence in order not to arouse rebellion, then, it must have fallen into such disrepute that it was of no functional relevance to the life of the *Golah* community.

54. For a fuller discussion of this see Murray, "Dynasty, People, and the Future," 71–92; Newsome, "The Chronicler and his Purpose," 201–17; and Williamson, "Eschatology in Chronicles," 115–54. Indeed, Dumbrell in his comment on this draws the reader's attention to the idealization of David and Solomon by the Chronicler. This idealization, he insists, was not "intended by the Chronicler to magnify the dynasty that had been established so much as they were aimed at pointing to the splendor of the temple, which endorsed the character of Israel as a theocracy. David and Solomon are thus merely the architects of the theocratic policy to which all good southern kings thereafter in Chronicles rigidly adhered . . . It is therefore more probable that the function of the Davidic–Solomonic narratives in Chronicles are theocratic (kingdom of God) in their nature rather than that they are dynastic" (Dumbrell, "The Purpose of the Books of Chronicles," 257–66).

55. Murray, "Dynasty, People, and the Future," 75–76.

quences for, the people and the priests.⁵⁶ In this new work that Yahweh is doing with his people, the king he chooses as the builder of the new temple is not a Davidide, but Cyrus the Persian ( 2 Chron 36:23; Isa 45:13). Indeed, Cyrus is the new David; he is given the titles previously preserved for either Yahweh or his chosen leaders of Israel: The shepherd of God's people (Isa 44:24–28; cf. 2 Sam 5:2; 7:7–8; 1 Chr 11:2; Ps 23:1; 28:9; 78:70–72) and Yahweh's anointed (Isa 45:1–4; cf. 1 Sam 12:5; 16:6; 24:6–6; 2 Sam 1:14–16; Ps 18:51 [ET, 18:50]).

The diminishing role for the Davidides in post-exilic Judah observed in Chronicles is further accentuated in books written much later in the post-exilic era. The hope of a revived Davidic kingdom is completely absent in Ezra-Nehemiah.⁵⁷ The priest assumed a much more prominent role than Zerubbabel (the Davidide). It is instructive that there is no appellation appended to Zerubbabel in Ezra-Nehemiah, while the title of governor is repeatedly used of Nehemiah. Besides, Nehemiah's leadership is cast in the Deuteronomic mold: one who does not exalt himself above his brothers, nor exploit the people for personal gain, but executes justice for all (Neh 5:1–18); he is a ruler under the law (Neh 8); he enacts covenant renewal between Yahweh and the people, just like all the ideal Deuteronomic leader (Moses, Joshua, and Josiah) did (Neh 9:1—10:28 [ET, 10:27]); and he reorganizes the temple *cultus*, like David (Neh 10:29–40 [ET, 10:28–39]). Indeed, Nehemiah indicts the Davidides Shesh-bazzar and Zerubbabel, who had been governors of the Persian province of Judah prior to him, for oppressing and exploiting the people (Neh 5:15; cf. vv. 1–5)—the very problematic matter with kingship in

---

56. Note the swiftness with which the Chroniclers raced through the affairs of four kings in just thirteen verses in 36:1–13 (Jehoahaz, Eliakim/Jehoiakim, Jehoiachin, and Zedekiah, all of whom are shown to have been evil and disobedient to the word of the Lord). The Chronicler concludes his narrative with his focus squarely on the people, spotlighting their flagrant violations of God's commands and how they defied his word through his prophets and the consequences they faced (36:14–21). In that same light, in the restoration, at the beginning of the Persian era, the focus again is on the exilic community. It is the exilic community, not the Davidic line, who are being challenged to go build Yahweh's temple in Jerusalem (36:22–23).

57. All the important references to David and Solomon in Ezra-Nehemiah relate to their prescriptions for services in the temple (cf. Ezra 3:10; 8:20; Neh 12:24, 36, 45), highlighting their significance as temple builders, and to Solomon's apostasy (Neh 13:26), underscoring the people's turn to the evils under the Davidic dynasty, the very cause of their exile in the first place.

general (1 Sam 8:11–17; cf. 2 Sam 20:24; 1 Kgs 4:6; 12:3–4, 10–14, 18; 2 Chr 16:10).

In Esther, the Writings have gone full circle: The existence of the Jewish people in the Persian Empire, like their forebears, was imperiled by the Amalekite Agagite Heman. It was the Benjaminites, Mordecai and his cousin Esther (perhaps, Saulides, cf. Est 2:5), not Davidides, that forever silenced the Amalekite threat, thereby completing the job that Saul had begun several centuries earlier (1 Sam 15). One wonders if there was a sense of nostalgia for the era of Saul at this point. Indeed, it raises the question of whether there was even a resurging sympathetic Benjaminite (Saulide) feeling in the exile, in view of the gross failure of the Judahite (Davidic) dynasty. The failures of kingship, besides cultic matters, were linked to the oppressiveness that Samuel was worried might arise with kingship. While the oppression of the people was not recorded against Saul (except for Saul's vain pursuit of David, which may have been warranted by David's insurgency against Saul), it was entrenched in the Davidic dynasty—beginning with David himself.[58]

The possibility of a resurgent Saulide nostalgia among the exiles seems plausible when we remember that while this narrative is about David, there is an interestingly persistent interjection of Saulide affairs at critical junctures, some aspects of which I may have already called attention to above. With the exception of the one instance of the investiture of Mephibosheth with his grandfather's patrimony (which by my analysis is not actually different from the other Davidic injustices against Saulides), every mention of a Saulide in this story has a significant potential of damaging public relations for David. At the center of the chiasm below, which shows the compositional interlacing of Saulide misfortunes in the story of David, is found the report of the singular act of seeming goodness that David performed for a Saulide—the rehabilitation of Mephibosheth (D).

The first half of the chiastic structure is rather subtle in its implication of David in the misfortunes of the Saulides, while the second half is more direct in placing blame at David's doorsteps. The outer rings of the chiasm show that David began his reign over Israel only after the elimi-

---

58. Most of the abuses that Samuel was concerned about first appeared in David's reign: David confiscated one Israelite's property to give to his surrogate (2 Sam 16:4), instituted forced labor (2 Sam 20:24; cf. 1 Kgs 4:6; 12:18), in addition to being a wife snatcher (Michal from Paltiel and Bathsheba from Uriah).

nation of Abner, albeit with a loud protestation of David's complicity (A), while David's era closed with the extirpation of the only surviving Saulide voice, Shimei, at David's instigation (A'). Similarly, in the next pair, an alibi is trotted out as evidence that Ishbosheth's death occurred without David's knowledge (B), while David's authorization of the execution of the Saulide Seven is touted as proof of David's culpability (B') in that event. Likewise, in the first half of the story, the reader is left to guess who deprived Michal of children (C), in the second half, the narrator informs the reader that it was David that confiscated Mephibosheth's patrimony (C').

A   Saul's commander (Abner) murdered by David's commander (Joab) (2 Sam 3:27)
    B   Saul's Son (Ishbosheth) dies at the hands of Davidic sympathizers (2 Sam 4:6-8)
        C   Saul's Daughter (Michal) deprived of progeny by David (2 Sam 6:23)
            D   Saul's grandson (Mephibosheth) invested with his grandfather's Patrimony by David (2 Sam 9:7-10)
        C'  Saul's son (Mephiboseth) divested of grandfather's patrimony by David (2 Sam 16:4)
    B'  Saul's sons and grandsons die at David's command (2 Sam 21:8-9)
A'  Saulide sympathizer (Shimei) murdered by Solomon at David's instigation (1 Kgs 2:8-9, 44-45)

Thus, the increasing overt acknowledgment of this series of evil deeds that David perpetrated against the Saulides could have possibly raised doubts, or, perhaps, is indicative of increasing doubts, about him and his dynasty, while at the same engendering sympathy for the Saulides.

Finally, the figure of David looms large over the entire Psalter, accompanied by a strong Messianic expectation of a renewed Davidic monarchy. The theme of the Davidic monarchy, in the Psalms, is found predominately in Books I–III (Pss 2–89). Understanding Psalm 1 as an introduction to the entire Psalter, Ernst-Joachim Waschke observes that the Davidic Psalms 2 and 89 constitute the outer boundaries of Books

I–III.⁵⁹ Psalm 89, which ends Book III, consists of a lament and prayer: Lamentation over the unenviable plight of the Davidic monarchy and its fallen kingdom, and a prayer for God to renew his grace to his servant David. The answer to this prayer is found in Books IV and V. Waschke points out that as a sequel to the lament and prayer in Psalm 89, the person praying is made to know that "human power and earthly deeds are transitory, whereas God has established his own kingdom before the beginning of time forever and ever (compare the very next psalm, Ps 90). In this light, the move from Book III to Book IV marks a change from the Davidic monarchy to the kingly rule of God."⁶⁰

The apocalyptic inclination of the redactors of the Psalter, as evident from the shape their arrangement gave to it, reflects the way the late post-exilic community dealt with disappointment about their existential situation. The pious among the exiles had sought to correct the ills of their predecessors, and therefore strove to set their lives straight by living in strict conformity to Yahweh's law: The reforms recorded in Ezra-Nehemiah testify to this. Yet the fortunes of the Jews seemed not to have changed for the better—the prophecies of the past seemed to have failed. It became increasingly difficult to translate the prophetic word, such as the promised renewal of the Davidic kingdom, in historical terms.⁶¹

The frustration generated by this cognitive dissonance is captured in the lament of Pseudo-Ezra: "If the world has indeed been created for

---

59. Waschke, "The Significance of the David Tradition," 413–20.

60. Waschke, "The Significance of the David Tradition," 419–20. The last two books of the Psalter do, indeed, make frequent references to God's rule (Pss 90:1–4; 93:2; 95:1–6; 96:10–13; 99:1–4; 106:47–48; 145:1, 11–13). Furthermore, Waschke shows that the evidence that the focus of the redactors of the Psalter shifts from human Davidic kingship to divine kingship can be "seen by (among other things) the fact that the first three books consist largely of psalms of lament and petition, whereas the last two are defined by hymns and other psalms with hymnic structure" (ibid., 420).

61. On this, Ladd writes, "The centuries which followed the restoration from Babylon involved the Jewish people in a historical and theological dilemma whose dark meaning they could not easily interpret. The prophet had proclaimed God's judgments in history upon Israel for her apostasy and disobedience and had held out the hope of repentance, conversion, and the Kingdom of God. When the Jews returned to their land, they renounced their former idolatry, giving themselves devotedly in obedience to the law as never before, separating themselves from sinful alliances with their pagan neighbors (Neh. 8–10). Never had Israel displayed more heroic devotion to the law than in the days of the Maccabees when many devout Jews gladly suffered torture and martyrdom rather than betray their devotion to God and the law (II Macc 5–7)" (Ladd, *The Presence of the Future*, 76).

us, why do we not possess our world as an inheritance? How long will this be so?" (4 Ezra 6:59). Old explanations could no longer adequately address the present mystifying state of affairs. As a result, prophetic eschatology was reinterpreted in apocalyptic terms, wherein the expected kingdom of God was transcendental in character and the king to come was the heavenly Son of Man (Dan 7:13-14; 9:25; cf. 4Q246).

The transcendental Son of Man is later shown as arising from the Davidic line so that he is seen as a divine Davidic Messianic eschatological redeemer. Indeed, the hope of the rise of the root of David was sustained in the Second Temple era, as can be seen in the non-canonical literature of the period, in keeping with the belief in Yahweh's eternal covenant with David in 2 Sam 7:11-14 (cf. Sir 47:11, 22; *Pss* Sol. 17:4, 21; 4QpGena V, 1-4).[62] This Second Temple apocalyptic tradition was one of the wellsprings that fed into the riverbed of New Testament Christianity (Luke 1:30-35; cf. Matt 24:27-32; 25:31-32; Acts 7:56; Rev 1:12-18).

What is fascinating about this is that in the Second Temple literature that deals with this issue, the Davidic redeemer figure (Messiah) shares his duties with the priest. As in the Chronicler, he is important as a religious reformer. Besides, he wields not the power of the sword but the power of the word, and his victory is ensured by the enabling power of the Holy Spirit (*Pss* Sol. 17:21-37). And as in the DtrH, he is subject to the Law and thus subject to the sacral leadership—the priesthood (4QpGena II, 5-6; 1 QSa II, 11-21; Sir 45:25-26; 2 Esd 12:31-32; T. *Sim.* 7:1-2; T. *Jud.* 21:2-4a).[63] The unique development the NT brings

---

62. For a fuller discussion of this see Fitzmyer, *The One Who is to Come*, 82-145; Kuhn, "The 'One like a Son of Man' Becomes the 'Son of God,'" 22-42; Cross, "Notes on the Doctrine of the Two Messiahs at Qumran," 1-13; Owen and Shepherd, "Speaking up for Qumran," 81-122; and Luz, "The Son of Man in Matthew," 3-21.

For opposing views see Casey, "Aramaic Idiom and the Son of Man Problem," 3-32; Casey, *The Solution of the 'Son of Man' Problem*; Vermes, *Jesus and the World of Judaism*; Lindars, *Jesus Son of Man*; and Lindars, "Re-enter the Apocalyptic Son of Man," NTS 22 (1976), 52-72.

63. In the Qumran community, the separation of the offices of the priest, prophet, and king (as in Deuteronomy) leads to the expectation of priestly, kingly, and possibly prophetic messiahs. We are already acquainted with the priestly Messiah embodied by the Righteous Teacher, also called the Interpreter of the Law, and the stately Davidic Messiah, who works alongside the Teacher or Interpreter (cf. 4QFlor I, 10-13; 4Q285 V, 1-6; CD XIX, 35-XX, 1). The idea of a prophetic Messiah comes from the portrayal of an expected Davidic leader who will not be occupied with stately duties (with the exception of judging, in which the priest also participated even in Deuteronomy), but rather will execute the sacral duties associated with the prophetic ministry—such as

to all this is the convergence in one Messiah—Jesus of Nazareth—of the stately (or royal) and the sacral (priestly and prophetic) offices, differentiated in Deuteronomy. In this way, the NT takes to a whole new level the convergence of the three offices in one individual.[64]

## The New Testament and David's Story

Margaret M. Daly-Denton aptly sums up the essence of the considerations in this section: "The gospel presentations of Jesus are shot through with motifs associated with Davidic kingship."[65] That the Gospel writers set out to show that Jesus was the expected "Son of David" needs no proving. Within the limitations of the scope and space of this project, I will highlight the themes and motifs in the NT that assert that Yahweh's eternal promise to David (2 Sam 7:11-16) has now come to fruition in Jesus of Nazareth. Then, I will outline some of the themes that connect the negative portrayal of David in the narratives examined in this study with key themes in New Testament Christianity.

The trajectory of the other-worldly character of the expected Davidic monarch that began in the Latter Prophets and developed through Second Temple literature finally comes to completion in the NT.

---

teaching precepts and working miraculous healings, including raising the dead (cf. 4Q521 II, 1-12; cf. Isa 42:5-7, 16; 61:1-2; Luke 4:18-19; 7:20-23; Matt 11:2-6). 1 QS IX, 9-11 mentions a prophet along with the two messiahs. Even though he is not called a messiah, this prophet appears to be at par with the two messiahs. The prophetic nature of the Messiah is also taught by 1 Enoch (48:2-8), where he is shown to have revelatory qualities (the New Moses) and is a light to the Gentile (as in Isaiah's Servant Songs), he is pre-existent, endowed with the Spirit of the Lord, and there is salvation in his name.

On Qumran text dealing with prophetic messiah figures without employing the epithet messiah, Martínez, similarly observes, "General consensus seems to indicate that the Dead Sea Scrolls can refer to these eschatological agents of salvation without using the term *messiah*. In fact texts vary in their use of the technical term when talking about the *same* eschatological figure. After all, the Old Testament texts, which later on will be used to express the hope of an eschatological savior, do not use the word *messiah*, and in none of the thirty-nine instances in which the Hebrew Bible uses the word *messiah* does this word have the precise technical meaning of the title used later to denote one of the figures who would bring eschatological salvation" (Martínez, "Two Messiah Figures in the Qumran Texts," 14–40).

64. The first manifestations of this convergence of all the offices in one person is seen in no less significant figures in Scripture, Moses and Samuel, though neither of them bore the titles of king and priest. During David's reign, the dividing lines between the offices were somewhat blurred as David (the king) performed both priestly and prophetic functions (cf. 2 Sam 6:11-14, 17-18; 23:1-4) in addition to reigning as king.

65. Daly-Denton, "David in the Gospels," 421-29.

In the birth narratives of Jesus, the birth of the expected Davidic king, promised through the agency of the prophets, is heralded by the very angels of heaven, thereby underscoring the surpassing excellency of this latter Davidide (Matt 1:18–23; Luke 1:26–38; 2:8–14). The genealogies of Jesus also demonstrate that he is a descendant of David on the physical plane, while efforts are made to exhibit his heavenly origin (Matt 1:20; Luke 1:35); thus, he is both the Son of David (or Son of Man) and the Son of God (Luke 1:32; Acts 13:22–23; Rom 1:3–4; 9:5).

In terms of the Messiah's work, the NT writers also understood the work of temple building as part of the work of the Messiah, a trend we have seen beginning in the DtrH but becoming more pronounced from Zechariah's time forward. Jesus himself reportedly made statements about a temple he was going to build (Matt 26:61; John 2:19–20). Yet, since the kingdom of this Davidide was not this-worldly, the temple he was building was also not physical; it was his *body*, which has a dual reference—to his bodily resurrection (John 2:21–22) and to his Church (Matt 16:18; Rom 12:4–5; 1 Cor 10:16–17; Eph 1:22–23).

The temple as the church, which Jesus, the expected Davidic Messiah, began to build in his life, ministry, death, and resurrection, continues to be built through the ministry of the Holy Spirit who empowers the members of Christ's body (Eph 2:14–22; 1 Pet 2:4–9). As the NT understands it, Jesus the Messiah is building a royal city beyond this life, wherein his church will one day eternally live with him in the presence of God the Father. As the temple in Jerusalem was "the temple" because of the presence of the deity there, symbolized by the Ark of the Covenant, the presence of the Godhead with his people in the New Jerusalem will in itself be constitutive of this new temple (John 14:1–3; Rev 21:2–3, 22–23; 22:3–5).

The point at which the NT writers have made the most comparisons between David and Jesus is at the intersection of David's suffering and Jesus' passion. In making this connection, the NT writers were not dependent solely on the narratives of the DtrH but assumed the Davidic authorship of the Psalms.[66] Some of the themes that interconnect these

---

66. In that assumption, the Gospel writers, for instance, seamlessly interwove the David story found in the DtrH narratives with that of the Psalms. To illustrate this, Daly-Denton writes, "Turning momentarily to Luke's 'Volume 2,' when Stephen says that David wanted 'to find a dwelling for the God of Jacob,' Luke is not drawing on the narrative traditions (2 Sam 7:2–6; 1 Kings 8:17–18; 1 Chr 17:1–14; 2 Chr 6:7–8) but on Ps 132:5, where David the psalmist says that he will not rest until he has found 'a place

two narratives include the motifs of a mournful walk across the Kidron Valley toward the Mount of Olives (2 Sam 15:30; John 18:1); the betrayal by a close confident (Ahithophel and Judas; 2 Sam 15:31; Matt 26:20–25); and the suicide of the traitor (2 Sam 17:23; Matt 27:3–5). Similarly, Ahithophel's plan to take David by night corresponds to Judas' leading the mob to take Jesus by night (2 Sam 17:1; John 18:3); Ahithophel's plan to strike only at David and to leave the people in peace finds its counterpart in Caiaphas' statement about one man dying for the people (2 Sam 17:3; John 11:50); the loyalty of David's followers and the alleged desertion of Mephibosheth (2 Sam 15–16) inversely corresponds to Jesus' prediction of his disciples' desertion and their avowed loyalty (Mark 14:27–31); Ittai's words of loyalty to the king during his crossing of the Kidron are echoed in John's record of Jesus' demands of his followers at the onset of the passion events (2 Sam 15:21; John 12:26); and David's temporary exile to the east and his eventual return to Jerusalem is a type of Christ's death and resurrection.[67] These parallels between the sufferings of David and the passion of the Christ found in the Gospels go a long way in demonstrating that Jesus is the coming Son of David, who would build the enduring temple of God and inherit an everlasting kingdom.

David is renowned for his repentant attitude (cf. 2 Sam 12:13; 24:10; Ps 32:1–5; 51:1–17). This is one thing that differentiates him from most of the kings of Israel and Judah, including those who may seem to be morally more upright than David. While he would readily admit his faults and own up to them, most of the other kings would not (cf. 1 Sam 15:13–28; 2 Chr 16:1–12; 2 Kgs 20:12–19). David, therefore, foreshadowed a cardinal teaching of the NT, that people are damned not because they have sinned but because of their unwillingness to repent (cf. Luke 13:1–5; John 3:17–19). Indeed, the NT Kerygma as a whole is centered on calling sinners to repentance.[68] Thus, the new Davidide (Jesus the Messiah) opened the way for the nations to share in this all-important aspect of David's story.

---

for the Lord, a dwelling for the God of Jacob' (Acts 7:46)" (Daly-Denton, "David in the Gospels," 427).

67. For more comprehensive discussion of these themes see Daly-Denton, "David in the Gospels," 425–29; and Doble, "David and his Psalms in Luke–Acts," 267–83.

68. For the centrality of repentance in the kerygma of the Church see the following passages: Matt 3:1–2; 4:17; Luke 5:32; 15:7, 10; 24:46–47; Acts 2:38; 3:19; 11:18; 17:30; 20:21; 26:20; 2 Tim 2:25–26.

## CONCLUSION

I began this chapter by evaluating David's dealings with the Saulides in light of the law. My conclusion is that David was a violator of the law as he was very unjust to Saul's progeny. I have also grappled with the negativity of the portrayal of David in Samuel vis-à-vis his positive depiction in the segments of the Bible subsequent to the books of Samuel. My conclusions are that within the DtrH, David was employed as a limiting concept not the ultimate model, and his repentant character trait dovetails well into the paramount call to repentance made in the DtrH to the *Golah* community. Besides, David's image was recreated by later generations, who were a battered people seeking a national icon around which to fashion and anchor a new self-identity. The rich Zion traditions of the Davidic dynasty provided the ready material that would inspire hope in Judean exiles.

Additionally, I have traced the themes arising from David's story, and connected them with similar themes in the rest of Scripture. Such resonances serve as elaborate demonstrations of our emergent perspectives on David and the monarchical era that followed him. First, the comparison between the story of David's dealings with Saulides in Samuel and the rest of Scripture shows that though our characterization of David goes against the grain of the traditional image of David, such character traits are not unique to him. Other biblical characters also share similar failings, even though David possesses them in more generous amounts. Second, it supplies the evidence that the failings of David laid the foundations for the final fall of the monarchy and Israel with it. Third, it manifests the revulsion of latter generations, especially the exilic and post-exilic generations, toward the injustices of the monarchical era. Fourth, it explains the unusual phenomenon of criticizing David but at the same time not disowning him. Indeed, the *Golah* community maintained this paradoxical dualism of disowning the monarchy but holding tenaciously to its most renowned king, while not sparing the latter from criticism. All this demonstrates how the dissatisfaction with the "old" David and his era would birth a new dimension in the development of the themes arising from the Davidic dispensation, and how this new direction itself would eventually lead to the "new" David (the Messiah) and his kingdom.

# 8

# Conclusion

## Truths from David's Dealings with the Saulides

THIS BOOK SET OUT to address comprehensively and holistically the fate of Saul's progeny after Saul's demise. Since there is no separate narrative of Saul's descendants in the Bible, it traced the story of David and how that story interconnected with the fate of the Saulides to determine whether the ills that befell the Saulides were due to continuing divine retribution, pure happenstance, or Davidic orchestration. The specific passages analyzed for this purpose are 1 Sam 18:17—19:17; 25:39-44; 2 Sam 2-4, 6, 9, 16:1-4; 19:25-31 [ET 19:24-30]; 21:1-14. The investigation revealed David's complicity in most of the Saulide tragedies, which portrayed David as being unjust on the basis of the provisions in Deuteronomy for justice in the covenant community. Viewing the injustices that David perpetrated against the Saulides from a biblical theological perspective makes plain that God's sovereign elective grace is not based on human deserts, that divine election does not translate automatically into virtuous character, and that less than full attention to the multiple testimonies of Scripture makes the church more susceptible to participating in, abetting, or, at the least, acquiescing to injustice.

Narrative criticism was my chosen analytical methodology for this study. In using narrative critical theory, questions of facticity gave place to concerns for truth. Narrative criticism, as a method, focuses the reader on the content of the final form of the text, as this book has demonstrated. The truth of a narrative, the case is made, is located at the intersection of facts, artistry, and ideology. Thus, the *historarity*[1] of biblical narrative and its threefold axes of history, literary artistry, and theological concerns are to be borne in mind in the attempts to explicate the world of the biblical narrative text. In the case of the Saulides, the injustices they suffered from David and his sympathizers is made manifest when one understands the historical context of the final redaction of Samuel to be exilic; pays attention to the rhetorical devices employed in the text such as narrative echo or analogy, intertextuality, key words, and point of view; and allows for the theological implications of a Deuteronomistic redaction of Samuel. All this underscores the utility of narrative criticism in helping the reader pay attention to the multiple voices in the text.

In my engagement with the books of Samuel, I sought to answer the following four questions: What was the fate of the Saulides? What was David's role in the fate of the Saulides? In light of the Torah, how should we regard David's role in the fate of the Saulides? How can we situate the conclusions of this research in the larger context of the biblical canon?

## DAVID AND THE FATE OF THE SAULIDES

### *The Fate of Abner and Ishbosheth*

The civil war years were the first substantive matter to engage our attention. The relocation of David from Ziklag to Hebron sent shock waves to Gibeah that consequently dislodged the imperiled Saulides from Gibeah to Mahanaim in Transjordan. Beginning with the skirmishes at the pool of Gibeon, David's men thrust deep into Benjaminite territory to prosecute the war their master had levied against Saul's house. At the end of the day, the two foremost Saulide figures, Abner and Ishbosheth, were exterminated, accompanied by David's loud protestations of innocence. Consequently, leaderless Israel capitulated to David's superior war machine, just as the Hebronites had done a few years earlier. David emerged as the king of Israel.

### *The Fate of Michal and the Saulide Seven*

Exploring the story of David as it interconnects with Michal, the wife of his youth, we saw David's underhanded dealing with her. He showed no affection for the only woman who is reported as having loved him.

---

1. See footnote 92 in chapter 3 of this book.

He made no attempts to rescue from the palace of a bitter father the woman who had saved his life from certain death: As David fled from eminent death, he never looked back. When it suited him, for the purpose of laying claim to Saul's throne, David remembered Michal—more as property he had purchased with a repugnant price to be repossessed than as a cherished wife whom he missed.

Michal's story paints a pathetic picture of a woman bedeviled by double jeopardy, being a woman in a man's world—a mere pawn in men's game of power—and belonging to a fated house. Thus, all her strivings for an independent assertion of herself were as successful as swimming against the tide could be. She loved a man who never loved her back. She defied her father to save a husband who was a loss to her anyway. She dared to rebuke her husband in an apparent defense of the honor and dignity of the institution in which she was raised, to protest her husband's usurpation of her father's throne, and possibly, to object to the bastardization or subversion of her people's cultic practices. All these actions only incurred for her the wrath of her husband, who invoked the name of the deity to have her five sons and two half-brothers impaled at a Gibeonite sanctuary.

### The Fate of Mephibosheth

The study showed David's interactions with Mephibosheth to be devious, to say the least. The loud proclamation of David's intended *ḥesed* for Jonathan's sake did not square up with his actions toward Jonathan's only son. Rather, as far as Davidic *ḥesed* to Mephibosheth is concerned, it is a matter of "the more you look the less you see." In his singular act of kindness toward a Saulide, David fished Mephibosheth out of hiding, brought him to the palace and restored to him his grandfather's estate, at least so he said. Yet, all these very actions are fraught with doubts about David's intentions. The requirement that Mephibosheth eat at the king's table daily smacks more of political hostage taking than of honoring. This becomes evident when it is remembered that Saul had required the daily presence of David at his dinner table as a way of keeping a watchful eye on the suspected southern insurgent. Jonathan, on the other hand, had released David from Saul's requirement for the latter's safety. That David chose to act in consonance with Saul rather than Jonathan raises questions about the integrity of his intentions. Similarly, the supposed return of Saul's estate to Mephibosheth appears to have been a ploy to supply the king's kitchen with produce, as David was the one who appointed the estate manager, whom he required to bring the yield of the fields to the palace under the pretext of providing food for Mephibosheth. We found these doubts all the more confirmed when we considered David's unjust actions against the Saulides such as his expropriation of Mephibosheth's patrimony and his later grudging return of half of it: Both actions were flagrant violations of the law. It is interesting that, somehow, Mephibosheth's fate, underscored by the motif of disability, prefigured the fate of the Davidic dynasty.

## DAVID'S DEALINGS WITH THE HOUSE OF SAUL IN LIGHT OF THE LAW

This section of the study evaluated, on the basis of Deuteronomic legislation, David's dealings with the Saulides, all of which are redolent with Torah violations. It particularly paid attention to David's action against Abner's murderers, contrasting it with Deuteronomic sanctions against murderers; David's jilting and later repossessing of Michal contrary to Deuteronomic provisions on both divorce and a wife's defilement to her husband upon being with another man; the execution of the Saulide Seven versus Deuteronomic proscription of collateral guilt; and David's judicial verdicts concerning Mephibosheth both during and after David's flight from Jerusalem vis-à-vis Deuteronomic prescriptions for ensuring due process of law and fair trial within the covenant community. In each of these cases, David is shown to have brazenly violated provisions in the Deuteronomic Code that guarantee justice for everyone in the covenant community.

## DAVID'S MORAL FAILURES IN THE CONTEXT OF THE BIBLICAL CANON

Reviewing the research findings from a biblical theological perspective entailed tracing themes or motifs found in the intertwined story of David and the Saulides and identifying their interconnections with similar themes and motifs in the rest of Scripture. By implication, these interconnections help explain the perplexing phenomenon of finding David criticized in Samuel but hailed in the subsequent books of the Bible; or the monarchy being vilified both in the Former and Latter Prophets, but its most prominent monarch eulogized.

The exilic experience of the Judeans furnished the soil in which the traditions of David flourished. As modern experiences show, those who live in exile or diaspora, whether they are forced or freely choose to do so, are plagued with a sense of being uprooted from their native soil. Concomitant with such feelings is identity crisis. Exiles are haunted by their experience of the interstitiality of the loss of connectedness with their old "home," and marginalization and/or liminality in the new.[2] Put differently, they are caught, as it were, dwelling at the cusps of both worlds but belonging to neither. Coupled with this is the fear that their heritage may be lost through the assimilation of their posterity into the host culture. A primary way of dealing with this dilemma is to seek reconnection with "home" through memory—memory of the traditions of their ancestors. In the diaspora, the telling, re-telling and even re-enactment of remembered traditions supply the forge in which a new identity is fashioned and then handed down to succeeding generations.

The Judean exiles, having been deprived of their temple, sovereign, Jerusalem, and land—the very things that had come to define their identity—turned to the memories of the traditions of David, the founder of their temple, dynasty, city, and the man who had also rid the land of its foreign invaders. The memories of David, therefore, became all the more cherished in the late pre-exilic and exilic eras. Moreover, the traditions of David's invincibility in war were morale boosting, ego enhancing, and hope generating to a defeated, harassed, and brutalized people. At the same time, being in exile also provided the opportunity for reflection: How did they get where they were? At once, the evils of the monarchy come to the fore. David, being among the chief sinners of that institution, therefore, is also subject to critique, giving pause to the enthusiasm about the renewal of the Davidic dynasty and its kingdom in the post-exilic era. Herein lies the basis for the Deuteronomists' paradoxical relation to David as one who is eulogized but criticized at the same time—criticized but never disowned all the same.

The twofold themes of leadership and justice were shown to have undergirded the concerns of the Deuteronomists. As they contemplated the direction the *Golah* community should follow, they saw themselves

---

2. For a fuller discussion of these themes see Bundang, "Home as Memory, Metaphor, and Promise"; Gluck, "Jewish Music or Music of the Jewish People?"; Pulido, "Engraving Emotions: Memory and Identity"; Tiessen, "Beyond the Binary"; and Wiesel, "A God Who Remembers."

at crossroads similar to those faced by their forebears. At the point of transition from judges to kings, there was the pending question of whether the Deuteronomic model of leadership that serves the interest of the people and glorifies God, set forth by Moses (Deut 17:14–20) and modeled by Samuel (1 Sam 12:1–4), would be found amongst Israel's kings. The choice of Saul as the first king was greeted with doubts right from the beginning (1 Sam 10:27); and even before his reign commenced in earnest, he was censured by the prophet Samuel (1 Sam 13:13–14). This critical stance of the prophet would dog and undermine Saul throughout his reign. After the demise of Saul, great hopes were raised with the ascent of David. However, these hopes were soon dashed, as David himself proved to be as depraved as any other person. Things only spiraled downward with the succession of kings that followed David, resulting first in the division of the kingdom and, ultimately, in the exile. After the return from exile, when the prophecies of the past seemed to have failed, the hopes of the people were gradually weaned from the prophetic eschatological expectation of the restoration of a this-worldly kingdom of David and directed toward the apocalyptic eschatological expectation of the inauguration of the other-worldly kingdom of the heavenly Son of Man, who is nonetheless descended from David. This accounts for the progressively waning interest in the monarchy in the second temple period. The NT writers understood the arrival of the Son of David, who inaugurates the kingdom of God, to have been realized in the Christ-event.

The interdigitated narration of David's story and the fate of Saul's progeny manifests the intersecting operations of law and grace. Law operates on the principle of equitability (being requited for one's deserts), while grace operates on the principle of superabundance (receiving what one does not deserve).[3] Saul was subjected to the equitability principle, and as such he and his house were rejected. This rejection resulted in the withdrawal of divine protective presence from them. Consequently, his house was exposed to pillaging bands (David and his gang and the Rimmon brothers, cf. 2 Sam 3:22; 4:2).

David, however, was accorded the superabundance principle despite his shortcomings, hence the endurance of his dynasty. The principle of superabundance, nevertheless, is not without boundaries. When the house of David crossed those boundaries with impunity and continued

---

3. See Ricoeur, "The Logic of Jesus, the Logic of God."

on that path without repentance, it fell within the domain of equitability, so it was truncated, its subjects sent into exile, and the hope it promised deferred until the rise of the Messiah.

## THE IMPLICATIONS OF THE STUDY

Until recently, Christian tradition has been unable or unwilling to come to terms with the atrocious conduct of its superheroes, David included, because of their prominence in redemptive history. The natural consequence of such selective listening to Scripture is the church's unspeakable lack of self-criticism at pivotal junctures in its checkered history. Studies of this nature are reminders that the witness of biblical narratives was not given in a single voice, but in multiplicity of voices. This awareness summons us to allow the word of God to instruct us from the perspectives of all the voices that bear testimony within it: We must listen not only to the dominant testimony but also to the counter-testimony, which cries out stridently for the oppressed. The fact that biblical narrative does not stifle counter-testimonies points to the ongoing prophetic ministry of the church, which is to be a counter-testimony in the midst of the dominant oppressive cultures of our time.

This research underscores the fact that David's choice as Israel's king and his place in redemptive history are manifestations of divine sovereign elective grace. It is a common fact of life that church tradition tends to be oblivious of the humanness of its biblical heroes. Yet, Scripture has not shied away from the darker sides of its most celebrated human characters. Scripture clearly shows that since the fall, all those who have been called and used of God have been only beneficiaries of his sovereign grace (or the superabundance principle): none could have merited it. David was no exception. He was a flawed man who was shown grace. David's repentant attitude was the means by which he renewed his hold onto the grace extended to him even when he fell. It is rather curious that he never applied such change of heart in far reaching ways to matters affecting the Saulides.

This awareness of divine grace for fallen humanity is very liberating. It frees us to live authentically. No longer wrapped in the hubris of a rehearsed life, we need not live in persistent denial of our failings. Instead, the awareness of sovereign grace gives us the audacity to critique freely the lives and works of the heroes of our faith traditions; it also affords us the courage to apply reflectively such critiques to our own lives and times. In the act of reading the biblical text, this step of appropriation that results in the experiencing of a transformative new self-understanding is the culminating rung of the hermeneutical spiraling ladder.

Another implication of the truth of David's story is that good people have a capacity for evil. Therefore, the people who are otherwise thought to be good could surprisingly turn out to be bad, or, at the least, behave badly. The awareness of this truth summons us to live with the consciousness of the gap that often exists between our noble aspirations and the passions of our lower nature. Such awareness challenges us to draw upon divine superabundance so as to ever so slowly narrow the yawning gap between our private and public faces so that we may constantly be straining toward their concurrence (Phil 3:12–14). That notwithstanding, David's unparalleled ability to accept his faults (when he became aware of them) and to repent readily is worthy of emulation.

## CONCLUSION

While much of the literature reviewed in this book argues that the genre of 1 and 2 Samuel is an apology for David, though one that is not uncritical of him, I understand the issue differently. Perhaps the sources of Samuel, especially the HDR, may have served the purpose of an apology when they were first composed. However, it is hard to reconstruct the sources precisely as they existed. Thus, we are left with the final form of the text as redacted in the exilic period. In this new form, the narratives serve a different purpose. David is critiqued, but the critique is not made without reserve. By this time, the exilic community was seeking what would both help define its identity and provide a sense of direction. The glories of the past, especially the united kingdom era, provided the memories upon which to attempt self-redefinition and to forge a new corporate identity. Yet, these memories also pointed painfully to the perturbing pitfalls of the old order that brought the exiles into their present predicament. If they were to move forward, then, they had to live above the deplorable oppressiveness of the monarchical era. The foregoing, to my mind, is a better explanation for the catalogue of evils attributed to David and his house in Samuel and, indeed, the DtrH as a whole.

The study has also shown that the driving force behind the stories in the books of Samuel can be better appreciated when attention is given to the books' concern with power, passion, prospects for renewal, and preservation that correspond respectively to politics, people, piety, and progeny. Power in Samuel has a magnetic attraction, comparable to that of the ring in Tolkien's trilogy, such that everyone in the narratives who comes within its purview goes grasping desperately after it—from the initially hesitant Saul, to the pretentious David, to the ambitious Absalom, to the loyal but brutal Joab, and to the powerful but witless Abner. In all their ways, they are shown to have lost out on God's way of possessing power, which is divine bestowal not human grasping.

Without exception, passion, with its contradictions and ambivalence, reveals the humanity of all the characters. For example, passion led Abner to appropriate Saul's concubine, an act that created division within Saul's camp, which in turn precipitated the liquidation of Saul's house; it propelled David to overreach and snatch other men's wives; and it drove Absalom to the rooftop with his father's concubines. Even the ruthlessness with which Joab held onto his position of power was passion driven.

Prospect for renewal is underscored in the pietistic concerns of the Deuteronomists. In the context of the exilic experience of the *Golah* community, the Deuteronomists channeled their piety into a clarion call to abandon all pretensions and return to the faith of the fathers as contained in the covenant document, Deuteronomy. This was done in the hope that Yahweh might see their repentance and bring about the promised restoration.

The desire for preservation is manifested in the concern with progeny. Both Saul and Jonathan earnestly besought David on oath to preserve their progeny. Preservation was also the theme of the Tekoite wise woman's parable, and of the fasting and prayer of David for the life of the son of his adulterous relationship with Bathsheba. The viciousness with which Saul's house was decimated is all part of the grand design to preserve David's dynasty.

This research fulfilled its primary purpose of providing a comprehensive study of the fate of the progeny of Saul after his death. The analysis of the Samuel narratives has shown that the tragedies that befell the Saulides were not pure happenstance neither is there any warrant to attribute them to divine retribution. On the contrary, there is ample evidence to suggest that they were victims of the combined forces of such human vices as unfettered political ambition, crass opportunism, and barefaced avarice.

Finally, I have evaluated the narratives of Samuel on the basis of their underpinning fundamental assumptions found in the book of Deuteronomy. In other words, I have evaluated these biblical texts not by an extraneous standard, but by their undergirding presuppositions. On this basis, in his interactions with the Saulides, David has been shown to be calculating, exploitative, and oppressive. In a number of his offenses against the Saulides, David violated such Deuteronomic laws that have the implication of incurring guilt and curses upon the land. The study thus has shown that the ill fate of Saul's progeny was the direct product of the efforts of David and his sympathizers to neutralize the house of Saul as they strained to secure the ascent of David and his house to Israel's throne.

Furthermore, I have also made modest additions to the tools and vocabulary of literary critical theory, especially as it relates to biblical narrative. I have introduced such concepts and terms as the *historarity* of biblical narrative, *plotlet*, stitch-word, intra-textual consciousness, and the Saulide Seven.

# Bibliography

Aberbach, Moses, and Bernard Grossfeld. *Targum Onkelos to Genesis: A Critical Analysis together with an English Translation of the Text.* New York: Ktav, 1982.
Abler, Ronald, John S. Adams, and Peter Gould. *Spatial Organisation: The Geographer's View of the World.* Englewood Cliffs, N.J: Prentice-Hall, 1971.
Ackerman, James S. "Knowing Good and Evil: A Literary Analysis of the Court History in 2 Samuel 9–20 and 1 Kings 1–2." *JBL* 109 (1990) 41–60.
Ackroyd, Peter R. *The First Book of Samuel.* Cambridge: Cambridge University Press, 1971.
———. *The Second Book of Samuel.* Cambridge: Cambridge University Press, 1977.
Adamiak, Richard. *Justice and History in the Old Testament: The Evolution of Divine Historiographies of the Wilderness Generation.* Cleveland: Zubal, 1982.
Alexander, T. Desmond. "Royal Expectations in Genesis to Kings: Their Importance for Biblical Theology." *TynBul* 49 (1998) 191–212.
Alter, Robert. *The Art of Biblical Narrative.* New York: Basic, 1981.
———. *The David Story: A Translation with Commentary of 1 and 2 Samuel.* New York: Norton, 1999.
———. "How Convention Helps Us Read: The Case of the Bible's Annunciation Type-Scene." *Prooftexts* 3 (1983) 115–30.
Anderson, A. A. *2 Samuel.* WBC 11. Waco, TX: Word, 1989.
Archer, Gleason L. *Encyclopedia of Bible Difficulties.* Grand Rapids: Zondervan, 1982.
Arnold, Bill T. "Necromancy and Cleromancy in 1 and 2 Samuel." *CBQ* 66 (2004) 199–213.
Auerbach, Erich. *Mimesis: The Representation of Reality in Western Literature.* Translated by W. Trask from the German edition of 1946. Garden City, NY: Doubleday, 1957.
Austin, John. *How to Do Things with Words.* 2nd ed. Cambridge: Harvard University Press, 1975.
Bal, Mieke, and David Jobling. *On Storytelling: Essays in Narratology.* Sonoma, CA: Polebridge, 1991.
Bal, Mieke. *Narratology: Introduction to the Theory of Narrative.* Toronto: University of Toronto Press, 1985.
Bar-Efrat, Shimeon. *Narrative Art in the Bible.* Sheffield: Almond, 1988.
Barton, John. *Ethics and the Old Testament.* Harrisburg, PA: Trinity, 1998.
———. *Reading the Old Testament: Method in Biblical Study.* 2nd ed. Louisville: Westminster John Knox, 1996.
Beardslee, William A. *Literary Criticism of the New Testament.* GBS. Philadelphia: Fortress, 1969.
Beckwith, Roger T. "Formation of the Hebrew Bible." In *Mikra: Text, Translation, Reading, and Interpretation of the Hebrew Bible in Ancient Judaism and Early Christianity.*

Edited by Martin Jan Mulder and Harry Sysling, 39–86. Peabody, MA: Hendrickson, 2004.

Begg, Christopher T. "The Significance of Jehoiachin's Release: A New Proposal." *JSOT* 36 (1986) 49–56.

Ben-Barak, Zafrira. "The Legal Background to the Restoration of Michal to David." In *Telling Queen Michal's Story: An Experiment in Comparative Interpretation*, edited by David J. A. Klines and Tamara C. Eskenazi, 74–90. JSOTSup 119. Sheffield: Sheffield Academic, 1991.

Bergen, Robert D. *1, 2 Samuel*. TAC vol. 7. Nashville, TN: Broadman & Holman, 1996.

Berlin, Adele. *Religion and Politics in the Ancient Near East*. Bethesda, MD: University of Maryland Press, 1996.

———. *Poetics and Interpretation of Biblical Narrative*. Winona Lake, IN: Eisenbrauns, 1983.

———. "Characterization in Biblical Narrative: David's Wives." *JSOT* 23 (1982) 69–85.

Berman, Joshua A. *Narrative Analogy in the Hebrew Bible: Battle Stories and Their Equivalent Non-battle Narratives*. Leiden: Brill, 2004.

Biddle, Mark E. "Ancestral Motifs in 1 Samuel 25: Intertextuality and Characterization." *JBL* 121 (2002) 617–38.

Birch, Bruce C. *Let Justice Roll Down: The Old Testament, Ethics and Christian Life*. Louisville: Westminster John Knox, 1991.

Blenkinsopp, Joseph. "Biographical Patterns in Biblical Narrative." *JSOT* 20 (1981) 27–46.

Block, Daniel I. "Echo Narrative Technique in Hebrew Literature: A Study in Judges 19." *WTJ* 52 (1990) 325–41.

Blomberg, Craig L. *Historical Reliability of John's Gospel*. Downers Grove: IVP, 2001.

———. *Interpreting the Parables*. Downers Grove, IL: IVP, 1990.

Bodner, Keith. "Is Joab a Reader-Response Critic?" *JSOT* 27 (2002) 19–35.

Borgman, Paul. *David, Saul, and God: Rediscovering an Ancient Story*. New York: Oxford University Press, 2008.

Bosworth, David A. "Evaluating King David: Old Problems and Recent Scholarship." *CBQ* 68 (2006) 191–210.

Bottéro, Jean. *Religion in Ancient Mesopotamia*. Translated by Teresa Lavender Fagan. Chicago: University of Chicago Press, 2001.

Bright, John. *A History of Israel*. Philadelphia: Westminster, 1981.

———. Review of R. A. Carlson, *David, The Chosen King: A Traditio-Historical Approach to the Second Book of Samuel*. *Interpretation* 19 (April 1965) 247.

Brueggeman, Walter. *David's Truth in Israel's Imagination and Memory*. 2nd ed. Minneapolis: Fortress, 2002.

———. *Deuteronomy*. AOTC. Nashville: Abingdon, 2001.

———. *A Commentary on Jeremiah: Exile and Homecoming*. Grand Rapids: Eerdmans, 1998.

———. *First and Second Samuel*. Interpretation. Louisville: John Knox, 1990.

———. "Narrative Intentionality in 1 Samuel 29." *JSOT* 43 (1989) 21–35.

———. "2 Samuel 21–24: An Appendix of Deconstruction?" *CBQ* 50 (1988) 383–97.

———. "Introduction: The Word in Particularity and Power," In *The Vitality of Old Testament Traditions*, edited by Walter Bruggemann and Hans Walter Wolf, 11–12. 2nd ed. Atlanta: John Knox, 1982.

———. "On Trust and Freedom: A Study of Faith in the Succession Narrative." *Interpretation* 26 (1972) 3–19.
Brunet, A.-M. "La théologie du Chroniste: théocratie et messianisme." *Sacra Pagina* Vol. 1, edited by J. Coppens, 384–97. Gembloux: Duculot, 1959.
Buber, Martin, and Franz Rosenzweig, eds. *Scripture and Translation*. Translated by Lawrence Rosenwald and Everett Fox. Bloomington: Indiana University Press, 1994.
Buber, Martin. "Leitwort and Discourse Type: An Example." In *Scripture and Translation*, by Martin Buber and Franz Rosenzweig, 143–50. Translated by Lawrence Rosenwald and Everett Fox. Bloomington: Indiana University Press, 1994.
Buchanan, Mark A. "Dance of the God-Struck: There's Something about Worship That Can Drive Even a King to Strip Down and Leap Up." *Christianity Today* 46.11 (2002) 51–54.
Budde, K. *Die Bücher Samuel*. Tübingen: Mohr, 1902.
Budde, Karl Ferdinand Reinhardt. *Die Bücher Richter und Samuel: Ihre Quellen und ihr Aufbau*. Giessen: Ricker, 1890.
Bundang, Rachel A. R. "Home as Memory, Metaphor, and Promise in Asian/Pacific American Religious Experience." *Semeia* 90–91 (2002) 87–104.
Campbell, Anthony F. *2 Samuel*. FOTL 8. Grand Rapids: Eerdmans, 2005.
Carlson, R. A. *David, The Chosen King: A Traditio-Historical Approach to the Second Book of Samuel*. Stockholm: Almqvist & Wiksell, 1964.
Carroll, Robert P. "Twilight of Prophecy or Dawn of Apocalyptic?" *JSOT* 14 (1979) 3–35.
Cartledge, Tony W. *1 & 2 Samuel*. Smyth & Helwys Bible Commentary. Macon, GA: Smyth & Helwys, 2001.
Casey, Maurice. *The Solution of the "Son of Man" Problem*. LNTS 343. London: T. & T. Clark, 2007.
———. "Aramaic Idiom and the Son of Man Problem: A Response to Owen and Shepherd." *JSNT* 25 (2002) 3–32.
———. "Re-enter the Apocalyptic Son of Man." *NTS* 22 (1976) 52–72.
Chapman, Mark D. *Ernst Troeltsch and Liberal Theology: Religion and Cultural Synthesis in Wilhelmine Germany*. CTC. Oxford: Oxford University Press, 2001.
Chatman, Seymour Benjamin. *Story and Discourse: Narrative Structure in Fiction and Film*. New York: Cornell University Press, 1978.
Childs, Brevard S. *Introduction to the Old Testament as Scripture*. Philadelphia: Fortress, 1979.
Wright, John Wesley. "The Legacy of David in Chronicles: The Narrative Function of 1 Chronicles 23–27. *JBL* 110 (1991) 229–42.
Clements, R. E. *Deuteronomy*. Old Testament Guides. Sheffield: JSOT Press, 1989.
———. "The Deuteronomic Interpretation of the Founding of the Monarchy in 1 Sam VIII." *VT* 24 (1974) 398–410.
Clines, David J. A. *On the Way to the Postmodern: Old Testament Essays, 1967–1998*. Sheffield: Sheffield Academic, 1998.
———. *Interested Parties: The Ideology of Writers and Readers of the Hebrew Bible*. Sheffield: Sheffield Academic, 1995.
———. *The New Literary Criticism and the Hebrew Bible*. Sheffield: JSOT, 1993.
Clines, David J. A., and Tamara C. Eskenazi, eds. *Telling Queen Michal's Story: An Experiment in Comparative Interpretation*. JSOTSup 119. Sheffield: Sheffield Academic, 1991.

Coates, William L. "A Study of David, the Thoroughly Human Man Who Genuinely Loved God: Selected Texts for Preaching and Teaching from 2 Samuel." *Review & Expositor* 99 (2002) 237–53.
Cogan, Mordechai, and Hayim Tadmor. *II Kings: A New Translation with Introduction and Commentary*. AB 11. Garden City, NY: Doubleday, 1988.
Combrink, H. J. Bernard. "The Rhetoric of Sacred Scripture." In *Rhetoric, Scripture and Theology: Essays from the 1994 Pretoria Conference*, edited by Stanley E. Porter and Thomas H. Olbricht, 102–23. JSNTSup 131. Sheffield: Sheffield Academic, 1995.
Conroy, C. *Absalom Absalom! Narrative and Language in 2 Sam 13–20*. AnBib 81. Rome: Biblical Institute Press, 1978.
Cook, Albert. "Fiction and History in Samuel and Kings." *JSOT* 36 (1986) 27–48.
Cremer, H. *Biblisch-theologisches Wörterbuch*. 7th ed. Gotha: 1893.
Crenshaw, J. L. "Method in Determining Wisdom Influence upon 'Historical' Literature." *JBL* 88 (1969) 138.
Cross, Frank Moore, Jr. "A Fragment of a Monumental Inscription from the City of David." *IEJ* 51 (2001) 44–47.
———. "Notes on the Doctrine of the Two Messiahs at Qumran and the Extracanonical Daniel Apocalypse (4Q246)." In *Current Research and Technological Developments on the Dead Sea Scrolls: Conference on the Texts from the Judean Desert, Jerusalem, 30 April 1995*. Edited by Donald W. Parry and Stephen D. Ricks, 1–13. STDJ 20. Leiden: Brill, 1996.
———. "Newly Found Inscriptions in Old Canaanite and Early Phoenician Script." *BASOR* 238 (1980) 8–15.
Cryer, Frederick H. "David's Rise to Power and the Death of Abner: An Analysis of 1 Samuel 26:14–16 and its Redaction-Critical Implications." *VT* 35 (1985) 385–94.
Culley, Robert C. *Studies in the Structure of Hebrew Narrative*. Philadelphia: Fortress, 1976.
Daly-Denton, Margaret M. "David in the Gospels." *Word & World* 23 (Fall 2003) 421–29.
Daniel Hawk. Review of Gillian Keys, *The Wages of Sin: A Reappraisal of the Succession Narrative*. *CBQ* 60 (1998) 332–33.
Daube, David. "Absalom and the Ideal King." *VT* 48 (1998) 315–25.
David, A. Rosaline. *The Ancient Egyptians: Religious Beliefs and Practices*. London: Routledge & Kegan Paul, 1982.
Davis, P. R. *In Search of "Ancient Israel."* JSOTSup 148. Sheffield: JSOT Press, 1992.
Day, John, ed. *King and Messiah in Israel and the Ancient Near East: Proceedings of the Oxford Old Testament Seminar*. JSOTSup 270. Sheffield: Sheffield Academic, 1998.
De Lamartine, Alphonse. *Saül, Tragédie*. Paris: Lévy, 1879.
Deleuze, Gilles. *Logique du sens*. Paris: Minuit, 1969.
Demsky, A. "A Proto-Canaanite Abecedary Dating from the Period of the Judges and Its Implications for the History of the Alphabet." *Tel Aviv* 4 (1977) 14–27.
Dillard, Raymond B., and Tremper Longman III. *An Introduction to the Old Testament*. Grand Rapids: Zondervan, 1994.
Doble, Peter. "Luke 24.26, 44—Songs of God's Servant: David and His Psalms in Luke-Acts." *JSNT* 28 (2006) 267–83.
Drinkard, Joel F., Jr. "An Understanding of Family in the Old Testament: Maybe Not as Different from Us as We Usually Think." *Review & Expositor* 98 (Fall 2001) 485–501.

Driver, S. R. *Notes on the Hebrew Text and the Topography of the Books of Samuel*. 2nd ed. Oxford: Clarendon, 1913.

Dumbrell, William J. "The Purpose of the Books of Chronicles." *JETS* 27 (1984) 257–66.

Edelman, Diana Vikander. "Did Saulide-Davidic Rivalry Resurface in Early Persian Yehud?" In *The Land that I Will Show You: Essays on the History and Archaeology of Ancient Near East in Honor of J. Maxwell Miller*, edited by J. A. Dearman and M. P. Graham, 69–91. JSOTSupp 343. Sheffield: Sheffield Academic, 2001.

———. *King Saul in the Historiography of Judah*. Sheffield: Sheffield Academic, 1991.

———. "The Deuteronomist's Story of King Saul: Narrative Art or Editorial Product?" In *Pentateuchal and Deuteronomistic Studies: Papers Read at the XIIIth IOSOT Congress, Leuven 1989*, edited by C. Brekelmans and J. Lust, 207–20. BETL 94. Leuven: Peeters, 1990.

Epzstein, Léon. *Social Justice in the Ancient Near East and the People of the Bible*. London: SCM, 1986.

Eshelbach, Michael A. *Has Joab Foiled David? A Literary Study of the Importance of Joab's Character in Relation to David*. New York: Lang, 2005.

Eskenazi, Tamara Cohn. "The Chronicler and the Composition of 1 Esdras." *CBQ* 48 (1986) 39–61.

Evans, Mary J. *1 and 2 Samuel*. NIBC. Peabody, MA: Hendrickson, 2000.

Exum, J. Cheryl. *Plotted, Shot, and Painted: Cultural Representations of Biblical Women*. Sheffield: Sheffield Academic, 1996.

———. "Bathsheba Plotted, Shot, and Painted." *Semeia* 4 (1996) 47–73.

———. *Fragmented Women: Feminist (Sub)Versions of Biblical Narratives*. Sheffield: JSOT Press, 1993.

———. *Tragedy and Biblical Narrative: Arrows of the Almighty*. Cambridge: Cambridge University Press, 1992.

———. *Signs and Wonders: Biblical Texts in Literary Focus*. Atlanta: Scholars, 1989.

Feldman, Louis H. *Josephus's Interpretation of the Bible*. Berkeley: University of California Press, 1998.

Finkelstein, Israel, and Neil Asher Silberman. *David and Solomon: In Search of the Bible's Sacred Kings and the Roots of the Western Tradition*. New York: Free, 2006.

———. *The Bible Unearthed: Archaeology's New Vision of Ancient Israel and the Origin of its Sacred Text*. New York: Free, 2001.

Firth, David G. *1 & 2 Samuel*. Apollos OTC. Edited by David W. Baker and Gordon J. Wenham. Nothingham, UK: Apollos, 2009.

Fitzmyer, Joseph A. *The One Who is to Come*. Grand Rapids: Eerdmans, 2007.

Flanagan, James W. "Chiefs in Israel." *JSOT* 20 (1981) 47–73.

Fohrer, George. *Introduction to the Old Testament*. Initiated by Ernst Sellin. Translated by David E. Green. Nashville: Abingdon, 1968.

Fokkelman, J. P. *Narrative Art and Poetry in the Books of Samuel: A Full Interpretation Based on Stylistic and Structural Analyses*. Vol. 1: King David (II Sam 9–20 & I Kings 1–2). Assen: Van Gorcum, 1981.

———. *Reading Biblical Narrative: An Introductory Guide*. Louisville: Westminster John Knox, 1999.

Frei, Hans W. *The Eclipse of Biblical Narrative: A Study in Eighteenth and Nineteenth Century Hermeneutics*. New Haven, CT: Yale University Press, 1974.

Friedman, Richard Elliott. "From Egypt to Egypt: Dtr1 and Dtr2." In *Traditions in Transformation: Turning Points in Biblical Faith*, edited by Baruch Halpern and Jon D. Levenson, 168–74. Winona Lake, IN: Eisenbrauns, 1981.

Friedmann, Daniel. *To Kill and Take Possession: Law, Moralilty, and Society in Biblical Stories*. Peabody, MA: Hendrickson, 2002.

Frolov, Serge. "Succession Narrative: A 'Document' or a Phantom?" *JBL* 121 (2002) 81–104.

Frye, Northrop. *The Great Code: the Bible and Literature*. New York: Harcourt Brace-Harvest, 1983.

Fuchs, Esther. "Structure and Patriarchal Functions in the Biblical Betrothal Type-Scene: Some Preliminary Notes." *JFSR* 3 (Spring 1987) 7–13.

Gaebelein, Frank E., ed. *The Expositor's Bible Commentary*. Grand Rapids: Zondervan, 1992.

Galán, José M. "What Is He, the Dog?" *UF* 25 (1993) 173–80.

Garbini, G. *History and Ideology in Ancient Israel*. New York: Crossroad, 1988.

Garret, Duane A. *Hosea, Joel*. NAC. Edited by E. Ray Clendenen. Nashville: Broadman & Holmes, 1997.

Garsiel, Moshe. *The First Book of Samuel: A Literary Study of Comparative Structures, Analogies and Parallels*. Ramat Gan, Israel: Revivim, 1985.

George, Mark K. "Yhwh's Own Heart." *CBQ* 64 (2002) 442–59.

Gluck, Bob. "Jewish Music or Music of the Jewish People?" *Reconstructionist* 62 (1997) 34–47.

Glück, J. J. Von. "Merab or Michal?" *ZAW* 77 (1965) 72–81.

Goldingay, John. *Men Behaving Badly*. Carlisle, UK: Paternoster, 2000.

———. *Theological Diversity and the Authority of the Old Testament*. Grand Rapids: Eerdmans, 1987

Good, Edwin Marshall. *Irony in the Old Testament*. 2nd ed. Sheffield: Almond, 1981.

Gordon, Robert P. *I & II Samuel: A Commentary*. LBI. Grand Rapids: Zondervan, 1986.

———. "David's Rise and Saul's Demise: Narrative Analogy in 1 Samuel 24–26." *TynBul* 31 (1980) 37–64.

Goulder, Michael Douglas. "David and Yahweh in Psalms 23 and 24." *JSOT* 30 (2006) 463–73.

Grabbe, Lester L. *Priests, Prophets, Diviners, Sages: A Socio-Historical Study of Religious Specialists in Ancient Israel*. Valley Forge, PA: Trinity, 1995.

Green, Barbara. *How Are the Mighty Fallen? A Dialogical Study of King Saul in 1 Samuel*. JSOTSup 365. Sheffield: Sheffield Academic.

Gressmann, H. *Die älteste Geschichtereibung und Prophetie Israels: von Samuel bis Amos und Hose*. Die Schriften des Alten Testaments. 2 vols. Göttingen: Vandenhoeck & Ruprecht, 1921.

Gunn, David M. "Narrative Criticism." In *To Each Its Own Meaning: An Introduction to Biblical Criticisms and Their Application*, edited by Steven L. McKenzie and Stephen R. Haynes, 201–29. Louisville: Westminster John Knox, 1999.

———. "Bathsheba Goes Bathing in Hollywood: Words, Images, and Social Locations." *Semeia* 74 (1996) 75–101.

———, ed. *Narrative and Novella in Samuel: Studies by Hugo Gressmann and Other Scholars, 1906–1923*. Translated by David E. Orton. JSOTSup 116. Sheffield: Almond, 1991.

———. "New Directions in the Study of Biblical Hebrew Narrative." *JSOT* 39 (1987) 65–75.

———. "From Jerusalem to the Jordan and Back: Symmetry in 2 Samuel 15-20." *VT* 30 (1980) 109-13.

———. *The Story of King David: Genre and Interpretation*. Sheffield: University of Sheffield, 1978.

———. "David and the Gift of the Kingdom (2 Sam 2-4, 9-20, 1 Kings 1-2)." *Semeia* 3 (1975) 14-45.

Haelewyck, Jean-Claude. "L'Assassinat D'Ishbaal (2 Samuel IV 1-12)." *VT* 47 (1997) 145-53.

Halpern, Baruch. *David's Secret Demons: Messiah, Murderer, Traitor King*. Grand Rapids: Eerdmans, 2001.

———. *The Constitution of the Monarchy in Israel*. HSM 25. Chico, CA: Scholars, 1981.

Hanson, Paul D. *The Dawn of Apocalyptic: The Historical and Sociological Roots of Jewish Apocalyptic Eschatology*. Philadelphia: Fortress, 1975.

Hardy, Thomas. *The Mayor of Casterbridge*. New York: Modern Library 1917.

Hasel, G. F. "Caleb, Calebites." *ISBE* 1 (1979), 573-74.

Hawk, L Daniel. "Violent Grace: Tragedy and Transformation in the Oresteia and the Deuteronomistic History." *JSOT* 28 (2003) 73-88.

Henn, T. R. *The Bible as Literature*. New York: Oxford University Press, 1970.

Hess, Richard S. "Writing about Writing: Abecedaries and Evidence for Literacy in Ancient Israel." *VT* 56 (2006) 342-46.

———. "Literacy in Iron Age Israel." In *Windows into Old Testament History: Evidence, Argument, and the Crisis of "Biblical Israel,"* edited by V. P. Long, D. W. Baker, and G. J. Wenham, 82-100. Grand Rapids: Eerdmans, 2002.

Herbert, Edward D. "2 Samuel v 6: An Interpretative Crux Reconsidered in the Light of 4QSam<sup>a</sup>." *VT* 44 (1994) 340-48.

Hertzberg, Hans Wilheim. *I & II Samuel: A Commentary*. OTL. Philadelphia: Westminster, 1964.

Hexter, J. H. *Doing History*. London: Allen and Unwin, 1971.

Hill, Andrew E. "On David's 'Taking' And 'Leaving' Concubines (2 Samuel 5:13; 15:16)." *JBL* 125 (2006) 129-50.

Holloway, Steven W. *Aššur is King! Aššur is King! Religion in the Exercise of Power in the Neo-Assyrian Empire*. Leiden, The Netherlands: Brill, 2002.

Hoy, David Couzens. *The Critical Circle: Literature, History, and Philosophical Hermeneutics*. Berkeley: University of California Press, 1982.

Hubbard, R. L., Jr. "Caleb, Calebites." In *DOTHB*, 120-22.

———. "The Eyes Have It: Theological Reflections on Human Beauty." *Ex Auditu* 13 (1997) 57-72.

Humphreys, W. Lee. Review of David M. Gunn, ed. *Narrative and Novella in Samuel: Studies by Hugo Gressmann and Other Scholars, 1906-1923. CBQ* 54 (1992) 746-47.

Iser, Wolfgang. *The Range of Interpretation*. New York: Columbia University Press, 2000.

———. *The Act of Reading: A Theory of Aesthetic Response*. Baltimore: Johns Hopkins University Press, 1978.

———. *The Implied Reader: Patterns of Communication in Prose Fiction from Bunyan to Beckett*. Baltimore: John Hopkins Universtiy Press, 1974.

Ishida, Tomoo. *The Royal Dynasties in Ancient Israel: A Study on the Formation and Development of Royal-Dynastic Ideology*. BZAW 142. Berlin: de Gruyter, 1977.

Jamieson-Drake, D. W. *Scribes and Schools in Monarchic Judah: A Socio-Archeological Approach*. JSOTSup 109. Sheffield: Sheffield Academic, 1991.
Jobling, David. *1 Samuel*. Berit Olam. Collegeville, MN: Liturgical, 1998.
———. Review of Robert Polzin, *Samuel and the Deuteronomist*. Interpretation 44 (1990) 416.
Josephus. *The Complete Works of Josephus: Complete and Unabridged*. Translated by William Whiston. New updated ed. Peabody, MA: Hendrickson, 1987.
Keil, C. F., and F. Delitzsch. *Commentary on the Old Testament*. Vol. 10. Reprint. Peabody, MA: Hendrickson, 2001.
Kermode, Frank. "New Ways with Bible Stories." In *Parable and Story in Judaism and Christianity*, edited by Clemens Thoma and Michael Wyschogrod, 121–35. New York: Paulist, 1989.
Kessler, John. "Sexuality and Politics: The Motif of the Displaced Husband in the Books of Samuel." *CBQ* 62 (2000) 409–23.
Keys, Gillian. *The Wages of Sin: A Reappraisal of the Succession Narrative*. Sheffield: Sheffield Academic, 1996.
Kidner, Derek. *Genesis: An Introduction and Commentary*. TOTC. Leicester, UK: IVP, 1967.
King, Philip J. *Amos, Hosea, Micah—An Archaeological Commentary*. Philadelphia: Westminster, 1988.
Kirsch, J. *King David: The Real Life of the Man Who Ruled Israel*. New York: Ballantine, 2000.
Kittel, R. "Das erste Buch Samuel." In *Die Heilige Schrift des alten Testaments*. Vol. 1. 4th ed. Edited by A. Bertholet, 407–51. Tübingen: Mohr, 1922.
———. *Geschichte des Volkes Israel*. Vol. 2. Gotha: Perthes, 1922.
Kirkpatrick, Alexander Francis. *The Second Book of Samuel*. The Cambridge Bible for Schools and Colleges. Rev. ed. London: Cambridge University Press, 1930.
Klein, Ralph W. *1 Samuel*. WBC 10. Waco, TX: Word, 1983.
Klement, Herbert H. "Structure, Context and Meaning in the Samuel Conclusion (2 Sa 21–24)." *TynBul* 47 (1996) 367–70.
Knowles, Melody D. "The Flexible Rhetoric of Retelling: The Choice of David in the Texts of the Psalms." *CBQ* 67 (2005) 236–49.
Koopmans, William T. "The Testament of David in 1 Kings 2:1–10." *VT* 41 (1991) 429–49.
Kuhn, Karl A. "The 'One like a Son of Man' Becomes the 'Son of God.'" *CBQ* 69 (2007) 22–42.
Laato, Antti. "Psalm 132 and the Development of the Jerusalemite/Israelite Royal Ideology." *CBQ* 54 (1992) 49–66.
Ladd, George Eldon. *The Presence of the Future: The Eschatology of Biblical Realism*. Grand Rapids: Eerdmans, 1974.
Lambdin, Thomas. O. *Introduction to Biblical Hebrew*. New York: Scribner, 1971.
Lawton, R. B. "1 Samuel 18: David, Merab and Michal." *CBQ* 51 (1989) 423–25.
Leithart, Peter J. "Counterfeit Davids: Davidic Restoration and the Architecture of 1–2 Kings." *TynBul* 56 (2005) 19–33.
———. *A Son to Me: An Exposition of 1 & 2 Samuel*. Moscow, ID: Canon, 2003.
———. *From Silence to Song: The Davidic Liturgical Revolution*. Moscow, ID: Canon, 2002.
Lemche, Niels Peter. "David's Rise." *JSOT* 10 (1978) 2–25.

Levenson, Jon D. "1 Samuel 25 as Literature and as History." *CBQ* 40 (1978) 11–28.
Levenson, Jon D. and Baruch Halpern. "The Political Import of David's Marriages." *JBL* 99 (1980) 507–18.
Levin, Richard. *The Multiple Plot in English Renaissance Drama*. Chicago: University of Chicago Press, 1971.
Lewis, Theodore J. "The Ancestral Estate (נחלת אלהים) in 2 Samuel 14:16." *JBL* 110 (1991) 597–612.
Licht, J. *Storytelling in the Bible*. Jerusalem: Magnes, 1986.
Lindars, Barnabas. *Jesus Son of Man: A Fresh Examination of the Son of Man Sayings in the Gospels in the Light of Recent Research*. London: SPCK, 1983.
———. "Re-enter the Apocalyptic Son of Man," *NTS* 22 (1976) 52–72.
Long, Burke O. Review of Gillian Keys. *The Wages of Sin: A Reappraisal of the Succession Narrative*. *Biblica* 79 (1998) 130.
Long, V. Philips *The Art of Biblical History*. Foundations of Contemporary Interpretation. Grand Rapids: Zondervan, 1994.
———. "First and Second Samuel." In *A Complete Literary Guide to the Bible*, edited by L. Ryken and T. Longman, 165–81. Grand Rapids: Zondervan, 1993.
———. *The Reign and Rejection of King Saul: A Case for Literary and Theological Coherence*. Atlanta: Scholars, 1989.
Longacre, Robert. *The Grammar of Discourse*. 2nd ed. New York: Plunum, 1996.
Longman, Tremper. *Literary Approaches to Biblical Interpretation*. Grand Rapids: Academie, 1987.
Lothe, Jakob. "Reptition and Narrative Method: Hardy, Conrad, Faulker." In *Narrative From Malory to Motion Pictures*, edited by Jeremy Hawthorn, 117–32. London: Edward Arnold, 1985.
Louis, Kenneth R. R. Gros. "The Difficulty of Ruling Well: King David of Israel." *Semeia* 8 (1977) 15–33.
Luz, Ulrich. "The Son of Man in Matthew: Heavenly Judge or Human Christ." *JSNT* 48 (1992) 3–21.
MacKenzie, R. A. F. "The City and Israelite Religion," *CBQ* 25 (1963) 60–70.
Malchow, Bruce V. *Social Justice in the Hebrew Bible: What is New and What is Old*. Collegeville, MN: Liturgical, 1996.
Malina, Bruce J. "Rhetorical Criticism and Social-Scientific Criticism: Why Won't Romanticism Leave Us Alone?" In *Rhetoric, Scripture and Theology: Essays from the 1994 Pretoria Conference*, edited by Stanley E. Porter and Thomas H. Olbricht, 72–101. JSNTSup 131. Sheffield: Sheffield Academic, 1995.
Martínez, Florentino García. "Two Messiah Figures in the Qumran Texts." In *Current Research and Technological Developments on the Dead Sea Scrolls: Conference on the Texts from the Judean Desert, Jerusalem, 30 April 1995*, edited by Donald W. Parry and Stephen D. Ricks, 14–40. STDJ 20. Leiden, The Netherlands: Brill, 1996.
Mauchline, John. *1 and 2 Samuel*. NCB. Greenwood, SC: Marshall, Morgan & Scott, 1971.
Mays, James Luther. *Micah: A Commentary*. OTL. Philadelphia: Westminster, 1976.
———. *Hosea: A Commentary*. OTL. Philadelphia: Westminster, 1969.
McCarter, P. Kyle. "The Books of Samuel." In *The History of Israel's Traditions: The Heritage of Martin Noth*, edited by Steven L. McKenzie and M. Patrick Graham, 260–80. JSOTSup 182. Sheffield: Sheffield Academic, 1994.
———. *1 Samuel: A New Translation with Introduction and Commentary*. AB 8. New York: Doubleday, 1980.

———. *2 Samuel: A New Translation with Introduction and Commentary.* AB 9. New York: Doubleday, 1984.
McCarthy, Dennis J. "The Use of *wᵉhinnēh* in Biblical Hebrew." *Bib* 61 (1980) 330–42.
McComiskey, Thomas Edward. "Amos." In *The Expositor's Bible Commentary: Daniel and the Minor Prophets.* Vol. 7, edited by Frank E. Gæbelein, 269–334. Grand Rapids: Zondervan, 1985.
McConville, J. Gordon *Deuteronomy.* Apollos OTC. Downers Grove, IL: IVP, 2002.
———. *Grace in the End: A Study in Deuteronomic Theology.* Grand Rapids: Zondervan, 1993.
———. "King and Messiah in Deuteronomy and the Deuteronomistic History." In *King and Messiah in Israel and the Ancient Near East: Proceedings of the Oxford Old Testament Seminar,* edited by John Day, 271–95. JSOTSup 270. Sheffield: Sheffield Academic, 1998.
McKenzie, John L. *The Old Testament Without Illusion.* Chicago: Thomas More, 1979.
McKenzie, Steven L. "Who Was King David?" *Word & World* 23 (2003) 357–64.
———. *King David: A Biography.* New York: Oxford University Press, 2000.
McKenzie, Steve L., and M. Patrick Graham. *The History of Israel's Traditions: The Heritage of Martin Noth.* JSOTSup 182. Sheffield: Sheffield Academic, 1994.
*Merriam-Wesbster's Collegiate Dictionary.* 10th ed. Springfield, MA: Merriam-Webster, 1994.
Merrill, Eugene H. *Deuteronomy.* NAC 4. Nashville. Broadman & Holman, 1994.
Mettinger, Tryggve N. D. *King and Messiah: The Civil and Sacral Legitimation of the Israelite Kings.* Lund: Gleerup, 1976.
Miller, Hillis. *Fiction and Repetition: Seven English Novels.* Oxford: Blackwell, 1982.
Miscall, Peter D. "Texts, More Texts, a Textual Reader and a Textual Writer." *Semeia* 69–70 (1995) 247–60.
———. *The Workings of Old Testament Narrative.* Philadelphia, PA: Fortress, 1983.
Moulton, Richard G., et al. *The Bible as Literature.* 3rd ed. New York: Crowell, 1896.
Muilenburg, James. "Form Criticism and Beyond." *JBL* 88 (1969) 1–18.
Murray, Donald F. *Divine Prerogative and Royal Pretension: Pragmatics, Poetics and Polemics in a Narrative Sequence about David (2 Samuel 5.17—7.29).* Sheffield: Sheffield Academic, 1998.
———. "Dynasty, People, and the Future: The Message of Chronicles." *JSOT* 58 (1993) 71–92.
———. "Of All the Years the Hopes—or Fears? Jehoiachin in Babylon (2 Kings 25:27–30)." *JBL* 120 (2001) 245–65.
Na'aman, Nadav. *Ancient Israel's History and Historiography: The First Temple Perriod.* Collected Essays 3. Winona Lake, IN: Eisenbrauns, 2006.
Newsome, J. D. "Toward a New Understanding of the Chronicler and his Purpose," *JBL* 94 (1975) 201–17.
Niccacci, Alveiero. "Basic Facts and Theory of the Biblical Hebrew Verb System in Prose." In *Narrative Syntax and the Hebrew Bible: Papers of the Tilburg Conference 1996,* edited by Ellen Van Wolde, 167–202. Leiden: Brill, 1997.
Nicholson, Sarah. *The Three Faces of Saul: An Intertextual Approach to Biblical Tragedy.* JSOTSup 339. Sheffield: Sheffield Academic, 2002.
Niditch, S. *Oral Word and Written Word: Ancient Israelite Literature.* Louisville: Westminster John Knox, 1996.
Noble, Paul R. "Esau, Tamar, and Joseph: Criteria for Identifying Inner-Biblical Allusions." *VT* 52 (2002) 219–52.

Noll, K. L. *The Faces of David*. JSOTSup 242. Sheffield: Sheffield Academic, 1997.
North, Robert. "Theology of the Chronicler." *JBL* 82 (1963) 369–81.
Noth, Martin.*The Deuteronomistic History*. JSOTSup 15. Translated by J. Doull, et al. Sheffield: JSOT, 1981.
———. *The History of Israel*. Translated by P. R. Ackroyd. New York: Harper & Row, 1960.
O'Connell, R. H. *The Rhetoric of the Book of Judges*. SVT 63. Leiden: Brill, 1996.
Olyan, Saul. "Zadok's Origins and the Tribal Politics of David." *JBL* 101 (1982) 177–93.
Oswalt, John N. *The Book of Isaiah: Chapter 1–39*. NICOT. Grand Rapids: Eerdmans, 1986.
Owen, P., and D. Shepherd. "Speaking up for Qumran, Dalman and the Son of Man: Was Bar Enasha a Common Term for 'Man' in the Time of Jesus?" *JSNT* 81 (2001) 81–122.
Oyen, Hendrik van. *Éthique De L'Ancien Testament*. Geneve: Labor Et Fides, 1974.
Palache, J. L. "The Nature of Old Testament Narrative." In *Voices from Amsterdam: A Modern Tradition of Reading Biblical Narrative*, edited by Martin Kessler, 3–22. Atlanta: Scholars, 1994.
Parry, Robin. "Narrative Criticism," In *Dictionary of Theological Interpretations of the Bible*, edited by Kevin J. Vanhoozer, 528–31. Grand Rapids: Baker Academic, 2005.
Patrick, Dale, and Allen Scult. *Rhetoric and Biblical Interpretation*. JSOTSup 82. Sheffield: Almond, 1990.
Payne, David F. *I & II Samuel*. DSB. Philadelphia: Westminster, 1982.
Peleg, Yaron. "Love at First Sight? David, Jonathan, and the Biblical Politics of Gender." *JSOT* 30 (2005) 171–89.
Perrin, Norman. *Literary Criticism for New Testament*. GBS. Philadelphia: Fortress, 1978.
Perrine, Laurence. *Story and Structure*. 4th ed. New York: Harcourt, Brace, Jovanovich, 1974.
Peterson, Eugene H. *First and Second Samuel*. Westminster Bible Companion. Louisville: Westminster John Knox, 1999.
Pfeiffer, R. H. *Introduction to the Old Testament*. New York: Harper, 1948.
Phillips, Anthony. "David's Linen Ephod." *VT* 19 (1969) 485–87.
Polzin, Robert. *David and the Deuteronomist: 2 Samuel*. Bloomington: Indiana University Press, 1993.
———. *Moses and the Deuteronomist: A Literary Study of the Deuteronomic History. Part One: Deuteronomy, Joshua, Judges*. New York: Seabury, 1980.
———. *Samuel and the Deuteronomist Samuel: 1 Samuel*. San Francisco: Harper & Row, 1989.
Pomykala, Kenneth E. *The Davidic Dynasty Tradition in Early Judaism: Its Significance for Messianism*. SBLEJL 7. Atlanta: Scholars, 1995.
Powell, Mark Allan. *What is Narrative Criticism?* GBS. Minneapolis: Fortress, 1990.
Preston, Thomas R. "The Heroism of Saul: Patterns of Meaning in the Narrative of The Early Kingship." *JSOT* 24 (1982) 27–46.
Propp, V. *Morphology of Folktale*. Austin: University of Texas Press, 1968.
Provan, Ian, V. Philips Long and Tremper Longman III. *A Biblical History of Israel*. Louisville: Westminster John Knox, 2003.
Pulido, Alberto López. "Engraving Emotions: Memory and Identity in the Quest for Emotive Scholarship." *Cross Currents* 54.2 (2004) 45–50.

Pyper, Hugh S. *David as Reader: 2 Samuel 12:1-15 and the Poetics of Fatherhood.* Leiden: Brill, 1996.

Rad, Gerhard von. *Deuteronomy: A Commentary.* OTL. Philadelphia: Westminster, 1966.

———. *Old Testament Theology.* Vol. 1. Translated by D. M. G. Stalker. New York: Harper, 1962.

———. *Studies in Deuteronomy.* Studies in Biblical Theology. Chicago: Regnery, 1953.

Ramsey, Janet L. "'Once in Royal David's City': David's Story in Preaching and Pastoral Care." *Word & World* 27 (2007) 444–50.

Reis, Pamela Tamarkin. "Killing the Messenger: David's Policy or Politics?" *JSOT* 31 (2006) 167–91.

Rhoads, David, and Donald Michie. *Mark as Story: An Introduction to the Narrative of a Gospel.* Philadelphia: Fortress, 1982.

Ricoeur, Paul. *Time and Narrative.* 3 vols. Translated by Kathleen Blamey and David Pellauer. Chicago: University of Chicago Press, 1984–88.

———. "Hermeneutics of Testimony." In Paul Ricoeur, *Essays on Biblical Interpretation*, edited by Lewis S. Mudge, 119–54. Translated by David E. Stewart and Charles E. Regan. Philadelphia, PA: Fortress, 1980.

———. "The Logic of Jesus, the Logic of God." *Criterion* 18 (1979) 4–6.

———. *The Role of Metaphor: Multi-Disciplinary Studies of the Creation of Meaning in Language.* Translated by Robert Czerny. Toronto: University of Toronto Press, 1977.

———. *Interpretation Theory: Discourse and the Surplus of Meaning.* Fort Worth: Texas Christian University Press, 1976.

———. "Philosophical Hermeneutics and Theological Hermeneutics." *Studies in Religion* 5 (1975/76) 14–33.

Robbins, Vernon K. "The Present and Future of Rhetorical Analysis." In *The Rhetorical Analysis of Scripture: Essays from the 1995 London Conference*, edited by Stanley E. Peter and Thomas H. Olbricht, 24–52. JSNTSup 146. Sheffield: Sheffield Academic, 1996.

Roberts, J. J. M. *David and Zion: Biblical Studies in Honor of J. J. M. Roberts.* Winona Lake, IN: Eisenbrauns, 2004.

———. "The Enthronement of Yhwh and David: The Abiding Theological Significance of the Kingship Language of the Psalms." *CBQ* 64 (2002) 675–86.

Robinson, Gnana. *Let Us Be Like the Nations: A Commentary on the Books of 1 and 2 Samuel.* ITC. Grand Rapids: Eerdmans, 1993.

Robinson, James McConkey. 'Breaking the Cycle: Jesus' Alternative to Vengeance." *Christian Century* 122:19 (Sept 20, 2005) 10–11.

———. *The New Hermeneutic.* New York: Harper & Row, 1964.

Rogers, Cleon L. "The Promises to David in Early Judaism." *BibSac* 150 (1993) 285–302.

Rogers, Jeffrey S. "Narrative Stock and Deuteronomistic Elaboration in 1 Kings 2." *CBQ* 50 (1988) 398–413.

Roland E. Murphy, and O. Carm. "Reflections on Contextual Interpretation of the Psalms." In *The Shape and Shaping of the Psalter*, edited by J. Clinton McCann, 21–28. JSOTSup 159. Sheffield: Sheffield Academic, 1993.

Römer, Thomas. "Deuteronomy in Search of Origins." In *Reconsidering Israel and Judah: Recent Studies on the Deuteronomistic History*, edited by Gary N. Knoppers and J. Gordon McConville, 112–38. Winona Lake, IN: Eisenbrauns, 2000.

Römer, Thomas C., and A. de Pury. *The So-Called Deuteronomistic History: A Sociological, Historical and Literary Introduction*. London: T. & T. Clark, 2005.

Rost, Leonhard. *The Succession to the Throne of David*. Translated by Michael D. Rutter and David M. Gunn, with introduction by Edward Ball. Sheffield: Almond, 1982.

Rudman, Dominic. "The Patriarchal Narratives in the Books of Samuel." *VT* 54 (2004) 239–49.

———. "The Commissioning Stories of Saul and David as Theological Allegory." *VT* 50 (2000) 519–30.

Ruthven, Pam. "The Feckless Later Reign of King David: A Case of Major Depressive?" *Journal of Pastoral Care* 55 (2001) 425–32.

Ryken, Leland. *How to Read the Bible as Literature*. Grand Rapids: Zondervan, 1984.

———. *The Literature of the Bible*. Grand Rapids: Zondervan, 1974.

Ryken, Leland, and Tremper Longman. *A Complete Literary Guide to the Bible*. Grand Rapids: Zondervan, 1993.

Sailhammer, John. "Genesis." In *The Expositor's Bible Commentary*, vol. 2, edited by Frank E. Gaebelein, 1–284. Grand Rapids: Zondervan, 1990.

Sakenfeld, Katharine Doob. *Just Wives? Stories of Power and Survival in the Old Testament and Today*. Louisville: Westminster John Knox, 2003.

Sayce, A. H. *The Religions of Ancient Egypt and Babylon*. Edinburgh: T. & T. Clark, 1902.

Scalise, Charles J. *From Scripture to Theology: A Canonical Journey into Hermeneutics*. Downers Grove, IL: IVP, 1996.

———. *Hermeneutics as Theological Prolegomena: A Canonical Approach*. Macon, GA: Mercer University Press, 1994.

Schipper, Jeremy. "'Significant Resonances' with Mephibosheth in 2 Kings 25:27–30: A Response to Donald F. Murray." *JBL* 124 (2005) 521–29.

———. "Reconsidering the Imagery of Disability in 2 Samuel 5:8b." *CBQ* 67 (2005) 422–34.

———. "'Why Do You Still Speak of Your Affairs?' Polyphony in Mephibosheth's Exchanges with David in 2 Samuel." *VT* 54 (2004) 344–51.

Schmidt, Karl Ludwig. *Der Rahmen der Geschichte Jesu*. Darmstadt: Wissenschaftliche Buchgesellschaft, 1964.

Schulte, Hannelis. *Die Die Entstehung der Geschichtsschreibung im Alten Israel*. BZAW 128. Berlin: de Gruyter, 1972.

Segal, H. H. "The Composition of the Books of Samuel." *JQR* 56 (1965) 137–56.

Shemesh, Yael. "David in the service of King Achish of Gath: Renegade to His People or a Fifth Column in the Philistine Army?" *VT* 57 (2007) 73–90.

Shepherd, P. Owen, and D. "Speaking up for Qumran, Dalman and the Son of Man: Was Bar Enasha a Common Term for 'Man' in the Time of Jesus?" *JSNT* 81 (2001) 81–122.

Smith, Gary V. *Hosea, Amos, Micah*. NIVAC. Grand Rapids: Zondervan, 2001.

Smith, Henry Preserved. *A Critical and Exegetical Commentary on the Book of Samuel*. ICC. Reprint. Edinburgh, T. & T. Clark, 1977.

Smith, Morton. "The So-Called 'Biography of David' in the Books of Samuel and Kings." *Harvard Theological Review* 44 (1951) 167–69.

Soggin, J. Alberto. *Old Testament and Oriental Studies*. BO 29. Rome: Biblical Institute Press, 1975.

Spielman, Larry W. "David's Abuse of Power." *Word & World* 19 (1999) 251–59.

Stern, David. *Parables in Midrash: Narrative and Exegesis in Rabbinic Literature.* Cambridge: Harvard University Press, 1991.

Sternberg, Meir. *The Poetics of Biblical Narrative: Ideological Literature and the Drama of Reading.* Bloomington: Indiana University Press, 1985.

———. "The Bible's Art of Persuasion: Ideology, Rhetoric, and Poetics in Saul's Fall." *HUCA* 54 (1983) 45–82.

Steussy, Marti J. "David, God, and the Word." *Word & World* 23 (2003) 365–73.

Taggar-Cohen, Ada. "Political Loyalty in the Biblical Account of 1 Samuel XX–XXII in the Light of Hittite Texts." *VT* 55 (2005) 251–68.

Terrien, Samuel. *The Elusive Presence: Toward a New Biblical Theology.* Religious Perspectives 26. 1979. Reprint Eugene, OR: Wipf & Stock, 2000.

Thiselton, Anthony C. *New Horizons in Hermeneutics: The Theory and Practice of Transforming Biblical Reading.* Grand Rapids: Zondervan, 1992.

Thompson, J. A. *Deuteronomy: An Introduction & Commentary.* TOTC. Downers Grove, IL: IVP, 1974.

Thompson, T. L. *Early History of Israelite People from the Written and Archaeological Sources.* SHANE 4. Leiden: Brill, 1992.

Tidwell, N. L. "The Linen Ephod: 1 Sam II 18 and 2 Sam VI 14." *VT* 24 (1974) 505–7.

Tiessen, Hildi Froese. "Beyond the Binary: Re-Inscribing Cultural Identity in the Literature of Mennonites." *MQR* 72 (1998) 491–501.

Todorov, Tzvetan. *Poetics of Prose.* Ithaca, NY: Cornell University Press, 1977.

Trible, Phyllis. *Rhetorical Criticism: Context, Method, and the Book of Jonah.* Minneapolis: Fortress, 1994.

Troeltsch, Ernst. *Religion in History.* FTMT. Minneapolis: Fortress, 1991.

Tsevat, Matitiahu. "Ishbosheth and Congeners: The Names and Their Study." *HUCA* 46 (1975) 77–85.

———. "Marriage and Monarchical Legitimacy in Ugarit and Israel." *JSS* 3 (1958) 237–43.

Tsumura, David Toshio. *The First Book of Samuel.* NICOT. Grand Rapids: Eerdmans, 2007.

Tull, Patricia K. "Jonathan's Gift of Friendship." *Interpretation* 58 (2004) 130–43.

———. "Rhetorical Criticism and Intertexuality." In *To Each Its Own Meaning: An Introduction to Biblical Criticisms and their Application*, edited by Steven L. McKenzie and Stephen R. Hayness, 156–80. Louisville: Westminster John Knox, 1999.

Uspensky, Boris. *A Poetics of Composition: The Structure of the Artistic Text and Typology of a Compositional Form.* Berkeley: University of California Press, 1973.

Vandergriff, Kenneth Lynn. "Re-creating David: The David Narratives in Art and Literature." *Review & Expositor* 99 (2002) 193–205.

VanderKam, James C. "Davidic Complicity in the Deaths of Abner and Eshbaal: A Historical and Redactional Study." *JBL* 99 (1980) 521–39.

Van Seters, John. "The Composition of the Books of Samuel." *JQR* 55 (1965) 318–39.

———. "The Composition of the Books of Samuel." *JQR* 56 (1965) 32–50.

———. *Abraham in History and Tradition.* New Haven, CT: Yale University Press, 1975.

———. *In Search of History: Historiography in the Ancient World and the Origin of Biblical History.* New Haven, CT: Yale University Press, 1983.

———. "The Terms 'Amorite' and 'Hittite' in the Old Testament." *VT* 22 (1972) 65, 78–81.

Vargon, Shmuel. "The Blind and the Lame." *VT* 46 (1996) 496–514.
Vermes, Geza. *Jesus and the World of Judaism*. London: SCM, 1983.
Via, Dan O. *The Parables: Their Literary and Existential Dimensions*. Philadelphia: Fortress, 1967.
Waltke, Bruce K. and M. O'Connor. *An Introduction to Biblical Hebrew Syntax*. Winona Lake, IN: Eisenbrauns, 1990.
Walton, John H., and Victor H. Matthews. *The IVP Bible Background Commentary: Genesis–Deuteronomy*. Downers Grove, IL: IVP, 1997.
Waschke, Ernst-Joachim. "The Significance of the David Tradition for the Emergence of Messianic Beliefs in the Old Testament." Translated by Frederick J. Gaiser. *Word & World* 23 (Fall 2003) 413–20.
Watson, Francis. *Text and Truth: Redefining Biblical Theology*. Edinburgh: T. & T. Clark, 1997.
Watts, James W. "Rhetorical Strategy in the Composition of the Pentateuch." *JSOT* 68 (1995) 3–22.
Watts, Rikki E. "Echoes from the Past: Israel's Ancient Traditions and the Destiny of the Nations in Isaiah 40–55." *JSOT* 28 (2004) 481–508.
Webb, Barry G. *The Message of Isaiah*. BST. Downers Grove, IL: IVP, 1996.
Weima, Jeffrey A. D. "What Does Aristotle Have to do with Paul?" *CTJ* 32 (1997) 459–61.
Weinfeld, Moshe. "Book of Deuteronomy." In the *Anchor Bible Dictionary*, vol. 2, edited by D. N. Freedman, 168–83. New York: Doubleday, 1992.
———. *Deuteronomy and the Deuteronomic School*. Oxford: Clarendon, 1972.
Weinsheimer, Joel C. *Gadamer's Hermeneutics: A Reading of 'Truth and Method*. New Haven, CT: Yale University Press, 1985.
Wellhausen, J. *Prolegomena to the History of Ancient Israel*. 4th ed. Cleveland, OH: World, 1965.
———. *Der Text de Bücher Samuelis untersucht*. Göttingen: Vandenhoeck & Rupert, 1871.
Wesselius, J. W. "Joab's Death and the Central Theme of the Succession Narrative (2 Samuel 9–1 Kings 2)." *VT* 40 (1990) 336–51.
White, Ellen. "Michal the Misinterpreted." *JSOT* 31 (2007) 451–64.
Whitelam, Keith W. *The Invention of Ancient Israel: The Silencing of Palestinian History*. London: Routledge, 1996.
Whybray, R. N. *The Succession Narrative: A Study of II Samuel 9–20, and I Kings 1 and 2*. London: SCM, 1968.
Wiesel, Elie. "A God Who Remembers." On NPR's *All Things Considered*, April 7, 2008. Online: http://www.npr.org.
Williams, Roland J. *Hebrew Syntax: An Outline*. 2nd ed. Toronto: University of Toronto Press, 1978.
Williamson, H. G. M. "Eschatology in Chronicles." *TynBul* 28 (1977) 115–54.
Willis, John T. "The Song of Hannah and Psalm 113." *CBQ* 35 (1973) 139–54.
Wilson, Gerald H. "The Structure of the Psalter." In *Interpreting the Psalms: Issues and Approaches*, edited by David Firth and Philip S. Johnston, 229–46. Downers Grove, IL: IVP, 2005.
Wimsatt, W. K., Jr., and M. C. Beardsley, "The Intentional Fallacy." *Sewanee Review* 54 (1946) 468–88.
Wright, Christopher. "נחל." In *NIDOTTE*, 77–81.

———. *Deuteronomy*. NIBCOT. Peabody, MA: Hendrickson, 1996.

———. *Living as the People of God: The Relevance of Old Testament Ethics*. Leicester, UK: IVP, 1983.

Wright, G. R. H. "Dumuzi at the Court of David." *Numen* 28 (1981) 54–63.

Wright, John Wesley. "The Founding Father: The Structure of the Chronicler's David Narrative." *JBL* 117 (1998) 45–59.

———. "The Legacy of David in Chronicles: The Narrative Function of 1Chronicles 23–27. *JBL* 110 (1991) 229–42.

Wyatt, Nicolas. David's Census and the Tripartite Theory. *VT* 3 (1990) 352–60.

———. "'Araunah the Jebusite' and the Throne of David." *Studia Theologica* 39 (1985) 39–53.

Young, I. M. "Israelite Literacy and Inscriptions: A Response to Richard Hess." *VT* 55 (2005) 565–67.

———. "Israelite Literacy: Interpreting the Evidence, Part I." *VT* 48 (1998) 239–53.

———. "Israelite Literacy: Interpreting the Evidence, Part II." *VT* 48 (1998) 408–22.

Youngblood, Ronald F. "1, 2 Samuel," In *The Expositor's Bible Commentary*, vol. 3, edited by Frank Gaebelein, 553–1104. Grand Rapids: Zondervan, 1992.

Zewi, Tamar. "The Particles הִנֵּה and וְהִנֵּה. in Biblical Hebrew." *Hebrew Studies* 37 (1996) 21–37.

# Index

Abiathar, 211
Abigail, 115, 118, 119, 127, 141, 174–76, 181, 186, 256, 276
Abinadab, 183–84, 219
Abishai, 130, 139, 220, 245
Abner, xiii, 46, 47, 52, 112–15, 118, 123–44, 146–48, 152, 154–56, 158–59, 165, 177–78, 181, 211, 217–18, 225, 271, 273, 277–78, 296, 307, 315, 317, 322
Absalom, 46, 51, 127, 156, 192, 200, 217, 226–30, 253–57, 261–63, 265–66, 269, 280, 294, 322
Achish, 38, 112, 120, 154, 262, 265, 274
Adonijah, 92–93, 127
Advocacy, 13, 58
Ahinoam, 51, 115, 118–19, 127, 174–76
Ahio, 184
All Israel, 9, 14, 16, 113, 116–17, 119–20, 129, 131, 135–36, 138, 144, 155, 162–63, 177, 187, 193, 201, 207–8, 211, 213, 226, 257, 298, 301
Amalek, Amalekite, 6, 10, 141, 153–55, 157, 162, 306
Ambiguity, 9, 14–15, 39, 58, 60, 62, 101, 103, 106, 142, 147, 164, 170, 178, 200–201, 210, 233, 237–38
Ambition, 114, 134, 138, 142, 159, 179, 198, 219, 236, 296, 322

Amnon, 46, 51, 92, 127, 174, 226
Anachronies, 32
ANE, 34, 45, 176, 178, 193–94
Annihilate, 149, 172
Apology/apologia, 47, 49–50, 52, 54–55, 112, 140, 150, 213, 262, 321
Araunah, 17, 283
Archaeology, archaeological, 1, 45–46, 51, 53–57
Ark, Ark Narrative, Ark Procession, xiii, 8–9, 11, 27, 34, 40, 52, 119, 183–95, 197–98, 203–4, 221, 224, 229, 283, 296, 297, 311
Asahel, 126, 130, 140, 144, 156
Ascend, ascendency, 15, 113, 122, 125, 155, 159, 169, 193, 211, 223–24, 229, 251, 269, 285, 290

Background, 23, 38, 39, 46, 52, 54, 56, 69, 98, 109, 123, 147, 175, 180–81, 227, 230, 235, 250, 262, 275, 299
Bathsheba, 16, 37, 93, 200, 208, 217, 226–27, 306, 322
Beeroth, Beerothite, 144–45, 147–49, 151
Benjamin, Benjaminite, 109, 113, 116–17, 129, 135, 137–38, 144, 147–49, 153–54, 173–74, 189, 207, 218, 241–42, 262, 268, 270, 306, 315

Canon, canons, 4, 10, 66, 69, 114, 280, 315, 317
Carnival, carnivalizing, carnivalization, carnivalizers, 184, 187, 195
Centralization, centralizing, centrality, 13, 41–42, 77, 89, 111, 312
Character, characteristics, characterized, characterization, ix, xii, 3, 16, 20, 23–24, 28, 30–32, 35–36, 38–39, 44, 47, 50–51, 53, 57–58, 61, 68, 70, 75–76, 79, 81–84, 88–101, 107, 109, 115, 117–18, 131, 142, 146, 163, 166, 169, 173, 176–77, 182, 187–88, 196, 208, 218, 220, 222, 225, 230, 235–39, 241–43, 248, 253–54, 258, 276, 281–82, 284, 290, 292, 293, 299–302, 304, 309–10, 313–14, 320, 322
Chiasm, chiastic, 18, 42, 164–67, 225, 228, 306
Confrontation, xiii, 14–15, 19, 104, 104, 120, 140, 158, 189, 203, 225–26, 267, 291
Covenant, covenantal, xi, 1, 3, 5, 7–8, 20–22, 24–25, 122, 129, 134–37, 139, 143, 147, 158, 173, 177, 180, 193, 204, 210, 226, 229, 231–33, 235–36, 240–43, 250, 268, 270–72, 279–81, 283, 286–87, 293, 295, 297–98, 301, 303–5, 309, 311, 314, 317, 322
Cult, *cultus*, cultic, xiii, 10, 13, 17, 24, 34, 98, 183–84, 186, 188, 194–97, 199, 215, 251, 273, 275–77, 283, 291, 296, 301, 303–6, 316
Culture, xi, 5, 37, 46, 49, 56, 64, 87, 99, 124, 176, 180–82, 318, 320

David's character, ix, 169, 237
Davidic hesed, 235, 270, 316

Davidic house/king/kingship/monarchy/dynasty/kingdom/throne, era/period, xi–xii, 3, 7, 23, 33, 35, 40, 53, 56–57, 118, 133, 140, 201, 250–51, 283, 287, 289, 289–90, 292, 295–311, 313, 317–18
Davidic tradition, 209, 296, 301
David's Rise, xiii, 4, 19, 27, 38, 111–13, 118–20, 126, 160, 164, 178, 200, 209, 220
David's wife/wives, 127, 132, 174, 196
Deconstruction, 29, 68, 70, 72–73
Demise, 4, 41, 61, 115, 125, 152, 158–59, 170, 209, 239–40, 242, 274, 314, 319
Descendant(s), xi, 61, 149–50, 216–17, 224, 287–88, 311, 314
Deuteronomic Code/Law(s), Legislation, x–xi, xiv, 270–71, 273–74, 276–80, 286–87, 291, 296, 317, 323
Deuteronomistic History/DtrH, xii, xiv, xvii, xx, 3, 9, 16, 19, 23, 25–26, 28, 33–34, 40, 42, 56, 62, 95, 109, 115, 123, 154, 180, 188, 234, 245, 272, 275, 277, 285–87, 290–91, 293–94, 296, 309, 311, 313
Deuteronomic leader/model, 16, 305, 319
Deuteronomic theology/ideology/perspective, 19, 23, 28, 33, 98, 204
Deuteronomy, xi, 2–4, 8–10, 16, 21–25, 28, 95, 271–77, 279, 286, 290, 309–10, 322–23
Deuteronomistic redaction, xi, 27, 61, 315
D-Group/D-work, 33–34, 54, 204
Dialogue, 36, 54, 62, 75, 81, 83, 98–100, 104, 178, 198, 233, 240, 245–46, 260, 287
Dishabille, 186, 199

# Index

Dishabilledly, xv, 186
Divine accommodation, 294
Dynasty, 8, 13, 15, 19, 52, 113, 123, 127, 132–33, 148, 153, 158–59, 178–79, 192, 194, 200, 211, 217, 250, 252, 261, 267, 281, 283–85, 287–90, 292, 295–307, 313, 317–19, 322

Election, xii, 44, 177–78, 193, 201, 281–83, 285–86, 288, 296–97, 300, 314
Eli, 14–15, 38, 92, 185, 189, 192, 224, 270, 273, 288
Emplotment, 30, 89
Ephod, 189–90, 195, 198–99, 211
Exile(s), xiv, 4, 6–7, 25, 112, 119, 146, 230, 253, 261, 279–89, 292–93, 296–99, 304–6, 308, 312–13, 318–21
Exodus, 6, 21, 79, 149, 229, 298, 304

Facticity, 58–60, 62, 85, 314
Famine, 18, 205, 209–11, 220, 277, 281–82
Form Criticism, 68
The Former Prophets, 10, 22–23, 25, 27–28, 98, 272
Fulfillment, 8–9, 16, 135, 138, 213, 236, 258, 283–84, 286, 288

Gath, 112, 120, 149, 262, 265, 274
Gibeon, Gibeonites, xiii, 6, 9, 130, 147–49, 153–54, 157, 180, 183, 187, 189–91, 203, 205–9, 212–17, 221, 224, 234, 252, 263, 277, 281, 315–16
*Golah*, xiv, 4, 23, 25, 28, 38, 302–4, 313, 318, 322

Hannah, 4, 11–12, 17, 38, 40, 185, 204–5
HDR, xiii, 4, 27, 31, 59, 111–14, 117–18, 126, 140, 145–46, 149–50, 158–59, 172, 177, 188, 219, 269, 321
Heir(s), xi–xii, 1
Hendiadys, 20, 241, 267
Hermeneutics, 40, 71, 77–78, 88, 139
Hermeneutical implication/significance/question, 31, 39, 61, 294
Hermeneutical key, 48, 219
Hermeneutical self-consciousness, 60
Hexateuch, 27
Historarity, History, xv, 83, 109, 111, 315, 323
Historiography, 44, 50, 60, 76, 79–81, 83, 86, 117

Ideology, 23, 28, 33, 37, 44, 58, 63, 65, 76, 83, 98, 193, 283–84, 292, 294–95, 297, 301, 315
Idolatry, 24, 279, 287, 297, 308
*Inclusio*, 11, 16, 19, 75, 152, 167, 171, 219, 249–50, 272
Integrity, xiv, 14, 20, 132, 154, 237, 263, 265, 267–68, 316
Interstitiality, 318
intertextuality, 70, 240, 242, 315
Intra-Textual Consciousness, xv, 95, 97, 277, 323
Ishbosheth, xiii, 47, 52, 112–14, 116–18, 122–25, 127, 129, 133–35, 137–38, 140, 144–54, 156–58, 177, 225, 231, 241, 251, 271, 278, 290, 307, 315
Israel, Isrealite, iv, viii, xii, xxi, 1–2, 4–10, 14–22, 24–25, 27–30, 35, 38–41, 44, 51–54, 56–58, 76, 79, 105, 109, 111, 113–17, 119–20, 125, 128–29, 131–39, 143–44, 146–50, 153–57, 162–63, 165–66, 168–69, 171–72, 176–87, 189–97, 199–202, 205, 207–15, 218–24, 226, 236, 241, 251, 254, 257, 262, 267–73, 275,

Israel, Isrealite (*cont.*)
278, 283, 285–88, 290–306, 308, 312–13, 315, 319–20, 323

Jebusites, 129, 252, 290
Jerusalem, 6–7, 13, 17–18, 40, 52–53, 55–57, 119, 146–47, 174, 184–85, 187, 191, 193–94, 199, 221, 224, 227–29, 233, 237, 249–54, 257, 259, 260–62, 279, 282–84, 290–91, 294–302, 304–5, 311–12, 317–18
Joab, 91, 114, 126, 130, 139–42, 144–45, 155–56, 159, 217, 243, 265–66, 273, 307, 322
Jonathan, xiv, 39, 44, 51, 91, 112, 124, 145, 147, 150, 162–67, 170–71, 189–90, 192, 206–7, 210, 215–16, 218–19, 222, 224, 231–33, 236–38, 240–43, 245, 247, 250, 256, 270, 274, 316, 322
Josephus, 11, 150, 162
Judah, Judahite, xii, xiii, xxii, 8, 41, 53–57, 60, 113, 115–23, 125, 128, 131, 137, 143, 149, 153, 165–66, 176, 183, 191, 193, 200, 205, 213, 218, 223, 260, 262, 281, 283–84, 286–87, 289–90, 292, 294–98, 300–302, 305–6, 312
Judgment, xiv, 6–7, 13, 19, 24, 35, 77, 79, 98, 100, 139, 151, 200, 209, 263–65, 269, 277, 288, 291, 294, 297–98, 308

Kingdom, 51, 53–54, 56–57, 116, 125, 130, 132–35, 137–38, 144, 147, 157, 159, 199–200, 208, 213, 229, 247, 251, 254, 285–86, 289, 296–98, 301–5, 308–9, 311–13, 318–19, 321

Kingship, xii, 7–9, 13, 18, 20, 22, 40, 45, 113, 119, 124, 128, 177, 193, 195, 261, 270, 272–73, 284–85, 287, 298–303, 305–6, 308, 310
Kiriath-jearim, 8, 183, 189

Land, 1–2, 5–7, 23, 25, 51, 56, 107, 117, 128, 134–36, 149, 153, 177, 180, 189, 207, 221–22, 225–26, 242, 245, 247, 257, 259, 268–70, 272–73, 275–78, 281, 298, 308, 318, 323
The Latter Prophets, 10, 292–94, 297, 299, 310, 317
Law, 16, 21, 24, 33, 48, 79, 179–80, 271–72, 273, 276, 278–79, 285–87, 296, 305, 308–9, 313, 317, 319
Legitimation, 101, 178–79, 193–94
Leitmotif(s), 7
Leitwort(er), leitwortsil, 75, 103, 105–6, 134, 137
Liminality, 318
Literary, ix, xi, xii–iii, xv, 4–6, 10–11, 17, 24–25, 29–33, 36–37, 39–43, 45, 47, 49–50, 55, 58–60, 62–63, 65–76, 82–83, 85, 87, 90, 92–94, 97, 101, 103, 106–7, 109–12, 114–15, 131, 135, 143, 158, 171–72, 188, 207, 209, 233, 249, 254, 265, 300, 315, 323
Literature, iv, ix, xi, xii, xxi, xxii, 3, 10, 26, 37, 42–43, 49–50, 53, 59, 61, 63–68, 76–79, 82, 89, 92–93, 99, 101, 104, 106, 112, 118, 129, 172, 197, 202, 219, 258, 265, 271, 281, 289, 309–10, 321

Masoretes, MT, xiii, 4, 11, 34, 50, 115–16, 120, 127–30, 133, 144, 146, 150, 161–63, 183,

Masoretes, MT (*cont.*)
185, 189–90, 203, 205–7, 210, 216, 218–19, 232–33, 246–47, 260, 278, 284, 288
Memory, 5, 57, 171, 176, 192, 224, 250, 269, 299, 318
Mephibosheth, vii, xiv, 34, 36, 51, 92, 127, 141, 144–47, 149–50, 206, 208, 215–16, 223–33, 235–71, 279–80, 288–90, 306–7, 312, 316–17
Michal, vii, xiii, 4, 15, 18–19, 31, 34, 36, 40, 48, 52, 54–55, 61, 119, 129, 134–38, 159–91, 193, 195–201, 203–11, 213–21, 223–26, 234, 252, 264, 271, 274–77, 287, 292–94, 296, 306–7, 315–17
Monarchy, xii, 9–10, 13, 17, 26, 31, 36, 38, 41, 44, 49, 55, 149, 193, 285–87, 294, 296, 298–99, 307–8, 313, 317–19
Motifs, motific, viii, xi–ii, 2, 10, 12, 14, 23, 26, 32, 33, 39, 42, 61–62, 75, 83, 106–9, 139, 172–73, 181, 191–92, 198, 200, 204, 220, 236, 240, 242, 251–52, 269, 276, 281–82, 287, 289–90, 294, 300, 310, 312, 317
Multivalence, multivalency, 39, 62, 105
Murder, murderer, xiii, 19, 51–52, 72, 93, 127, 139–40, 141, 147, 150–52, 154–60, 165, 192, 203, 211–14, 217, 220–21, 224, 226–27, 241, 243, 267, 271, 273, 277–78, 296
Nabal, 115, 127, 141, 174, 176, 182, 256
Nacon, 184
Narrative Criticism, xii–xiii, 63–64, 66, 68, 70–75, 83–91, 98, 104, 106, 109, 111, 314–15

The Nations, 8–9, 183, 194–95, 213, 215, 221, 275, 282, 285–86, 297–98, 312
Nathan, 37, 93, 182, 200, 226, 293, 296
Novella, 29–31, 42

Oppress, oppression, oppressor, the oppressed, 6, 10, 12–13, 20, 182, 226, 272–73, 277, 306, 320
Oracle, xiv, 18, 31, 34, 119, 189, 207, 210, 212–14, 222–23, 277, 288, 296, 298

Parallelism, 20, 30, 62, 121, 151
Partisan, 54–56
Pentateuch, 27–28, 64, 76
Philistine, 4, 7–9, 14–15, 46, 52, 54, 56, 112, 114, 116–18, 120–21, 129, 138, 149, 153–54, 160–65, 167–68, 172, 177–79, 181, 189–92, 194, 200, 206–7, 209, 219, 220, 233, 257, 262, 265, 270, 274
Plot, xv, 30, 62, 70, 75, 78, 81, 89–90, 92–93, 95, 99, 108–9, 113–14, 133, 170, 182, 187–88, 207, 254, 258, 264, 323
Plotlet, xv, 187–88, 323
Point of View, xv, 39, 62, 70, 75, 93–98, 100, 112, 127, 144, 199, 219, 289, 315
Polyvalence, 58, 60
Progenitor, 3–4, 218
Progeny, ix, 1–4, 25, 61, 98, 145, 150, 159–60, 162, 188, 207, 211, 223–24, 235, 238–40, 243, 247, 250–52, 269–70, 273, 278, 307, 313–14, 319, 322–23
Prophet(s), 5–6, 8, 10, 13, 15, 22–23, 25, 27–28, 37, 39, 42, 49, 67, 69, 88, 92–93, 98, 194, 211–12, 226, 258, 266, 270,

Prophet(s) (*cont.*)
272, 282, 287–88, 293–303, 305, 308–11, 317, 319
Punishment, 2, 42, 49, 200, 204, 214, 273, 279–80

Ranke, Leopold von, 78
Reader-Response, 29, 68, 70–71, 73–74, 102, 105, 139, 141–42
Reality, 30, 40, 47, 53, 58, 62, 66, 77–78, 84–85, 88, 91, 94, 109–10, 122, 200, 242, 268, 303
Reconstruction(s/ist[s]/ism), 4, 29, 69, 73, 189
Redaction, xi, xiv, 23, 27–28, 32, 34–35, 61–62, 272, 275, 315
Redaction Criticism, 62
Reign, reigning, ix, xii, 3–4, 7–8, 14–16, 19, 26, 43–45, 50, 54, 60–61, 107, 112, 116–17, 123–25, 130, 153, 159, 168, 188–90, 193–94, 205, 207–8, 210, 213–15, 220, 223–24, 226, 234, 239, 247, 250, 269, 272, 277, 281, 287–88, 290, 297, 299, 302, 306, 310, 319
Religion, religiosity, 10, 15, 17, 47, 49, 193, 194–96, 213, 215, 295–96,
Repetition, 1, 31, 32, 39, 62, 75, 103–5, 107, 142–44, 151–53, 169, 171, 186, 194, 233, 236, 248, 250, 253, 258, 264
Retainers, xiv, 15, 146, 155, 162, 165, 168, 170, 172, 240
Retribution, xi, 2, 3, 15, 42, 155, 200, 203, 258, 270, 272, 314, 322
Rhetorical Criticism, 58, 60, 68, 70–71, 73–74, 85, 106
Righteousness, 20–21, 148, 267, 302
Rimmon, 114, 141, 144–45, 147, 151–57, 159, 162, 278, 319
Ritual(s), 17, 34, 49, 184, 197, 199, 271, 277

Rizpah, 18, 124, 127, 133, 203, 206–7, 216, 221, 222

Sacrifice, xiii–xiv, xviii, 13, 34, 160, 185–86, 188, 195, 197, 199, 203, 207–9, 215, 221, 252
Samarian acropolis, 57
Samuel's role, 38
Samuel's reign, 190
Sanctuary, 8–9, 13, 17, 24, 183, 316
The Saulide Seven, 18–19, 208–10, 212, 215–16, 220–22, 225, 231, 241, 252, 267, 307, 315, 317, 323
Scenic Composition, 30, 235
Septuagint, LXX, 50, 115–16, 127–30, 144–46, 150, 160–63, 183, 185–87, 189, 205–7, 210, 216–19, 232–33, 246–47, 260–61
Shepherd, 6–7, 47–48, 92, 305, 309
Sibling(s), Sibling rivalry, 7, 36
Skepticism, 47, 49, 50–52, 62, 75–76, 141, 264
So-Called Appendix, the "appendix," xii, 9, 17–19, 25, 27, 42, 208–9, 220, 234
Solomon, 19–20, 35–37, 41–42, 50–55, 57, 112, 120, 140, 180, 200, 215, 221, 269, 283, 287, 288–89, 293, 304–5, 307
Stitch-Word(s), xv, 143–44, 323
Struggle(s), 14–15, 34, 114, 188, 193, 205
Succession Narrative, SN, xii, 4, 9, 17, 25, 27–28, 31–37, 41–43, 59, 114, 172, 188, 219
Successors-In-Waiting, 15

Temple, 9–10, 13, 17, 57, 194, 217, 283, 289, 295–296–298, 301–2, 304–5, 309–12, 318–19
*Tendenz* critics, 41
Tensive Complexity, 58, 60, 65

Testimony, 56, 58, 60, 157, 203, 208, 213, 279, 320
Tetrateuch, 28,
Threshing Floor, 17, 184, 209, 283
Torah, xii, xiv, 3–8, 10, 16, 21–26, 98, 155, 190, 197, 210, 214, 217, 221–22, 226, 267, 281–82, 287, 292, 315, 317
Traditio-historical approach/ research, 27–28, 32
Tradition, xii–xiii, 4–5, 9–10, 25, 27–28, 35, 44, 52–53, 55, 58, 62, 78, 128, 179–80, 182, 188, 193–95, 197, 204, 208–9, 211, 215, 270, 275, 280–81, 283–84, 291, 293–98, 300–301, 303, 308–9, 311, 313, 318, 320
Transjordan, 113, 153, 158, 207, 315
Troeltsch, 47, 49

Truth, 20, 57–60, 62–63, 75, 79–82, 84, 86, 88, 109, 140, 168, 179, 247, 257, 263–69, 296, 302, 314, 321
Usurpation, usurper(s), xi, 51, 54, 112–13, 177–78, 195, 241, 244, 254, 316
Uzzah, 184–85, 188

Woman at the Window, xiii, 172–73, 198
The Writings, 64, 295, 297, 303, 306

Ziba, xiv, 36, 141, 216, 225, 228–33, 235–36, 238–39, 241–42, 246–50, 253–69, 271, 279–80
Zion, xii, 192, 252, 283–84, 290, 292, 294–97, 301, 304, 313

www.ingramcontent.com/pod-product-compliance
Lightning Source LLC
Chambersburg PA
CBHW071149300426
44113CB00009B/1133